Decision-Making on Mega-Projects

TRANSPORT ECONOMICS, MANAGEMENT AND POLICY

Series Editor: Kenneth Button, *Professor of Public Policy, School of Public Policy, George Mason University, USA*

Transport is a critical input for economic development and for optimising social and political interaction. Recent years have seen significant new developments in the way that transport is perceived by private industry and governments, and in the way academics look at it.

The aim of this series is to provide original material and an up-to-date synthesis of the state of modern transport analysis. The coverage embraces all conventional modes of transport but also includes contributions from important related fields such as urban and regional planning and telecommunications where they interface with transport. The books draw from many disciplines and some cross disciplinary boundaries. They are concerned with economics, planning, sociology, geography, management science, psychology and public policy. They are intended to help improve the understanding of transport, the policy needs of the most economically advanced countries and the problems of resource-poor developing economies. The authors come from around the world and represent some of the outstanding young scholars as well as established names.

Titles in the series include:

Structural Change in Transportation and Communications in the Knowledge Society
Edited by Kiyoshi Kobayashi, T.R. Lakshmanan and William P. Anderson

Competition in the Railway Industry
An International Comparative Analysis
Edited by José A. Gómez-Ibáñez and Ginés de Rus

Globalized Freight Transport
Intermodality, E-Commerce, Logistics and Sustainability
Edited by Thomas R. Leinbach and Cristina Capineri

Decision-Making on Mega-Projects
Cost–Benefit Analysis, Planning and Innovation
Edited by Hugo Priemus, Bent Flyvbjerg and Bert van Wee

Port Privatisation
The Asia-Pacific Experience
Edited by James Reveley and Malcolm Tull

The Future of Intermodal Freight Transport
Operations, Design and Policy
Edited by Rob Konings, Hugo Priemus and Peter Nijkamp

North American Freight Transportation
The Road to Security and Prosperity
Mary R. Brooks

Decision-Making on Mega-Projects

Cost–Benefit Analysis, Planning and Innovation

Edited by

Hugo Priemus

Professor of System Innovation and Spatial Development, Delft University of Technology, The Netherlands

Bent Flyvbjerg

Professor of Planning, Aalborg University, Denmark and Chair of Infrastructure Policy and Planning, Delft University of Technology, The Netherlands

Bert van Wee

Professor and Head of Transport Policy and Logistics, Delft University of Technology, The Netherlands

TRANSPORT ECONOMICS, MANAGEMENT AND POLICY

Edward Elgar
Cheltenham, UK • Northampton, MA, USA

Published by
Edward Elgar Publishing Limited
The Lypiatts
15 Lansdown Road
Cheltenham
Glos GL50 2JA
UK

Edward Elgar Publishing, Inc.
William Pratt House
9 Dewey Court
Northampton
Massachusetts 01060
USA

Reprinted 2014

A catalogue record for this book
is available from the British Library

ISBN 978 1 84542 737 5

Printed and bound in Great Britain by T.J. International Ltd, Padstow

Contents

Contributors

Hans de Bruijn is Professor of Public Administration at Delft University of Technology, The Netherlands. His research is on processes of decision-making, in which many mutually dependent actors are involved, with different interests. He is involved in the development of concepts regarding this multi-actor decision-making and in applying it to numerous areas, e.g. large infrastructural projects, law enforcement, the relation between management and professionals, environmental policy and privatisation. His most recent book is *Managing Performance in the Public Sector* (Routledge, 2007).

Bent Flyvbjerg is Professor of Planning at Aalborg University, Denmark and Chair of Infrastructure Policy and Planning at Delft University of Technology, The Netherlands. He is Founder and Director of Aalborg University's research programme on large-scale infrastructure planning. His books include *Megaprojects and Risk* (Cambridge University Press, 2003, with Nils Bruzelius and Werner Rothengatter), *Making Social Science Matter* (Cambridge University Press, 2001) and *Rationality and Power* (The University of Chicago Press, 1998).

Karen Trapenberg Frick is a Lecturer at the University of California, Berkeley, USA, in the Department of City and Regional Planning and teaches courses on transportation planning, policy and finance. She also is a post-doctoral Research Scholar at the University of California Transportation Center.

Moshe Givoni is a Marie Curie Fellow at the Department of Spatial Economics, Free University, Amsterdam. He gained his PhD at the Bartlett School of Planning, University College London. His academic background also includes degrees in Economics (BA), Geography (BA) and Business Administration (MBA), from Tel-Aviv University, Israel. His main research interests relate to air and rail transport.0

Ernst F. ten Heuvelhof (Chair Public Management) is a Professor at the Department of Technology, Policy and Management of Delft University of Technology and at the Department of Public Administration of Erasmus University in Rotterdam, The Netherlands. His main research interests are the management of complex decision-making processes; and liberalisation, privatisation and internationalisation of network-based industries. He is Scientific Director of the Bsik research programme Next Generation Infrastructures.

W. Martin de Jong is Associate Professor of Policy, Organisation and Management at the Faculty of Technology, Policy and Management, Delft University of Technology, The Netherlands. He publishes and teaches on issues of cross-national institutional comparison, cross-national lesson-drawing, transport infrastructure planning and evolutionary approaches to the administrative sciences.

Joop Koppenjan is Associate Professor at the Faculty of Technology, Policy and Management of the Delft University of Technology, The Netherlands. His research topics include policy networks, decision-making, implementation, privatisation and public–private partnerships.

Donald R. Lessard is the Epoch Foundation Professor of International Management at the MIT Sloan School of Management, USA. His research interests are project management and global strategic management, with an emphasis on managing in the face of uncertainty and risk. He currently teaches courses on global strategy and organisation, and global strategy in the energy sector. Lessard is also the Faculty Director for the BP–MIT Projects Academy, a major executive education programme for major project leaders that spans management and engineering.

Martijn Leijten is a Researcher at the Faculty of Technology, Policy and Management of Delft University of Technology, The Netherlands. His research focuses on multi-actor systems, in particular in the management of complex infrastructure projects. In 2004 he worked for the Dutch Parliamentary Committee on Infrastructure Projects.

Roger Miller is the Jarislowsky Professor of Innovation and Project Management at École Polytechnique in Montreal, Canada, and a Founding Partner of SECOR, a strategy consulting firm with offices in Montreal, Toronto and Paris. He has been a Fellow at the Center for International Affairs of Harvard University and in MIT's International Motor Vehicle Program. His work has focused on (1) strategy and industry dynamics, (2) public policies in science and technology, and (3) large engineering project management. Roger Miller is a Fellow of the Canadian Academy of Engineering.

Hugo Priemus is Professor of System Innovation and Spatial Development at Delft University of Technology, The Netherlands. In 2004 he was Research Coordinator of the Dutch Parliamentary Committee on Infrastructure Projects. He is Honorary Doctor at the University of Uppsala, Sweden.

Piet Rietveld is Professor in Transport Economics and Head of the Department of Spatial Economics, Vrije Universiteit, Amsterdam, The Netherlands. He is the Chairman of NECTAR and Fellow of the Tinbergen Institute. He has conducted extensive research in the field of infrastructure and spatial development.

Werner Rothengatter is President of the World Conference on Transport Research (WCTR) and Head of the Institute of Economic Policy Research (IWW), University of Karlsruhe, Germany.

Knut Samset is Professor in Project Management at the Department of Civil Engineering and Transport, Norwegian University of Science and Technology in Trondheim, Norway, and Director of the Concept Research Program on Front-end Management of Major Investment Projects. His current research is on project governance, appraisal and quality assurance of major investments. He is the author of books on technology assessment, project design, evaluation and risk management.

Lóránt A. Tavasszy is Senior Adviser, Mobility & Infrastructure, at the TNO Institute in the Netherlands and Visiting Professor at the Radboud University in Nijmegen, The Netherlands. His research work in recent years has focused on freight transportation, and spatial policy and modelling. He has conducted several projects on the development of guidelines for cost–benefit analysis of transport projects and policies.

Didier van de Velde is Researcher at the Faculty of Technology, Policy and Management of Delft University of Technology and Senior Adviser at inno-V consultancy in Amsterdam, The Netherlands. His research work focuses on institutional reforms in public transport (urban, regional and national rail) and especially on the introduction of forms of competition in these sectors.

Roger W. Vickerman is Professor at the Centre for European, Regional and Transport Economics, and Head of the Department of Economics, Keynes College, University of Kent at Canterbury, UK.

Bert van Wee is Professor in Transport Policy and Logistics and Head of the section with the same name at Delft University of Technology, The Netherlands, in the faculty Technology, Policy and Management. His main interests are long-term developments in transport, the environment, safety and accessibility, and policy analysis.

Acknowledgements

The editors wish to acknowledge not only the authors of the chapters, who were extremely cooperative, but also the referees, who contributed greatly to the quality of the final publication.

Most authors have served as referees in cross-referee procedures. In addition, the following external referees have delivered valuable contributions: Peter Abelson, David Banister, Giampiero Beroggi, Antonio Estache, Andreas Faludi, Marina van Geenhuizen, Paul 't Hart, David Hensher, Toon van der Hoorn, Milan Janic, David Luberoff, Rico Maggi, Vincent Marchau, Barry Needham, Eric Pels, Dani Shafer, Folke Snickars, Arvid Strand, Barry Ubbels, Jose Viegas and Henk van Zuijlen.

1. Introduction: scope of the book

Hugo Priemus, Bent Flyvbjerg and Bert van Wee

1.1 INTRODUCTION

This book aims to enlarge understanding of the decision-making on mega-projects and to suggest recommendations for a more effective, efficient and democratic approach. This is not the first book published on this theme. But this is certainly a unique book, presenting an up-to-date and differentiated overview of the state of the art, based on experiences and visions of authors from Europe and North America.

Traditionally, it has been the job of the government to develop, finance and – often – to manage major investment projects, which we have bundled together in this book under the blanket definition of 'mega-project'. There are many successful mega-projects, most of which have taken some time to bear fruit – both directly and indirectly. However, there are also many potential problems, which could turn mega-projects into what Peter Hall labels 'planning disasters' (Hall, 1980). These problems include low transport performances, adverse environmental effects (landscape erosion, noise pollution, toxic emissions etc.), underestimated investment costs and disappointing returns.

In this book, authors from different scientific disciplines address various aspects of decision-making in mega-projects, such as management characteristics and cost–benefit analysis, planning and decision-making, and innovation, competition and institutions. Many cases are drawn from different parts of the world, both best and worst practices.

The subject matter is varied and highly differentiated, but certain questions crop up time and again. For example, how do we deal with protracted preparation processes, how do we tackle risks and uncertainties, and how can we best divide the risks and responsibilities among the private and public players in the different phases of the process?

The next section elaborates the scope of the book. The notion of mega-project will be explained. We will then present a brief review of recent publications on common pitfalls in decision-making processes on mega-projects

(Section 1.3). Section 1.4 presents the content of the book, divided into three parts: I   Management characteristics and cost–benefit analysis; II   Planning and decision-making; and III.   Innovation, competition and institutions.

1.2   SCOPE OF THE BOOK

Frisk's contribution in Chapter 12 identifies the following general characteristics of mega-projects, referred to as the 6 Cs:

1.   colossal in size and scope;
2.   captivating because of size, engineering achievements and aesthetic design;
3.   costly: costs are often underestimated;
4.   controversial: funding, mitigation packages, impacts on third parties;
5.   complex: risk and uncertainty in terms of design, funding and construction;
6.   control issues: who are the key decision-makers, funding, operation etc.

Mega-projects are often technological *tours de force* with an innovative and, not infrequently, an experimental character. They sometimes reflect the cutting edge of modern technology (Frick refers to the notion of 'the technological sublime' in Chapter 12), sometimes the initiators overreach themselves, and the problems and deficiencies become embedded in the project.

There is not only a question of technological complexity, but also of social complexity, as De Bruijn and Leijten argue in Chapter 2. There are often concerns about public support, and the rationality and consistency of political decisions. A question consistently raised is where private decision-making, private funding and private risk-taking should be preferred and where public decision-making is necessary, for example in order to safeguard public values, to have risks borne publicly, or to come to the aid with public finance. Until recently in the transport infrastructure sector, public decision-making, public finance and public risks were involved exclusively, which usually resulted in a weak orientation to the market and serious cost underestimates. The approach has shifted progressively towards arrangements between public and private institutions, in which the public institutions are required to safeguard public values, and private institutions usually ensure a better market orientation, more dynamism, and flexibility. There is a constant quest for the optimum balance between competition and collaboration, and a certain control of the transaction costs, which may be excessively high in innovative arrangements (Van de Velde and Ten Heuvelhof, Chapter 13).

We have opted to solicit contributions from the circle of independent, academic experts from Europe and North America. It was tempting also to request contributions from the banking world (such as the World Bank) or from the world of developers and contractors. The expertise of financers and practitioners is included in the scientific contributions in this book, but our preference is for this expertise to come from independent, academic sources.

It was likewise tempting to request contributions from authors who derive their insights from mega-projects in countries such as China, India and Korea, where the biggest known mega-projects are currently being planned and executed. However, we chose evidence-based contributions, embedded in the modern context of democratic governments and market-oriented private institutions. In some contributions (Chapter 7 by Flyvbjerg; Chapter 8 by Miller and Lessard), mega-projects in other continents are included, but in general there is insufficient empirical information available on mega-projects outside Europe and North America, and in many cases the context is still too specific and too traditional, as in China, where until recently the socialist regime dominated decision-making, and where the concept of private property was scarcely understood. All this is now changing rapidly. Globalisation is introducing an increasing number of Western institutions, companies and experiences into Asia, Africa and Latin America. We think that the experiences compiled in this book are relevant for the entire modern developed world, and to some extent also for the developing countries that have now embarked on a spectacular economic transition. None the less, in the course of time there will be enough data for a book compiling experiences with mega-projects outside Europe and North America. Whereas now many scientists and practitioners in Asia, Africa, Australia and South America are able to benefit from the findings and lessons in our book, soon scientists and practitioners in Europe and North America will likewise be learning lessons from the decision-making on mega-projects in other parts of the world.

Many of the cases in this book are related to major transport infrastructure projects. This mega-project category is highly relevant, and an abundance of research has been undertaken to gather empirical evidence on them. But there is more to mega-projects. This is stated explicitly in Chapter 8 (Miller and Lessard) and Chapter 9 (Samset), which deal with a broader set of large engineering projects, including nuclear plants, offshore constructions, water treatment plants, military weapons systems, ICT systems and complex real-estate projects (e.g. hospitals, offices, shopping malls and urban centres). The scope of this book is certainly wider than large transport infrastructure projects. Where general phenomena, concepts, findings and lessons are involved, we always have the broader set of mega-projects in mind, which extends beyond the infrastructure projects: technological complexity, social complexity, cost overruns, strategic behaviour, contested information: all these phenomena apply not only to transport infrastructure projects, but also to mega-projects in a broader sense.

1.3   COMMON PITFALLS IN DECISION-MAKING ON MEGA-PROJECTS

Introduction

Various recent studies on mega-projects have identified certain characteristics that are typical of decision-making processes for those projects. In this section we shall discuss the findings of researchers who each studied a large number of mega-projects: the American researchers Altshuler and Luberoff (2003), and Miller and Lessard (2001), followed by the European researchers Flyvbjerg, Bruzelius and Rothengatter (2003). Then we examine the approach of Short and Kopp (2005) from the Joint OECD/ECMT Transport Research Centre. Finally, the conclusions of the Dutch Parliamentary Committee on Infrastructure Projects (Tijdelijke Commissie Infrastructuurprojecten; TCI, 2004) are summarised.

Mega-Projects According to Altshuler and Luberoff (2003)

Altshuler and Luberoff (2003: 6–7), who investigated three types of mega-projects – highways, airports and rail transit systems – search for a broader approach spanning four dimensions. First, the authors integrate their findings with leading theories on urban politics and empirical research by others on urban renewal. Second, they address national patterns. Although the authors make substantial use of case studies, they take them from multiple sources to illustrate broad themes and intersperse them with discussions on national developments. Third, Altshuler and Luberoff examine the situation from an intergovernmental perspective. Most urban mega-projects in the latter half of the twentieth century were undertaken with substantial federal funding and within contours of opportunity defined by federal programmes. The authors delineate the multilevel dynamics of these cases, highlighting the roles of federal, state and local players. Finally, they trace developments over half a century, long enough for considerable evolution to have occurred.

   Altshuler and Luberoff (2003: 219–47) identify a number of common patterns:

1. Urban mega-projects ceased to be routine after 1970. Implementation depended far more on the case-by-case initiative and style of the advocates.
2. Mega-project support coalitions were, with rare exceptions, spearheaded by business enterprises with immediate interests at stake. The exceptions were led by environmental groups promoting mass transit projects.
3. Mega-project ideas frequently originated in the public sector and were then 'sold' to prospective constituencies. Even when the initial impetus came from private groups, energetic and skilful public-sector leadership was still required in most cases to widen the base of public support, mollify critics, secure resources at higher levels of government, and generally manage conflict. The authors dub this kind of leadership 'public entrepreneurship'.
4. However broad their support coalitions, mega-project proposals were rarely implemented if they imposed substantial costs on neighbourhoods or the natural environment. Altshuler and Luberoff call this the 'do-no-harm' paradigm.
5. But even the most sensitively planned mega-projects generated some negative impacts, so it became widely accepted that these should be 'mitigated' as far as possible. The mitigation norm frequently became a major source of leverage for groups with agendas that went beyond damage limitation.
6. Though urban mega-projects were often founded mainly by the federal government, they almost invariably originated locally, where they also drew their main constituency of support with little or no regard for national objectives. Altshuler and Luberoff refer to this as 'bottom-up federalism'.
7. The whole point of mega-project finance was to avoid increases in broad-based local taxes – particularly if levied on host-city residents alone – and, more specifically, property and income taxes. Alternative sources of funding included local taxes designed mainly for visitors, state and regional sales taxes, and sometimes lottery revenues. Altshuler and Luberoff describe this as 'locally painless project financing'.
8. Finally, the costs of mega-projects rose spectacularly in 1970–2000 and surpassed official estimates by a considerable margin at the time of authorisation. The causes of this development seem to lie in the realm of politics rather than in engineering or accounting.

Mega-Projects According to Miller and Lessard (2001)

In Chapter 8, Roger Miller and Donald Lessard present an overview of the IMEC study, an assessment of 60 mega-projects (IMEC = International

Program in the Management of Engineering and Construction). These projects include 15 hydroelectric dams, 17 thermal and nuclear power plants, 6 urban transport facilities, 10 civil infrastructure investments, 4 oil platforms and 8 technology initiatives. Per project, seven to eight participants–sponsors, bankers, contractors, regulators, lawyers, analysts and others were interviewed. Particular emphasis was placed on front-end development decisions, but execution and initial ramp-up to operation were also studied.

The goal of the IMEC study was to understand the changes that were occurring (increasing financial, political and social complexity), and to identify the practices that, in the experience of executives involved in projects, really made a difference. The study reflects the collective experience from Europe, North and South America, and Asia. The study involved systemic and strategic perspectives, and focused on themes such as coping with uncertainly through risk analysis, institution-shaping and strategies.

Mega-projects or large engineering projects (LEPs) are presented as high-stakes games characterised by substantial irreversible commitments, skewed reward structures when they are successful, and high probabilities of failure. Their dynamics also change over time. The journey from initial conception to ramp-up and revenue generation takes ten years, on average. While the 'front end' of a project – project definition, concept selection and planning – typically involves less than one-third of the total elapsed time and expense, it has a disproportionate impact on outcomes, as most shaping actions occur during this phase. During the ramp-up period, the reality of market estimates and the true worth of the project are revealed. Sponsors may find that actual conditions are very different from expectations, but only a few adaptations are possible. Once built, most projects have little flexibility in use beyond the original intended purpose. Managing risks is thus a real issue.

Successful projects are not selected but shaped. Successful sponsors appear to start with project ideas that have the potential to become viable. These sponsors then embark on shaping efforts to influence risk drivers ranging from project-related issues to broader governance. The seeds of success or failure of individual projects are thus planted early and nurtured over the course of the shaping period as choices are made. Successful sponsors, however, do not escalate commitments, and they abandon quickly when they recognise that projects have little possibility of becoming viable.

Two other key concepts related to risk that emerge from the study are governability – the creation of relationships that allow a project to be reconstituted and proceed even after major changes in project drivers and the resulting payoffs to the various parties involved – and turbulence – the tendency for risks to compound dramatically once things begin going off track.

Miller and Lessard argue that projects are dynamic, iterative and often chaotic systems. Project-management architectures must reflect this. While projects tend to resemble a spiral more than the classic waterfall, even this metaphor may be too orderly. Projects are better viewed as evolutionary and path-dependent systems composed of episodes displaying different dynamics.

These findings apply equally, albeit in somewhat different ways, to the three distinct classes of risk (in terms of their causes) encountered in most projects: those emanating from the dynamics of the project itself (technical and operational risks); those associated with the markets with which the project interacts (market risks); and those related to the political, social and economic setting of the project (institutional/social risks).

Chapter 8 informs the reader in more depth about the findings of the IMEC study.

Mega-Projects According to Flyvbjerg, Bruzelius and Rothengatter (2003)

Flyvbjerg et al. (2003) base their analysis on a unique database comprising 258 large infrastructure projects spread over many years in all continents and involving a total investment of €90 billion. Despite the geographical and temporal spread and the wide differences in the characteristics of the projects, Flyvbjerg et al. (2003) identified some common features.

The most important finding is that in nine out of ten cases the costs of mega-projects are underestimated. Cost overruns are in particular a problem in the development of rail infrastructure. On the other hand, the demand for transport, and hence the actual performance of transport, are invariably overestimated. This conclusion confirms the findings of previous studies by Wachs (1989; 1990) and Pickrell (1989; 1992). The actual costs for rail projects are, on average, 45 per cent higher than the projected costs. The differences are so great and so consistent that Flyvbjerg et al. (2003) rule out the likelihood of coincidence. The World Bank refers to this phenomenon as 'appraisal optimism' (Short and Kopp, 2005: 366); Flyvbjerg et al. (2003) call it 'misinformation' (TCI, 2004: 41).

Misinformation undermines Parliament's ability to exercise democratic control. Flyvberg et al. stress that the effects of misinformation are not confined to the political arena; for example:

- misinformation destabilises the decision-making on a project. It is bound to emerge sooner or later that the information was incorrect;
- setbacks disrupt the process; for example, new research may be needed and the political and market players might start getting edgy;

- incorrect information can also lead directly to squandering of tax-payers' money.

If the actual costs had been known beforehand, the project could have been abandoned, and other projects with a higher societal yield per invested euro could have been considered. As Flyvbjerg et al. say: 'The wrong projects are being chosen and implemented.'

The dividing line between misinformation and prevarication is wafer-thin. According to Flyvbjerg et al. (2003), misinformation is essentially the wilful and deliberate telling of untruths – which is tantamount to lying.

The central challenge when defining decision-making processes for mega-projects is to create incentives that deliver more reliable information – particularly in the early stages. This may be achieved through second opinions, hearings, workshops and independent experts. Flyvbjerg et al. (2003) maintain that cost–benefit prognoses should be left to the organisations that will actually suffer the consequences of any inaccuracies. Accordingly, they also argue that private parties should be allowed to participate in the preparations for mega-projects provided they bear at least 30 per cent of the total investment risk.

The conclusions of Flyvbjerg et al. (2003) do not bode well for political decision-making. They imply that governments and parliaments base their decisions on (deliberately fabricated) incorrect information. The costs are underestimated and the benefits overestimated: there are too many mega-projects with far lower returns than predicted, and nowhere near enough economic benefits. Moreover, huge differences exist between projects: while some are prepared on the basis of the grossly exaggerated predictions of the initiators, others are prepared on the basis of (more or less) accurate information. So it makes no sense to argue that the impacts of the mistakes cancel each other out.

Mega-Projects According to Short and Kopp (2005)

Short and Kopp (2005: 362–3) have assembled data that show long-run trends (1975–2000) in the ratio of investment in different modes of transport. In Western European countries the percentage invested in road transport is declining slightly while the percentage that goes to rail transport is on the increase. Conversely, in Central and Eastern European countries investment in rail transport is declining, standing at around 37 per cent in 2000. Short and Kopp (2005: 363) write: '[T]he fact that the rail market share has been constantly declining and that its share of investment is increasing in Western European countries is certainly worth noting.' It looks as if the renaissance of rail investment in Western Europe is tied in with the popularity of the high-speed railway and light rail (ECMT, 1994).

Short and Kopp (2005: 363) have misgivings about the recent rise in investment in rail infrastructure in Western Europe. Considering the sharp fall in the railway's market share in the modal split (lower than 10 per cent in many West European countries), the low rates of return on rail investment, the relatively large sums needed to make an impact, and the high maintenance consequences of rail investments (in Germany it is estimated that every €100 invested in rail means annual maintenance costs of €40), Short and Kopp (2005: 363) ask 'whether we can afford this'. Rail investment and user charge in rail transport without accompanying policy measures are likely to be costly and ineffective (Affuso et al., 2003).

Short and Kopp (2005: 363) refer to Bonnafous (2003), who points out that the costs per kilometre of high-speed railway lines are far higher than in the past. In fact, they have almost doubled in real prices, from €5.03 million for the first lines to over €9.91 million for more recent ones. Though the first high-speed rail projects in Japan and France (Bonnafous and Crozet, 1997) were successful, recent ones show more dubious results.

Short and Kopp (2005: 363) compiled a set of proposals for improving planning and decision-making in transport infrastructure mega-projects:

- Greater efforts should be made to explain the planning methods to a broad expert audience. Secrecy about forecasting methods, modelling assumptions, model selection criteria and, in particular, the determination of planning objectives, can make people suspicious of the planning outcomes.
- Quality checks on the planning outcomes, similar to reviews by scientific journals, could help to improve the reputation of planning agencies.
- Even if the quality of a planning process is beyond reproach, it is not always certain that the outcomes will be directly translated into political decisions and then implemented. If this is due to defects in the planning, information should be relayed back to improve the planning process in general and move it forward to an interactive planning–policy learning process.
- The rejection of planning outcomes should be justified. The reasons for political non-acceptance of planning outcomes should be backed by a broad audience.

In general, Short and Kopp (2005) observe a lack of transparency in decision-making on transport infrastructure projects on a national and European scale. The methodological underpinning of decision-making on these projects also left much to be desired. Short and Kopp (2005: 364) even say that no use is made of traffic forecasts or economic analyses. Neither data nor costs are publicly available. There is also a dire shortage of reliable and competent *ex-post* evaluations (Quinet, 2000; Rothengatter, 2000). As European decision-making is sometimes geared exclusively to projects worth at least €500 million, a bias has emerged towards mega-projects. Short and Kopp (2005: 364) write: '[T]hese international processes did not make enough use of economics, became over-politicised and biased towards mega-projects, and had no close links with financing or implementation.'

Unfortunately, the findings with regard to decision-making in international projects apply likewise to decision-making in national transport infrastructure projects. There is a pressing need at both levels for better data, better economic appraisal and more transparency (Mackie and Preston, 1998).

In tram and light-rail projects the costs also tend to be underestimated and the benefits overestimated (Pickrell, 1989). Even so, Short and Kopp (2005: 365) concede that, at the end of the day, sensible decisions are still taken: 'Some cities, for example, Strasbourg, Nantes and Grenoble believe that their visions of accessibility and liveability have been achieved and that their light rail systems have enhanced them. Other cases are much less convincing – Sheffield in the UK is one example and there are several more in the US.'

Short and Kopp (2005: 366) write: 'It is clear that an evaluation framework for light rail needs to address broader aims: better accessibility to cities and particular groups, more attractive cities, revitalised city districts and more users of other modes to reduce congestion and pollution.' The question is how all these effects can be credibly determined in advance.

Short and Kopp (2005: 366) draw six general conclusions on investment in and planning of transport infrastructure projects:

1. Policy and research need good data. The broad information that is currently available allows some analysis but it is still insufficient and in need of fundamental improvement. Often, project data are not collected or made available, and *ex-post* monitoring of projects and policies needs to be systematically introduced and strengthened.
2. Even at this level, important questions can be raised about appropriate levels of investment and how the investments are allocated to the various modes. The search for answers will involve more in-depth analyses and may prove a rich topic for research.
3. National investment planning methods are flawed in several respects, the most serious being lack of transparency, not differences in appraisal methods.

4. International planning is growing in importance but it risks inheriting all the flaws of national planning and some new ones as well. But that does not alter the fact that there are areas where infrastructure has to be planned on an international scale. We therefore need better analyses and a clearer understanding of where international planning might apply and how it could work effectively.
5. Project appraisal is still inconsistent and weak. Strategic appraisal is in its infancy. *Ex-ante* appraisal is often biased and *ex-post* analysis rarely takes place.
6. Research into planning and decision-making processes could, given their ever-increasing complexity and duration, be of great value to society.

Mega-Projects According to the Duivesteijn Commission (2004)

The experience of the Dutch Duivesteijn Commission (TCI, 2004) confirms the findings of Short and Kopp (2005).

In 2004 the Dutch Parliamentary Commission on Infrastructure Projects published its official report (TCI, 2004). The conclusions of the Duivesteijn Commission are based on the decision-making process for two major infrastructure projects: the dedicated High Speed Rail Link South (Amsterdam–Belgian border – HSL-South) and the dedicated Freight Railway Link, connecting Rotterdam and the Ruhr Area (Betuwe Line). The TCI (2004) also turned its attention to recent international analyses of decision-making in large infrastructure projects. The central concern of the TCI study (2004) is the role of the Dutch Parliament.

In the Netherlands, empirical evidence drawn from the two cases mentioned bears out the findings of Altshuler and Luberoff (2003): the Port Authority of Rotterdam, the Dutch Railways and the ECT Terminal in Rotterdam strongly backed the Betuwe Line (no. 2). Public entrepreneurship was observable in both the HSL-South and the Betuwe Line (no. 3). The do-no-harm approach was adopted by municipalities and action groups in both cases. This led to a number of extra tunnels and other plans for mitigating negative impacts, incurring substantial cost overruns. With the exception of the province of Gelderland, no local or regional authority made a financial contribution (no. 4). Mitigation of negative impacts played an important role in the Betuwe Line in particular, but HSL-South also generated some interesting and costly mitigation programmes, including the Green Heart Tunnel (no. 5). 'Bottom-up federalism' was observed in HSL-South (Amsterdam–Schiphol) and even more so in the Betuwe Line (Port Authority of Rotterdam) (no. 6). 'Locally painless project financing' occurred in both cases (no. 7). Finally, it was the huge cost overruns in both cases that prompted the TCI to launch a parliamentary inquiry (no. 8). In comparing the USA and the Netherlands we have to keep in mind that the finance of local projects in the Netherlands is much more dependent on the national public budget than in the USA.

The TCI (2004: 15) observed that mega-projects are often contested during preparation and implementation. They are characterised by dynamism and complexity, as is reflected in systematic budget overruns. Large projects are one-off events in public administration and therefore require an individualised approach.

The frequent budget overruns point to a financial complexity which is intertwined with the immense technological and social complexity of mega-projects. The decision-making on complex projects takes place in a policy arena of interdependent parties (TCI, 2004: 18). Teisman (1998) writes: 'The players are stuck with each other. Mutual dependence creates relationships. The policy field evolves into a network of interdependent ties. . . . Initiatives come under fire in systems founded on checks and balances – which could lead to better policy proposals.'

Any number of obstacles can crop up and obstruct political management and monitoring of the decision-making process. A huge problem is that the Lower House is not involved in the decision-making procedure in the initiation phase of mega-projects and, in effect, acquiesces. In the later stages it seems to be primarily committed to pushing through spatial adjustments.

The government has set its course and is holding fast; it is subject to a process of entrapment (Brockner and Rubin, 1985). The government has shown that it is hardly capable of learning lessons. Hence the government is also to blame for the many overrun budgets.

There was no overall appraisal at the start of the decision-making process. There was no scope for weighing up the alternatives. Sometimes the decision-making was prematurely included in the text of a coalition agreement. However, since the start of the Betuwe Line and the HSL-South much has improved by introducing the OEEI method in calculating *ex-ante* costs and benefits (Eijgenraam et al., 1999).

The main obstacles to management and monitoring in the implementation phase are the project organisers, project control, risk management, contracting, and the public–private partnership. In all these areas the ambitions were found to be too high and the achievements too low, partly because of a lack of professionalism in the public sector.

The findings of the TCI (2004) bear out the conclusion of Short and Kopp (2005: 366), who call the role of government into question: '[I]n many cases, its role as protector of the public interest has become subordinate to its role as promoter of projects. Achieving the right balance requires an urgent redefinition of the job of Transport Minister . . .'.

1.4 CONTENT OF THE BOOK

The book is structured in three parts, which relate to the three components of the subtitle of the book: I   Management Characteristics and Cost–Benefit Analysis; II   Planning and Decision-Making; and III   Innovation, Competition and Institutions.

Part I   Management Characteristics and Cost–Benefit Analysis

Part I starts with Chapter 2, 'Management characteristics of mega-projects' (Hans de Bruijn and Martijn Leijten). In this contribution the authors discuss the most common pitfalls for managers of mega-projects and ways to avoid them. Projects may be unmanageable (in terms of time and money) as a result of a challenging design or a complex social system, or impoverished as a result of a safe design to prevent this unmanageability. In addition, this chapter focuses on the characteristics of the technical and social complexity, and how projects can be managed to avoid these pitfalls. This leads to the central question whether the manager should be mainly involved with the substance of his project or rather with the process that should lead to its completion.

Chapter 3 is on the '*Ex-ante* evaluation of mega-projects: methodological issues and cost–benefit analysis' (Bert van Wee and Lóránt Tavasszy). This chapter discusses methodological issues from the cost–benefit analysis (CBA) perspective. Several of the issues, however, are also relevant for other evaluation frameworks such as multi-criteria analysis (MCA). The issues include both the more technical/methodological issues as well as modelling issues.

'Cost–benefit analysis and the wider economic benefits from mega-projects' is the topic of Chapter 4 (Roger Vickerman). Wider benefits, going beyond the direct benefits to the users of transport infrastructure, are frequently claimed as the basis for justifying projects that have only marginal rates of return based on user benefits. This chapter reviews the basis for such claims, referring to empirical evidence from European, Dutch and UK studies. It assesses the way in which such evidence can be used to refine the appraisal process for mega-projects. There is a particular emphasis on the value of the new economic geography, especially the impacts on the labour market. The chapter argues that there is no simple rule of thumb that can be applied to such projects, and that the data requirements, although demanding, are feasible for mega-projects.

Chapter 5, written by Hans de Bruijn and Martijn Leijten, is on 'Mega-projects and contested information'. Good information is key to good decision-making on mega-projects. Decision-making is information-sensitive and empirical research shows that, in many cases, a lack of information has resulted in poor decision-making. This chapter deals with three issues related to mega-projects:

1. The concept of contested knowledge will be introduced. The stronger the different interests of the main actors are, the stronger the incentives will be to make information more contested and devalue it.
2. If the contested character of information is denied, what are the implications for decision-making? Denying the contested character of information will make decision-making a free fight. This is a paradoxical conclusion: if information is contested and actors look for objective information, the role of information will be devalued rather than strengthened.
3. A number of strategies will be introduced to cope with the contested character of information. Their essence is not finding objective information but negotiating on what the right information for correct decision-making might be. The result of these strategies is negotiated knowledge rather than objective knowledge.

Part II   Planning and Decision-Making

Chapter 6, by Hugo Priemus, tries to explain 'How to improve the early stages of decision-making on mega-projects'. The author argues that the decision-making process on mega-projects is mostly at its weakest in the early stages.

Very often a solution is presented without a valid analysis of the problems. In addition, feasible alternatives are not put forward, because lobby groups work hard mobilising support for the 'superior' solution. Alternatives are only later suggested by others than the promoters, and are often whittled down to nothing.

The systems analysis methodology is presented in this chapter and strongly recommended: at an early stage alternatives are generated, ranked according to the *ex-ante* calculations of costs and benefits, and finally selected. This methodology is certainly not new among scientists, but in practice governments and other promoters of mega-projects seldom use this well-known approach, let alone more advanced techniques such as actor modelling, simulation and gaming, which could very well be combined with systems analysis.

'Public planning of mega-projects: overestimation of demand and underestimation of costs' is the theme of Chapter 7 by Bent Flyvbjerg. This chapter presents evidence that forecasters generally do a poor job of estimating travel demand and construction costs for new transportation infrastructure. For travel demand, in nine out of ten rail projects passenger forecasts are over-estimated; actual ridership is on average 51 per cent less than that forecasted. In 50 per cent of road projects the difference between actual and forecasted traffic is more than ±20 per cent; for 25 per cent of roads the difference is greater than ±40 per cent. For construction costs, nine out of ten projects have underestimated costs and cost overruns.

Forecasting inaccuracy appears to be constant over time and space. Estimates of travel demand have not improved for 30 years, cost estimates and overruns not for 70 years. Inaccuracy exists across the 20 nations and five continents included in the study. Measures developed to improve this sorry state of affairs include improved governance structures with incentives that better reward valid estimates of demand, costs and risks, and punish deceptive estimates. Measures also include better forecasting methods, for example the use of 'reference class forecasting', based on theories of decision-making under uncertainty.

Chapter 8 is on 'Evolving strategy: risk management and the shaping of mega-projects' (Roger Miller and Donald Lessard). The authors argue in this chapter that the succession of shaping episodes that form the front-end process to cope with risks can be reinterpreted in terms of the real-options framework that is currently revolutionising academic treatments of project evaluation. In fact, as is often the case with cutting-edge practice, managers have been successful at creating value through the development and exercise of sequential options without explicitly framing the process in options terms. Academics have simply codified this practice in the form of a new conceptual framework.

The real-options framework is based on the same logic as that of financial options as developed by Black and Scholes (1974). It recognizes that the decisions that determine project cash flows are made sequentially over many episodes. The key insight of this approach is that uncertainty or volatility may actually increase the value of a project, as long as flexibility is preserved and resources are not irreversibly committed. As a result, the economic value of a project when it is still relatively unformed is often greater than the discounted present value of the expected future cash flows. Value is increased through the creation of options for subsequent sequential choices and exercising these options in a timely fashion. Thus sponsors seek projects that have the potential for large payoffs under particular institutional and technical circumstances. The study in this chapter illustrates the rich varieties of mechanisms through which these options are shaped and exercised over the life of the project – the real management that is integral to real options.

'How to overcome major weaknesses in mega-projects: the Norwegian approach' is the theme of Chapter 9, by Knut Samset. This chapter takes a broad view on decisions made at different stages, up front and during implementation, of mega-projects – and their effects during the implementation and operational phases. The author discusses characteristics of the decision-making process and the basis for decisions during these phases. Some general requirements are outlined, and cases used to illustrate the points. The presentation focuses on basic generic principles, and only to some extent goes into further discussion of the complexities and restrictions that might apply when the principles are implemented. The quality assurance scheme applied by Norwegian authorities to improve up-front decision-making, management and the effect of major public investment projects is presented as one type of governance regime that might help overcome some of the problems observed. Current and potential effects and spin-offs of the regime are discussed.

Joop Koppenjan discusses 'Public–private partnership and mega-projects' in Chapter 10. This contribution concentrates in particular on the Private Finance Initiative (PFI) – as in arrangements in the transport and water sectors. The author discusses what public–private partnership (PPP) is about: definitions, motives and form. Then an overview is given of experiences with PPP. The central question is: does PPP live up to expectations? The author discusses a number of typical problems that occur in PPP processes which will have to be dealt with in order to make PPP schemes work.

Finally, a number of lessons are formulated regarding the conditions for successful PPP in mega-projects. The author argues that the current emphasis on PFI-like models in the world of infrastructure projects should be complemented with other experimental models: the variety of infrastructure projects calls for the development of a variety of PPP options, which makes the task for parties to learn to handle these options even more challenging.

Part III   Innovation, Competition and Institutions

Chapter 11 (Werner Rothengatter) is on 'Innovations in the planning of mega-projects'. The focus is the aspects of new institutional arrangements and innovative assessment tools to improve on the performance of the planning process for mega-projects.

Wrong procurement is a major cause of public failure; the problems of high risk and long life of mega-projects deserve particular consideration in the procurement process. Innovations in planning approaches start at this point of departure and first suggest a different organisation structure. Important issues are the establishment of a project company under private law and the participation of private risk capital. Furthermore, the integration of preferences of different stakeholder groups from the beginning is important to minimise conflicts in the procurement process. This can be supported by particular methodological approaches such as logic constraint programming. Finally, a dynamic assessment scheme is necessary, which includes the most important feedback loops between infrastructure use and the economy. One possibility is to apply system dynamics, which is illustrated by the example of the ASTRA model.

The basic message is that improved success of mega-projects is not so much a matter of better methods or more accurate calculations. Major progress can be achieved by changing the institutional environment so that the incentives of the stakeholders work in the direction of generating real economic benefits within the budget. Once the incentives are set right, the players will almost automatically be interested in using the best technologies and methods, as is suggested.

Chapter 12, written by Karen Trapenberg Frick, is on 'The cost of the technological sublime: daring ingenuity and the new San Francisco–Oakland Bay Bridge'. The 'technological sublime' refers to the repeated experiences of awe and wonder, often tinged with an element of terror, which people have had when confronted with particular natural sites, architectural forms and technological achievements. This chapter uses this concept of the sublime to contribute a new dimension to understanding the evolution of mega-project design and optimism bias. The case of the new San Francisco–Oakland Bay Bridge in Northern California is used to demonstrate how the technological sublime dramatically influenced bridge design, project outcomes, public debate and lack of accountability for its excessive cost overruns. The new Bay Bridge case raises several important additional dimensions that should be considered in policy analyses about mega-projects: the sublime, aesthetics and funding.

Chapter 13 (Didier van de Velde and Ernst ten Heuvelhof) is on 'Provision and management of dedicated railway systems: how to arrange competition'. The main aim of using contracting under competition in the case of infrastructures was the introduction of additional incentives for budget control in infrastructure realisation and a better inclusion of trade-offs between building costs and maintenance costs in infrastructure design and operation. Further in-depth studies are required to identify the relative performance of these different arrangements.

The authors observe that, although the advantages may seem substantial from a theoretical perspective, innovative contracting is difficult to get off the ground. The main issue, identified as the vertical dimension in their framework of analysis, is whether production stages that are conceptually separable (such as infrastructure management and train operations) should be separated, or whether interdependencies between these or other stages require integration to guarantee optimisation. These critical interface problems require specific attention when the use of competition is contemplated to realise one or several parts of a railway system. This is the fundamental issue of transaction-cost economics. One feature of the current reform practices in the railway sector is that they are, to a large extent, dictated by political or economic dogma rather than by optimal outsourcing decisions. Furthermore, many of the reforms go beyond simple outsourcing, as they introduce several non-hierarchically related initiative-takers along the various layers, adding to the complexity and requiring further coordination between these new actors.

Two questions present themselves in a horizontal sense: to what extent should the various activities (designing, building, operating, maintaining) and their financing be kept in one hand and how much room should private parties be given in their role as contractors? Successes appear to be scored mainly in effectiveness, better project control and innovation. Most problems occur in the areas of transaction costs, transparency, legitimacy and accountability. Many of the disadvantages might perhaps have been prevented if the process had been better organised.

Chapter 14 deals with a specific case: 'Rail infrastructure at major European hub airports: the role of institutional settings'. This contribution by Moshe Givoni and Piet Rietveld compares different approaches to intermodality. The authors argue that the development of rail networks around the world is directly linked to the development of cities. Large airports generate demand which is often even larger than that of city centres. Big airports are ideal places for developing railway services. Nevertheless, the connection of the world's largest airports to the rail network is a recent development.

The different degrees of rail development at airports which are big enough to justify investments in rail infrastructure are very context-specific. In terms of intermodal policies and more specifically rail services at airports, the cases of Schiphol (seamless intermodality) and Heathrow (limited intermodality) represent two extremes. The case of Charles de Gaulle (Paris) illustrates an intermediate position. These three cases are presented and compared. The different institutional settings contribute strongly to the explanation of the differences in outcomes.

The authors conclude that in countries with large airports and a developed rail network, airports should be a stop on the main rail lines. It is helpful to recognise large airports as cities. The role and function of these cities in a regional-economic perspective depend on their connection to the surface transport network. It is important not only to improve the interconnectivity between air networks and road networks, but also the interconnectivity between air networks and rail networks.

Chapter 15 draws institutional lessons across countries on making transport infrastructure policy. The author, Martin de Jong, argues that institutions and institutional systems are hard to change, but it is not impossible.

When congestion on the infrastructure networks or annual investment/ maintenance costs are considered to have grown out of hand, or when citizens feel they should be more involved in the decision process, drawing lessons from policies in other countries can prove a helpful source of inspiration for institutional changes at home. This does not imply, however, that following good examples from elsewhere also results in policy successes at home. Political, legal, administrative and cultural practices differ among countries, and so do their economic, geographical and practical potential. In the end, each country can benefit immensely from experiences abroad, but policy actors will always have to take into account that a transplant must function in one's own institutional context, in one's own practical circumstances and in collaboration with other domestic policy actors. The chances that such a situation comes about is low when policy models are copied literally and without making the necessary amendments.

Four examples of promising policy transplants are presented. All four may prove invaluable sources of inspiration for policy entrepreneurs apt to provoke changes in their national systems for infrastructure decision-making, albeit in various directions. But in none of them can transfer be considered something automatic. It will require political and policy struggles among proponents and opponents, and in all cases intelligent thought and careful manoeuvring in negotiations will lead the transplants to deviate substantially from their examples.

REFERENCES

Affuso, L., J. Masson and D.M.G. Newbery (2003), 'Comparing investments in new transport infrastructures', *Fiscal Studies*, **24** (3): 273–315.

Altshuler, Alan and David Luberoff (2003), *Mega-Projects. The Changing Politics of Urban Public Investment*, Washington, DC: Brookings Institution Press.

Black, Fischer and Myron Scholes (1974), 'From theory to a new financial product', *Journal of Finance*, **29** (2): 399–412.

Bonnafous, A. (2003), 'Assessing our expertise', in European Council of Ministers of Transport (ECMT) (ed.), *Fifty Years of Transport Policy. Successes and New Challenges*, Paris: ECMT.

Bonnafous, A. and Y. Crozet (1997), 'Evaluation, dévaluation ou réévaluation des lignes à grande vitesse?', *Les Cahiers Scientifiques du Transport*, **32**: 45–56.

Brockner, J. and J.Z. Rubin (1985), *Entrapment in Escalating Conflicts: A Social Psychological Analysis*, New York: Springer Verlag.

Eijgenraam, C.C.J., C.C. Koopmans, P.J.G. Tang and A.C.P. Verster (1999), *Evaluatie van infrastructuurprojecten. Leidraad voor kosten–batenanalyse. Deel I:*

20   *Introduction: scope of the book*

Hoofdrapport [Evaluation of infrastructure projects. Guide for cost–benefit analysis. Part 1: Main report]. Onderzoeksprogramma Economische Effecten Infrastructuur (OEEI), The Hague: Ministerie van Verkeer en Waterstaat en Ministerie van Economische Zaken.
European Council of Ministers of Transport (ECMT) (1994), *Light Rail Transit Systems*, Paris: ECMT.
Flyvbjerg, B., N. Bruzelius and W. Rothengatter (2003), *Megaprojects and Risk: An Anatomy of Ambition*, Cambridge: Cambridge University Press.
Hall, P. (1980), *Great Planning Disasters*, Berkeley, CA: University of California Press.
Mackie, P. and J. Preston (1998), 'Twenty-one sources of error and bias in transport project appraisal', *Transport Policy*, **5** (1): 1–8.
Miller, R. and D. Lessard (2001), *The Strategic Management of Large Engineering Projects: Shaping Risks, Institutions and Governance*, Cambridge, MA: MIT Press.
Pickrell, D. (1989), *Urban Rail Transit Projects. Forecast versus Actual Ridership and Costs*, Washington, DC: US Department of Transportation.
Pickrell, D. (1992), 'A desire named streetcar–fantasy and fact in rail transit planning', *Journal of American Planning Association*, **58** (2): 158–76.
Quinet, E. (2000), 'Evaluation methodologies of transportation projects in France', *Transport Policy*, **7** (1): 27–35.
Rothengatter, W. (2000), 'Evaluation of infrastructure investments in Germany', *Transport Policy*, **7** (1): 17–27.
Short, J. and A. Kopp (2005), 'Transport infrastructure: investment and planning. Policy and research aspects', *Transport Policy*, **12**: 360–67.
Teisman, G.R. (1998), *Complexe besluitvorming, een pluricentrisch perspectief op besluitvorming over ruimtelijke investeringen* [Complex decision-making, a pluricentred perspective on spatial investments], The Hague: Elsevier.
Tijdelijke Commissie Infrastructuurprojecten (TCI) (2004), *Grote projecten uitvergroot. Een infrastructuur voor besluitvorming* [Large projects under the magnifying glass. An infrastructure for decision-making], Tweede Kamer (Dutch Lower House), 2004–2005, 29.283 nos 5–6, The Hague: Sdu Uitgevers.
Wachs, M. (1989), 'When planners lie with numbers', *APA Journal*, **55** (4): 476–9.
Wachs, M. (1990), 'Ethics and advocacy in forecasting for public policy', *Business and Professional Ethics Journal*, **9** (1&2): 141–57.

PART I

Management Characteristics and
Cost–Benefit Analysis

2. Management characteristics of mega-projects

Hans de Bruijn and Martijn Leijten

2.1 INTRODUCTION

Over the years the development of mega-projects has presented us with some of the most persistent problems of our times. Cost overruns, delays, use and revenues falling short, and even technical failure – sometimes with devastating consequences – plague our progress. In this chapter we provide an overview of the uncertainties and the management dilemmas many project owners or commissioners encounter.

There are at least two generically formulated pitfalls in the implementation of mega-projects:

- The project is *unmanageable in terms of time or money*. This can have many causes that often have to do with the technical and social complexity of the project and its environment. Most implementation problems come into this category. An example of an important factor in technical complexity is the extent of technical uncertainty. In social complexity such a factor can be, for instance, the extent to which there is disagreement between the parties involved regarding the desirability and design of the project. The costs involved in a project may be well managed during the setting up of the project, but after the planning has been completed it turns out that the project is much less cost-effective than originally thought – for example because the number of users of the completed project falls short. This is also an aspect of manageability.
- The project is *impoverished as to its substance*: to prevent unmanageability it has too little ambition, is not sufficiently future-oriented. The outcome would have had greater added value if – for example – the choice had been of a different scope, if the wishes of the users or local inhabitants had been better exploited or if use had been made of the latest expertise.

In this chapter we search for possible explanations for these pitfalls. In simple terms, three types of explanation can be offered:

1. Explanations stemming from the *decision-making process* for a mega-project. The classic example here is the strategy of making too low an estimate of the costs involved in the mega-project in order for the decision-making to go more smoothly at this stage.
2. Explanations stemming from the *nature of the project* decided upon. Thus a project requiring a great deal of innovative and as yet undeveloped technology will probably be less manageable than a project that mainly makes use of 'proven technology' (technical complexity).
3. Explanations stemming from the *implementation* of the mega-project. Here we can expect that a project meeting little opposition is more rapidly implemented than a project that can look forward to a great deal of opposition and thus generates a great deal of blocking power (social complexity).

The (political) decision-making process that leads to a decision to carry out a mega-project has already been dealt with extensively (see, e.g., Hall, 1980 and Altshuler and Luberoff, 2003). In this chapter we concentrate mainly on the latter two explanations: the nature of the project and the implementation path.

The chapter is organised as follows: first the management characteristics of the project will be examined more closely. These can be divided into technical and social characteristics (Sections 2.2 and 2.3 respectively). It is pointed out that certain characteristics make projects more manageable while others make them less so. When projects are easily manageable there is the risk that they are less rich and innovative as to their substance, because they must comply with standards already available. We then examine the question of how potential unmanageability or impoverished substance can be dealt with, which leads to further elaboration (Section 2.4). Some conclusions are formulated in Section 2.5.

2.2   TECHNICAL COMPLEXITY

We distinguish between technical complexity (complexity with regard to the project's technical system) and social complexity (complexity with regard to the social system, such as the constellation of players involved) (cf. Cleland and King, 1983: 39).

Table 2.1 gives an overview of the most important factors in determining the technical complexity of a project. The underlying thought is that

Table 2.1   Technical characteristics of projects affecting manageability

Manageable if . . .	Less well manageable if . . .
Robust (overdesign)	Less robust (underdesign)
Proven technology (tame technology)	Innovative technology (unproven technology, unruly technology)
Divisible	Indivisible
Loose coupling	Tight coupling
Fallback option	No fallback option
Monofunctional	Multifunctional
Incremental implementation	Radical implementation

the characteristics on the left are positive in their effect on the manageability of a project. We discuss these characteristics briefly and provide an example of each.

Robustness: Overdesign or Underdesign

The robustness of a project refers to the lifespan and the solidity of a technical design and its realisation. The more technically robust a project is, the less chance there is of unforeseen developments. Robustness is often accompanied by a certain measure of overdesign: there is a standard for the robustness of a particular design, but the project is made more robust and more detailed than the standard. This brings about a greater chance of manageability (though no guarantee). The opposite side of the coin is underdesign. The project is less robust and thus less predictable and less manageable, as failure becomes a serious possibility. Underdesigning can be an attractive strategy since it offers opportunities for realising the project at a lower cost or for adjusting the design in the course of its implementation. This can enrich the project's substance and innovative character. Unexpected and unforeseen chances of a better implementation of the project's substance can be included without difficulty. It can also turn out, in hindsight, that an underdesign is sufficiently robust after all. Overdesign is more easily manageable; underdesign can be cheaper.

The Central Artery/Tunnel project of Boston, MA demonstrates the possible risks of underdesigning (assuming that the leakages were the result of a design problem, as suggested by some engineers). The Central Artery/Tunnel project was the first US project to use slurry walls (usually temporary walls to prevent the excavation from flooding and collapsing) as permanent walls. Moreover, the tunnel was being constructed in a vulnerable area, within a stone's throw from Boston's Inner Harbor. After opening, the tunnel experienced structural leakage problems, allegedly as a result of this design. However, there has not been a unanimous judgement on the causes so far, and the commissioner has been discussing responsibility and solutions with the many parties involved.[1]

An example of overdesign is also found in Boston, at the Post Office Square underground car park, where engineers made very thick walls in order to reduce to a minimum the risk of collapse or subsidence in the complex inner-city area where the project was planned. This was decided after the discovery of minor subsidence at one of the abutting buildings.[2] The extent to which overdesign is successful is almost always the same: usually nothing goes wrong technically, but costs are higher and the opportunities for innovation (e.g. development of a cheaper or better technology or application, inherent to underdesign) are more limited than when overdesign is not employed.

Proven Technology or Innovative Technology

An innovative technology is one that is being used for the first time. There are different grades:

- A technology is specifically devised and developed for a project and then applied. This is the most extreme form of innovation.
- A technology has already been developed but not yet applied.
- A technology that has been applied previously, but not under the same conditions (manageability can then be reduced by – for example – unfavourable soil conditions, a more complex project environment, larger scale etc.).

The use of a proven technology provides greater certainty than the use of innovative technology. Result: the project is more manageable but the potential for innovation suffers, as does the enrichment of the project's substance.

An example of the application of innovative technology in infrastructure construction is the New Austrian Tunnelling Method, developed in the 1950s and 1960s in Austria to build tunnels (with the use of surrounding soil; see Golser, 1976). It is now regularly applied all over the world. An example of the use of a known technology under new conditions is the drilling of tunnels in the boggy Dutch soil. Tunnels had been drilled world-wide for many years before it was done for the first time under the difficult Dutch conditions in the construction of the Tweede Heinenoordtunnel. This was clearly seen as a test project, and its implementation was planned with a great deal of redundancy and checks and balances (see also Section 2.4), later turning out to be reasonably manageable.

The Tacoma Narrows Bridge in the US state of Washington is one of the best-known examples of an infrastructure where the application of an innovative design went wrong. It was the first suspension bridge with plate girders, rather than open-lattice beams under the roadbed. In the old design, the wind would go through the truss, but in the new design the wind was diverted above and below the structure. Soon after the bridge opened in 1940 it was discovered that the roadbed would start to sway and buckle in windy conditions. A few months later, the bridge collapsed (Ammann et al., 1941).

Divisibility or Indivisibility

A divisible project consists of different functional elements or sub-projects, working independently of one another; an indivisible project consists of a single functional whole that can no longer function if one part is removed. Divisible projects usually have more simultaneous processes (activities that can be carried out at the same time), which can reduce the consequences of time and cost overruns in the course of the project (shorter critical path). If activities are carried out sequentially, any slow-down in a particular activity automatically causes delay in the subsequent activity. Also, in a divisible project any problems in one part of the project can more easily be isolated or a part of the project can even be cancelled without any consequences for the rest of the project. For these reasons divisibility ensures more certainty and manageability during the implementation of the project (Van Gigch, 1991; Simon, 1996).

Both divisibility and indivisibility can have benefits and disadvantages. A divisible project is less vulnerable to failures, because in general any failure can easily be isolated. On the other hand, a divisible project is prone to downsizing. If circumstances make it attractive, the owner of a project can opt to scrap part of the project, thereby enhancing the manageability of the rest. Seen from the point of view of the project owner, this can be regarded as an advantage, but supporters of the project may see it as a disadvantage. The situation is precisely the opposite in the case of an indivisible project: downsizing is often impossible and failures can bring down the entire project system.

An example of an indivisible project in which all parts are required to render the project useful is a tunnel. By the time a tunnel is only half completed, it cannot be used for the end envisaged in its construction, namely to be able to cross over, by a fixed link, that which is being tunnelled under. If failures occur in the tunnel, the crossing is blocked and the rest of the tunnel cannot be used.

Tight or Loose Coupling

Projects are systems consisting of components or subsystems with couplings (mutual links) between them. To say that a coupling is tight or loose is to refer to the intensity with which two system components are tied to one another. An extremely tight coupling between two system components means that an occurrence in one element always affects the other. This is not so if the coupling is loose: any occurrence in an element there is isolated. With a tight coupling the risks can be greater because an incident in a particular element or sub-project can have a negative effect on another element or sub-project. Problems with tight coupling therefore often lead to an 'oil-slick' mechanism or a domino effect. When a loose coupling is involved, a problem of this nature can more easily be isolated (Perrow, 1999). A suspension bridge is an example of a project with tight couplings. A weak stay cable, for instance, can lead to problems with the road surface.

The constellation of couplings in a technical system is also important. Systems with linear coupling are the easiest to oversee. Here system elements are linked in series. This has the disadvantage that if a failure occurs, generally the entire system collapses. But the system's simple structure means that problematic couplings or failing systems can often be repaired relatively easily. The reverse side of the coin is the system with complex couplings, with parallel connections. A failure in this type of system can often be solved by using an alternative link in the system. This means that a failure does not necessarily cause the entire system to collapse, but it does mean that an error is sometimes more complicated to correct because of the many complex links between the system's elements. And in this type of system it is more difficult for managers and even for engineers to be familiar with and to understand all the system's characteristics. The difference between linear and complex couplings is not only found in infrastructure projects.

This can be shown most clearly by taking the example of an electricity network. When an electrical connection simply runs from A to B and the connection is damaged at a particular point along this line, the entire connection fails. But it is a fairly simple matter to restore the connection. However, if the damage occurs in a complex network of electrical connections, this can be compensated by the current being drawn from elsewhere in the system. Then, however, it is more difficult to discover the site of the problem. The blackout that occurred in north-eastern America on 14 August 2003 is a good example of the second situation. A problem in the network made it necessary for other power stations to supply more current so that they became overloaded and a chain reaction occurred causing the electricity supply to fail in a large part of the north-eastern USA and the

Canadian province of Ontario. It took two days to restore power to most places, and a further three months for the official investigating committee to establish the cause.

Fallback Option Available or Not

A fallback option is a reserve solution offering the possibility of completing a project if something goes wrong with the original option. If a fallback option has been provided for, a simple transfer takes place to another option in the case of a failure. This can happen either because the technology bears its own alternative or because provision has been made for an alternative before to the project was implemented. In the case of the Souterrain tram tunnel project in The Hague, for instance, it took two-and-a-half years for a decision to be made regarding an alternative technology after leakage occurred when the original technology was applied. If a prior decision had been made to keep an alternative to hand, the project would have experienced far less delay after the leakage had occurred.

Monofunctionality or Multifunctionality

A multifunctional project serves a variety of functions, while a monofunctional project has only one. In theory no limit can be placed on multifunctionality (perhaps there are projects in which an endless number of functions can be combined). Multifunctionality can be advantageous for manageability: the more functions a project has, the smaller the risk of total failure. Of course there are limits to this. An excessive accumulation of functions can have an adverse effect on the manageability of the project. There will, in fact, always be at least one function that is realised in the end; the project cannot fail completely. Many railway links are monofunctional: high-speed tracks often serve only for high-speed trains. Many ICT projects are multifunctional. Certain types of e-enforcement, such as Weigh in Motion (the automatic weighing of a freight truck via loops in the road to detect whether the truck is overloaded) are multifunctional. The ICT serves not only to detect lawbreakers but also to measure road wear.

Incremental versus Radical Implementation

Incremental implementation implies phased transfer to the new infrastructure/service. Radical implementation means that transfer is achieved in a 'jump'. Incremental implementation is often advantageous to the project's manageability: it is possible to learn and the project can – if necessary – be halted or adjusted at an early stage in implementation. The advantage of radical implementation is that all the technological and social complexity involved in implementation is concentrated on a single moment. If a project manager is absolutely certain that this is possible and that no learning is required, then radical implementation is the preferred strategy. However, this will hardly ever be the case with a large-scale project, and there is a strong risk of a radical implementation turning into a big bang and giving birth to something other than has been expected.

The Dutch C2000 project illustrates this well. C2000 is a new communications system for the emergency services in the Netherlands. Given the crucial function the new information system plays in disasters, it is almost a necessity that it should be subjected to radical implementation since all the relevant emergency services have to be connected up to it the moment it comes into service. Add to this the system's indivisibility (see above) and the use of innovative technology, and it is clear that this is a difficult project to manage. At the start the introduction of the system in the Netherlands led to major problems (Tweede Kamer der Staten-Generaal, 2002).

In the construction of – for instance – drilled tunnels with two practically identical tunnel tubes, lessons that can be applied to work on the second tube can be learned from the drilling of the first. During construction of the Herrentunnel in the northern German city of Lübeck, problems of delay arose in the first tube largely caused by obstacles in the soil that damaged the drill head. An evaluation and subsequent adjustments led to the drilling of the second tube going much more rapidly (Assenmacher, 2003).

2.3   SOCIAL COMPLEXITY

The social complexity of a project also has various dimensions. These are summed up in Table 2.2.

Limited or Major Dependence on Users

A first dimension is that of the role of the user. Is the user someone who plays an active part in the implementation or someone who is completely absent? The greater the influence of the user on the completion of the project, the smaller the chances of manageability. At the same time, the quality of the substance of a mega-project can increase if the user can feel satisfaction at the final outcome. For many large-scale government ICT projects this is an important variable. An important role was played by the users in the implementation of the C2000 project already mentioned, since they regularly voiced strong criticism of the system or did not wish to use

Table 2.2   Manageability and unmanageability of projects

Manageable if . . .	Less well manageable if . . .
Limited dependence on user preferences	Major dependence on user preferences
Uniformity between preferences and aims of commissioning party/users	Variety between preferences and aims of commissioning party/users
Stability of preferences and aims of commissioning party/users	Dynamic in preferences and aims of commissioning party/users
Little blockage power held by third parties	Great deal of blockage power held by third parties
Short transformation time	Long transformation time
Limited influence of project on social environment	Major influence of project on social environment

it as yet. The reason is easy to guess. A system of this type is closely bound up in the primary processes of the relevant organisation and thus pushes the users into action. In the case of rail infrastructure the influence of the user during implementation is generally more limited. Uncertainties about the use to be made of rail infrastructure can put its public or private financing on a shaky basis. Insufficient participation and lack of commitment on the part of operators and end users of rail infrastructure can have major undesirable consequences.

A Great Deal or Little Variety in User Preferences

As far as the preferences and aims of users are concerned, it is not only important to know the extent to which a commissioning party or project manager is dependent on them, but also the extent to which the users have come to a shared assessment. This can vary from complete unanimity to strong divisions of opinion and thus to variety. Here too C2000 can serve as an example. Various bodies that were expected to work with C2000 turn out to have different preferences. What is good for the police is not necessarily so for the fire service.

A Great Deal or Little Dynamics in User Preferences

As far as users are concerned, whether their relevant preferences and aims are stable or dynamic can make a difference. During the process a change can occur in preferences or aims – for instance, because of changes in the conditions, progress in technical developments or progress in technology.

When stability is extreme, the preferences and aims of all users remain fixed for the entire duration of the project. When dynamics are extreme, the preferences/aims are subject to constant change, the upper limit of the dynamics being difficult to indicate. A project with dynamic preferences and aims on the part of users is, for instance, the Channel Tunnel. It was thought that the tunnel would be subject to mass use by travellers by car and train as an alternative to the cross-channel ferries, but the rise of budget airlines ensured a shift in the users' preferences from the high-speed train and car to the cheap flight.

A Great Deal or Little Third-party Blocking Power

Various external players can exert a great deal of influence on a project, depending on their blocking power. If they have major blocking power they can make many demands. Blocking power is related to position in a process (e.g. a local council with infrastructure of national importance on its territory) or it can be forcibly acquired (e.g. citizens that penetrate a process). When there is very little blocking power, a commissioning party alone can determine the implementation of a project, whereas in the presence of a great deal of blocking power everything has to be laid before third parties. Blocking power can be the result of a wide variety of factors, such as formal positions (landowners), political power, formal authorisations (local councils) and expertise.

Long or Short Transformation Time

A project's transformation time is the length of the period required for implementation. A long transformation time increases uncertainty since new technological and social developments can occur in the interim. An example familiar in the Netherlands is the Oosterschelde Zeewering (Eastern Scheldt Storm Surge Barrier). The long period required for the construction made it possible for social players to change the design during implementation from a closed dam (which would have changed the Oosterschelde from a saltwater to a freshwater reservoir) into a semi-open dam (better able to maintain the ecosystem). This dynamic also often occurs in large-scale military projects: the length of time required for completion enables changed technological and social conditions to have a major effect on the project.

A Great Deal or Little Influence on the Social Environment

The influence a project has on its social environment can contribute to uncertainty. The greater the impact on the existing environment, the greater the chance that players are activated and attempt to exert influence on the project's implementation. The classic example here is the extensive spatial changes in inner-city areas (underground rail lines, tram tunnels) or the threatened damage to nature and landscape (the Green Hart tunnel in the Dutch section of the Paris to Amsterdam high-speed rail link), which is not without an effect in the social environment.

2.4 MANAGEMENT OF IMPLEMENTATION

If a project's implementation can be well managed, a simple project-based approach to the job is often sufficient. In simple terms: the project can be clearly and unambiguously described, has a clear planning in a number of phases, has a transparent budget and has been organised as efficiently as possible. But if many technical and social uncertainties appear, an approach of this kind is not only insufficient but also misleading. It suggests management and manageability that, in fact, cannot be realised. There are two concrete points that need attention: interaction and redundancy.

Interaction: is there any Process Design and Process Management Present?

If there are many uncertainties due to technical and social complexity, the ways to manage are:

- to involve actors:
    - those who create social complexity, e.g. stakeholders who try to block the project;
    - those who have expertise to solve technical uncertainty (Miller and Lessard, 2000);
- to shift the attention of managers from a well-defined project to a process of interaction.

This requires a process design, one that makes clear who will be involved and when. Excluding players who create complexity may at times seem attractive (it avoids a great deal of 'messing about', discussion etc.), but is a very risky business in the situations referred to. The actual facilitation of the interaction we call process management. Process design and process management can lead to players being activated, including players who oppose the project. If they are not activated, there is a risk that they will emerge later in the process and still manage to use their blockage power. The social complexity (many players, many different interests) requires that the players clearly recognise how they can play a part in the implementation. If this is not clear, many players will simply penetrate the implementation process at a time convenient to themselves. Result: increasing chaos and further unmanageability of the process.

If the decision-maker faces many technical uncertainties, a solution can be found in process management. In fact, innovation can come about by not having the project implemented in a closed circuit (by a limited group of implementers), but by admitting third parties with their expertise at crucial moments.

A process approach is the opposite of two other styles of decision-making: command-and-control and project management. The process approach focuses on organisation and management of a project, rather than its substance. This approach takes the way managers and engineers act and organises the project and its technology as the explaining factor for the performance of a project. Successful project implementation requires a well-organised process in which all actors with important powers (production power, blocking power) and competences cooperate from an equal position, rather than just being hired without responsibilities on the whole project.

Process versus command-and-control

A process approach is the opposite of command-and-control (De Bruijn and Ten Heuvelhof, 2000). As soon as a government (body) has to function within a network of interdependencies (and when is this not the case?), it cannot simply rely on hierarchical management mechanisms. Indeed, such a body depends on other parties, whose support is far from being guaranteed. Any government (body) recognising this fact will not take unilateral decisions but will come to a conclusion in a process of discussion and negotiation with other parties. Such a process does justice to the mutual dependencies in a network.

Process versus project

A process approach can also be opposed to a project approach (De Bruijn et al., 2002). The assumption in a project approach is that problems and solutions are (within certain limits) reasonably stable. This makes it possible to use project-management techniques: a clearly defined aim, a time path, clear conditions and a previously defined end product. Naturally, this type of approach works only in a static world. If an activity is dynamic rather than static, a project approach is not possible and thus a process approach is desirable. These dynamics can have both an external and an internal cause (Morris and Hough, 1987).

● *External dynamics* An activity starts out as a project but develops into a process because external parties, all of whom contribute their own definitions of and solutions to the problem, interfere with the project. This is a familiar pattern in many infrastructural projects. What starts as a project (e.g. laying down part of a rail track) ends up as a process in which all manner of parties become involved with the rail track, a process that has its own dynamic. After a time there is a chance that the parties are no longer discussing the rail track but totally different subjects.

- *Internal dynamics*   An activity starts out as a project but develops into a process because during the project its owner learns that the problem is wider or more complex than originally thought. A neat illustration of this – once given to us by a process manager at the DHV engineering consultancy – is that of a house owner who decides one fine morning to hang a painting in his house. He discovers that the wall is discoloured and repaints the entire wall – which has repercussions for the rest of the interior and finally involves a full-scale renovation of the house. Subsequently he discovers that this desire for renewal is connected to the phase of life he is in and he ends up consulting a psychologist. What starts as a simple project ends as a complex process involving many parties (other people in the house, contractor, neighbours, psychologist).

Much decision-making on infrastructure and transportation is developed and funded unilaterally by government institutions. An owner of, say, a transportation problem makes an exact formulation of its problem (e.g. traffic jams), a goal is set (e.g. reduction of traffic jams by 20 per cent), information is gathered (what are the possibilities for a solution, what are their economic benefits and environmental impact etc.) and a decision is taken (e.g. expansion of highway lanes) that subsequently has to be implemented and evaluated. The decision is imposed unilaterally on other players, some of whom have an interest in the project while others do not, and sometimes they possess blocking power. The gridlock is a typical problem for commuters and government institutions but is not gratuitously recognised by other parties such as environmentalists or people who live nearby who experience nuisance from fast-driving cars if the gridlock is dissolved by road expansion. It is also imaginable that while other parties may recognise the problem, they give it a different priority. Each step in the project-based approach, therefore, can be disputed. Instead of unilaterally defining and fixing a problem, a government body has to accept that different parties define the realities of the situation differently and (can) also have good arguments in their favour. Parties should have to go through a process of negotiation in which they make efforts to arrive at a package of solutions that does justice to the various definitions of the problem advanced by the different parties.

Clearly an approach of this kind has little chance of success. The Bay Area model of decision-making is a famous example of a more process-oriented approach. The model was developed in the San Francisco Bay Area (hence the name). The area was characterised by a disparate group of public authorities that needed each other for the realisation of their goals. Rather than applying the common substance-oriented, hierarchical approach, the Metropolitan Transportation Commission developed a model in which 17 relevant regional actors participated, focusing on values and arguments, which matches better the perceptions of the actors (Chisholm, 1989).

Redundancy: has the Project Sufficient Organisational Redundancy?

A redundant organisation is one in which some overlap has been deliberately created. There is no question of clearly separate tasks between – for example – designer or constructor, or between constructors among themselves. This may seem inefficient: the designer should design and the constructor should construct. The constructor of an ICT system for a fighter plane should not interfere with the company building the engines.

However, the idea is that a separation of tasks of this nature only works when the project is completely manageable (Lerner, 1986; Low et al., 2000). If major technical uncertainties arise, strict separation leads to 'over-the-wall-engineering' (Payne et al., 1996). The designer delivers his design to the constructors, who then have to see whether the design can be realised. The constructors can then become involved in a rat race: the one with his part of the project completed first determines the conditions within which the others have to work. In consequence of this and similar mechanisms, this sort of project becomes increasingly unmanageable. Major problems often arise and there are strong incentives for the engineers involved to blame one another for their problems. Redundancy implies that – for instance – the constructors are involved in the design of the project or that they are mutually involved with one another's projects, and that clear prior agreements are arrived at. Redundancy creates the opportunity for mutual checks and stimulates the implementers involved to assume shared responsibility for an appropriate outcome.

A step further is when explicit counter-forces are organised within a project – for instance by subjecting crucial technical options to counter-expertise. Redundancy and checks and balances can also be beneficial for the innovative nature of a project. It is precisely in the confrontation between designers and constructors, between constructors among themselves or between constructors and peers (providers of counter-expertise) that innovations can come about. Or, to put it another way: if, with the available expertise, no innovation comes about, then innovation is probably not possible.

In the case of the Central Artery/Tunnel project in Boston, the commissioning party (Massachusetts Highway Department, later Massachusetts Turnpike Authority) lacked the technical knowledge required for a project of such complexity. For this reason the commissioning party got as close as possible to the contractor. The Federal Highway Authority, which was financing the project, also turned out (according to a report by the Inspector-General of Massachusetts) to have been very close to the other organisations, so that the work of control was jeopardised (Cerasoli, 2001). In the end this led to a situation where nobody could offer any counterweight to the contractor on the basis of (technical) expertise. This meant that not only was there no redundancy in difficult technical issues, but the costs could also rise in an uncontrolled manner (Leijten, 2004).

In the construction of a subway tunnel in the German city of Dortmund we see exactly the opposite. In this project the commissioning party (Stadtbahnbauamt Dortmund) not only had a great deal of in-house expertise itself, but it also had a reference design made by a specialist engineering consultancy, redundant to its own designs. During implementation it allowed itself to be assisted by the same consultancy and checked the contractor's work on a permanent basis. Up to the present the technical uncertainties have not led to any problems in this project.

2.5 CONCLUSIONS

Modern mega-projects are commonly plagued by technical and social complexity. Preferred solutions do not always result in the most manageable projects. Sometimes projects even demand a less favourable design, introduction or implementation. Both possibilities may result in fierce uncertainty. In addition to that, decision-making, design and implementation regularly take place in a complex social environment of actors helpful or even needed for successful implementation, but also of actors with blocking power. This requires a trade-off determining whether a project is still manageable with traditional project management. A process-oriented approach does more justice to the complexity and the uncertainties. The involvement of a network of relevant parties may be better at providing the insights required to make good trade-offs on technical and social issues than a hierarchically acting commissioner or manager.

NOTES

1. *Boston Globe* article: 'Big Dig began with a critical decision; Novel technique may be behind troubles' (19 December 2004).
2. Author's (ML) interview with R. Weinberg, director of the Friends of the Post Office Square Trust, 30 January 2004.

REFERENCES

Altshuler, A. and D. Luberoff (2003), *Mega-projects: The Changing Politics of Urban Public Investment*, Washington, DC: Brookings Institution Press.

Ammann, O.H., T. Von Karman and G.B. Woodruff (1941), *The Failure of the Tacoma Narrows Bridge*, Report to the Federal Works Agency.

Assenmacher, S. (2003), 'The Herren Tunnel's Learning Curve', in *T and T International*, **35** (11): 20–22.

Cerasoli, R. (2001), *A History of Central Artery/Tunnel Project Finances 1994–2001: Report to the Treasurer of the Commonwealth*, Boston, MA: Commonwealth of Massachusetts.

Chisholm, D. (1989), *Coordination without Hierarchy: Informal Structures in Multiorganizational Systems*, Berkeley, CA: University of California Press.

Cleland, D.I. and W.R. King (1983), *Systems Analysis and Project Management*, 3rd edn, McGraw-Hill Management Series, Singapore: McGraw-Hill.

De Bruijn, J.A. and E.F. ten Heuvelhof (2000), *Networks and Decision Making*, Utrecht: Lemma.

De Bruijn, J.A., E.F. ten Heuvelhof and R.J. in 't Veld (2002), *Process Management. Why project management fails in complex decision making processes*, Boston, MA: Kluwer Academic Publishers.

Gigch, J.P. van (1991), *System Design Modeling and Metamodeling*, New York: Plenum Press.

Golser, J. (1976), *New Austrian Tunneling Method (NATM), Theoretical Background & Practical Experiences*, 2nd Shotcrete Conference, Easton, MD.

Hall, P. (1980), *Great Planning Disasters*, Berkeley, CA: California University Press.

Leijten, M. (2004), 'Big Dig: Een halve eeuw Central Artery in Boston', in H. de Bruijn, G.R. Teisman, J. Edelenbos and W. Veeneman, *Meervoudig ruimtegebruik en het management van meerstemmige processen*, Utrecht: Lemma.

Lerner, A.W. (1986), 'There is more than one way to be redundant', *Administration and Society*, **18** (3): 334–59.

Low, B., E. Ostrom, C. Simon and J. Wilson (2000), *Redundancy and Diversity in Governing and Managing Common-pool Resources*, Bloomington, IN: IASCP.

Miller, R. and D. Lessard (2000), *The Strategic Management of Large Engineering Projects: Shaping Institutions, Risks and Governance*, with S. Floricel and the IMEC Research Group, Cambridge, MA: MIT Press.

Morris, P.W.G. and G.H. Hough (1987), *The Anatomy of Major Projects: A Study of the Reality of Project Management*, Chichester, UK: John Wiley & Sons.

Payne, A.C., J.V. Chelsom and L.R.P. Reavill (1996), *Management for Engineers*, Chichester, UK: John Wiley & Sons.

Perrow, C. (1999), *Normal accidents: Living with High-Risk Technologies*, Princeton, NJ: Princeton University Press.

Simon, H.A. (1996), *The Sciences of the Artificial*, 3rd edn, Cambridge, MA: MIT Press.
Tweede Kamer der Staten-Generaal (2002), *Communicatienetwerk C2000 en Geïntegreerd Meldkamersysteem* (Communication Network C2000 and Integrated Emergency Room System), Kamerstuk 28970, no. 2, vergaderjaar 2002–2003, The Hague (Sdu) (in Dutch).

3. *Ex-ante* evaluation of mega-projects: methodological issues and cost–benefit analysis[1]

Bert van Wee and Lóránt A. Tavasszy

3.1 INTRODUCTION

Mega-projects play a major role in most Western and non-Western countries, in several respects. First, they are heavily under debate at the political level, the assumed economic impacts and important budget implications being the major issues. Such projects often cost several billions of euros or dollars. Second, there is an important scientific debate about these projects, mainly because of the huge cost escalations (Flyvbjerg et al., 2003; Odeck, 2004) but also because of the uncertainty of the wider economic effects (in addition to direct user benefits). Because of the important role of mega-projects a sound *ex-ante* evaluation of a possible new project is crucial for the quality of decision-making. In most Western countries cost–benefit Analysis (CBA) is the method used for *ex-ante* evaluations of transport infrastructure projects (Hayashi and Morisugi, 2000). In literature the discussion on the CBA of infrastructure projects focuses on methodological issues, as well as on more principal items. In recent years the attention paid to non-methodological issues has gained more attention, including issues related to the position of CBA in decision-making, the complex multi-actor context of mega-projects and governance issues. The purpose of this chapter is to discuss the current state of the art with respect to CBA as well as to discuss possible improvements with respect to costs, benefits and modelling. However, we do not discuss wider economic effects because these are extensively discussed in Chapter 4.

Section 3.2 discusses the state of the art of CBA for transport infrastructure projects. Sections 3.3, 3.4, 3.5 and 3.6 deal with possible improvements in CBA methodology on costs, benefits, discount rates and modelling. Section 3.7 presents the main conclusions.

3.2 CBA FOR TRANSPORT INFRASTRUCTURE PROJECTS: STATE OF THE ART

CBA: an Overview

Basically a CBA is an overview of all the pros (benefits) and cons (costs) of a project. These costs and benefits are as far as possible quantified and expressed in monetary terms. Benefits are based on consumer preferences.[2] Costs and benefits occur in different years within the time horizon of the CBA. To deal with this, they are presented as so-called net present values, implying that taking into account interest and inflation it is better to have 1 euro or dollar nowadays than in, for example, 2020. The discount rate is used to express this valuation. Final results are often presented in sum-marising tables. The main indicators that are presented are the difference between costs and benefits, the return on investment, and the cost–benefit ratio. Almost every handbook on transport economics includes CBA in transport (see Button, 1993).

   There are several explanations for the popularity of CBA in the *ex-ante* evaluation of infrastructure projects and its role in decision-making. First, most of the costs and benefits are relatively well known, at least the-oretically. Investment, maintenance and operation costs can be derived from data from projects constructed in the past, or from tenders. The most important benefits are travel time savings, for both travellers and freight transport. Models are generally used to estimate the demand of passengers or volume of goods transport that will benefit from a new project. In addition, in the case of passengers, the travel time savings per trip can easily be estimated by comparing travel times with and without the proposed infrastructure project using changes in network character-istics. Next, the so-called value of time (VOT) is used to express shorter travel times in monetary terms. VOT is higher for business travel and goods transport than for commuting, and leisure travel has the lowest value of time. VOT differs between modes, income classes and some other characteristics of travel and travellers (e.g. Gunn, 2001). In the past much more research has been carried out on the VOT for passengers than for goods transport, especially for rail, making VOT estimates for rail goods transport relatively uncertain. There is far more debate about the indirect effects (effects additional to the direct effects due to a reduction in gener-alised transport costs; see Chapter 4 by Vickerman) and environmental effects. The second reason for the popularity of CBA is its often-assumed 'neutral' characteristic compared to its main competitor: multi-criteria analysis (MCA). In MCA effects are presented and weighed using weights per effect. Setting the weights is not at all value-free. It is therefore much easier to manipulate the final outcomes of an MCA compared to a CBA. However, CBA is not completely value-free either, for example because of the use of the utilitarian concept, the assumption that price tags should be based on consumer preferences, and because several methodologies exist to obtain these price tags, the choice often having a major impact on the outcomes. In addition, the models to estimate the transport effects can be manipulated (which of course is also true for MCA). Nevertheless, there is a broad consensus that CBA is much more value-free than MCA.

Travel time savings, often the most important benefits of infrastructure projects, are not fully expressed in GDP. Travel time savings for business trips and goods transport lead to higher productivity and lower costs and have an impact on GDP, but if a commuter can leave home later because commuting times are reduced, or because it takes less time to travel to a relative, GDP is not affected. In CBA it is common to have a broad approach to welfare, implying that all benefits for consumers are included, even if they are not expressed in GDP.

Next to travel time savings, additional travel (induced demand) is an important category in the benefits of transport infrastructure projects; these benefits are generally estimated using the so-called rule of half. This rule can be explained using an example. Let us assume a rail project reduces the travel time between cities A and B, for example, because a short cut is made. It is also assumed that person X living in city A commutes to city B by train, both with and without the reduced travel time. It is assumed that all other variables, such as monetary travel costs, safety etc., are not influenced by the project. For this person the benefits of the project for each trip consist of the travel time saved multiplied by his (marginal) value of time. Let us now assume that his neighbour only starts travelling to city B once the new line is constructed. We do not know at which level of travel time reduction he might have made the decision to travel. It might be that even a very small reduction in travel time would have induced the change, but it might also have only occurred if almost the full reduction in travel time occurred. Assuming many persons, the average break-even reduction in travel time is half of the actual reduction in travel time, assuming a linear demand function. For the new travellers the benefits are therefore half of the reduction in travel time multiplied by the number of trips and the VOT of these persons. As stated before, in transport economics this phenomenon is referred to as the rule of half.

In addition, extra benefits may occur due to changes in the timetable (see also Section 3.4).

Figure 3.1 visualises demand with (Q_1, GTC_1 – GTC: generalised transport costs, including at least time and money) and without (Q_0, GTC_0) a

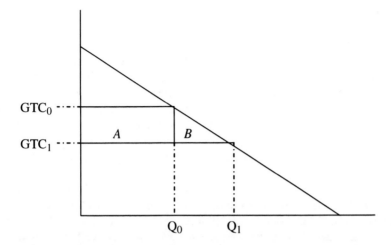

Figure 3.1   Increase in consumer surplus due to a decrease in generalised transport costs

new infrastructure project. A refers to the benefits (increase in consumer's surplus) of those people who travel both with and without the new line, B to the benefits of the extra demand. The surface of B can easily be calculated as $(Q_2 - Q_1 * T_2 - T_1) * \frac{1}{2}$, the factor $\frac{1}{2}$ referring to the 'rule of half' as presented above.

Other benefits of rail and tolled road projects might be the gains of the company operating the service or road section. Also relevant in *ex-ante* evaluations are environmental and safety impacts. Changes in safety and the environment might be both positive and negative, implying that safety and environmental changes can be listed under both the costs and the benefits.

For CBA (as well as for other evaluation methods) the spatial and temporal system boundaries are of crucial importance. If the spatial boundaries as used are too tight, relevant effects might occur outside the area under consideration. All non-marginal effects at the network level should be included. Temporal boundaries are relevant, as it is only after the opening of a new infrastructure project that the benefits can be realised. Also there may be important disbenefits from the building activities during the construction of the project. Due to the generally used discount rates, longer construction periods can significantly reduce the benefits of a project. It is therefore important that a relatively long time horizon is included in a CBA. This should be at least two or three decades. Benefits in the very long term hardly affect the net present value due to the generally used discount rates.

CBA and Modelling

The main output of a CBA is an overview of economic, ecological and social impacts, as far as possible in quantitative and monetary terms. The categorisation of these three impact types is generally used for all kinds of developments and policies, partly as a result of the use of it by the World Bank. The most important impact categories of transport projects are related to accessibility, safety and the environment. Accessibility has both economic as well as social impacts. The same is true for safety. Therefore in CBAs for transport projects the World Bank categorisation is not often used explicitly.

For the evaluation of transport infrastructure projects the main question is: which changes are due to the project? Then the question arises: compared to what? The comparison should certainly not relate to the current situation, because some changes will occur anyway. Nevertheless, for communication reasons it can be interesting to compare results with the current situation. The comparison should normally also not relate to the 'do-nothing' option: several changes will occur anyway. For example, if the discussion is about a new infrastructure project in an area where infrastructure will be extended or changed anyway, these changes should be included in the comparison. In economic literature it is suggested that the best alternative for comparison is the best alternative for the projects or alternatives under consideration.

The overview of CBA-relevant impacts is preferably based on state-of-the-art methods, modelling being the first priority in most cases. In most cases two categories of models are used, the first one being transport models and the second being impact models. Here we have a broad scope of transport models: they include both traditional transport models as well as models for vehicle ownership and characteristics, distribution of traffic over infrastructure classes, etc.

Transport models are used to provide outputs for CBAs. Outputs include: first, the number of vehicles, wagons, vessels etc. as well as their characteristics (age, fuel type, emission class etc.). These numbers and characteristics are important in modelling transport and traffic flows, as well as their environmental impact; second, outputs include the origins, destinations and distances over which vehicles travel, in order to calculate route choice, to estimate the use of specific segments of the networks to related environmental impacts, and partly also social and economic impacts; third, outputs include a classification of road types. This classification is important because substantial differences between road types exist with respect to energy use per kilometre, noise emissions and safety impacts. A fourth category of outputs is travel times for both passengers and freight transport.

As stated before, changes in travel times are a major benefit category of infrastructure improvements. Characteristics of passengers and freight are important; for instance, the value of time for business trips on average is higher than for leisure trips, and the added value of transport is often higher in the case of high-value goods compared to low-value goods.

These outputs depend in different ways on the impacts that the infrastructure changes will have. These impacts include: *residential choices and location choices of firms*. These location choices have an impact on mode choice and travel distances.

- *Destination choices*: the lower the generalised transport costs (time, money, trouble), the easier it becomes to reach destinations at a greater distance.
- *Trip frequencies*: the choice of vehicle types may be influenced by infrastructure changes; e.g. the more important the position of motorways in the road network is, the more attractive it becomes to own a big, comfortable, fast car.
- *Driving behaviour*, which is relevant for safety impacts.
- *Emissions and related concentrations of pollutants*.
- *Noise*.
- *Route choice* and *freight routing* may be influenced by the quality of infrastructure networks, being relevant for travel times, travel costs, and impacts on the environment and safety and congestion levels.

These changes interact in a dynamic way and there are many different types of users that will all react differently as individuals and in interaction with each other. Transport models are needed to combine one or more of these responses.

The output of transport models is relevant, first, because it provides results that are directly included in a CBA, such as travel time changes. Second, this output is needed for the calculation of impacts on society and the environment caused by the change in the transport system. In other words: transport models provide input for impact models, such as noise, safety and pollution models. Finally, the monetary expression of CBA-relevant output is often obtained using external data, such as the value of time for discrete modes, motives, income classes and categories of goods.

For economic impacts a distinction is often made between direct and indirect effects. The effects that are incurred by the users of the transport system are called direct effects. As these users are part of chains of consumption and production, effects propagate widely into the economy.

Through the course of this propagation process, new, i.e. additional, welfare effects can be generated, if prices do not equal marginal social costs. This can happen if markets are subsidised, if there are externalities, benefits of scale, etc. Mainstream economics tells us that if prices are equal to marginal social costs, indirect effects will not occur. In that case changes in, for example, economic output and land use are only passed-through direct effects. Then the monetary effects should not be added to the direct effects, to avoid double counting. In practice, however, prices are never equal to marginal social costs. Therefore indirect effects may occur. We reflect on indirect effects in more detail in the next section and refer also to Chapter 4. Here, the focus is on modelling. In our opinion, in addition to conventional models, for CBAs of infrastructure projects, models are needed to provide outputs with respect to both the passed-through direct effects as well as indirect effects.

A problem arises because traditional transport models often do not include some of these passed-through effects, nor do they describe indirect effects. They do however sometimes include changes in origins, destinations and trip frequencies, within a given land-use context. Land-use and transport interaction (LUTI) models have a broader scope because they do include land-use implications. However, these do not give output with respect to the related utility changes, which is a drawback in the case of their use in a CBA context. Other, non land-use-related impacts, e.g. with respect to job productivity, are not included in traditional land-use models, nor in LUTI models. These models are therefore not sufficiently well equipped to calculate indirect effects. For these impacts, models based on new economic geography, also called spatial computable general equilibrium (SCGE), models, are helpful and are sometimes used in a CBA context. Examples include the Dutch RAEM model and the CGEurope model (see Gunn, 2004 for a review). These models are explicitly designed to deal with indirect effects, expressed in monetary units, so that effects can be easily included in a CBA. A more detailed comparison between LUTI and SCGE models can be found in Oosterhaven et al. (2001). As these models require regional economic data to estimate indirect effects of transport policies, their use requires additional investments in analytical work. Therefore, their application to address wider economic effects in addition to the conventional transport modelling approach needs to be carefully considered.

From this section it appears that the main costs and benefits of possible new infrastructure projects are relatively easy to estimate, making CBA an attractive tool for the *ex-ante* evaluation of such projects. But is this true? We think many challenges to improving current practice are available and present some of these in the next sections.

3.3 METHODOLOGICAL ISSUES ON COSTS

Research Methods for Construction Cost Estimations

On the basis of an impressive database containing 258 projects, Flyvbjerg et al. (2003) concluded that cost overruns are very common for transport infrastructure projects, the average for roads being 20 per cent and for rail 45 per cent. Causes are of a methodological nature as well as the result of strategic behaviour by actors that benefit from a positive decision to construct the project. In the first case improvements in the methods of cost estimations can strengthen the quality of these estimations. Improvements can be obtained by choosing another methodology or – even better – by applying different types of methodologies. These types might be engineering methods, econometric methods and case studies comparing actual costs in practice. In addition, within each of these methods improvements can be made. There are several suggestions for research. First, an analysis or meta-analysis can be carried out once a database is available including the real costs of projects and many possible project characteristics, linking these characteristics to the real costs. This is what Flyvbjerg et al. (2003) did. Extending the database both with respect to the number of projects as well as project characteristics allowed the researchers to increase their insights into the importance of project characteristics. Note that Flyvbjerg et al. found several relationships to be not statistically significant at the 0.95 level, possibly due to the low number of cases. Second, research can focus on the impact of the market situation on tenders. For example, it is generally recognised that a tight market results in higher prices in the tenders, a phenomenon that makes sense according to conventional economics. Relevant variables might be the number of competitors that could be included as well as those that were actually included in the tender procedure, the market itself (are there enough projects or is it difficult for construction companies to acquire projects?), and market prices for materials. The outcomes could be used for the simultaneous planning of the construction of more than one major infrastructure project at a regional or even national level. In search of an 'optimum', one could compare lower tender prices with discounted costs for construction and travellers' benefits. For a CBA a national perspective is generally used, implying that higher costs for the government or private parties to construct a project lead to additional profits for construction companies. These 'additional costs' are only a transfer caused by market power, and are not additional costs for the economy as a whole. On the other hand, it is also possible that market power encourages construction companies to work less efficiently. This effect would indeed be a loss to society.

Costs Estimates in CBA and Strategic Behaviour

Apart from research improvements, a major challenge relates to the reduction of strategic behaviour. Strategic behaviour is found to be a major cause of the underestimation of the costs and the overestimation of the benefits of possible new infrastructure projects, a phenomenon that is even more important for rail projects than for roads (see Trujillo et al., 2002; Flyvbjerg et al., 2005; Wachs, 1989; 1990; Bruzelius et al., 2002). Possibilities for reducing strategic behaviour, as found in the literature, include the establishment of an independent committee evaluating the forecasts, including an uncertainty analysis for all forecasts, more transparency in documentation with respect to costs and benefits, the introduction of 'better' institutional arrangements (e.g. which institutions or actors have which responsibilities, how to avoid manipulation or strategic behaviour by some of the actors, what should be done when manipulation does occur and by whom), and finally the application of the method of 'reference class forecasting' (comparing the project under discussion with other comparable projects constructed in the recent past, using a database with data on such projects), making use of an 'outside view' and data from other, comparable projects. Strategic behaviour is relevant for 'costs' as well as for 'benefits'. To avoid overlap we include this subject only under 'costs'.

Optimism Bias

Because cost overruns are so common, estimates can be corrected for optimism. Unfortunately not only the average cost escalation is high but so is the standard deviation (Flyvbjerg et al., 2003), which implies that it is not appropriate to use a simple methodology; for example, applying a general correction factor for the difference between the estimated costs and actual costs is too simple. Flyvbjerg and COWI (2004) developed a method to deal with optimism for the UK. This method includes the use of data from other projects and distinguishes between project type, such as several types of rail (metro, light rail, conventional rail, high-speed rail). Implementing such methods would really improve the quality of CBA. An average cost escalation of 20–50 per cent has a major impact on the quality of CBA and its usefulness in decision-making. To avoid the methodological problem of *ecological fallacy* (general conclusions are not necessarily applicable to specific cases) it is preferable to include the country-specific situation in the method.

Construction Period

CBAs in general take into account the fact that the construction period covers several years, leading to costs preceding benefits. As already mentioned, using discount rates compensates for these time aspects. A longer construction period results in lower (discounted) benefits but also reduces the discounted costs, because part of the costs is spent later. However, we have hardly seen any CBA including the extra costs in the construction period related to the inconvenience for other travellers, such as adaptations to the timetables (i.e. fewer trains), speed reductions and route changes for roads. These costs should be included in CBA as well.

Changes in Project Specification

The specification of projects at the time of decision-making often differs from the final project. Changes might occur due to cost escalations, reducing the money available at later stages and leading to adaptations that reduce costs (less money for the reduction of environmental impacts, simpler layout). But project adaptations might also result from opposition at a later stage than at the time of decision-making. For example, in the case of the Dutch Betuwe Line, a dedicated rail freight line from Rotterdam Harbour to the German Ruhr area, many adaptations were made as a result of local and regional opposition, leading to additional tunnels, noise-reducing measures and other adaptations, making the project much more expensive than assumed at the time of political decision-making. Not only are these adaptations relevant for the cost estimations, but also for the estimations of impacts, such as environmental or safety impacts.

Life-cycle Costs and Implications for Project Alternatives

Project alternatives are often not compared on a life-cycle basis. A life-cycle approach includes the whole life cycle of a product or project. Focusing on infrastructure, it not only includes the first decades of its use (the period often included in CBAs), but the whole period of use, all maintenance and repair and sometimes modifications needed, and even the stage after its use period, e.g. the removal of the infrastructure.[3] A life-cycle approach for infrastructure projects might lead to other conclusions with respect to the best project specifications than only including the first decades of its use. Sometimes a trade-off exists between construction costs on the one hand and the total life span, as well as costs for maintenance and repairs on the other hand. Lower construction costs might result in higher costs for maintenance and replacement and a shorter life span of the infrastructure (see Zoeteman, 2004 for the relevance for rail projects). Replacement costs (or in some cases even major maintenance costs) might be necessary in a year after the time horizon of a CBA, as a result of which they are not included in the CBA. CBA might explicitly put project alternatives on the agenda that result in the lowest life-cycle costs. The construction costs are not necessarily paid by the same actor as the costs for replacement or maintenance. Therefore adding alternatives based on life-cycle perspectives is not only a technocratic issue but may have an impact on the costs and benefits for the actors involved.

Uncertainty in the Costs of New Technology

One of the aspects that Flyvbjerg et al. (2003) pay attention to is the importance of technology: new technologies, such as maglev, have higher uncertainties with respect to costs, the continuous increase in estimated costs of maglev in Germany in the 1990s being an illustration of this. This is not a plea never to propose unconventional plans, but a plea to include uncertainty with respect to new technologies in cost forecasts for CBA.

3.4   METHODOLOGICAL ISSUES ON BENEFITS

In this section we present an overview of challenges related to benefits. The importance of strategic behaviour for benefits has already been described in Section 3.3.

Demand Forecasting: the Link with Land Use

Transport and land use interact: changes in travel times and costs (e.g. due to new infrastructure projects, changed prices or subsidies) for distinguished modes may affect land use, and land-use changes may affect travel behaviour (Wegener and Fürst, 1999). Many models as used for CBA do not include this two-way interaction. If possible, using a land-use and transport interaction (LUTI) model would allow the researchers to indicate the land-use changes resulting from transport changes, and then the related economic, social and environmental impacts. We realise that a reliable LUTI model is often not available. If this is the case, an alternative might be to use expert judgement to estimate the land-use changes due to the transport changes. And even if a LUTI model is available, the question is whether the benefits of applying it exceed the costs. We note that LUTI models do not provide the necessary outputs for CBA in terms of additional indirect effects. We treat this subject in more detail in Section 3.6 on modelling.

Other Land-use Issues

Apart from the importance of land-use and transport interactions for demand forecasting, the link between land use and transport offers more challenges, some of which are discussed below.

First, it is important to realise that better transport reduces transport costs, which influences the advantages of agglomeration. Agglomeration effects refer to advantages of economic density, which may or may not yield additional benefits in CBA. The consequences of agglomeration are well known, but its causes, its specific nature and quantitative relations are not. Finding out more about the causes is an important challenge for CBA, and even more for spatial economics.

Second, intensive use of land reduces urban sprawl and makes it possible to preserve open space. In CBA the valuation of open space is still a challenge, because not only the agricultural value of land is important, but also its recreational use and external effects.

The third issue relates to rail. Rail is a 'land-use-efficient' transport mode, compared to road transport, not only because of the efficient use of infrastructure space, but also because of a lower claim for car parking. Measuring and valuing these benefits is an important issue.

Importance of Indirect Effects

Indirect effects occur if transport prices are not equal to the marginal social costs of transport. As transport prices are seldom equal to marginal social costs, indirect effects mostly occur; the question is, however, how high these indirect effects are. Indirect effects can be both positive and negative. When positive, earlier empirical research has found indirect effects up to about 38 per cent (Elhorst et al., 2001). Theoretical research seems to indicate that these benefits can be lower (Venables and Gasiorek, 1998) or higher (FHWA, 2001). As their estimation requires a substantial extra analysis effort, these impacts are seldom taken into account. However, we argue that their consideration can be vital for a good CBA because they can provide important information to decision-makers on the socioeconomic impacts, in terms of both overall changes and the redistribution of welfare. Assumed indirect effects often play an important role in the policy discussion on large infrastructure projects. Therefore even if they are absent or negligible it is very valuable to present them explicitly. Indirect effects are discussed in more detail in Chapter 4.

Value of Time

The value of time is a well-known subject of debate, partly because of the big impact it has on the benefits of infrastructure projects. Recent publications include Gunn (2001) and Wardman (2001), who focus on public transport. Tavasszy and Bruzelius (2005) provide an international overview of VOT studies for freight transport. Important challenges include the impact of ICT on the VOT, especially for rail, and the impact of the journey length in combination with travel purpose. Challenges for freight include taking into account the dependence between time and reliability values and the effect of changes in logistics variables on time valuation.

Value of Reliability and Variations in Travel Times

In recent years the reliability of travel times has received more attention both in research and in policy-making. Research shows that the negative value of unreliability is roughly in the order of magnitude or at least a substantial percentage of the negative value of travel-time losses due to congestion (see Lam and Small, 2001; Bates et al., 2001; Rietveld et al., 2001). Challenges relate to getting more insights into the determinants of unreliability, the determinants of its negative value for travellers, the possibility of forecasting unreliability and insights into possible future changes in its valuation. In addition, the link between the negative value of unreliability and information provision is of great importance, since variations in travel times are valued more negatively if the traveller does not know them beforehand. If the traveller is informed before or during the trip, this might reduce the negative value of travel-time variations. Travel-time variations are not equal to unreliability: once they are known to the traveller before he starts his trip, the travel time might be very reliable, although travel times for the same trip at different times of the day can vary significantly.

Life-cycle Energy Use and Emissions; Indirect Energy Use and Emissions

To estimate energy use and emissions per alternative, CBAs generally ignore the impacts of construction and maintenance, and focus only on the stage when infrastructure projects are actually being used. Indirect energy use and emissions may also be substantial. Relevant sources of indirect energy use and emissions are those related to the production of vehicles, including the 'gain' due to materials being reused when vehicles are discarded. A much more difficult-to-tackle source of indirect energy use and emissions is related to the 'overhead' connected to transport. Examples are offices of railway (and bus) companies, and of vehicle manufacturers and vehicle import companies. Energy use and emissions related to the mainte-nance and repair of vehicles may also be relevant. Since it seems to us to be very complicated to obtain data and avoid 'double-counting' problems, we think that it will not be easy to gain new insights by carrying out new research in this area. For more insights into the life-cycle aspects as well as indirect energy use and emissions, see Van Wee et al. (2005).

Location of Emissions

For the impact on climate change the location of emissions is not relevant: 1 kg of CO_2 has the same impact on climate change, regardless of location. But for several other impacts the location is relevant. For instance, for pollutants that have health impacts, such as PM, NO_2 and CO, the spatial distribution of vehicles (or power plants) in relation to the spatial distribution of the pop-ulation is relevant. The average distances between a power plant providing electricity for trains and the population will in general be much larger than the distance between them and road vehicles. The same emission level may have more health impacts if emitted by lorries than by power plants. As a result, 1 kg of NO_x emissions of road traffic may be valued higher compared to 1 kg of NO_x emissions of electricity plants. For acidification and noise the location of emissions is also relevant. We have found only a few studies that include the impact of location of emissions on their effects (e.g. Dorland and Jansen, 1997; Eyre et al., 1997; Newton, 1997); we have found, however, only one CBA that has included this aspect (Koning et al., 2002).

Non-conventional Environmental Impacts

In current practice the environment is included in CBA to a limited extent. Several impacts are stated as *pro memory* (PM) (not valued) in the CBA, and in decision-making processes PM effects are often ignored, or they get much less attention compared to effects that are valued in monetary terms. Van Wee et al. (2005) suggest several ways to improve current practice.

The first improvement is to include the emission of other pollutants. CO_2 and NO_x, and sometimes SO_2, emissions are often seen as being the most important, or at least as good indicators for all emissions. Valuing only these emissions, however, leads to a possible underestimation of all emis-sion impacts. For example, PM10 emissions are very important, and for health effects these emissions are probably the most important pollutants.

The second improvement is that changes in emission factors over time are generally not included because emission factors for one or two future years only are used. If two future years are included, then in general only regulations that are already decided upon are taken into account. Emission

factors for motor vehicles, however, will change, for example due to EU regulations that are as yet partly undecided. Emissions from electricity production will also change, due to fuel-mix changes, efficiency improvements,
changes in the import or export of electricity, and possibly the combination
of heat and power. Changes partly depend on country-specific policies. See
Van Wee et al. (2005) for a further discussion on the importance of this
subject.

The third improvement is related to the energy use of trains. In the
Netherlands, at least, there is hardly any information on this. We find it
strange that the environment forms a political reason to subsidise rail passenger transport (and goods transport as well), while the government lacks
reliable data on environmental performance (energy use, emissions of diesel
trains). Far more data are available on noise.

Fourth, a major shortcoming of current practice is the limited attention
paid to the impacts of infrastructure on the landscape and on nature.
Because such impacts can be huge, more research into these impacts is
needed. In addition, more research into methods to value these impacts
might result in a more equal treatment of them in CBAs. However, we realise
that there is still a long way to go before these impacts can be valued. And
it is questionable whether methods to value these impacts in a satisfactory
way can be developed at all. For such impacts a combination of CBA and
multi-criteria analysis (MCA) might be a better tool to facilitate decision-
making than only a CBA with its questionable values or PM estimations.

Robustness of Policies

Another issue is the robustness of infrastructure and land-use concepts.
How vulnerable are we to, for example, an expected or unexpected limitation in energy availability for transport? Such limitations may be the result
of political instability in oil-producing countries, much higher prices for
fuels or stringent environmental policies. The preferences of consumers
and firms may also change in the future. What will happen if sustainably
produced energy becomes available at reasonable prices? The environmental pros and cons of project alternatives might then change dramatically.

Cross-border Harmonisation

Because cross-border rail links are heavily under discussion, especially in the
EU, cross-border issues are becoming more and more important. These
include, first, general methodological issues such as the discount rate to be
used and the linking of demand models to be used to estimate travel impacts.
Second, 'real-life' issues are relevant. For example, in the case of electrical

traction, differences in power generation between countries should be included. Another issue relates to the differences in the value of time. The EU HEATCO project (Developing Harmonised Approaches for Transport Costing and Project Assessment – see http://heatco.ier.uni-stuttgart.de/ hstart.html), focusing on the harmonisation of appraisal methods for cross-border projects, expresses the importance for the European Commission of such *ex-ante* evaluations. HEATCO provides guidelines for such projects with respect to decision criteria, the treatment of non-monetarised impacts, the project appraisal evaluation period, the treatment of future risk and uncertainty, discounting, intragenerational equity issues, non-market valuation techniques, value transfer, the treatment of indirect socioeconomic effects, marginal costs of public funds, and the producer surplus of transport providers. Next to these general guidelines, it elaborates on the value of time and congestion, the value of changes in accident risks, environmental costs, and costs and indirect impacts of infrastructure investments. In order to reduce the amount of ambiguity and uncertainty in cross-border project assessments, guidelines are needed that are internationally consistent, transferable and easily executable. As a first step towards this objective, the HEATCO project proposed a set of internationally harmonised methodological guidelines for project evaluation. These guidelines are based on the state of the art in project evaluation and also include default values where data limitations prohibit the application of comprehensive evaluation methods. The EU BEACON project also focuses on cross-border aspects related to the strategic environmental assessment of transport plans, policies and projects (see www.transport-sea.net).

Environmental Performance and Mode Choice

In CBA for the environmental performance of modes, average values are often used, ignoring specific characteristics of the situation under consideration. Van Wee et al. (2005) emphasise the importance of detour factors (difference between overland distance and distance as the crow flies), the characteristics of the goods to be transported, speed and many other factors on the values for energy use and emissions. The challenge is in both research and application: it is highly recommended that the methodologies to estimate energy use and emissions per mode are improved as well as applying insights in CBA practice.

Power Generation

Since in many countries most rail transport uses electricity as the source of energy, one has to consider in CBA the expected changes in emissions from power plants. But these may be relatively uncertain due to the liberalisation of the electricity market in many countries. Developing scenarios for the next decades focusing on energy production will probably become available from experts in that research area, and should be used in CBAs of rail projects. Such scenarios may include the use of biofuels or other sustainably produced energy sources to generate electricity, as well as technologies to store CO_2 under ground.

Non-user Benefits

Current CBAs focus on user benefits only. There is the question, however, of whether non-user benefits might be relevant. The first category of non-user benefits relates to the so-called option value. The option value can be described as an individual's valuation of the opportunity to use a particular transport mode or piece of infrastructure in the future that is not being used in the present. For example, car-owners may value the ability to use a public transport service when, for whatever reason, they cannot make use of the car due to unavailability or a breakdown, bad weather, increases in fuel prices or other car costs, or the loss of the ability to operate a car. Other non-use benefits relate to altruistic and existence values: a person may value a rail network even if he never uses it, because he appreciates that others have the possibility of using it (altruistic value) or even its very existence (a classic example is the South Pole: people value the existence of it even if nobody, including themselves, ever visits it).

3.5   DISCOUNT RATES

Discount rates are discussed in a separate section because they are not exclusively related to only costs or benefits. Because costs and benefits occur in future years and are discounted, the discount rate has a major impact on the outcomes of a CBA, the importance for benefits and costs of operations being even higher than for construction costs because they occur at a later stage. The general tendency in most countries is that official guidance is given for public-sector projects. Another tendency is to lower the official discount rates, mainly as a result of the long-term decrease in inflation rates. A problem with discounting, or at least a consequence, is that benefits or costs in the very long run hardly have any impact on the outcomes. Intuitively this does not always seem to be correct. One can argue whether it is correct that saving one tree now is equally important to saving 50 trees in 100 years (the result of a discount rate of 4 per cent), or that climate change effects that occur after 50 years are hardly relevant. An option to deal with benefits or costs in the very long-term could be the tapering of rates for long-term benefits, as well as assuming increases in the value of units, e.g. the value of a ton of CO_2.

3.6 MODELLING

Until the mid-1990s, in CBA, the analysis of the transport system was mostly limited to those effects that occurred for passenger transport and took place on a limited geographical scale. However, network effects may occur on not-included infrastructure elements, such as local roads, as well as outside the study area and in the short to medium term. There was generally no account of freight transport, of network effects that occurred over a wider geographical area and of long-term effects (related to, e.g., residential choice). Practice in these areas has improved as since the mid-1990s many new models have become available. In addition, such improvements as well as their implications are discussed in the literature; see for example Gille et al. (2004). An example of such new models are the SCGE models described in Section 3.2. Challenges still remain, however, and below we discuss some important ones.

Freight Demand Modelling

Freight transport is an important source for the environmental and economic effects of transport projects and policies. Despite a large amount of research in the past decade (see Tavasszy, 2006), reviews of modelling practice often show that freight transport is seldom treated with as much detail and attention as passenger transport (see the UK Department for Transport (2002) for a comprehensive international review of freight modelling). In particular, the following subjects are not yet well understood:

- *Light goods vehicle (LGV) movements* In order to understand how increasing freight flows put pressure on car network capacity, the increase in the use of LGVs needs to be understood. This requires new measuring approaches which can distinguish between passengers and freight as motives for an LGV trip, and models which explain the trade-offs with other vehicle types.
- *Links between freight trips and logistics systems* The future growth in freight transport (in terms of total volumes, spatial patterns and functional characteristics) depends to a large extent on the underlying development of logistics networks. The supply chain management and operations disciplines drive this development, and form part of the behavioural explanation of changes in these networks.

- *Relations between freight and the economy*   Freight transport is an important determinant of welfare, competitiveness and social equity. The evaluation instruments (models) needed to assess the impacts of freight transport policy in these dimensions are usually inadequate or unavailable. At various spatial levels, the challenges to understanding the influence of transport policy on the economy are great, and are strongly dependent on our knowledge of interregional and intersectoral interactions, as described by freight models.

New research into the modelling of freight transport should not just include work on new mathematical model specifications, but focus also on the empirical challenges of accurately representing freight flows. Data acquisition, preferably at the level of individual firms, is a prerequisite for advances in this area. While proprietary data are difficult to acquire and employ for public policy purposes, they are needed for specific facilities such as container terminals or industrial site development.

Models of global freight flows are still underdeveloped. Although trade data do exist, our forecasting abilities for international flows are still limited. Part of the problem lies in the difficulty of measuring freight flows in detail, including, for example, contents of containers. Also, as port regions combine various different functions in the supply chain, including transit, value-added logistics, production, import and export clearance, re-exporting etc., the available statistics are often insufficiently detailed to support the development of freight flow databases and models around ports.

Demand Estimations: Technology-specific Aspects

Models that forecast travel demand often include travel costs, travel time and an alternative specific constant. Data are generally obtained from research (revealed preference or stated preference). However, in the case of unconventional technologies, such as maglev, it can be questioned whether these data are applicable. It is recommended that research is carried out that aims explicitly to take into account the technologies used. Technologies may also include the options on board a train, such as power supply for laptop computers and internet connections, which could be wireless.

Network Effects

When looking at various sorts of models, the distinction between direct effects and direct network effects cannot be clearly made. It is now common understanding that a good transport model will include the effects that occur through an interaction between users over a network. More practically, a transport model will treat network effects if it

- covers a geographical study area sufficiently large and a network of sufficient detail to include re-routing responses;
- includes various multimodal responses, both in terms of modal competition and in terms of complementarity (services or modes feeding each other);
- allows for changes in departure times of network users;
- takes into account interaction in the responses between passengers and freight transport;
- includes adequate indicators for congestion and describes changes in congestion levels, or, maybe better: travel-time losses compared to free flow;
- expresses traffic in the right units to establish environmental impacts;
- includes adequate indicators for reliability and expresses changes in their levels.

Although the above requirements are theoretically not difficult to meet, few models are generally available that combine these features.

Modelling Traveller Benefits via Logsums

As described in Section 3.2, travel-time gains are an important benefit category of infrastructure improvements, as well as the benefits of induced demand. Calculating the benefits of travel-time gains is normally the result of a simple methodology in which the number of travellers is multiplied by the travel-time gains and the (mode and income-specific) value of time. The benefits of induced demand are calculated using the rule of half. Other benefits, such as changes in departure time, or the combination of changes in behaviour (e.g. time and destination) are often ignored. Koopmans and Kroes (2003) propose a more advanced method to include all benefits as far as they are related to travel behaviour changes, based on changes in the logsum of transport models. The method is an option in case a generalised extreme value (GEV) model is used to forecast changes in travel behaviour due to the infrastructure project. Basically it calculates the overall consumer surplus in a consistent way. It is beyond the scope of this chapter to discuss the method in more detail. Although the results of applying this method are more complicated to communicate, theoretically it is more advanced than current practice. The further development of this method, including communication improvements, might contribute to a better modelling of benefits of infrastructure changes.

Modelling Wider Economic Effects

As introduced earlier in this chapter, models are useful to study the wider economic effects of transport infrastructure changes. From a policy perspective, these models can show the total change in welfare due to infrastructure policy as well as the distribution of this change over regions and population groups. In order to prevent double counting in CBA, these models should deal in a consistent manner with wider economic effects that are additional to the direct effects (which we defined here as indirect effects), and those that are simply the propagated direct effects. As discussed in Section 3.2, there are a number of alternative models, all of which are being developed further alongside each other. Below we summarise four specific research challenges in the area of modelling of indirect effects. We again refer readers to Chapter 4 for a more elaborate discussion of issues related to the assessment of wider economic effects.

The modelling of wider economic effects offers the following challenges:

1. The impact of transport on the economy can be modelled in different ways, for example using direct cost elasticities or explicit production functions. SCGE models require a separate transport model to supply the production functions with transport inputs, and as the conventional ways of dealing with transport costs in CGEs introduce problems for CBA applications, alternatives need to be found (see Tavasszy et al., 2002).
2. Indirect effects can be positive or negative, depending on the nature of market imperfections in various markets. There are various markets outside the goods markets which are affected by new infrastructure, such as labour markets, housing markets and land markets. Despite the fact that these can each contribute significantly to the total impacts, most models provide no or only a limited account of some markets (Oosterhaven et al., 2005), and models are continuously being extended.
3. Most models of wider economic effects are static, while it is clear that the dynamics of the responses in the system are relevant (because of non-linearities in the system) or simply useful (for discounting purposes in CBA) to know. However, as very little is known empirically about typically dynamic phenomena such as lagged responses or the role of expectations in behaviour, dynamic models are being developed based, for example, on the theory of evolutionary economics (Rothengatter, 2002).
4. Models that show economic effects outside the transport sector can have different theoretical backgrounds. Next to the neoclassical and

NEG (new economic geography) (microeconomic) based models, we also know the neo-Keynesian (macroeconomic) approaches. The former typically show sectoral and regional details, while macro models work at country level. Linking these models to get the best of both worlds is a new direction of research (see Varga et al., 2006).

Consistency between Modelling and Valuation

Transport flows and travel-time changes are the key drivers for the calculation of economic impacts, while changes in vehicle movements are used to assess the environmental effects. In addition, vehicle and traveller characteristics are needed to derive the economic and environmental effects. As in practice different data are used in traditional transport models than in effect models to calculate changes in transport flows themselves, an issue of consistency arises. For example, transport models generally have travel-time-related variables and parameters to calculate traffic flows, which are used in (variables) or obtained from (parameters) model calibration. In contrast, guidelines for CBA typically prescribe another source of values of time, for example as derived from recent empirical (stated-preference) willingness-to-pay (WTP) studies. In addition, both theory and guidelines conclude that values should be indexed over time to reflect income changes. Therefore consistency in VOTs between the models used and the values used in CBAs is rather the exception, based on coincidence, than the rule due to consistency procedures.

3.7 CONCLUSIONS

The most important conclusions of this chapter are first that large infrastructure projects are heavily under debate in many countries. Second, CBA is a standardised and popular approach to evaluate *ex ante* the effects of transport projects, including large infrastructure projects, with a large body of practice/experience. Its popularity can partly be explained by the (at least seemingly) well-known monetary expressed costs and also benefits. Third, this experience tells us that there are many alternative ways to obtain the input for CBAs, but also many possibilities for 'wrong' input. Fourth, recent studies also show that this can occur easily as a result of ignorance or misjudgement, rather than manipulative politics. Fifth, the main problems with respect to costs lie in the areas of construction cost estimates, optimism bias, changes in the project specifications, ignorance of life-cycle aspects and uncertainty in the costs of new technology.

Sixth, the main problems with respect to benefits relate to the poor estimates of links between transport and land use, the inclusion of indirect effects, including double counting of effects, value-of-time and reliability estimates, the inclusion of environmental aspects, cross-border harmonisation, non-use benefits and the limited time horizon of *ex-ante* evaluations. Our final conclusion is that modelling challenges include freight modelling, demand estimates in the case of unconventional technology, network effects, indirect effects and the consistency between modelling and valuation.

Important questions that arise are: what is the impact of all the improvements as discussed in this chapter? And: does it have any impact on decision-making? The aim of this chapter is not to fully answer these questions. Here we will discuss them briefly. We think that better insights into construction costs can really change the outcomes of a CBA and may have an important impact on decision-making. We think all aspects as discussed may contribute significantly to better estimates of costs. It is more difficult to stress the importance of the challenges related to demand in general terms, e.g. land-use implications might be important for one project, but not for another project. Our first impression is that the challenges that might be of most importance for the outcomes of a CBA and therefore perhaps also for decision-making are those related to the value of time and value of reliability, and non-user benefits. For some projects indirect effects and land-use change might be relatively important. Effects in the long term, related to the robustness of policies and long-term environmental impacts, hardly have any impact on the outcomes of a CBA unless changes in the discount rate are made, or if these impacts are valued higher in the long term. We have the impression that improvements in modelling might be important, but the impacts on the outcomes of a CBA are probably of less importance than changes in cost estimates, some benefit categories, and discount rates. This does not imply that we suggest not emphasising modelling improvements. On the contrary: because the costs and benefits of infrastructure projects are generally huge, the additional costs of developing and applying better models are marginal compared to the size of the costs and benefits, and are therefore highly recommended. And next to the content, several improvements with respect to the process can be made. For example Gille et al. (2004) conclude that in an early stage it is necessary to combine the insights of the client, the CBA specialist and the modeller to discuss the level of detail and specific policy questions so that agreement exists on the sort of model output to be used. The process is another area of improvements, strongly linked to the content, that we consider as an important area for further research.

NOTES

1. This chapter is based partly on Van Wee (2007) and Tavasszy et al. (2002).
2. In some cases benefits are based on other assumptions than consumer preferences. Examples include the valuation of CO_2 emissions; current consumer preferences are generally much lower than estimates based on political choices.
3. This removal stage is an important one in the case of nuclear power plants, and therefore is often included in discussions on energy supply. For vehicles (e.g. Bouwman and Moll, 1997; ECMT, 1999) and infrastructure projects (Bos, 1998) it is sometimes discussed as well.

REFERENCES

Bates, J., J. Polak, P. Jones and A. Cook (2001), 'The valuation of reliability for personal travel', *Transportation Research Part E*, **37** (2–3): 191–229.
Bos, S. (1998), *Direction Indirect. The Indirect Energy Requirements and Emissions from Freight Transport*, Groningen: Groningen University.
Bouwman, M.E. and H.C. Moll (1997), 'Status quo and expectations concerning the material composition of road vehicles and consequences for energy use', IVEM Research Report no. 91, Groningen: Groningen University.
Bruzelius, N., B. Flyvbjerg and W. Rothengatter (2002), 'Big decision, big risks. Improving accountability in mega projects', *Transport Policy*, **9** (2): 143–54.
Button, K.J. (1993), *Transport Economics*, 2nd edn, Aldershot, UK and Brookfield, MA, USA: Edward Elgar.
Dorland, C. and H.M.A. Jansen (1997), 'ExternE Transport – the Netherlands. Dutch case studies on transport externalities', Institute for Environmental Studies (IVM), Amsterdam: Free University.
ECMT (1999), *Cleaner Cars. Fleet Renewal and Scrappage Schemes*, Paris: European Conference of Ministers of Transport.
Elhorst, J.P., J. Oosterhaven and W.E. Romp (2001), 'Integral cost–benefit analysis of MAGLEV technology under market imperfections', Research Report 04C22, Groningen: University of Groningen, Research Institute SOM.
Eyre, N.J., E. Ozdemiroglu, D.W. Pearce and P. Steele (1997), 'Fuel and location effects on the damage costs of transport emissions', *Journal of Transport Economics and Policy*, **31** (1): 5–24.
FHWA (2001), *Freight Transportation Improvements and the Economy*, Washington, DC: US Department of Transport.
Flyvbjerg, B. and COWI (2004), *Procedures for Dealing with Optimism Bias in Transport Planning: Guidance Document*, London: UK Department for Transport.
Flyvbjerg, B., N. Bruzelius and W. Rothengatter (2003), *Megaprojects and Risk: An Anatomy of Ambition*, Cambridge: Cambridge University Press.
Flyvbjerg, B., M.K. Skamris Holm and S.L. Buhl (2005), 'How (in)accurate are demand forecasts in public works projects? The case of transportation', *Journal of the American Planning Association*, **71** (2): 131–46.
Gille, J., A.I.J.M. van der Hoorn and F.A. Rosenberg (2004), 'Transport models as an input for cost benefit analysis', paper presented at the European Transport Conference, Strasbourg, 4–6 October.

Gunn, H. (2001), 'Spatial and temporal transferability of relationships between travel demand, trip cost and travel time', *Transportation Research E*, **37**: 163–89.

Gunn, H. (2004), *SCGE Models: Relevance and Accessibility for Use in the UK, with Emphasis on Implications for Evaluation of Transport Investments*, London: UK Department for Transport.

Hayashi, Y. and H. Morisugi (2000), 'International comparison of background concept and methodology of transportation project appraisal', *Transport Policy*, **7**: 73–88.

Koning, M., E. Verkade and J. Hakfoort (2002), *Implications of Expanding Schiphol Airport. A Quick Scan CBA*, The Hague: Centraal Planbureau (in Dutch).

Koopmans, C.C. and E. Kroes (2003), 'Estimation of congestion costs in the Netherlands', paper presented at the European Transport Conference, Strasbourg, 8–10 October.

Lam, T.C. and K.A. Small (2001), 'The value of time and reliability: measurement from a value pricing experiment', *Transportation Research Part E*, **37** (2–3): 231–51.

Newton, P.N. (ed.) (1997), *Reshaping Cities for a More Sustainable Future – Exploring the Link between Urban Form, Air Quality, Energy and Greenhouse Gas Emissions*, Research Monograph 6, Melbourne: Australian Housing and Research Institute (AHURI). www.ea.gov.au/atmosphere/airquality/urban-air/urban air docs.html.

Odeck, J. (2004), 'Cost overruns in road construction – what are their sizes and determinants?', *Transport Policy*, **11** (1): 43–53.

Oosterhaven, J. and K.C. Koopmans (2005), 'NEG modelling in cost–benefit analysis – the Netherlands experience', paper presented at the 'Economic impacts of changing accessibility' seminar, Heriot-Watt University, Edinburgh, 27 October.

Oosterhaven, J., T. Knaap, C.J. Ruijgrok and L.A. Tavasszy (2001), 'On the development of RAEM: the Dutch spatial general equilibrium model and its first application', paper presented at the 41st European Regional Science Association Conference, Zagreb, 29 August–1 September.

Rietveld, P., F.R. Bruinsma and D.J. van Vuren (2001), 'Coping with unreliability in public transport chains: a case study for Netherlands', *Transportation Research Part A*, **35** (6): 539–59.

Rothengatter, W. (2002), 'The role of CBA in assessing European transport projects and strategies', unpublished paper for the IASON project, Karlsruhe: IWW, Universität Karlsruhe.

Tavasszy, L.A. (2006), 'International experiences with freight modelling', *Proceedings of the Transportation Research Board Conference on Freight Modelling*, 25–27 September, Washington, DC.

Tavasszy, L.A. and N. Bruzelius (2005), 'The value of freight transport time: a logistics perspective – state of the art and research challenges', in OECD, *Report of the ECMT Round Table No. 127, Time and Transport*, Paris: OECD.

Tavasszy, L.A., M.J.P.M. Thissen, A.C. Muskens and J. Oosterhaven (2002), 'Pitfalls and solutions in the application of spatial computable general equilibrium models for transport appraisal', paper prepared for the 42nd European Congress of the Regional Science Association, Dortmund, 27–31 August.

Trujillo, L., E. Quinet and A. Estache (2002), 'Dealing with demand forecasting games in transport privatization', *Transport Policy*, **9** (4): 325–34.

UK Department for Transport (2002), *Review of Freight Modelling*, London: UK Department for Transport.

Van Wee, B. (2007), 'Rail infrastructure: challenges for CBA and other ex ante evaluations', *Transportation Planning and Technology*, **30** (1): 31–48.

Van Wee, B., P. Janse and R. van den Brink (2005), 'Comparing environmental performance of land transport modes', *Transport Reviews*, **25** (1): 3–24.

Varga, A., A. Koike, M.J.P.M Thissen and L.A. Tavasszy (2006), 'Endogenizing spatial economic structure in a macro-regional modeling framework', paper presented at the 2006 European Regional Science Association Conference, Volos, Greece, 30 August–3 September.

Venables, A. and M. Gasiorek (1998), 'The welfare implications of transport improvements in the presence of market failure', Report to SACTRA, London: UK Department for Transport.

Wachs, M. (1989), 'When planners lie with numbers', *APA Journal*, **55** (4): 476–9.

Wachs, M. (1990), 'Ethics and advocacy in forecasting for public policy', *Business and Professional Ethics Journal*, **9** (1&2): 141–57.

Wardman, M. (2001), 'A review of British evidence on time and service quality valuations', *Transportation Research Part E*, **37** (2–3): 107–28.

Wegener, M. and F. Fürst (1999), 'Land-use transport interaction: state of the art. Deliverable D2a of the project TRANSLAND' (Integration of Transport and Land Use Planning), Dortmund: Universität Dortmund, Institut für Raumplanung.

Zoeteman, A. (2004), *Railway Design and Maintenance from a Life-cycle Cost Perspective. A Decision Support Approach*, Delft: Delft University of Technology.

4. Cost–benefit analysis and the wider economic benefits from mega-projects

Roger W. Vickerman

4.1 INTRODUCTION

The potential for mega-projects to generate a social surplus, benefits above and beyond those accruing to users, has been recognised for a long time. The standard cost–benefit approach to the appraisal of transport infrastructure has tended to ignore such wider benefits, arguing that a well-defined cost–benefit analysis will ensure that the benefits to users will adequately capture all economic benefits. This has led to the situation where project promoters will attempt to reinforce the justification for projects by adding a mark-up to the user benefits to reflect these supposed wider benefits to the economy. This practice has then been extended to using such wider benefits as a means of justifying projects that would not be acceptable on the basis of the user benefits alone.

Over the last 15 years considerable effort has been expended on providing a more rigorous theoretical basis for including such wider effects and on gathering empirical evidence to assess whether the magnitude of any errors from ignoring them is sufficient to justify the added complexity of widening the appraisal framework. In Section 4.2 we examine the theoretical justification for including any wider economic impacts; in Section 4.3 we assess empirical evidence on the extent of such impacts; and in Section 4.4 we consider the implications for the appraisal process, especially in the situation where not just public funds are used for the investment. Section 4.5 presents some conclusions.

4.2 THE CASE FOR INCLUDING WIDER ECONOMIC BENEFITS

Microeconomic and Macroeconomic Arguments

The argument for relying on the user benefits from a project to justify its value to society is a simple one. The demand for transport is a derived demand; thus transport infrastructure will only be used for journeys that can be justified in terms of their value to the activities for which they are undertaken. Since these activities will only be undertaken up to the point where the willingness to pay is just equal to the price that has to be paid, the derived benefit to the user is expressed exactly by the revealed consumer surplus, no more and no less. This is the standard microeconomic argument identified by Dodgson (1973) and formalised by Jara-Diaz (1986).

Nevertheless there has always been a rather more macroeconomic argument that significant infrastructure development could have an impact on the overall rate of growth of the economy. This finds support particularly in the argument over the role that the development of the railways played in the development of the American West (Fogel, 1964; Fishlow, 1965). Here it was argued that the power of new infrastructure to unlock the economic potential of a region generated total economic benefits well above the sum of the benefits to individual users. This social surplus might of course be difficult to realise if reliance were placed on the market to provide infrastructure, a market that would only be able to generate its revenue from direct users. Thus the argument about a social surplus could very quickly become an argument for social involvement in the provision of infrastructure.

There is a microeconomic argument that would also support this view. Going right back to Dupuit (1844), it has been recognised that once infrastructure was constructed, the marginal cost for its use by the individual user would be very small (effectively zero in most cases). Thus the efficient price for using an uncongested infrastructure would also be zero. In such a situation it would not be possible for a private operator to develop and operate the infrastructure profitably. This did not, however, necessarily mean that the infrastructure was not worthwhile in the aggregate, as there might be externalities arising from its use that could not be internalised (Pigou, 1920).

Although these wider benefits were recognised as a theoretical possibility, particularly as Jara-Diaz (1986) identified where there were monopolistic tendencies in industries in the locations served by the infrastructure, there was little quantitative evidence confirming the actual extent of such inaccuracies in a standard analysis of transport user benefits. A well-defined transport CBA would thus always be the best estimate of overall benefits. This view was reinforced from the macroeconomic perspective by a desire not to use the wider benefits argument as an excuse for public-sector subsidy of such projects. In particular the 'crowding-out' argument was advanced to accuse public-sector-financed projects of increasing the cost, and reducing the rate of return, of the private sector in productive industries. Thus even if there were wider social benefits from an infrastructure project, securing these benefits would involve a reduction in output elsewhere in the economy. Again, however, although there was no empirical evidence of the relative sizes of these effects, the argument suited the political mood of the time with a desire to find any excuse to reduce the size of the public sector.

These views were confronted by Aschauer (1989), who set out to provide robust empirical evidence on the magnitude of the output effects of public infrastructure. Using a standard aggregate production function approach, Aschauer claimed that in practice the positive long-term effects of infrastructure on output were so large that they more than outweighed any short-term crowding-out effects. Aschauer's general findings based on evidence from US states were supported by some parallel work on European regions by Biehl (1986). Biehl's work went further, however. Instead of simply estimating an overall production function with a parameter that measured an average output elasticity with respect to aggregate infrastructure in a region, it tried to identify the conditions under which infrastructure did and did not have an impact in a particular region. Thus Biehl identified that there were regions, many with quite significant amounts of infrastructure, where infrastructure remained a constraint on growth, but other regions seemingly lacking in infrastructure would provide in effect a very poor return on further investment in infrastructure as other factors, such as private capital and skilled labour, were the main constraints on growth (Biehl, 1991).

Aschauer's work in particular did not go unchallenged. There was criticism of the econometric specification, and a raft of further studies (including several by Aschauer himself) was undertaken on a variety of data sets which confirmed, or in some cases failed to confirm, positive effects, although few produced estimates as large as those in Aschauer's original study (for a review see SACTRA, 1999; Vickerman, 2000; 2002). The consensus that has emerged is that there is evidence of an overall positive effect, with an output elasticity that is probably of the order of 0.1 (Lynde and Richmond, 1993).

The problem with all these studies is that the output elasticity of a volume of infrastructure is not a particularly useful measure of the wider economic effects that can be associated with any particular project. As Gramlich (1994) suggests, the real impact of infrastructure can only be identified at a much more micro or specific level. Depending on the nature of the project, the wider benefits could be very different in magnitude. In cases where the lack of infrastructure was a serious constraint on the integration of a local economy into wider markets, the overall benefits could be large relative to the direct user benefits. In other cases, even significant changes in accessibility could have only marginal impacts on the overall level of activity. But this assumes that all transport infrastructure changes are pro-competitive in the sense that they reduce transport costs in such a way as to lower the overall costs of transport-using activities, promoting competition and increased welfare. This also implies that lower transport costs are neutral in their impact on different regions.

Imperfect Competition

Jara-Diaz (1986) recognised that if the degree of monopoly were different in the two regions connected by a new infrastructure, there could be differential effects, but the further demonstration of this came from the development of the so-called new economic geography approach, following Krugman (1991). The key issue here is that in an imperfectly competitive world there will be agglomeration forces that enable firms with larger markets and enjoying scale economies to take more advantage of any reduction in transport costs. Hence reductions in transport costs can lead to more agglomeration and to unequal impacts on regions connected by the same infrastructure (Venables and Gasiorek, 1999). However, the nature of this approach means that the impact of any particular reduction of transport costs cannot be determined *a priori*. It will depend on the initial level of transport costs, the degree of agglomeration already present, the size of each market, the extent of scale economies and of the backward and forward linkages within that market (Fujita et al., 1999; Fujita and Thisse, 2002).

What becomes relevant here is the extent of the mark-up over marginal cost in the transport-using industries. In perfectly competitive sectors there is no mark-up and hence any changes in transport costs will have to be passed on directly to the final activity, so the extent of the impact on the wider economy is dependent on the elasticity of demand for that final activity. Since the amount of transport demanded depends directly on the demand for the final activity, the direct user benefits capture all the economic benefits. As mark-ups increase, a wedge is driven between the market for the transport-using activity and the transport associated with it. Any reduction in transport costs from new infrastructure does not need to be passed directly on to the customers of the final activity, but firms can use the opportunity to increase or reduce the mark-up. Reducing the mark-up by passing on more than the reduction in transport costs could be a way of increasing a firm's market area and gaining market advantage over firms in a more competitive market. On the other hand, firms may use the fall in transport costs to increase the mark-up, for example to invest so as to reduce other costs, and gain from potential scale economies. The net impact can also be negative. If the mark-up is negative, for example where there are industries with significant subsidies, such as in economically lagging regions, then the direct user benefits may overestimate the total economic benefit. Hence the ultimate impact from any infrastructure project is likely to be unpredictable, in terms of both magnitude and sign.

Components of the Total Economic Impact

How then can the total economic impact be assessed? There are three main elements to this. First, there is the impact on competition in the affected regions; second, there is the impact on the ability to gain benefits from the change in market power through agglomeration: and third, there is the impact on the linkages, and in particular on backward linkages such as the labour market. Once these have been assessed, we need to identify how to include them in a full cost–benefit framework.

The impact on competition is ambiguous. In perfectly competitive markets, as we have seen, the impact of increased competition is essentially neutral and should be adequately captured by the direct user benefits. In imperfectly competitive markets, the direct effect of any increased competition resulting directly from lower transport costs is also likely to be essentially neutral in its impact. It is traditionally argued that monopoly power is derived from the effective barriers to competition provided by higher transport costs so that reductions in such barriers are pro-competitive, reducing monopoly mark-ups and hence there is a wider benefit resulting from the reduction of prices. On the other hand, such competitive pressures if they do exist may also drive firms out of the market, and the effect of lower transport costs is to reduce the number of firms able to compete in the market in the long run. It is likely that such effects cancel each other out in most cases, and thus there is little in the way of wider economic benefits that can be added.

There may be some exceptions to this where new links are created that have such a significant impact on transport costs (which are already very high) that significant market restructuring takes place, introducing competition to previously protected local monopolies. This is the 'unlocking' argument advanced by SACTRA (1999) and reaffirmed in its latest guidance by the UK Department for Transport (2005). These are likely to be rare in most developed market economies.

Much more significant than the market competition effects are the agglomeration benefits that may result from the change in transport costs. The argument here is that the rise in output that follows from the lower transport costs has cumulative effects through the way in which firms interact in a market. This involves both localisation economies, in which firms within the same industry benefit from proximity to each other through such factors as specialised labour pools or shared R&D, and urbanisation economies, in which firms obtain a form of public-goods benefit from the existence of an urban infrastructure including knowledge, research and culture, as well as the physical infrastructure. The larger the market, the greater the likely net additional impact that arises because there is an additional impact on productivity. There has been a long debate over the extent to which urban size and productivity are related, and the direction of causality, but there is an increasing consensus that there is a strong positive relationship that can have a significant additional impact on the benefits from transport improvements (Fujita and Thisse, 2002; Venables, 2004; Graham, 2005). This argues that although the lower transport costs may cause firms to increase the size of their market, that increased size provides an incentive for the firm to enjoy scale economies and to benefit from proximity to other more efficient firms. Typical productivity elasticities are in the range 0.01 to 0.1. Ciccone (2002), using data for EU regions, finds an elasticity with respect to employment density of 0.05. Graham (2005) finds for UK industries a weighted average elasticity of 0.04 for manufacturing, but significant variations between industries, with some as high as 0.2, and an average of 0.12 for service industries. Graham also identifies some important variations between regions, reflecting different degrees of localisation of industry groups.

Labour-market Effects

A further element of this output benefit under imperfect competition is that because productivity is increasing, the direct user benefits will also be greater than would be the case under an assumption of perfect competition. The largest direct user benefits from most projects are time savings, valued relative to the wage level assuming that wages reflect productivity. The increase in productivity implies that a higher value of time savings should be applied. But the increased productivity enables firms to increase output (or produce the same output with fewer workers), which implies that an uplift needs to be applied to the time savings.

The basic advantage that some regions obtain in an imperfectly competitive world derives from a larger market size, which enables firms to increase both output (scale) and productivity. However, it is useful to break that larger market size effect up into a pure market size effect, and the backward and forward linkages associated with agglomeration. One of the key backward linkages relates to the labour market. As transport costs are reduced, labour markets become larger as commuting times are reduced and firms have access to a larger labour supply. This enables firms to benefit both from wage levels lower than they might be as a result of more competition in the larger market, and access to more skilled labour, which will be more productive for the reasons discussed above.

Normally a wage premium would be expected at the market centre reflecting its greater accessibility, scale and productivity effects, but also reflecting the wage necessary to attract labour to commute in from across the wider region. As transport is improved, more workers find it attractive to work in the market centre, because of the larger catchment area from which commuting is feasible, and because of the increased opportunities for work in the centre rather than elsewhere (or not at all). Workers in the centre may also be prepared to work longer hours. Hence an output effect arises because of the increased size of the labour market. Where there is also a productivity effect due to agglomeration effects at the market centre, the output effect from the expansion of employment is added to by the increased output of all existing workers.

This is illustrated in Figure 4.1, derived from Venables (2004). The W curve represents the mark-up of wages at the market centre relative to the edge of the city. This increases with city size, reflecting the productivity effect of agglomeration. The C function represents total commuting costs (assuming for simplicity a constant transport cost per unit distance). In the initial situation with commuting costs given by C_0, the city is of size L_0 in terms of numbers of workers, and the unit benefit (the equilibrium wage mark-up) is B_0. Transport improvements lead to commuting costs falling to C_1 and thus the equilibrium size of the city increases to L_1, at which size the wage gap at the centre increases along the W function to B_1. The total net benefit is composed of an increase in output from the existing workers facing lower commuting costs (α), an increase in the output from the additional workers ($\beta + \gamma$), less the additional transport costs (γ), and finally the increase in output due to the productivity enhancement from agglomeration (δ). Note that if there were no productivity enhancement, the wage gap would remain at B_0 and hence, with commuting costs at C_1, the city would only increase to size L_1', areas β and γ would be smaller and δ would not exist.

Note in all this discussion that it is not the size of the infrastructure project that determines the scale of the wider economic benefits. Mega-projects are likely to have a wider impact in terms of greater direct user benefits, but the wider benefits are not simply proportional to the direct

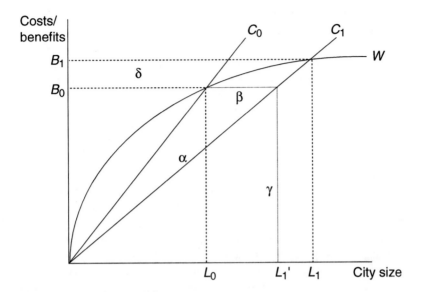

Source: Based on Venables (2004).

Figure 4.1   Labour-market benefits from transport improvement

user benefits. Some relatively minor projects, the 'unlocking' projects, can have disproportionately large wider benefits, whereas some very large projects may have relatively little impact on the key scale, productivity and linkage effects. This is why there is no *a priori* reason to apply a simple wider benefits multiplier. It also demonstrates that seeking a simple output elasticity as in the macro-analyses can be misleading.

4.3   EMPIRICAL EVIDENCE ON WIDER EFFECTS

It is clear from the previous discussion that identifying the source of wider benefits involves greater complexity than the simple approaches might suggest. In particular, it will be much more difficult to model a situation in which there are imperfectly competitive sectors as the equilibrium outcome is not easy to determine. Finding evidence of such effects empirically may thus be difficult. The approach that has become key to this is the use of computable equilibrium models, which can allow for the actual mark-ups observed in the affected sectors and thus for the differential impacts that a given change in transport costs can have on different regions, depending on their sectoral and competitive structures.

In their general equilibrium form, such models can allow for differences between regions in industrial structure and linkages to model the differential impact on each region. However, this approach is dependent on significant data resources, which has so far led to considerable reluctance to use the approach as a general evaluation tool. In the UK, SACTRA (1999) identified the value of such an approach, but suggested that it would be more useful for overall network evaluation or very large projects than for routine investment appraisal, a view reinforced in a more recent assessment (Gunn, 2004).

It is not proposed to go into detail here on the structure of computable general equilibrium (CGE) models (see Bröcker, 2004; Gunn, 2004, for valuable introductions), and we use only a selection of examples from the large number of case studies to illustrate key points. Given our focus on developed-country cases where even mega-projects have only a marginal impact on overall networks, we ignore the large number of examples applied to developing countries.

The basic structure involves a demand system that expresses final consumers' preferences over a range of differentiated goods, a social accounting matrix that expresses the input–output structure of the economy, and a profit function for firms. The input–output structure distinguishes tradable and non-tradable goods. The demand for non-tradables has to be satisfied by regional production; that for tradables can be satisfied by importing goods from other regions, the delivered price of such goods depending on the price of transport. Firms are assumed to be in imperfect competition producing differentiated goods. In order to make the system more tractable, the typical assumption is that of monopolistic competition so that although there is a mark-up over marginal cost, the possibility of entry ensures that firms produce where price equals average cost. A further important element is the labour market. It must be ensured that the demand for labour necessary for a region's production is matched by the available labour force. In the longer run this requires the recognition of migration between regions to achieve labour-market balance, but in other cases there will be a need to accommodate commuting between regions as a key element.

The advantages of the CGE approach over other modelling approaches lie in its ability to incorporate imperfectly competitive markets and differentiated goods. Central to the model structure are the final consumers' preferences for these goods, and hence the output of the model, as well as sets of demands for these goods and the implicit flows between regions which these demands generate, is a direct measure of changes in consumer welfare in terms of the equivalent variation in income (the income equivalent of the change in welfare resulting from a change in any input, such as the cost of transport). Moreover, the structure of the model is such that it determines a higher proportion of critical variables endogenously without the need for further assumptions.

Although CGE models have been used increasingly widely in the analysis of international trade, such trade does not involve the complexity of spatial relationships which are implicit in most passenger transport applications. The approach has been used to demonstrate the way in which the spatial distribution of the benefits from transport developments are parameter-dependent (see Venables and Gasiorek, 1999), but such demonstrations use highly simplified numerical simulations with a small number of sectors and regions. Applications of CGE models to specific transport investment projects are still relatively scarce. This is not surprising given the difficulty in deriving the detailed data requirements for a specific project, not least in determining the relevant spatial scale of the area of study. The availability of social accounting data at the small area level is particularly problematic. There is also a difference between the use of CGE models to refine evidence on Aschauer-type macro-questions of the role of aggregate infrastructure from those trying to answer micro-type questions about the specific impact on flows of a given infrastructure improvement.

In between these two extremes is the case of the overall benefits of transport network improvements. These require us to model the impact of differential changes on specific links, but are aimed more at identifying the overall benefits of improvements to the network and their spatial distribution than at the appraisal of an individual investment. Thus, for example, the CGEurope model developed by Johannes Bröcker has been used in a number of research projects looking at the impact of the Trans-European Networks (TENs; see, for example, Bröcker et al., 2004a; 2004b). This uses a detailed representation of the European transport network mapped onto a detailed regional structure of Europe at the NUTS3 level.

The model generates three important results. First, it demonstrates that despite significant changes in transport costs and accessibility occasioned by the development of the TENs, the impact on welfare is relatively modest (equivalent typically to less than 2 per cent of regional GDP). Second, it shows that the network as a whole has both positive and negative impacts and, although the largest positive impacts relative to regional GDP are in the more peripheral, poorer regions, it is difficult to claim that, despite significant investment expenditures, the TENs are a major force for convergence and cohesion. Third, specific investments can be seen to have differential impacts both on the specific regions they serve and on the added value they bring to the European economy as a whole. Thus, even using a fairly aggregated modelling structure, much of parameter dependence and variety of impact predicted by the theoretical model can be identified.

More specific project applications include an evaluation of the regional impacts of highway developments in Japan (Miyagi, 1998; 2001), and of the impact of a high-speed rail link between the Randstad and the Northern Netherlands, including the possibility of using an ultra-high-speed maglev system (Oosterhaven and Elhorst, 2003; Elhorst et al., 2004). The Dutch model focuses not just on the output and welfare implications, but also very specifically on the labour market since the improvement to transport will affect not only the location of employment but also the residential location decision. This introduces further difficulties because it requires not just a balance of production and consumption in the goods markets, with a potential response through migration to long-term imbalances, but a period-by-period balancing of labour-market demands and supplies, zone by zone. Furthermore, once the key benefiting users of the system are passengers rather than goods, some of the simplifying assumptions used in the typical CGE structure become less plausible. For example, the use of 'iceberg' transport costs, in which the cost of transport of a good is subsumed into the value of the goods moved such that they are worth less at the destination than at the origin by the amount of the cost of transport, is inappropriate for passengers. Similarly the assumption of constant costs of transport per unit of distance is even less appropriate for passenger transport.

Nevertheless, the application of a CGE model to this project has produced an interesting set of results. The wider benefits are shown to vary significantly as a result of the precise nature of the project and the region studied (especially core–periphery differences), and constitute a higher proportion of direct benefits than earlier studies suggested, of the order of 30–40 per cent. These wider benefits are higher than theoretical simulation models have suggested; SACTRA (1999) suggested that a figure of 10 to 20 per cent was a likely range, following the conclusion by Venables and Gasiorek (1999) that 30 per cent was likely to be exceeded in only a few cases. (It is worth noting, however, that in the earlier version Oosterhaven and Elhorst had produced a figure of 83 per cent.) What is clear from Elhorst et al. (2004) is that the degree of detail in the modelling of labour market responses may be crucial here. These employment effects arise by linking areas of surplus labour to those of labour shortages, rather than through the productivity effects arising as a result of agglomeration benefits, which have been argued elsewhere (Venables, 2004).

4.4   LESSONS FOR APPRAISAL

There is a significant difference between a theoretical model that tries to explain the relationship between investment in transport infrastructure and economic welfare, and a method of appraisal to be used for individual projects. We have already suggested that the nature of CGE models makes them more suitable for mega-projects which are more likely to have the sort of complex effects which CGE models attempt to disentangle. As Gunn (2004) has identified, the applications thus far have been largely in this category. But identifying economic impacts is not the same as appraisal. SACTRA (1999) pointed out the way in which appraisal using traditional cost–benefit analysis would require an increasingly complex move from the standard transport CBA to a more sophisticated analysis that incorporated environmental and wider economic effects, including recognising imperfect competition, if the total impact were to be correctly appraised.

The advantage of the CGE model approach is that it allows us to assess the sensitivity of the overall outcome to varying the assumptions about inputs. This identifies which are the most critically sensitive values and relationships included in the model. These are the areas of the appraisal process that have to be tackled most carefully and thoroughly. In a recent summary of the implications for appraisal of work by Venables (2004) and Graham (2005), the UK Department for Transport (2005) has outlined the steps for appraisal of these wider benefits in large-scale transport investment improvements.

Apart from the usual appraisal of user benefits in terms of journey-time savings, four wider effects are identified: productivity effects, agglomeration effects, competition effects and labour-market effects. Productivity effects aim to measure the way in which journey-time savings and increased reliability for business travel affect productivity and GDP. These are in addition to the benefits to the users themselves and can lead, for example, to firms employing fewer staff or fewer vehicles because of the greater speed in the network. Agglomeration effects are those we have already identified, where productivity among firms increases because of an increasing concentration of firms or increasing density of employment. Competition effects include the pro-competitive effects of increased competition and, under imperfect competition, the impacts of increasing returns to scale. Finally, labour-market effects arise from three possible sources. First, more people may be willing to enter the labour market because of the improved transport. Second, workers may be willing to work longer hours. Third, and of greatest significance, employment may relocate from a lower-productivity area to a higher-productivity area.

The key to estimating all these impacts is good data on the relationship between employment density and productivity, and the way in which labour supply may adjust in imperfect markets to changing patterns of transport costs. This requires evidence at a much more detailed level than the type of approach typically available for CGE studies. Detailed

Table 4.1   Welfare and GDP impacts of Crossrail

Benefits	Welfare (£m)	DGP (£m)
Business time savings	4847	4847
Commuting time savings	4152	
Leisure time savings	3833	
Total transport user benefits – conventional appraisal	**12832**	
Increase in labour force participation		872
People working longer		0
Move to more productive jobs		10772
Agglomeration benefits	3094	3094
Increased competition	0	0
Imperfect competition	485	485
Exchequer consequences of increased GDP	3580	
Additional to conventional appraisal	**7159**	
Total (excluding financing, social and environmental costs and benefits)	**19991**	**20069**

Source: UK Department for Transport (2005).

evidence on price–cost mark-ups has been provided by Graham (2005), and this, together with the labour market evidence produced by Venables (2004), enables some estimates of wider benefits to be calculated from transport projects. Table 4.1, taken from UK Department for Transport (2005), shows some estimates for the likely impact of introducing Crossrail, a major new cross-London rail link which would provide much faster transport along an east–west corridor for commuters into central London.

Table 4.1 presents these benefits in two ways, as an impact on GDP and as an impact on welfare so as to include those things which would not be measured in GDP measures. It can be seen that in this case the difference is not great, but the incidence changes somewhat. The welfare measure includes as gains to users the time savings that have an impact on labour supply, which appear as additional benefits in the GDP measure. Particularly important in both measures is the likely agglomeration effects, amounting to some 25 per cent of direct user benefits, suggesting again that omitting this factor would lead to a serious underestimate of the total economic benefit of a project. But notice also that over 50 per cent of the GDP benefits arises from the redeployment of employment to more productive jobs. This approach is based essentially on putting together the findings of a set of data from complementary sources, but it produces overall results that are not dissimilar from the full modelling approach of Oosterhaven and Elhorst (2003) and Elhorst et al. (2004) discussed above.

However, care must be taken not to assume that every new infrastructure project will produce wider benefits on this scale. Most of the studies we have discussed above are *ex-ante* modelling studies of projects which have not yet been developed. Hay et al. (2004) have shown, in a rare *ex-post* study of impacts, how a very significant mega-project, the Channel Tunnel, has not produced significant wider benefits, at least on the regional economies close to the tunnel. In fact it is suggested that any wider benefits are so dispersed and so long term as not to be easily detectable.

Most appraisal methods have been developed for simple link improvements. Such methods require the definition of a well-behaved demand function for a clearly defined link or origin–destination pair in order to assess the user benefits. Major infrastructure developments raise the question of how to handle network effects. This is not just an issue that arises in the case of how to measure the added value of a network such as the European Union's Trans-European Networks. Major infrastructures, particularly fixed links such as the Channel Tunnel, have widespread repercussions on the networks they link together, causing a significant redistribution of traffic. This goes beyond the question of simply recognising induced traffic as it can lead to a complex interaction with the economy in the way discussed earlier in this chapter. This complexity precludes a simple method of handling such effects and, as Laird et al. (2005) have argued in a detailed analysis of the issue, these need to be considered on a case-by-case basis.

The identification of these network effects may also be critical in identifying the most appropriate sources of finance for such mega-projects. Most CBAs ignore the origin of the funds used to finance the project. The assumption is generally that if a CBA is being carried out, then the main source of funding is the public sector, in which case the only real consideration is the relevant discount rate, which must reflect both the social time preference and the marginal cost of the public funds used. It is usually (implicitly) assumed that such funds are raised by some form of lump-sum tax that does not distort the allocation of resources elsewhere in the economy. Where taxes are raised otherwise, for example via an income tax, there may be further complications (see, for example, Venables, 2004). If a new transport infrastructure leads to an increase in the size of labour-market areas and an increase in productivity, and hence increased wage rates, then the increased tax take may have an effect on the willingness of workers to respond to the new situation. If the tax falls mainly on employers through some form of payroll tax, then the willingness of employers to respond to the new situation may change. Such a situation may be changed if any increase in such taxes is hypothecated to the transport improvements so that beneficiaries see that they are contributing directly to the improvement.

Where the funding needs to go outside the public sector to involve private finance, either independently or through some form of public–private partnership, identifying the beneficiaries may be critical to making the finance available (see Vickerman, 2007a; 2007b, for a further discussion). Private investors may be interested in the overall rate of return they will receive on the project, but may also need to justify it in terms of the distribution of those benefits. The distribution of benefits may thus become a key element in the appraisal process.

4.5   CONCLUSIONS

There are three clear conclusions from the discussion in this chapter:

1. Significant wider economic effects which can be identified from large-scale transport infrastructure mega-projects that cannot be captured by conventional CBA methods, which concentrate on the change in the consumers' surplus of users.
2. The nature of these economic effects will vary considerably between projects, in both magnitude and direction.
3. Although methods exist to capture these effects, principally the development of spatial computable general equilibrium models, these are complex and demand significant data resources, which means that they may only be viable in cases of mega-projects.

This implies that for many small projects a conventional CBA may remain the most effective means of decision-making. This is not to argue that wider benefits are in any way proportional to the scale of the project. It is quite feasible that a very large investment may be able to capture virtually all of its benefits as user benefits, for example where any wider impacts are very widely dispersed and there is little scope for the generation of agglomeration effects or significant impacts on local labour markets.

The overriding conclusion is that there is unlikely to be any possibility of adopting simple rules of thumb for determining whether a project needs a wider evaluation than CBA or what that might mean in the way of potential additional benefits. The nature and extent of imperfect competition by sector at the regional level and the scope for thickening labour markets through better accessibility are likely to be the key indicators. Both of these require more and better data than are currently available at the regional level in most cases.

REFERENCES

Aschauer, D.A. (1989), 'Is public expenditure productive?', *Journal of Monetary Economics*, **23**: 177–200.

Biehl, D. (ed.) (1986), *The Contribution of Infrastructure to Regional Development*, Luxembourg: Office of Official Publications of the European Communities.

Biehl, D. (1991), 'The role of infrastructure in regional development', in R.W. Vickerman (ed.), *Infrastructure and Regional Development*, European Research in Regional Science, Vol. 1, London: Pion.

Bröcker, J. (2004), 'Computable general equilibrium analysis in transportation economics', in D.A. Hensher, K.J. Button, K. Haynes and P. Stopher (eds), *Handbook of Transport Geography and Spatial Systems: Handbooks in Transport Volume 5*, Oxford: Elsevier.

Bröcker, J., R. Meyer, N. Schneekloth, C. Schürmann, K. Spiekermann and M. Wegener (2004a), *Modelling the Socio-economic and Spatial Impacts of EU Transport Policy*, IASON (Integrated Appraisal of Spatial, Economic and Network Effects of Transport Investments and Policies) Deliverable 6. Funded by 5th Framework RTD Programme, Kiel/Dortmund: Institut für Regionalforschung, Christian-Albrechts-Universität, Kiel/Institut für Raumplanung, Universität Dortmund.

Bröcker, J., R. Capello, L. Lundquist, T. Pütz, J. Rouwendal, N. Schneekloth, A. Spairani, M. Spangenberg, K. Spiekermann, R. Vickerman and M. Wegener (2004b), *Territorial Impact of EU Transport and TEN Policies*, Final Report of Action 2.1.1. of the European Spatial Planning Observation Network ESPON 2006, Kiel: Institut für Regionalforschung, Christian-Albrechts-Universität.

Ciccone, A. (2002), 'Agglomeration effects in Europe', *European Economic Review*, **46**: 213–27.

Dodgson, J.S. (1973), 'External effects in road investment', *Journal of Transport Economics and Policy*, **7**: 169–85.

Dupuit, J.A. (1844), 'De la mesure de l'utilité des travaux publics', *Annales des Ponts et Chaussées*, **8**.

Elhorst, J.P., J. Oosterhaven and A.E. Romp (2004), 'Integral cost–benefit analysis of maglev technology under market imperfections', SOM Research Report, University of Groningen, available at http://irs.ub.rug.nl/ppn/268887764.

Fishlow, A. (1965), *American Railroads and the Transformation of the Ante-Bellum Economy*, Harvard Economic Studies, Vol. 127, Cambridge, MA: Harvard University Press.

Fogel, R.W. (1964), *Railroads and American Economic Growth: Essays in Econometric History*, Baltimore, MD: Johns Hopkins University Press.

Fujita, M., P. Krugman and A.J. Venables (1999), *The Spatial Economy: Cities, Regions and International Trade*, Cambridge, MA: MIT Press.

Fujita, M. and J. Thisse (2002), *The Economics of Agglomeration*, Cambridge, MA: Cambridge University Press.

Graham, D. (2005), *Wider Economic Benefits of Transport Improvements: Link between Agglomeration and Productivity. Stage 1 Report*, London: Department for Transport, available at www.dft.gov.uk/stellent/groups/dft_econappr/documents/page/dft_econappr_038895.pdf.

Gramlich, E.M. (1994), 'Infrastructure investment: a review essay', *Journal of Economic Literature*, **32**: 1176–96.

Gunn, H. (2004), *SCGE Models: Relevance and Accessibility for Use in the UK, with emphasis on Implications for Evaluation of Transport Investments*, Final Report to Department for Transport, London, Cambridge: RAND Europe.

Hay, A., K. Meredith and R. Vickerman (2004), *The Impact of the Channel Tunnel on Kent and Relationships with Nord-Pas de Calais*, Final Report to Eurotunnel and Kent County Council, Canterbury: Centre for European Regional and Transport Economics, available from www.kent.ac.uk/economics/research/Full%20Report.pdf.

Jara-Diaz, S.R. (1986), 'On the relations between users benefits and the economic effects of transportation activities', *Journal of Regional Science*, **26**: 379–91.

Krugman, P.R. (1991), 'Increasing returns to scale and economic geography', *Journal of Political Economy*, **99**: 483–99.

Laird, J.J., J. Nellthorp and P.J. Mackie (2005), 'Network effects and total economic impact in transport appraisal', *Transport Policy*, **12**: 537–44.

Lynde, C. and J. Richmond (1993), 'Public capital and long-run costs in UK manufacturing', *Economic Journal*, **103**: 880–93.

Miyagi, T. (1998), 'A spatial computable general equilibrium approach for measuring multiregional impacts of large scale transportation projects', in L. Lundqvist, L.-G. Mattsson and T.F. Kim (eds), *Network Infrastructure and the Urban Environment: Advances in Spatial Systems Modelling*, Heidelberg: Springer: 224–44.

Miyagi, T. (2001), 'Economic appraisal for multi-regional impacts by a large scale expressway project', Tinbergen Institute Discussion Paper TI 2001-066/3, Amsterdam: Tinbergen Institute.

Oosterhaven, J. and J.P. Elhorst (2003), 'Indirect economic benefits of transport infrastructure investments', in W. Dullaert, B. Jourquin and J.B. Polak (eds), *Across the Border: Building on a Quarter Century of Transport Research in the Benelux*, Antwerp: De Boeck.

Pigou, A.C. (1920), *The Economics of Welfare*, London: Macmillan.

SACTRA (Standing Advisory Committee on Trunk Road Assessment) (1999), *Transport and the Economy*, London: Stationery Office.

UK Department for Transport (2005), *Transport, Wider Economic Benefits, and Impacts on GDP*, Technical Paper, available at www.dft.gov.uk/stellent/groups/dft_econappr/documents/page/dft_econappr_038893.pdf.

Venables, A.J. (2004), 'Evaluating urban transport improvements: cost–benefit analysis in the presence of agglomeration and income taxation', mimeo, London School of Economics.

Venables, A. and M. Gasiorek (1999), *The Welfare Implications of Transport Improvements in the Presence of Market Failure Part 1*, Report to Standing Advisory Committee on Trunk Road Assessment, London: DETR.

Vickerman, R.W. (2000), 'Economic growth effects of transport infrastructure', *Jahrbuch für Regionalwissenschaft*, **20**: 99–115.

Vickerman, R.W. (2002), 'Transport and economic development', in *Transport and Economic Development*, Round Table 119, Economic Research Centre, European Conference of Ministers of Transport, OECD, Paris: 139–77.

Vickerman, R.W. (2007a), 'Private sector finance of transport infrastructure: progress and prospects', in P. Rietveld and R. Stough (eds), *Institutions and Sustainable Transport: Regulatory Reform in Advanced Economies*, Cheltenham, UK and Northampton, MA, USA: Edward Elgar.

Vickerman, R.W. (2007b), 'Cost–benefit analysis and large-scale infrastructure projects: state of the art and challenges', *Environment and Planning B*, **34** (4): 598–610.

5. Mega-projects and contested information

Hans de Bruijn and Martijn Leijten

5.1 INTRODUCTION

Information is crucial to good decision-making on mega-projects. No matter whether such decision-making concerns the technical aspects of implementation, the economic and ecological impact or the risks of a project, it is highly information-sensitive. It seems reasonable to assume that no proper decision-making can take place without the right information.

The reality tends to be different, however. Many decisions on large infrastructural projects have been insensitive to information. Flyvbjerg et al. have demonstrated the poor quality of cost–benefit analyses (Flyvbjerg, 2004; Flyvbjerg et al., 2002; 2003a; 2003b; 2004; 2005). This seems easy to explain: the proponents of a project have an interest in low-cost estimates and therefore show behaviour that is qualified as 'strategic misrepresentation, i.e. lying' (Flyvbjerg et al., 2002). The remedies often suggested follow naturally from these findings. In some of the literature, we find a decisionistic remedy, consisting of two elements:

1. The right information must, and can, be gathered.
2. Decision-making follows analyses; there is no decision-making without the right information and analysis. We find this remedy in the older literature (Hall, 1980), but it can also be found in the more recent literature (Bell, 1998).

Other authors point out that it is impossible to gather 'the right information'. Flyvbjerg et al. reconfirm a general fact about mega-projects: rarely is there a simple truth about them. What is presented as reality by one set of experts is, in many cases, 'a social construct that can be deconstructed and reconstructed by other experts' (Flyvbjerg et al., 2003a: 61).

In theory, the absence of a 'simple truth' and the conclusion that facts tend to be 'mere' social constructs may lead to the extreme relativism of 'anything-goes' decision-making. 'Strategic misinterpretations' or 'lies' do not exist in such a view, because any picture of reality is justified. Information is unable to play its disciplining role; decision-making will degenerate into a free fight between proponents and opponents of a project. In such a free fight, information can freely be ignored or the wrong information can be used to discipline the decision-making.

A difficult dilemma arises if such relativism is not an option. On the one hand, there is no 'truth' and the decisionistic approach to mega-projects is too simple. Much crucial information is 'contested' at the time of decision-making. It is controversial, disputable, difficult to measure objectively or even non-existent. On the other hand, researchers should seek information of the best possible quality. Flyvbjerg's study we referred to is full of examples (2003: 49–64) of the disastrous consequences of the use of poor information. In more prosaic terms, although there is no holy grail, we have to continue the quest for it.

In this chapter, we focus on this dilemma. First, we shall introduce the concept of 'contested knowledge' (Sections 5.2, 5.3 and 5.4). Then we shall point out that the paradoxical effect of denying the contested nature of information may be that the quest for the right information to structure decision-making will, in fact, incentivise chaotic decision-making (Section 5.5). We shall conclude with a number of recommendations for dealing with contested information and the above dilemma. The essence of these recommendations is that attention should be paid not only to the *substance* of analyses and information that are used, but also to the *process* of generating these analyses and this information (Section 5.6). Short conclusions are formulated in Section 5.7.

5.2   WHAT IS CONTESTED INFORMATION?

Douglas and Wildavsky (1983) identify four types of problems of risk that influence decision-making on, for example, mega-projects. Two factors are of the utmost importance in these problems: knowledge and consensus on the desired prospects (see Table 5.1).

- *Tamed problems* Problems with a high certainty of the knowledge available, i.e. with facts that can be measured objectively. Furthermore, there is consensus on standards and a normative trade-off of standards is possible. These problems are guaranteed to be fully solvable.
- *(Un)tameable ethical problems* Problems with a high certainty of the knowledge available, i.e. with facts that can be measured objectively. However, either there is no consensus on standards or a

Table 5.1   Different types of policy problems

	Certainty about knowledge	Little certainty about knowledge
Consensus on normative standards	Tamed problems	(Un-)tameable scientific problems
Little consensus on normative standards	(Un-)tameable ethical problems	Untamed political problems

normative trade-off of standards is impossible. Many ethical issues come under this category. Problems can only be solved by more coercion or more discussion.

- *(Un)tameable scientific problems*   Problems with a high consensus on standards (normative trade-offs are possible), but the level of knowledge causes uncertainty. There are no facts that can be measured objectively. These problems can be tamed if knowledge is developed to a sufficient level. The solution lies in more research.
- *Untamed political problems*   Problems with high uncertainty of the knowledge available and little consensus on standards. There is no *ex-ante* hard scientific information on, for example, the economic and ecological performance of a project. In addition, there is a conflict of values. Different actors will make different trade-offs between the values of, for example, economic profit, ecologic sustainability and safety.

Untamed political problems are those in which basically any type of information is contested. Both the underlying facts and the underlying values or normative standards are controversial. Many mega-projects are subject to untamed political problems. Goals a project should achieve and problems it should solve are unclear or disputed, and methods to calculate to what extent those problems are solved and goals are achieved are contested as well. The following section will deal with this subject in more depth.

5.3   CONTESTED INFORMATION: FACTS

First, creating sufficient objective information is impossible in this type of decision-making. For example, when the economic and ecological effects of a mega-project have to be estimated, the following four problems may arise.

Data

Data used in calculations are always disputable. In many cases, they are simply not available, because data about future developments – i.e. from *ex-ante* analyses – just do not exist; data are mere expectations or predictions. Flyvbjerg et al. also acknowledge the contested character of data by stating that 'mega-project development is currently a field where little can be trusted, not even – some would say especially not – numbers produced by analysts' (Flyvbjerg et al., 2003a: 5). They attribute the distrust fully to wrongdoing, however. As we saw in Section 5.1, this is not always the only valid explanation. Although the use of data from *ex-ante* analyses for decision-making may be acceptable in practice, the fact that it describes a future state automatically makes it anything but facts and therefore contestable, no matter how fair-minded an analyst may be. This makes any use of data in decision-making, obtained either justly or unjustly, automatically disputable. A railway project, for example, depends on factors such as transport volume, economic growth and the development of competing modes; both decision-making and construction take many years. Data used with regard to these variables are always disputable. Some private projects where the owner himself made the cost–benefit analysis show that wrong data are not always the result of wrongdoing. Private owners do not have an incentive to misrepresent estimates, which makes them a good example. The privately built and operated Warnow tunnel in North German Rostock, for instance, attracts less traffic than estimated by its private owner, which, in hindsight, makes it a bad investment (*Ostseezeitung*, 2004).

Methods

Another question is what method is used to calculate the findings from an analysis. Different actors tend to use different methods as they regard the methods of other actors as less suitable. The views of the various parties about the economic effects of a mega-project – both direct and indirect – often differ sharply, because each may adopt different calculating methods in the cost–benefit analysis. Given the difference in views, reaching scientific consensus about the method by which the effects are best calculated may then appear to be impossible.

The different methods may then lead to completely different conclusions about the societal feasibility of a project. There are examples of attempts to arrive at a joint analysis that resulted in academic discussions about the calculation of indirect effects (Ministerie van Verkeer en Waterstaat, 2004).

System Boundaries

The third question concerns the system boundaries: when we consider the effects of an infrastructural decision, how broadly will the system be defined? In most cases, the effects included in cost–benefit analyses are those on a country or state as a whole. However, proponents of certain regionally orientated projects may point out that the value of the infrastructure they propose lies in the shift of jobs and people *within* the country or state (for instance in order to achieve economic growth in one region in particular). If this can be counted as a positive effect (although, on balance, there is hardly any effect on the country or state as a whole), the question of the system boundaries becomes even more crucial. The point of departure may be the effect on the immediate surroundings of the infrastructure, but also the effect on the areas further away, or even the entire region. If the decision is made to account for the effects on the region, the decision-makers may ignore the fact that areas in the immediate proximity of an infrastructure line (such as a motorway or railway) absorb economic activity from areas in the same region, but located further away from a motorway exit or railway station. Including those peripheral or deprived areas in the economic analyses will, of course, present a picture that is completely different from the one that emerges when the system boundaries of the analysis are drawn more narrowly.

Moreover, the wider the system boundaries are, the greater the uncertainties will be. The effect of a high-speed rail link on the immediate surroundings of a railway station proves to be easier to calculate than the effect on the area on a greater scale level. In the case of high-speed rail links in France and Japan, the expected positive economic effect round the railway stations was indeed found, but there was hardly any effect on the wider area as economic activities moved from the city's surroundings to the immediate proximity of the high-speed railway station. This effect appeared for example in and around the French city of Lyon after the opening of the Paris–Lyon TGV (train à grande vitesse) connection (Bonnafous, 1987; Rietveld et al., 2001).

Optimisations

Finally, there is the issue of optimisation of the desired effects. Decision-making about mega-projects tends to be decision-making in which several options have to be compared. An important question in analyses of this kind is what possibilities the various modes offer for further optimisation: what innovative potential does the mode have, what are the possibilities for a mode to improve the economic and ecological performance? At one stage, mode A may score better than mode B, but if mode B has far more innovative potential, it may be attractive to opt for mode B. Again, the problem here is easy to see: optimisations depend on a large number of variables, which cannot be measured objectively, so it is difficult to determine the innovative potential.

5.4 CONTESTED INFORMATION: NORMATIVE STANDARDS

In addition to this question about facts, a normative question arises in the event of contested knowledge. Decision-making about mega-projects always concerns a trade-off between different interests, and consensus about this trade-off is usually lacking. If we focus on the example of the economic and ecological performance of a mega-project, two trade-off issues arise, even when 'scientific analyses' have been made: a trade-off within the analysis and a trade-off between analyses.

A Trade-off Within the Analysis

For example, an ecological analysis may show that the construction of line infrastructure reduces CO_2 emission, but makes a heavier demand on scarce resources. This requires a trade-off. Which is more important? Similar issues arise in the event of an economic analysis. Although a project may bring economic growth, it may do so mainly in the segment of the highly educated, while the area served may need jobs for unskilled workers. Which is considered more important? Of course, this does not involve a simple trade-off between two components. In many cases, both economic and ecological analyses have a large number of components that have to be considered. The magnetic levitation (maglev) train connection between the Chinese city of Shanghai and its airport Pudong was very expensive and there were considerable technical uncertainties and even problems when the line was built. Once in use, it appeared to attract fewer travellers than expected or hoped. The Chinese government nevertheless attached great value to its construction, as it was the first commercial maglev railway line in the world, and many still consider this a dominant value (Associated Press, 2004).

A Trade-off Between Analyses

This concerns the question of how to weigh the findings from different analyses against each other. Such a question can hardly be formulated objectively, and depends heavily on political views and interests. A project may for example have a positive economic effect, but a negative effect on the natural environment (scenic values would be harmed). If scenic beauty is an asset of the region concerned, the value of the natural environment might be considered more important than economic growth. Apart from the fact that all these effects are difficult to measure objectively, the question about the trade-off arises: how can we weigh economic, ecological and possible other effects against each other? This is a normative question, for which there is no unambiguous method. The generally used cost–benefit analysis method monetarises all effects. Although experts in many countries agree that such an analysis is the proper instrument for this, decision-makers may attribute higher values to one effect than to the other. The region may be economically weak and the decision-makers might then consider the natural environment subordinate to the economy. Cost–benefit analyses do not take such normative issues into account. Both the trade-offs by politicians and the cost–benefit analyses may then be contested.

The first conclusion here must be that, although information is crucial to proper decision-making in complex projects of this kind, there is either hardly any objective information or there is none at all: information is 'contested'.

An important mechanism may be added. The more the political struggle round a mega-project increases, the more the amount of objectively established information will decrease (see also Noordsij and De Bruijn, 2004) because the more different views there are about the desirability of a mega-project, the more incentives there will be for the parties involved to regard very critically analyses that are being conducted. A party that is fiercely opposed to the construction of a mega-project will closely scrutinise any analysis that appears and check what data were used, what system boundaries were used, how the issue of optimisation was dealt with, what methods were used, and how the trade-off was made. The point is now that, given the contested nature of information, such a party will usually find sufficient ammunition to question the authority of the analysis.

5.5 CONTESTED KNOWLEDGE AND DECISION-MAKING

Now suppose a simple paradigm is used in mega-projects: correct and early information will result in good decision-making. Because of the contested nature of information, such a recommendation is insufficient, because, in many cases, correct and unambiguous information is not available, while the dynamic of decision-making means that by definition it contains many iterations. If, nevertheless, too much emphasis is placed on the requirement of good and early information supply, the following effects may be expected.

Accumulation of Contested Information

In the first place, it will produce soft information, which is neither authoritative nor sufficiently useful for decision-making. Such a conclusion may raise a call for even more information, to make the whole of the information no longer soft and insufficiently authoritative. This will result in an immense information overload: piles of reports that, eventually, still fail to provide the right information and, in the worst case, trigger a call for even more information. This may result in a 'report war'. As long as any debate is possible about data, methods, system boundaries and optimisations, there is no reason to assume that the next analysis will be authoritative if it is not agreed clearly beforehand how it will be set up and how the main actors will be involved in the *process*. These actors are not only the experts on cost–benefit analyses; they are also project-specific stakeholders. These stakeholders will have to accept the findings of the analysis because they have the power to influence the decision-making. There is every risk that they will not accept these findings if they have not been able to participate in the process of analysis. In addition, these stakeholders have 'local knowledge', which might be relevant to the analysis.

A good illustration of the need to involve these stakeholders is the set of new directives for cost–benefit analyses (OEI directives),[1] designed by Dutch experts and representatives of the government departments. Project-specific stakeholders were not involved systematically in the process of analysis, which led them to make their own analysis. This is not so difficult, because even the most advanced directives will leave room for discussion. The 2004 update of the OEI, for example, acknowledges that there are different methods to measure indirect project effects. Which method should eventually be used in which situation depends on the kind of indirect effects that can be expected, the kind of infrastructure for which the effects must be analysed and the economic conditions in which the effects take place (Ministerie van Economische Zaken, 2004). It is obvious that different actors will have different opinions on these issues, and that project-specific stakeholders that have not been involved in the process of analysis will use this room to criticise the findings. Actors usually only accept information as authoritative if they have been involved in the process of problem formulation and problem solution. These actors insert their own information and values. This leads to 'negotiated knowledge' (Salter, 1988; Jasanoff, 1990; De Bruijn and Heuvelhof, 2000; De Bruijn et al., 2002).

A Variety of Truths

In the second place, the fact that much information is either not authoritative or conflicting will cause each party to collect its own reports and facts. This may trigger a struggle of schools between various institutes or scientists. Given all these private views of political decision-makers' or scientists' predilections for particular models and data, everybody will ultimately put together their own facts. The call for more and correct information will thus politicise the decision-making rather than objectivise and depoliticise it. Everybody has their own facts and causalities, and feels that only they are right.

This makes the quest for the right information sensitive for the 'strategic misrepresentation, i.e. lying' of Flyvbjerg et al. When a particular party – an external consultant, for example – conducts an analysis and it is certain beforehand that it will influence the decision-making (as in the proposal of Flyvbjerg et al.), there will be strong incentives and possibilities for others to criticise these analyses. In the dynamic that will then develop, these critics will, in response, conduct their own analyses. The step to 'strategic misrepresentation' is then just a small one. The quest for correct information, although information is contested in itself, will have led to far-reaching reservations about the information. Concluding, the 'lying' is particularly problematic from an ethical point of view. For the consequences it does not really matter whether an actor is lying or not; in any case the outcome of analyses can and will be disputed.

In the latter situation, the risk is that the decision-making about mega-projects will turn into a 'free fight': wide-ranging reservations about the information and merely a conflict of views and interests; or the national government (as the main financier) makes a discretionary decision, but then the decision itself will be contested (see Figure 5.1).

5.6   HOW TO DEAL WITH THE CONTESTED NATURE OF INFORMATION

The above prompts a dilemma. On the one hand, information is always contested. Consequently, the idea that all information should be gathered first and decisions should be made subsequently is too simple. On the other hand, the contested nature of information may lead to an undesirable

Call for the right information

↓

Not authoritative/overload

↓

Reservation about the information

↓

Decision-making as a free fight

Figure 5.1   Sequence of events that lead to decision-making as a free fight

qualification of the significance of the right information and be a strong incentive for 'strategic misrepresentation, i.e. lying'. The question is how we should deal with this. How can we organise the information-gathering and the analysis so as to evade this dilemma? In our view, the essence of a strategy comprises the following elements.

Need for Procedural and Interactive Rationality

Lindblom and Cohen (1979) and Wildavsky (1980) distinguish between analytical rationality and interactive and procedural rationality. Whereas analytical rationality uses a purely cognitive analysis, interactive and procedural rationality concentrates on interpersonal relationships and communication processes with elements such as debate, deliberation and consultation (Lindblom and Cohen, 1979; Wildavsky, 1980; Van de Graaf and Hoppe, 1996). The essence of this is that, in a process of interaction, actors exchange their views on, for example, the data and system boundaries to be used, discuss them and try to reach a joint perception (interactive rationality). In the interest of a proper process, they agree a number of rules of the game or a procedure (procedural rationality). We will deal with this in more depth in the following subsections.

Emergence of 'Negotiated Knowledge'

The result of a process of interaction is called 'negotiated knowledge': findings about which the participating actors agree.[2] The essence is that participants should conduct a structured debate. Suppose the ecological impact of a new railway line has to be established. This dialogue may take the following course:

- There is dissensus between experts about the ecological impact.
- The experts debate the data, the system boundaries, the method they will use and the way they will reach a trade-off between values.
- They may manage to conclude this debate successfully and reach agreement.
- If not, they may conduct a 'sensitivity analysis': how sensitive are the findings from the analysis to the differences of opinion between the experts?
- If the findings prove to be highly sensitive to these differences, they may focus on 'opportunities for improvement': can they think of any measures that might limit the ecological impact and that may be interesting, regardless of views on data, system boundaries, method and values?
- If the findings are highly sensitive to the differences, and if there is no consensus about opportunities for improvement, experts can find out whether there is consensus about particular findings and opportunities for improvement, because there will hardly ever be total dissensus. Given this partial consensus, they may then propose decisions of a 'no-regret' nature (Etzioni, 1989). No regret means that the decisions in question are acceptable from any perspective.
- 'Third parties' may be brought in during each of these steps. Suppose there is dissensus about data, system boundaries and methods; suppose sensitivity analysis and opportunities for improvement bring no solution, leading to a deadlock. In such a situation, the experts may be asked to formulate this difference of opinion as accurately as possible. An expert third party may then be asked to give a judgement. This third party is not so much the arbitrator that decides about the dispute between the experts, but it may contribute new insights, breaking the deadlock between the experts and giving the debate a new chance of success.

The idea behind this procedural rationality is threefold. In the first place, structured interaction leads to unfreezing: experts become sensitive to other views on data, system boundaries, methods and values. Unfreezing creates room: those who are able to put their own views into perspective have the room to take the views of others into account. In the second place, if there is unfreezing, interaction is more than just challenging the opinions of other experts. Interaction may also lead to 'co-creation' (Teisman, 2001):

the joint creation of new knowledge, for example by improving datasets or adapting existing methods.

In the third place, a process of interaction gives rise to new relationships and interdependencies between the participants. This makes it difficult for the participants to withdraw from the process, which might imply contempt of other participants and harm relations with them. In other words, the process creates incentives for cooperative behaviour, which promotes the development of negotiated knowledge.

Results of Interaction: Types of Negotiated Knowledge

Negotiated knowledge of course has a certain variety. Discussions about mega-projects are complex, and are always multi-issue analyses. Ecological or economic analyses, for example, always contain a large number of subtopics, each requiring analysis. The degree of consensus may differ for each subtopic, and may take a number of forms:

- total consensus about the findings for each subtopic;
- partial consensus about the findings for each subtopic;
- total dissensus about the findings for each subtopic.

If there is either partial or total dissensus about the findings, there may be consensus about opportunities for improvement or no-regret decisions. This increases the variety of possible findings:

- partial consensus or dissensus on findings, but consensus or opportunities for improvement;
- partial consensus or dissensus on findings and opportunities for improvement, but consensus on no-regret decisions;
- total dissensus on findings, opportunities for improvement and no-regret options.

All sorts of other variants are possible (De Bruijn and Porter, 2004). Participants can also make agreements on how to define 'consensus' (there might also be consensus if some participants agree to disagree: they disagree with the findings, but they agree not to block the consensus among other participants). The message here is that the outcome of a process of interaction is hardly ever binary (either consensus or dissensus), but offers variety: there are hard findings and there are findings that are less hard. On the one hand this seems disappointing, but it makes the process also attractive to decision-makers. Suppose there were total consensus between the analysts. This would leave no room at all for decision-makers and would make the process very unattractive for them. The variety of findings leaves them 'decision-making space', which is very important for the acceptance of an interaction process. There is no longer a free fight, but there is still room for a fight between interests.

Need for Process Management

If the way out of the dilemma mentioned in the introduction of this section is to create negotiated knowledge, a number of important procedural questions arise, such as:

- Which experts will conduct the analyses and be involved in the interaction process?
- What will the role of stakeholders be? How will they be involved in the interaction process? For example, how will they be able to ask their questions and offer their criticism during the research?
- What is the research agenda? How will interim findings be reported? How will the discussion about system boundaries, data, etc. take place?
- If a deadlock arises, how shall we deal with it? How shall we report on it? How can we prevent a deadlock on an issue from blocking the whole process?
- How shall we keep the process from proceeding too slowly?
- How shall we report on the process?
- How shall we deal with new and unforeseen developments?

These and similar questions call for a set of rules of the game that the experts involved in the interaction process should observe. This set of rules is called a process design; managing such a process is called process management (De Bruijn et al., 2002).

A process design is necessary because it structures the interaction between experts. Interaction is necessary because there is no one single truth in processes with contested information. Moreover, such a design may boost the authority of the negotiated knowledge. If the rules of the game are fair and allow all players – be they experts or stakeholders – to participate in forming the negotiated knowledge, their commitment to it will be stronger or it will at least be less easy for players to distance themselves from it.

An important question is, of course, who will be allowed to participate and how participants will reach decisions. We cannot give a detailed answer to these partly operational questions (see De Bruijn et al., 2002; De Bruijn and Ten Heuvelhof, 2003), but the essence of the answer is twofold:

- The participants should be a representative reflection of types of expertise and views; lack of such representation may harm the process.

- An important aspect of the decision-making rules is that parties must accept them as sufficiently fair. This might imply that they can influence them. The initiator of a process may therefore propose that particular rules be used, but first submit these rules to the participants for their approval.

Incentives for Setting up a Process

A crucial question is what the incentives are for decision-makers to design a process as described above. The greater the consensus, the more such a process will diminish the room for decision-making. Why would a decision-maker, who holds strong views on the desirability of building a railway, for example, tolerate such a process?

- Because of the broad agenda, i.e. there are many different items on it. A wide agenda takes the complexity of mega-projects into account and forces different types of experts (for example environmental and economic experts) to start a debate with each other. Moreover, the wider the agenda, the greater is the chance that the decision-maker will still have sufficient decision-making space at the end of the process. A wide agenda therefore serves both substantive interests and the interests of the decision-maker.
- Because of the confrontation between experts. Suppose there is no process. Decision-makers will nevertheless be faced with the findings from analysts. There are two differences, however, compared to the situation in which there is a process: (1) researchers who present their findings need not face other researchers; and (2) these researchers decide for themselves when they will present their findings. This may be highly unpleasant for decision-makers, particularly if these research findings are unwelcome to them, are based on controversial assumptions and methods, and are presented at an inconvenient moment. A process will then be an attractive alternative, because it disciplines the behaviour of experts.
- Because decision-makers can play a role in the process of interaction. This is pointed out in a number of studies (De Bruijn and Porter, 2004; Van Eeten, 1995; 2001). They can play a role in asking critical questions of the experts, because decision-makers have their own data, 'local knowledge', knowledge of possible innovations, etc. This improves the quality of the findings.
- Because the process enriches the decision-making. From the perspective of the decision-maker with strong views, the expert will sometimes play the reactive role of the 'Mister Noman': the expert

tells him what is wrong with the decision. However, a process of interaction in which decision-makers can also participate may also be attractive to them, because they can ask questions of experts in such a way that they play a more proactive role. What innovations can be expected that alleviate the emissions problem? What forms of supplementary policy are there that make a rail link more cost-effective? What are the most cost-effective measures to enhance the safety of a rail link? These and similar questions allocate a proactive role to the experts and may enrich the decision-making agenda. De Bruijn et al. (2002) mention the example of a political discussion that focuses on issues A and B and results in a deadlock. The analysts in the process show that issues C and D are far more interesting. This is attractive for decision-makers because they do not have to continue the discussion about A and B, which leads only to stalemate.

- Because of the societal legitimacy. A process of interaction also promotes the legitimacy of the decision-making; decision-makers can point out that they have involved a great many experts in the decision-making and that these agreed or disagreed on particular points. This, too, serves the interest of the stakeholders, but also the interest of a proper substantive analysis. When there is consensus and decision-makers distance themselves from it, this is difficult to explain to other stakeholders or to society.

Each of these considerations is slightly ambiguous. On the one hand, they imply that room is created for a process of interaction to arrive at negotiated knowledge. On the other hand, they also serve the interests of the decision-makers, who retain sufficient room for their mutual struggle of interests. However, this is the essence of contested knowledge. On the one hand, it requires a quest for the negotiated knowledge that is necessary. On the other hand, where this is impossible, decision-making is a political game, a struggle between interests.

5.7   CONCLUSIONS

A dilemma arises about the necessary information supply in decision-making about mega-projects. On the one hand, there is not 'one simple truth'. On the other hand, this conclusion should not lead to 'anything-goes' decision-making.

This dilemma requires that, as regards the issue of information supply, attention should be given not only to the substance of the information, but also to the process by which information is generated. This process may result in negotiated knowledge. Paying attention to the design and the management of such processes may improve decision-making.

ACKNOWLEDGEMENTS

The authors were advisers to the Dutch Parliamentary Commission on Infrastructure Projects. They alone are responsible for this contribution.

The research for this chapter was conducted in the Research Centre for Sustainable Urban Areas, Delft University of Technology, The Netherlands.

NOTES

1. OEI = Overview Infrastructure Effects; directive for drawing up societal cost–benefit analyses (including non-monetary effects), drawn up as an initiative of the Dutch Ministry of Transportation, Public Works and Water Management and the Dutch Ministry of Economic Affairs (see Ministerie van Verkeer en Waterstaat, 2004; Eijgenraam et al., 2000). Other organisations in various countries make comparable attempts by drawing up guidelines for cost–benefit analyses; for example the European Commission, for its Trans-European Networks programme (see for instance the HEATCO project at http://heatco.ier.uni-stuttgart.de).
2. An example of the negotiated knowledge solution is the Orange County Landfill Selection Committee's choice for a landfill location. It is a choice between 17 potential locations, to be compared on 16 variables. It tenders its research, expecting to receive an objective answer on where to site the landfill. The research, however, leads to a different outcome. It indicates which judgements are objectifiable and where room for negotiation exists. The outcome was that in a comparison only four of the 16 variables proved relevant. Trade-offs on the other 12 would not have led to different locations. The scores on the remaining four variables were input for negotiation. See Miranda et al. (1996).

REFERENCES

Associated Press (2004), 'Shanghai maglev starts operating', 2 January.
Bell, Robert (1998), *Les Peches Capitaux de la Haute Technologie*, Paris: Editions du Seuil.
Bonnafous, A. (1987), 'The regional impact of the TGV', *Transportation*, **14**: 127–37.
Bruijn, J.A. de and E.F. ten Heuvelhof (2000), *Networks and Decision Making*, Utrecht: Lemma.
Bruijn, H. de and E. ten Heuvelhof (2003), 'Policy analysis and decision making in a network. How to improve the quality of analysis and the impact on decision making?', *Impact Assessment and Project Appraisal*, **20** (4): 232–42.
Bruijn, H. de and A. Porter (2004), 'Education of a technology policy analyst – to process management', *Technology Analysis and Strategic Management*, **16** (2): 261–74.

Bruijn, H. de, E. ten Heuvelhof and R. In 't Veld (2002), *Process Management: Why Project Management Fails in Complex Decision Making Processes*, Boston, MA: Kluwer Academic Publishers.

Douglas, M. and A. Wildavsky (1983), *Risk and Culture: An Essay on the Selection of Technological and Environmental Dangers*, Berkeley, CA: University of California Press.

Eeten, M.J.G. van (1995), *Ontwerp van een strategie naar aanleiding van majeure infrastructurele en bestuurlijke ontwikkelingen* [Design of a strategy in response to major infrastructural and administrative developments], Delft.

Eeten, M.J.G. van (2001), 'Recasting intractable policy issues: the wider implications of the Netherlands civil aviation controversy', *Journal of Policy Analysis and Management*, **20** (3): 391–414.

Eijgenraam, C.J.J., C.C. Koopmans, P.J.G. Tang and A.C.P. Verster (CPB/NEI) (2000), *Evaluatie van infrastructuurprojecten: Leidraad voor kosten–batenanalyse* [Evaluation of infrastructural projects: Directive for cost–benefit analysis], The Hague: Sdu Uitgevers.

Etzioni, A. (1989), 'Humble decision making', *Harvard Business Review*, **67** (4): 122–6.

Flyvbjerg, B. (2004), 'International experience with large infrastructure projects', presentation in the public hearing for the Dutch Temporary Commission on Infrastructural Projects, The Hague.

Flyvbjerg, B., M.S. Holm and S. Buhl (2002), 'Underestimating costs in public works projects', *Journal of the American Planning Association*, **68** (3): 279–95.

Flyvbjerg, B., N. Bruzelius and W. Rothengatter (2003a), *Megaprojects and Risk: An Anatomy of Ambition*, Cambridge, MA: Cambridge University Press.

Flyvbjerg, B., M.K. Skamris Holm and S.L. Buhl (2003b), 'How common and large are cost overruns in transport infrastructure projects?', *Transport Reviews*, **23** (1): 71–88.

Flyvbjerg, B., M.K. Skamris Holm and S.L. Buhl (2004), 'What causes cost overrun in transport infrastructure projects?', *Transport Reviews*, **24** (1): 3–18.

Flyvbjerg, B., M.K. Skamris Holm and S.L. Buhl (2005), 'How (in)accurate are demand forecasts in public works projects? The case of transportation', *Journal of the American Planning Association*, **71** (2): 131–46.

Graaf, H. van de and R. Hoppe (1996), *Beleid en Politiek: Een inleiding tot de beleidswetenschap en de beleidskunde* [Policy and politics: An introduction into policy science and policy analysis], Bussum: Countinho.

Hall, P. (1980), *Great Planning Disasters*, Berkeley, CA: University of California Press.

Jasanoff, S. (1990), *The Fifth Branch: Science Advisers as Policy Makers*, Cambridge, MA: Harvard University Press.

Lindblom, C.E. and D.K. Cohen (1979), *Usable Knowledge: Social Science and Social Problem Solving*, New Haven, CT: Yale University Press.

Ministerie van Economische Zaken (Ministry of Economic Affairs), Ministerie van Verkeer en Waterstaat (Ministry of Transportation, Public Works and Water Management) (2004), *Indirecte Effecten Infrastructuur-Projecten: Aanvulling op de Leidraad OEI*, The Hague (Ministerie van Economische Zaken).

Ministerie van Verkeer en Waterstaat (Ministry of Transportation, Public Works and Water Management), CPB (2004), *Aanvulling op de leidraad OEI (Supplement to the OEI directive)*, 8 parts, The Hague.

Miranda, M.L., J.N. Miller and T.L. Jacobs (1996), *Informing Policymakers and the*

Public in Landfill Siting Processes, Princeton, NJ: Institute of Electrical and Electronic Engineers, Technical Expertise and Public Decisions.

Noordsij, R.A. and H. de Bruijn (2004), 'Informatievoorziening aan de Tweede Kamer inzake grote infrastructuurprojecten (Supply of information to Parliament on large infrastructure projects)', in *Grote Projecten: Inzichten en Uitgangspunten; Achtergrondstudies*, Tijdelijke Commissie Infrastructuurprojecten, Tweed Kamer 2004–2005, 29.283, nr/10, The Hague: Sdu Uitgevers, pp. 208–31.

Ostseezeitung (2004), 'Warnowtunnel droht die Pleite', 6 December.

Rietveld, P., F.R. Bruinsma, H.T. van Delft and B. Ubbels (2001), *Economic Impacts of High Speed Trains: Experiences in Japan and France: Expectations in the Netherlands*, Amsterdam: Research Memoranda Series, Free University.

Salter, L. (1988), *Mandated Science: Science and scientist in the making of public policy*, Amsterdam: Kluwer.

Teisman, G.R. (2001), *Ruimte mobiliseren voor coöperatief besturen: over management in netwerksamenlevingen* [Mobilizing space for cooperative governing; about management in network societies], Rotterdam: Erasmus Universiteit.

Wildavsky, A. (1980), *The Art and Craft of Policy Analysis*, London: Macmillan.

PART II

Planning and Decision-Making

6. How to improve the early stages of decision-making on mega-projects

Hugo Priemus

6.1 INTRODUCTION

The research on decision-making in mega-projects tends to be dominated by the problem of cost overruns and disappointing operating results (Flyvbjerg et al., 2003; Altshuler and Luberoff, 2004; Pickrell, 1989; 1992; Morris and Hough, 1987; Short and Kopp, 2005; Bell, 1998; Wachs, 1989; 1990). This chapter will depart from this trend and explore another theme: the initial stages of decision-making on mega-projects. It is not uncommon in mega-projects for a solution to present itself early – the solution which suits the initiators and which then heads off in search of a problem. Hence the process rarely begins with a proper analysis of the problems involved and an impartial appraisal of the alternatives.

Often, in the earliest phases, we see lobby groups hard at work mobilising support for a particular solution that is thought to be superior. Feasible alternatives are not even put forward, let alone analysed. Any alternatives proffered by opposing camps further down the line are usually too late. It is not unusual for the government to back the – supposedly superior – solution at an early stage. Alternatives suggested by others in later stages of the process are often whittled down to nothing. This chapter looks at the problem analysis at the initial stage of the decision-making process and at the general problem of alternatives that are not generated early on and are therefore mostly not given serious consideration.

This chapter argues that, most of the time, the solution precedes the problem (Section 6.2). Section 6.3 presents the case for a valid problem analysis as a basis for decision-making. Section 6.4 concentrates on the generation and appraisal of relevant alternatives. Section 6.5 focuses on systems analysis, a well-known and trusted technique which has been around since the 1980s but has not been applied nearly enough in practice. Section 6.6 addresses the role of systems analysis in mega-projects. Finally, Section 6.7 presents some conclusions.

In this chapter we explain the systems analysis methodology, which in general begins with a detailed problem analysis and leads to an appraisal of alternatives generated to cope with the problems identified. The fact that systems analysis is hardly ever applied in the practice of decision-making on mega-projects is undesirable, as consistent and frequent application of systems analysis would certainly pay off, perhaps in combination with actor-oriented approaches such as actor modelling, simulation and gaming. Adoption of the systems analysis methodology is strongly recommended, in which a problem analysis is conducted right from the start, and in which alternatives are generated at an early stage, ranked according to the *ex-ante* calculations of costs and benefits and in which the 'best' alternative is finally selected.

6.2 JUMPING TO CONCLUSIONS: THE WRONG WAY

At the start of the decision-making process, the focus should be on the problem, not so much on the solution. In general, one can argue that a problem equals an objective plus an obstacle to achieving that objective. Generally speaking, the objective of creating an infrastructural connection in its simplest form is the linking of two points: towns/cities and/or regions. This is usually accompanied by further specification in the form of answers to certain questions: how many people and goods are transported or can be transported between a and b, and between b and a at present? How many people and goods need to be transported between a and b and b and a in the future (t_1, t_2, t_3 etc.)? How should this capacity be spread over 24 hours, the week (weekdays, weekend) and the seasons? How should the capacity of the existing infrastructure be adapted to achieve this? Is a large new infrastructure project needed to achieve this end? How far does the capacity of certain modalities need to be modified? (For the transport of people, these are cars, trains and planes and, for short distances, buses, trams, the metro and bikes. For goods, the modality options are trucks, trains, inland shipping, coastal shipping, planes and pipelines.) Do the traffic prognoses and the uncertainties that surround them make a large infrastructure project necessary all at once or would it be more appropriate to expand the capacity in phases?

In these situations it is essential not only to look at the linear connection between a and b; attention also needs to be paid to the level of infrastructure networks (see the publications by the Roundtable of European Industrialists on missing links and missing networks: Roundtable of European Industrialists, 1984; 1991). Ultimately, the objectives seldom relate exclusively to a link between two points; the aim is also to boost the economy in one or more regions. A generous helping of wishful thinking often comes into play at this point.

6.3 MOVING TOWARDS A VALID PROBLEM ANALYSIS

An infrastructure project is, at best, a solution. This implies that there are one or more problems to which an infrastructure project is the most expedient response. A valid problem analysis is essential in order to determine whether a proposed alternative is effective, efficient and legitimate. The first question that should be asked is: what is or what are the problem(s)? And then: what is the problem *now* and what is it likely to become in the short and the long term? And finally, who is affected by the problem? A problem for one actor might be a solution for another actor.

Pretty soon the problem will emerge in the form of locations that are insufficiently accessible at present or in the future. This may go hand in hand with an increased risk of stagnation (measured in lost vehicle hours) due to growing congestion. Sometimes there are additional health and/or safety problems as a result of emissions (air quality).

As all of this impinges on mobility, people tend to see the problem in wider terms than just accessibility or stagnation. They refer to the decline in residential and commercial appeal, and the prospect of a deteriorating living climate, reduced quality of life and a decline or stagnation in business leading to job insecurity and uncertain economic growth. This implicit connection between mobility and the living and economic climate is usually difficult to substantiate and often bears witness to a long list of policy ambitions which cannot be supported by valid insights.

In practice, it is barely possible – and usually impossible – to establish a causal relationship between improved accessibility and a boost to the regional economy (Rietveld, 1989; Vickerman, 1989; 2000; Banister and Berechman, 2000).

As problems are often perceived differently by different parties, it is not only essential to conduct a problem analysis but also to reach the strongest possible consensus. A generally shared problem analysis enhances the possibility that the selected alternative will still be endorsed by everyone at a later stage. If there is still a difference of opinion on the analysis, it is usually the authorised political body that decides on the problems that will serve as the departure point.

Any later alternatives must be tested against the problem analysis. Hence certain aspects need to be concretely and promptly specified:

- the values and criteria;
- the objectives of the parties and the political bodies who bear responsibility;
- the boundaries and constraints.

The various parties may have different ideas about these issues, so a conflict can easily arise. The best approach is to identify potential stumbling blocks at an early stage and to establish a workable consensus.

6.4   CONSIDERING ALTERNATIVES

Once the problem analysis has been sorted out, it is time to think seriously about potential solutions. It is best to appraise alternatives in the initial stages. After all, more than one road leads to Rome. An investment project is not always the right answer, so the Dutch Ministry of Transport, Public Works and Water Management (Ministerie van Verkeer en Waterstaat, 2004) differentiates between three types of solution related to transport infrastructure: utilisation, pricing and building. First, attempts can be organised to make better use of the capacity of the existing infrastructure. Congestion might easily arise on certain routes during the rush hour. But can capacity in the opposite direction be enlarged? Or capacity outside the rush hours? That is the first question. The second is whether a price tag can be attached to the use of infrastructure in the form of a user charge, such as road pricing. Experience has shown that people curtail their use of infrastructure if it costs money. If the price is differentiated in terms of time and place, pricing can lead to a (better) utilisation. If utilisation and pricing are not enough, then new infrastructure or expansions to the current infrastructure can be considered.

The 'construction' category embraces various alternatives: different routes, different modalities (e.g. road, rail, inland shipping), different cross-sections (e.g. two-lane, four-lane, six-lane) and different types of spatial integration (for instance, in order to conserve nature or prevent urban pollution).

Alternatives must not be put forward at the last minute by, for example, only opponents of the plan favoured by the government. Alternatives must be systematically recognised at a very early stage.

One classic illustration of a shameful state of affairs is the decision-making in the Netherlands on the Betuwe Link, the dedicated freight rail link between Rotterdam Harbour and the Ruhr Area (TCI, 2004a; 2004b). From the very start, the Dutch government had decided that a dedicated rail link would be the best (and only) response to the challenge to improve the hinterland connection between Rotterdam and the Ruhr Area, and to bolster the competitiveness of Rotterdam Harbour. Only in the very late stages were alternatives considered, mostly from opposing groups. Several options were not objectively considered at early stages:

1. Increase the utilisation of the existing rail network.
2. Increase the utilisation of inland shipping.
3. Increase the capacity of road traffic (by building new lanes and/or introducing road pricing) and reduce the emissions from trucks at the same time.
4. Phase the Betuwe Link, giving priority to the western part: the Havenspoorlijn, connecting Rotterdam Harbour and the marshalling yard Kijfhoek.
5. Lay a pipeline between Rotterdam and Germany.
6. Accept a lower growth of freight transport to and from the harbour and restructure the economy of the Rotterdam region: less freight and more ICT.

With hindsight it is clear that the capacity of the existing rail network was underestimated (1), as a result of which phasing (4) would have been a better, more cost-effective solution. Inland shipping (2) and road traffic with reduced emissions (3) would also have provided more cost-effective alternatives. Finally, when the costs of new infrastructure are higher than the benefits, it is better not to expand the infrastructure for freight transport (6). This last observation is relevant because the Netherlands Bureau for Economic Policy Analysis concluded that the variable costs of the freight rail link can be covered by income, but that the investment costs will probably never be covered (CPB, 2004).

A similar situation arose during the initial stages of the decision-making process on the Zuiderzee Link: the proposed high-speed railway between Amsterdam and Groningen. The main objective of this dedicated line was to increase the economic strength of the northern provinces of the Netherlands. Calculations by the Netherlands Bureau for Economic Policy Analysis (CPB et al., 2002) indicated that the regional economy would barely improve and that only a limited number of jobs would be created in the north after improvements of the rail connection to Groningen. If the primary aim was indeed to revitalise the economy in the north, then the strategic question was whether a rail link was the most cost-effective means of achieving it.

There are countless alternatives which were never explored and appraised, such as:

●   promote urban renewal and the restructuring of business areas in the north;

- promote rural vitality by stimulating economic activities in rural areas in the north;
- improve the road infrastructure in and to the north;
- improve the digital accessibility of the north;
- stimulate the knowledge economy in the north.

The decision-making process should have begun by identifying the problems and then appraising the options. Instead, it went in search of plausible variations on the theme of one favourite solution. No steps were taken to weigh up the alternatives even after the publication of the TCI report (TCI, 2004a). The analysis that was carried out after the publication of the TCI report only considered a few alternatives for improving the rail infrastructure and one new proposal: a track for an automatic Superbus, developed by Professor Wubbo Ockels. Only recently has a broader analysis been announced, including alternatives outside the realm of improving transport infrastructure.

One factor that tends to be underestimated is the effect of prices and pricing policy. The demand for mobility cannot be satisfied without a price-tag. Without a price, demand tends to be limitless. So, the higher the price, the lower the demand. This is where the substitution of one modality for another becomes crucially important. If, for example, discounts bring about a sharp fall in the cost of air travel, then the demand for plane tickets will probably increase dramatically, but the demand for high-speed rail travel could plummet at the same time. The government plays a key role here – wittingly and unwittingly – through taxation and policy on user charges. Airlines do not pay VAT on kerosene, the concept of 'user charge' has been introduced into the train system, and many countries are considering road-pricing. Pricing-policy initiatives like these can have a deep impact on the development of mobility through a particular modality such as the train. Evaluation studies *ex post* can determine how the use of infrastructure reacts to user charges (Affuso et al., 2003; Bonnafous, 2003; Bonnafous and Crozet, 1997; Nilsson, 1992; Quinet, 2000; Rothengatter, 2000; Priemus, 2005).

6.5   SYSTEMS ANALYSIS

For decades, systems analysis methodology has shown how decision-making on a new policy or project needs to begin by defining the problem. Certain questions need to be asked: what is the nature of the problem? Who is affected? Why is it a problem for one or more players?

The classic systems analysis procedure is shown in Figure 6.1. In Section 6.6 we will apply it to decision-making on a mega-project.

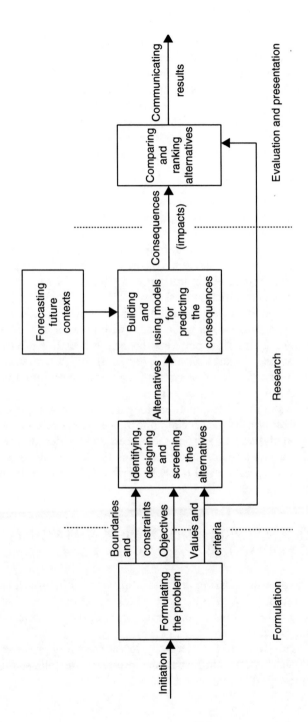

Source: Adapted from Miser and Quade (1985: 123).

Figure 6.1 The systems analysis procedure

Figure 6.1 is drawn from Findeisen and Quade (in Miser and Quade, 1985: 117–49), who provide an introduction and overview to the method-ology of systems analysis. Findeisen and Quade (1985) argue that besides formulating the problem, it is necessary to define the values and crite-ria, and map out the boundaries and constraints. The next step is to devise solutions that best meet the objectives, values and criteria of the decision-maker and other stakeholders, and take account of the bound-aries and constraints. The alternatives are then identified, designed and screened.

Next, models are built to predict the long- and short-term consequences of each alternative according to the forecasts for, among others, demo-graphic and economic trends and mobility dynamics. The impacts of each alternative are quantified on the basis of the models and assumptions. Finally, the alternatives are compared and ranked in advance according to their impact (costs and benefits). The results of the whole exercise are com-municated clearly and over time. An important dimension is the awareness and quantification of uncertainties and risks.

Figure 6.2 shows that, in reality, things are much more complicated than Figure 6.1 suggests, because many feedbacks with iteration loops are required. In addition, interaction between the analysis team and the decision-maker is essential. Figures 6.1 and 6.2 are basically 20 years old, making it all the more astonishing that systems analysis is so seldom used in current decision-making on mega-projects.

Systems analysis is still useful as a methodology for decision-making on mega-projects. It stresses for us the crucial importance of meticulous and exhaustive problem analysis at the start of the process and the design, gen-eration, appraisal and ranking of alternative solutions. The decision-makers who apply this procedure will rarely be confronted with solutions searching for a problem.

6.6   SYSTEMS ANALYSIS AND DECISION-MAKING ON MEGA-PROJECTS

The structure of the decision-making process on infrastructure projects is often criticised (Teisman, 1998; WRR, 1994; Mackie and Preston, 1998; Priemus, 2004). Several recommendations have been proposed to improve the decision-making process.

What can systems analysis offer modern-day decision-making processes on mega-projects, such as large infrastructure projects? We follow and explain the boxes presented in Figures 6.1 and 6.2.

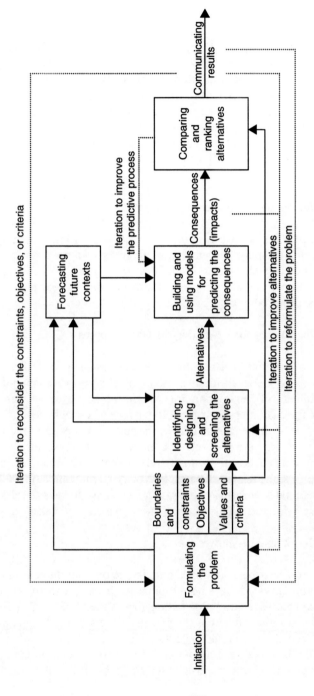

Note: The figure does not show the essential ongoing interaction between the analysis team and the decision-maker.

Source: Adapted from Miser and Quade (1985: 124).

Figure 6.2   The systems analysis procedure with iteration loops

113

Formulating the Problem

When an infrastructure project is being considered, the problem is usually formulated in terms of accessibility. This problem can manifest itself at the link level and at the network level. Sometimes it also has an economic dimension: perhaps new infrastructure will revitalise or boost the regional economy. A detailed analysis of the problem is both necessary and desirable at the start of a decision-making process. When different actors perceive different problems, energy has to be invested in communication and negotiations to reach a certain consensus about the problems perceived (see Chapter 5 in this book).

Identifying, Designing and Screening the Alternatives

The experience with the Betuwe Link and the Zuiderzee Link illustrates how crucial it is that the players identify, design and screen the options at an early stage. There are alternative modalities (train, truck, inland shipping), alternative tracks and alternatives in time (including a clear phasing of the alternative projects).

Building and Using Models for Predicting the Consequences

The effects of the alternative projects can only be determined *ex ante* if realistic assumptions are made about the length of the period taken into account, the numbers of persons and/or volume of goods to be transported, the price the customers are willing to pay, the investment costs, the price to be paid for using the infrastructure, the costs of energy and maintenance for the infrastructure and vehicles, the trend in interest rates and inflation, the financing costs and the costs and distribution of risk. As this exercise can lead to some heated debates, Flyvbjerg recommends (in TCI, 2004a) that the estimates be left to those players who have to bear the risks of under- and overestimation. This recommendation certainly makes sense.

Comparing and Ranking Alternatives

Once the alternatives have been identified and fleshed out and the costs and benefits (priced and unpriced) have been established in each case, the alternatives can be ranked. A separate issue altogether is the allocation of the costs and benefits in time and across the various players. It is not uncommon for (some) benefits to accrue to parties – generally known as 'free-riders' – who do not bear the costs. Sometimes the government can intervene so that the costs and benefits are redistributed fairly. But it is still perfectly conceivable that different rational players will arrive at a different ranking of alternatives when they consider only their own costs and benefits.

Coping with Surprises and Chaos: a Design Approach

At first glance, the diagram of the system analysis approach looks fairly straightforward and free of surprises. The description by Findeisen and Quade (1985) takes insufficient account of the fact that a mega-project can take a very long time to crystallise. Major shifts can take place in the composition of the public delegations and in the negotiating teams of the private parties. New policy guidelines and priorities may arise, not to mention changes in building techniques, spatial layout and the cost structure of the project. The process followed by a mega-project can be likened to a series of learning curves in which new, cutting-edge ideas are constantly casting a new light on the solution. An Echternach procession (two steps forward, one step back) may creep in from time to time and decisions may end up being taken more than once.

Often, in practice, it is much more difficult to define alternatives than Findeisen and Quade (1985) suggest. It takes vision and a design approach to come up with options that are unlikely to occur to players with no imagination. As Miller and Lessand comment in Chapter 8, mega-projects follow a dynamic, iterative and – often – chaotic course, which should be reflected in project-management architectures. This does not, however, dispense with the need to conduct a proper problem (and a risk–opportunity) analysis in the start phase and to formulate and flesh out alternatives from the earliest stages. A design approach, which partly reflects the initial preferences of the various stakeholders, will widen the range of alternatives. Alternatives may not be rejected until it has been conclusively established that the cost–benefit ratio is unfavourable. In fact, it is not inconceivable that all the plan alternatives will come adrift in the run-up phase – and there will be no mega-project.

Sometimes a mega-project is the solution, sometimes it is the problem.

6.7 CONCLUSIONS

Experience of decision-making in mega-projects in the Netherlands (TCI, 2004a) has exposed the general need for proper problem analysis at the start of the process. It has also revealed that alternatives are seldom generated and worked out at an early stage, which could solve or reduce the problem in other ways. Most of the time, the solution precedes the problem analysis, and any alternatives mooted at a later stage by opponents and observers are simply swept aside by the project initiators and the Ministry of Transportation. As a result, the role of Parliament is often marginalised, especially in the early stages. Mostly Parliament is unable to get a foothold in the decision-making. Any adaptation that Parliament pushes through at a later stage merely adds to the – already looming – excess costs. This is not a particular Dutch problem but a worldwide issue, if we compare the Dutch situation with experiences in other countries in different continents (Flyvbjerg et al., 2003).

Sörenson (oral presentation at a meeting of the Council on Engineering Systems Universities, Atlanta, USA, 14 December 2005) argues that the reason why most problems are never solved is because they are not formulated correctly in the first place. Far too often it is the wrong problem that is addressed. It is therefore imperative that each decision-making process for mega-projects starts with a sound problem analysis.

The flaws mentioned can be remedied by consistent application of systems analysis (Miser and Quade, 1985), which begins with a problem formulation and analysis, and the identification of the objectives, values, criteria, boundaries and constraints that the stakeholders attach to the prospective solution. Alternatives are identified, designed and screened with a view to meeting these objectives, values, criteria, boundaries and constraints as far as possible. The assumed effects of each variable are determined by a model. The priced and unpriced costs and benefits are quantified by a cost–benefit analysis as suggested in Chapter 3 in this book (Eijgenraam et al., 1999). The quantification of indirect effects is a particularly awkward business, as Chapter 4 in this book makes clear (see also Banister and Berechman, 2000; Elhorst et al., 2004; Oosterhaven et al., 2005). Finally, the alternatives can be ranked and the best one selected.

A clear structure of the decision-making process can be helpful in clarifying where go/no go decisions by Parliament or decentralised public representative bodies are needed to prevent entrapment or feelings of entrapment (Brockner and Rubin, 1985; TCI, 2004a).

Systems analysis methodology as devised by Findeisen and Quade in 1985 still has much to offer as a basis for decision-making. Hands-on experience, gleaned from numerous studies in Europe and North America, has shown that systems analysis is rarely applied in decision-making processes on mega-projects. It is important in the early phases to create plenty of scope for generating and working out alternatives. These would include options that would make the project unnecessary or too expensive, as well as alternatives for the project itself. The integrity of the decision-making – and even of the democratic procedure – is enhanced when the rejected as well as the selected alternatives are known (including the respective reasons). The adoption of systems analysis can therefore improve the results in decision-making processes on mega-projects.

REFERENCES

Affuso, L., J. Masson and D.M.G. Newbery (2003), 'Comparing investments in new transport infrastructures', *Fiscal Studies*, **24** (3): 273–315.

Altshuler, Alan and David Luberoff (2004), *Mega-Projects. The Changing Politics of Urban Public Investment*, Washington, DC: Brookings Institution Press.

Banister, D. and J. Berechman (2000), *Transport Investment and Economic Development*, London: University College London Press.

Bell, Robert (1998), *Worst Practices/De bodemloze put. Megaprojecten en manipulatie* [Worst Practices/The Bottomless Pit. Mega-Projects and Manipulation], Rotterdam: Aristos.

Bonnafous, A. (2003), 'Assessing our expertise', in European Council of Ministers of Transport (ECMT) (ed.), *Fifty Years of Transport Policy. Successes and New Challenges*, Paris: ECMT.

Bonnafous, A. and Y. Crozet (1997), 'Evaluation, dévaluation ou réévaluation des lignes à grande vitesse', *Les Cahiers Scientifiques du Transport*, **32**: 45–56.

Brockner, J. and J.Z. Rubin (1985), *Entrapment in Escalating Conflicts: A Social Psychological Analysis*, New York: Springer Verlag.

Centraal Planbureau (CPB) (2004), *Vooruitzichten voor spoorvervoer over de Betuweroute* [Prospects of rail transport on the Betuwe Rail Link], The Hague, CPB-notitie 2004/39, 24 September.

Centraal Planbureau (CPB), RIVM, RPB and SCP (2002), *Selectief investeren; ICES-maatregelen tegen het licht* [Selectively investing, ICES-measures in the spotlight], The Hague: CPB.

Eijgenraam, C.C.J., C.C. Koopmans, P.J.G. Tang and A.C.P. Verster (1999), *Evaluatie van infrastructuurprojecten. Leidraad voor kosten–batenanalyse. Deel I: Hoofdrapport* [Evaluation of infrastructure projects. Guide for cost–benefit analysis. Part 1: Main report]. Onderzoeksprogramma Economische Effecten Infrastructuur (OEEI), The Hague: Ministerie van Verkeer en Waterstaat, Ministerie van Economische Zaken.

Elhorst, J.P., A. Heyma, C.C. Koopmans and J. Oosterhaven (2004), *Indirecte Effecten Infrastructuurprojecten: Aanvulling Leidraad OEI* [Indirect Effects of Infrastructure Projects: Supplement to the OEI Guideline], Groningen/ Amsterdam: University of Groningen/Foundation for Economic Research.

Findeisen, W. and E.S. Quade (1985), 'The methodology of systems analysis: an introduction and overview', in H.J. Miser and E.S. Quade (eds), *Handbook of Systems Analysis. Overview of Uses, Procedures, Applications, and Practice*, Chichester, New York: John Wiley & Sons.

Flyvbjerg, B., N. Bruzelius and W. Rothengatter (2003), *Megaprojects and Risk: An Anatomy of Ambition*, Cambridge, MA: Cambridge University Press.

Mackie, P. and J. Preston (1998), 'Twenty-one sources of error and bias in transport project appraisal', *Transport Policy*, **5** (1): 1–8.

Ministerie van Verkeer en Waterstaat (2004), *Nota Mobiliteit* [Memorandum Mobility], The Hague: Ministerie van Verkeer en Waterstaat.

Miser, H.J. and E.S. Quade (1985), *Handbook of Systems Analysis. Overview of Uses, Procedures, Applications, and Practice*, Chichester, New York: John Wiley & Sons.

Morris, Peter W.G. and George H. Hough (1987), *The Anatomy of Major Projects. A Study of the Reality of Project Management*, Chichester, New York: John Wiley & Sons.

Nilsson, J.E. (1992), 'Second-best problems in railway infrastructure pricing and investment', *Journal of Transport Economics and Policy*, **26** (3): 245–59.

Oosterhaven, J., C.C. Koopmans and J.P. Elhorst (2005), 'Indirecte effecten van beleid: lastig, maar belangrijk' [Indirect effects of policy: difficult but important], *ESB*, **90**, 29 July: 335–7.

Pickrell, D. (1989), *Urban Rail Transit Projects. Forecast versus Actual Ridership and Costs*, Washington, DC: US Department of Transportation.

Pickrell, D.H. (1992), 'A desire named streetcar – fantasy and fact in rail transit planning', *Journal of American Planning Association*, **58** (2): 158–76.

Priemus, H. (ed.) (2004), *Grote projecten: inzichten en uitgangspunten. Achtergrondstudies* [Mega-projects: insights and starting points. Background studies], commissioned by the Temporary Committee for Infrastructure Projects, Tweede Kamer (Dutch Lower House), 2004–2005, 29.283 no. 10, The Hague: Sdu Uitgevers.

Priemus, H. (2005), 'Design & Construct bij de Hogesnelheidslijn-Zuid: De Wet van Murphy' [Design & Construct for the Southern High Speed Rail Link: Murphy's Law], *Building Business*, **7** (1): 42–9.

Quinet, E. (2000), 'Evaluation methodologies of transportation projects in France', *Transport Policy*, **7** (1): 27–35.

Rietveld, P. (1989), 'Infrastructure and regional development: a survey of multiregional economic models', *The Annals of Regional Science*, **23**: 255–74.

Rothengatter, W. (2000), 'Evaluation of infrastructure investments in Germany', *Transport Policy*, **7** (1): 17–27.

Roundtable of European Industrialists (1984), *Missing Links. Upgrading Europe's Transborder Ground Transport Infrastructure*, Paris: Roundtable Secretariat, Paris Office.

Roundtable of European Industrialists (1991), *Missing Networks. A European Challenge. Proposals for the Renewal of Europe's Infrastructure*, Paris: Roundtable Secretariat, Paris Office.

Short, J. and A. Kopp (2005), 'Transport infrastructure: investment and planning. Policy and research aspects', *Transport Policy*, **12**: 360–67.

Teisman, G.R. (1998), *Complexe besluitvorming, een pluricentrisch perspectief op besluitvorming over ruimtelijke investeringen* [Complex decision-making, a pluricentred perspective on spatial investments], The Hague: Elsevier.

Tijdelijke Commissie Infrastructuurprojecten (TCI) (2004a), *Grote projecten uitvergroot. Een infrastructuur voor besluitvorming* [Large projects under the magnifying glass. An infrastructure for decision-making], Tweede Kamer (Dutch Lower House), 2004–2005, 29.283 nos 5–6, The Hague: Sdu Uitgevers.

Tijdelijke Commissie Infrastructuurprojecten (TCI) (2004b), *Reconstructie Betuweroute. De besluitvorming uitvergroot* [Reconstruction Betuwe Rail Link. Decision-making under the magnifying glass], Tweede Kamer (Dutch Lower House), 2004–2005, 29.283 no. 7, The Hague: Sdu Uitgevers.

Vickerman, R.W. (1989), 'Measuring changes in regional competitiveness: the effect of international infrastructure investments', *The Annals of Regional Science*, **23**: 275–86.

Vickerman, R. (2000), 'Evaluation methodologies for transport projects in the United Kingdom', *Transport Policy*, **7** (1): 7–16.

Wachs, M. (1989), 'When planners lie with numbers', *APA Journal*, **476**: 476–9.

Wachs, M. (1990), 'Ethics and advocacy in forecasting for public policy', *Business and Professional Ethics Journal*, **9** (1&2): 141–57.

Wetenschappelijke Raad voor het Regeringsbeleid [Scientific Advisory Council on Government Policy] (WRR) (1994), *Besluiten over Grote Projecten* [Decisions on large projects], The Hague: Sdu Uitgevers.

7. Public planning of mega-projects: overestimation of demand and underestimation of costs

Bent Flyvbjerg

7.1 INTRODUCTION

Despite the enormous sums of money being spent on transportation infrastructure, surprisingly little systematic knowledge exists about the costs, benefits and risks involved. The literature lacks statistically valid answers to the central and self-evident question of whether transportation infrastructure projects perform as forecasted. When a project underperforms, this is often explained away as an isolated instance of unfortunate circumstance; it is typically not seen as the particular expression of a general pattern of underperformance in transportation infrastructure projects. Because knowledge is lacking in this area of research, until now it has been impossible to validly refute or confirm whether underperformance is the exception or the rule.

Knowledge about demand risk, cost risk and compound risk is crucial to planners and decision-makers when developing projects and deciding which to build and which not. For transportation infrastructure projects, the benefits and costs involved often run into hundreds of millions of dollars, with risks being correspondingly high. Estimates of the financial viability of projects are heavily dependent on the accuracy of traffic demand and construction cost forecasts (Pickrell, 1990; Richmond, 1998). Such forecasts are also the basis for socioeconomic and environmental appraisal of transportation infrastructure projects. According to the experiences gained with the accuracy of demand and cost forecasting in the transportation sector, there is evidence that such forecasting, despite all scientific progress in modelling, is a major source of uncertainty and risk in the development and management of large infrastructure projects (Van Wee, 2007; Priemus, 2007).

Nevertheless, rigorous studies of accuracy are rare. Where such studies exist, they are characteristically small-N research, that is, they are single-case studies or they cover only a sample of projects too small or too uneven to allow systematic, statistical analyses (Brooks and Trevelyan, 1979; Bruzelius et al., 2002; Fouracre et al., 1990; Fullerton and Openshaw, 1985; Hall, 1980; Kain, 1990; Mackinder and Evans, 1981; National Audit Office, 1988; 1992; Nijkamp and Ubbels, 1999; Pickrell, 1990; Richmond, 1998; 2001; Skamris and Flyvbjerg, 1997; Szyliowicz and Goetz, 1995; Walmsley and Pickett, 1992; Webber, 1976; World Bank, 1994). Despite their value in other respects, with these and other studies, it has so far been impossible to give statistically satisfying answers to questions about how accurate traffic and cost forecasts are for transportation infrastructure projects. The objective of the study presented here has been to change this state of affairs by establishing a sample of transportation infrastructure projects that is sufficiently large to permit statistically valid answers to questions of accuracy. The methodology and data of the study are described in detail in Flyvbjerg, Holm and Buhl (2003; 2006) and Flyvbjerg (2005).

The present study focuses on accuracy in demand and cost forecasts. It should be mentioned, however, that similar concerns and results as those presented here for demand and cost forecasts pertain to (in)accuracy in environmental and social forecasts made as part of major projects. The latter issue is covered in Flyvbjerg, Bruzelius and Rothengatter (2003).

7.2 INACCURACY IN TRAVEL DEMAND FORECASTS

Inaccuracy in travel demand forecasts is here measured as actual minus forecasted traffic as a percentage of forecasted traffic. Actual traffic is counted for the first year of operations. Forecasted traffic is the traffic estimate for the first year of operations as estimated at the time of decision to build the project. Thus the forecast is the estimate available to decision-makers on the basis of which they made the decision to build the project in question. With this standard definition of inaccuracy, perfect accuracy is indicated by zero; an inaccuracy of minus 40 per cent, for example, indicates that actual traffic was 40 per cent lower than forecasted traffic, whereas an inaccuracy of plus 40 per cent means that actual traffic was 40 per cent higher than forecasted traffic.

The study includes 210 transportation infrastructure projects with comparable data for forecasted and actual traffic. The sample comprises a project portfolio worth approximately US$62 billion in actual costs (2006 prices). The project types are urban rail, high-speed rail, conventional rail, bridges, tunnels, highways and freeways. The projects are located in 14 countries on five continents, including both developed and developing nations. The projects were completed during the 30 years between 1969 and

1998. The size of the projects ranges from construction costs of US$23 million to US$11 billion (2006 prices), with the smallest projects typically being stretches of roads in larger road schemes and the largest projects being rail links, bridges and tunnels.

Figure 7.1 shows the distribution of inaccuracy of traffic forecasts for the 210 projects in the sample split into rail and road projects. The most noticeable attribute of Figure 7.1 is the striking difference between rail and road projects. Rail passenger forecasts are much more inaccurate and biased (inflated) than are road traffic forecasts.

Tests show that of the 27 rail projects included in the statistical analyses, two German projects should be considered as statistical outliers. These are the two projects represented by the two right-most columns in the rail histogram in Figure 7.1. Excluding statistical outliers, the following results are found for the remaining 25 rail projects (results including the two statistical outliers are given in brackets):

- The data document a massive problem with inflated rail passenger forecasts. For more than nine out of ten rail projects, passenger forecasts are overestimated; for 72 per cent of all rail projects, passenger forecasts are overestimated by more than two-thirds [including statistical outliers: for 67 per cent of all rail projects, passenger forecasts are overestimated by more than two-thirds].
- Rail passenger forecasts were overestimated by an average of 105.6 per cent (95 per cent confidence interval of 66.0 to 169.9), resulting in actual traffic that was on average 51.4 per cent lower than forecasted traffic (sd = 28.1, 95 per cent confidence interval of −62.9 to −39.8) [including statistical outliers: rail passenger forecasts were overestimated by an average of 65.2 per cent (95 per cent confidence interval of 23.1 to 151.3), resulting in actual traffic that was on average 39.5 per cent lower than forecasted traffic (sd = 52.4, 95 per cent confidence interval of −60.2 to −18.8)].
- Eighty-four per cent of the rail projects have actual traffic more than 20 per cent below forecasted traffic and none have actual traffic more than 20 per cent above forecasted traffic. Even if we double the threshold value to 40 per cent, we find that a solid 72 per cent of all rail projects have actual traffic below that limit [including statistical outliers the figures are 85 per cent and 74 per cent, respectively].

For road projects, the tests show (see also Table 7.1):

- Fifty per cent of the road projects have a difference between actual and forecasted traffic of more than ±20 per cent. If we double the

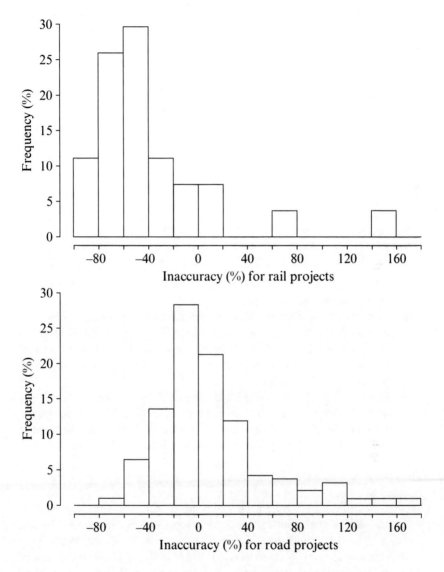

Figure 7.1 Inaccuracies of travel demand forecasts in transportation infrastructures projects split into 27 rail and 183 road projects

Table 7.1   Inaccuracies in forecasts of rail passenger and road vehicle traffic

	Rail (figures in brackets include two statistical outliers)	Road
Average inaccuracy (%)	−51.4 (sd = 28.1) [−39.5 (sd = 52.4)]	9.5 (sd = 44.3)
Percentage of projects with inaccuracies larger than ±20%	84 [85]	50
Percentage of projects with inaccuracies larger than ±40%	72 [74]	25
Percentage of projects with inaccuracies larger than ±60%	40 [41]	13

threshold value to ±40 per cent, we find that 25 per cent of projects are above this level.

- There is no significant difference between the frequency of inflated versus deflated forecasts for road vehicle traffic ($p = 0.822$, two-sided binominal test). A total of 21.3 per cent of projects have inaccuracies below −20 per cent, whereas 28.4 per cent of projects have inaccuracies above +20 per cent.
- Road traffic forecasts were underestimated by an average of 8.7 per cent (95 per cent confidence interval of 2.9 to 13.7), resulting in actual traffic that was on average 9.5 per cent higher than forecasted traffic (sd = 44.3, 95 per cent confidence interval of 3.0 to 15.9).

Thus the risk is substantial that road traffic forecasts are wrong by a large margin, but the risk is more balanced than for rail passenger forecasts. Testing the difference between rail and road, we find at a very high level of statistical significance that rail passenger forecasts are less accurate and more inflated than road vehicle forecasts ($p < 0.001$, Welch two-sample t-test). However, there is no indication of a significant difference between the standard deviations for rail and road forecasts; both are high, indicating a large element of uncertainty and risk for both types of forecasts ($p = 0.213$, two-sided F-test). Excluding the two statistical outliers for rail, we find the standard deviation for rail projects to be significantly lower than for road projects, although still high ($p = 0.0105$).

The striking difference in forecasting inaccuracy between rail and road projects documented above may perhaps be explained by the different procedures that apply to how each type of project is funded, where competition for funds is typically more pronounced for rail than for road, which creates an incentive for rail promoters to present their project in as favourable a light as possible, that is, with overestimated benefits and underestimated costs (Flyvbjerg, Holm and Buhl, 2002). One may further speculate that rail patronage will be overestimated and road traffic underestimated in instances where there is a strong political or ideological desire to see passengers shifted from road to rail, for instance for reasons of congestion or protection of the environment. Forecasts here become part of the political rhetoric aimed at showing voters that something is being done – or will be done – about the problems at hand. In such cases it may be difficult for forecasters and planners to argue for more realistic forecasts, because politicians here use forecasts to show political intent, not the most likely outcome.

All told, the traffic estimates used in decision-making for rail infrastructure development are highly, systematically and significantly misleading. Rail passenger forecasts are consistently and significantly inflated. For road projects the problem of misleading forecasts is less severe and less one-sided than for rail. But even for roads, for half the projects the difference between actual and forecasted traffic is more than ±20 per cent. Against this background, planners and decision-makers are well advised to take with a grain of salt any traffic forecast that does not explicitly take into account the uncertainty of predicting future traffic. For rail passenger forecasts, a grain of salt may not be enough. The data demonstrate to planners that risk assessment and management regarding travel demand must be an integral part of planning for both rail and road projects. The data presented above provide the empirical basis on which planners may found such risk assessment and management.

7.3   INACCURACY IN COST FORECASTS

Inaccuracy in construction cost forecasts is measured as actual cost minus forecasted cost as a percentage of forecasted cost. An inaccuracy of zero means that the forecasted cost for the project was correct and thus equalled actual cost. Forecasted cost is the estimate made at the time of decision to build, or as close to this as possible if no estimate was available for the decision to build. Actual cost is outturn construction cost measured after the project was completed. All costs are calculated in constant prices.

The study includes 258 projects with comparable data for forecasted and actual construction cost. Figure 7.2 shows histograms with the distribution of cost escalation for these projects. Table 7.2 shows the expected (average)

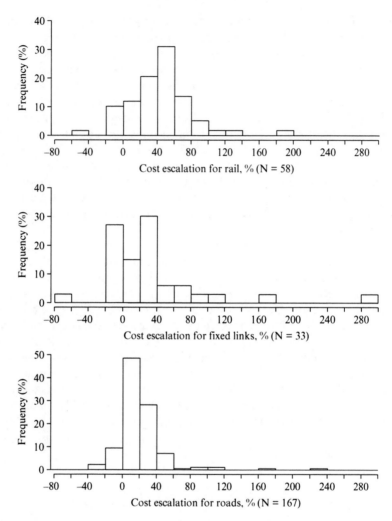

Figure 7.2   Cost overrun for rail, fixed links and roads (constant prices)

value of cost escalation and standard deviation for each type of project. The differences between rail, fixed links (bridges and tunnels) and roads are statistically significant. If errors in forecasts of cost were small, the histograms would be narrowly concentrated around zero. If errors in over-estimating costs were of the same size and frequency as errors in underes-timating costs, the histograms would be symmetrically distributed around zero. Neither is the case.

Table 7.2   *Average cost overrun for rail, fixed links (bridges and tunnels) and roads (for all project types average cost overrun is different from zero with very high significance, constant prices)*

Type of project	Number of cases (N)	Average cost overrun (%)	Standard deviation	Level of significance, p
Rail	58	44.7	38.4	<0.001
Fixed links	33	33.8	62.4	0.004
Road	167	20.4	29.9	<0.001
All projects	258	27.6	38.7	<0.001

The study shows:

- Cost escalation happens in almost nine out of ten projects. For a randomly selected project, the likelihood of actual costs being larger than forecast costs is 86 per cent.
- The thesis that the error of overestimating cost is as common as the error of underestimating cost is rejected with overwhelming significance ($p < 0.001$; two-sided test, using the binomial distribution). Forecasted costs are biased and the bias is caused by systematic underestimation.
- The thesis that the numerical size of the error of underestimating costs is the same as the numerical size of the error of overestimating costs is rejected with overwhelming significance ($p < 0.001$; non-parametric Mann–Whitney test). Costs are not only underestimated much more often than they are overestimated or correct; costs that have been underestimated are also wrong by a substantially larger margin than costs that have been overestimated.
- Rail infrastructure projects incur the highest difference between actual and estimated costs with an average of 44.7 per cent, followed by fixed links averaging 33.8 per cent and roads with 20.4 per cent. An F-test falsifies at a very high level of statistical confidence the null hypothesis that type of project has no effect on percentage cost escalation ($p < 0.001$). Project type matters.

If fixed links are split into tunnels and bridges, the average cost escalation for tunnels is 48 per cent (sd = 44) and for bridges 30 per cent (sd = 67). However, the difference is statistically non-significant due to too few observations in each category.

Similarly, if rail projects are subdivided into high-speed rail, urban rail and conventional rail, one finds that high-speed rail tops the list of cost escalation with an average of 52 per cent (sd = 48), followed by urban rail with 45 per cent (sd = 37) and conventional rail with 30 per cent (sd = 34). Again the differences are statistically non-significant, and again the reason is that the subsamples are too small.

In sum, cost escalation for rail, fixed links and roads is large and has large standard deviations. The cause is cost forecasts that are highly and systematically underestimated. Again, decision-makers – as well as investors, media and the public – are well advised to take any estimate of construction costs with a grain of salt.

7.4 HAVE FORECASTS BECOME MORE ACCURATE OVER TIME?

Figures 7.3 and 7.4 show how inaccuracy in traffic forecasts varies over time for the projects in the sample for which inaccuracy could be coupled with information about year of decision to build and/or year of completing the project. There is no indication that traffic forecasts have become more accurate over time. Quite the opposite is true for road projects, where forecasts appear to become highly inaccurate toward the end of the period. Statistical analyses corroborate this impression.

For rail projects, inaccuracy in forecasts is independent of both year of project commencement or year of project conclusion. This is the case whether two statistical outliers (marked with 'K' in Figure 7.3) are included or not. The conclusion is that forecasts of rail passenger traffic have not

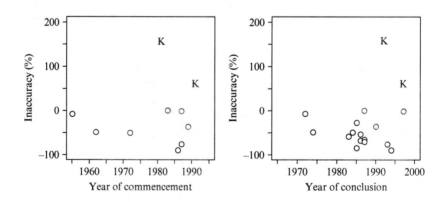

Note: K = statistical outliers.

Figure 7.3 Inaccuracies in number of rail passengers

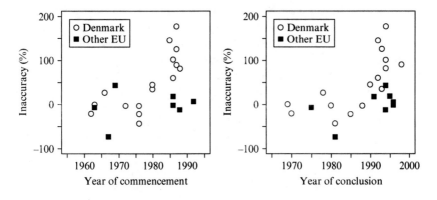

Figure 7.4   Inaccuracies in number of road vehicles

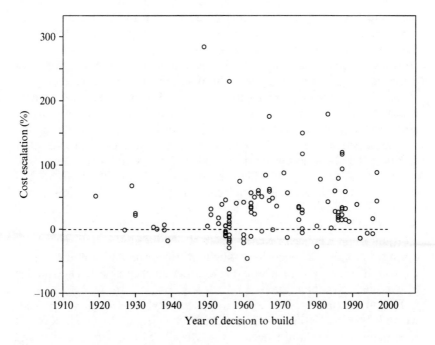

Figure 7.5   A century of cost escalation (constant prices)

improved over time. Rail passenger traffic has been consistently overestimated during the 30-year period studied.

For cost forecasts, Figure 7.5 shows a plot of cost overrun against year
of decision to build for the 111 projects in the sample for which these data

are available. The diagram does not seem to indicate an effect from time on cost overrun. Statistical analyses corroborate this impression. The null hypothesis that year of decision has an effect on cost overrun cannot be supported ($p = 0.22$, F-test). A test using year of completion instead of year of decision (with data for 246 projects) gives a similar result ($p = 0.28$, F-test).[1] Similar analyses have been carried out with year of decision combined with the logarithm of estimated cost as a measure of the size of projects, also split into rail, fixed links and road. Year of completion and logarithm of actual cost was also tried. In no case could any statistically significant result be established, neither with main effects nor with interactions (in no case was a p-value below 0.10 found). We see that cost performance has not improved over time. Cost overrun today is in the same order of magnitude as it was 10, 30 or 70 years ago.

In sum, accuracy in traffic and cost forecasting has not improved over time. Rail passenger forecasts are as inaccurate, that is, inflated, today as they were 30 years ago. Road vehicle forecasts even appear to have become more inaccurate over time, with large underestimations towards the end of the 30-year period studied. Accuracy in cost forecasts has not improved for 70 years. If techniques and skills for arriving at accurate traffic and cost forecasts have improved over time, this does not show in the data.

At first sight, it may seem strange that no learning and improvement appear to be taking place for forecasting demand and cost in this important and highly costly sector of public and private decision-making, and that apparent errors are allowed to continue unchecked decade after decade. After all, project promoters and forecasters seem to be as smart and as capable of learning as other people. But perhaps they have already learned what there is to learn. The behaviour of promoters and forecasters invites speculation that the persistent existence over time of significant and widespread bias and inaccuracy in demand and cost forecasts is a sign that an equilibrium has been reached where strong incentives and weak disincentives for inaccuracy may have taught project promoters that inaccuracy pays off. If this is the case, bias and inaccuracy must be expected and it must be expected to be intentional.

This and other explanations of 'inaccuracy' have been tested elsewhere (Flyvbjerg, Holm and Buhl, 2002; Flyvbjerg and COWI, 2004). It was found that bias and inaccuracy – typically cost underestimation and benefit overestimation – indeed often appear to be intentional and part of power games and rent-seeking behaviour among project promoters and forecasters aimed at getting projects started. Cost underestimation and benefit overestimation are used strategically to make projects appear less expensive and more beneficial than they really are in order to gain approval from decision-makers to build them. Such behaviour best explains why inaccuracy is so consistent over time (see also Wachs, 1986; 1989; 1990; Flyvbjerg, 1996; 1998).

This suggests to decision-makers and planners that the most effective means for improving forecasting accuracy is probably not improved methods but, instead, strong measures of accountability that would curb strategic misrepresentation in forecasts.

7.5   GEOGRAPHICAL VARIATIONS

In addition to testing whether forecasting accuracy varies with time, geographical variations were also tested. The geographical location of projects in the sample was defined as Europe, North America, or 'other geographical areas' (the last being a group of ten developing nations plus Japan).

Table 7.3 shows cost overrun for these geographical areas for fixed links (bridges and tunnels), rail and road, respectively. There is no indication of statistical interaction between geographical area and type of project. The effects from these variables on cost overrun are therefore considered separately.

Considering all projects, the difference between geographical areas in terms of cost development is highly significant ($p < 0.001$). Geography matters for cost overrun.

If Europe and North America are compared separately, which is compulsory for fixed links and roads because no observations exist for other geographical areas here, then comparisons can be made by t-tests (as the standard deviations are rather different, the Welch version is used). For fixed links, average cost overrun is 43.4 per cent in Europe versus 25.7 per cent in North America, but the difference is non-significant ($p = 0.414$). Given the limited number of observations and the large standard deviations for fixed links, one would need to enlarge the sample with more fixed links in Europe and North America in order to test whether the differences might be significant for a larger sample.

For rail, the average cost overrun is 34.2 per cent in Europe versus 40.8 per cent in North America. For roads the similar numbers are 22.4 per cent versus 8.4 per cent. Again these differences are non-significant ($p = 0.510$ and $p = 0.184$, respectively).

It is concluded that the highly significant differences in cost overrun we saw above for geographical location are due to 'other geographical areas', with their poor track record of cost overrun for rail, averaging 64.6 per cent. In addition to more data on projects in Europe and North America, a particularly interesting question for further research is whether data on bridges, tunnels and roads in 'other geographical areas' would show the same tendency at poor cost performance and high risk as does rail.

Table 7.3 *Cost overrun in Europe, North America and other geographical areas (constant prices)*

Type of project	Europe			North America			Other geographical areas		
	Number of projects	Average cost overrun (%)	sd	Number of projects	Average cost overrun (%)	sd	Number of projects	Average cost overrun (%)	sd
Rail	23	34.2	25.1	19	40.8	36.8	16	64.6	49.5
Fixed links	15	43.4	52.0	18	25.7	70.5	0	–	–
Roads	143	22.4	24.9	24	8.4	49.4	0	–	–
Total	181	25.7	28.7	61	23.6	54.2	16	64.6	49.5

For traffic forecasts, more data are needed in order to study the effect on inaccuracy from geographic location of projects. With the available data, there is no significant difference between geographical areas.

7.6 LESSONS IN HOW TO REDUCE INACCURACY, BIAS AND RISK

The first lesson to be learned from the results presented above is that it is highly risky to rely on forecasts of travel demand and cost in developing large transportation infrastructure schemes. Rail passenger forecasts are overestimated in nine out of ten cases, with an average overestimate above 100 per cent. Half of all road traffic forecasts are wrong by more than ±20 per cent; a fourth is wrong by more than ±40 per cent. Moreover, nine out of ten projects have underestimated costs and cost overrun. Average cost overrun for rail is 45 per cent in constant prices, for tunnels and bridges 34 per cent, and for roads 20 per cent. All averages have large standard deviations, indicating that risks of individual forecasts being very wrong are high. Finally, forecasts have not become more accurate over time.

This state of affairs points directly to better risk assessment and management as something planners could and should do to improve planning and decision-making for transportation infrastructure projects. Today, the benefit and cost risks generated by inaccurate forecasts of travel demand and cost are widely underestimated in project development and management (Flyvbjerg, Holm and Buhl, 2003).

However, when contemplating what planners can do to reduce inaccuracy, bias and risk in forecasting, we need to distinguish between two fundamentally different situations, namely, (1) the situation where planners and politicians consider it important to get forecasts right, and (2) the situation where they don't. We consider the first situation in this section and the second in the following section.

If planners and politicians genuinely consider it important to get forecasts right, it is recommended they use a new forecasting method called 'reference class forecasting' to reduce inaccuracy and bias.[2] This method was originally developed to compensate for the type of cognitive bias in human forecasting that psychologist Daniel Kahneman found in his Nobel prize-winning work on bias in economic forecasting (Kahneman, 1994; Kahneman and Tversky, 1979). Reference class forecasting has proven more accurate than conventional forecasting. For reasons of space, here only an outline of the method is presented, based mainly on Lovallo and Kahneman (2003). For details on how to use this method in practical demand and cost forecasting, see Flyvbjerg (2006).

Reference class forecasting consists in taking a so-called 'outside view' on the particular project being forecast. The outside view is established on the basis of information from a class of similar projects. The outside view does not try to forecast the specific uncertain events that will affect the particular project, but instead places the project in a statistical distribution of outcomes from a group of reference projects. Reference class forecasting requires the following three steps for the individual project:

1. Identify a relevant reference class of past projects. The class must be broad enough to be statistically meaningful but narrow enough to be truly comparable with the specific project.
2. Establish a probability distribution for the selected reference class. This requires access to credible data for a sufficient number of projects within the reference class to make statistically meaningful conclusions.
3. Compare the specific project with the reference class distribution, in order to establish the most likely outcome for the specific project.

Daniel Kahneman relates the following story to illustrate reference class forecasting in practice (Lovallo and Kahneman, 2003: 61). Some years ago, Kahneman was involved in a project to develop a curriculum for a new subject area for high schools in Israel. The project was carried out by a team of academics and teachers. In time, the team began to discuss how long the project would take to complete. Everyone on the team was asked to write on a slip of paper the number of months needed to finish and report the project. The estimates ranged from 18 to 30 months.

One of the team members – a distinguished expert in curriculum development – was then posed a challenge by another team member to recall as many projects similar to theirs as possible and to think of these projects as they were in a stage comparable to their project. 'How long did it take them at that point to reach completion?', the expert was asked. After a while he answered that not all the comparable teams he could think of ever did complete their task. About 40 per cent of them eventually gave up. Of those remaining, the expert could not think of any that completed their task in less than seven years, nor of any that took more than ten. The expert was then asked if he had reason to believe that the present team was more skilled in curriculum development than the earlier ones had been. The expert said no, he did not see any relevant factor that distinguished this team favourably from the teams he had been thinking about. His impression was that the present team was slightly below average in terms of resources and potential.

The wise decision at this point would probably have been for the team to break up, according to Kahneman. Instead, the members ignored the pessimistic information and proceeded with the project. They finally completed the project eight years later, and their efforts were largely wasted – the resulting curriculum was rarely used.

In this example, the curriculum expert made two forecasts for the same problem and arrived at very different answers. The first forecast was the inside view; the second was the outside view, or the reference class forecast. The inside view is the one that the expert and the other team members adopted. They made forecasts by focusing narrowly on the case at hand, considering its objective, the resources they brought to it, and the obstacles to its completion. They constructed in their minds scenarios of their coming progress and extrapolated current trends into the future. The resulting forecasts, even the most conservative ones, were overly optimistic. The outside view is the one provoked by the question to the curriculum expert. It completely ignored the details of the project at hand, and it involved no attempt at forecasting the events that would influence the project's future course. Instead, it examined the experiences of a class of similar projects, laid out a rough distribution of outcomes for this reference class, and then positioned the current project in that distribution. The resulting forecast, as it turned out, was much more accurate.

Similarly – to take an example from urban planning – planners in a city preparing to build a new subway would, first, establish a reference class of comparable projects. This could be the urban rail projects included in the sample for this chapter. Through analyses the planners would establish that the projects included in the reference class were indeed comparable. Second, if the planners were concerned about getting patronage forecasts right, they would then establish the distribution of outcomes for the reference class regarding the accuracy of patronage forecasts. This distribution would look something like the rail part of Figure 7.1. Third, the planners would compare their subway project to the reference class distribution. This would make it clear to them that unless they had reason to believe they were substantially better forecasters and planners than their colleagues who did the forecasts and planning for projects in the reference class, they were likely to grossly overestimate patronage. Finally, planners can then use this knowledge to adjust their forecasts for more realism.

The contrast between inside and outside views has been confirmed by systematic research (Gilovich et al., 2002). The research shows that when people are asked simple questions requiring them to take an outside view, their forecasts become significantly more accurate. However, most individuals and organisations are inclined to adopt the inside view in planning major initiatives. This is the conventional and intuitive approach. The traditional way to think about a complex project is to focus on the project itself and its details, to bring to bear what one knows about it, paying special attention to its unique or unusual features, trying to predict the events that will influence its future. The thought of going out and gathering simple statistics about related cases seldom enters a planner's mind. This is the case in general, according to Lovallo and Kahneman (2003: 61–2). And it is certainly the case for forecasts of travel demand and construction cost. Among the several hundred forecasts reviewed for the study presented here, not a single one was a genuine reference class forecast.[3]

While understandable, planners' preference for the inside view over the outside view is unfortunate. When both forecasting methods are applied with equal skill, the outside view is more likely to produce a realistic estimate. That is because it bypasses cognitive and organisational biases such as appraisal optimism and strategic misrepresentation, and cuts directly to outcomes. In the outside view planners and forecasters are not required to make scenarios, imagine events, or gauge their own and others' levels of ability and control, so they cannot get all these things wrong. Surely the outside view, being based on historical precedent, may fail to predict extreme outcomes, that is, those that lie outside all historical precedents. But for most projects, the outside view will produce more accurate results. In contrast, a focus on inside details is the road to inaccuracy.

The comparative advantage of the outside view is most pronounced for non-routine projects, understood as projects that planners and decision-makers in a certain locale have never attempted before – such as building an urban rail system in a city for the first time, or a new major bridge or concert hall where none existed before. It is in the planning of such new efforts that the biases toward optimism and strategic misrepresentation are likely to be large. To be sure, choosing the right reference class of comparative past projects becomes more difficult when planners are forecasting initiatives for which precedents are not easily found, for instance the introduction of new and unfamiliar technologies. However, most large-scale infrastructure projects are both non-routine locally and use well-known technologies. Such projects are, therefore, particularly likely to benefit from the outside view and reference class forecasting.

7.7   THE 'DARK SIDE' OF PROJECT DEVELOPMENT

In the present section we consider the situation where planners and politicians do not find it important to get forecasts right and where they, therefore, do not help to clarify and mitigate risk but, instead, generate and exacerbate it. Here planners are part of the problem, not the solution.

This situation needs some explication, because it may sound to many like an unlikely state of affairs. After all, it may be agreed that planners ought to be interested in being accurate and unbiased in forecasting. It is even stated as an explicit requirement in the American Institute of Certified Planners' (AICP) Code of Ethics and Professional Conduct that 'A planner must strive to provide full, clear and accurate information on planning issues to citizens and governmental decision-makers' (American Planning Association, 1991: A.3), and who would not agree with this? The British Royal Town Planning Institute (RTPI) has laid down similar obligations for its members (Royal Town Planning Institute, 2001).

Yet the literature is replete with things planners and planning 'must' strive to do, but which they don't. Planning must be open and communicative, but often it is closed. Planning must be participatory and democratic, but often it is an instrument to dominate and control. Planning must be about rationality, but often it is about power (Flyvbjerg, 1998; Watson, 2003). This is the 'dark side' of planning and planners identified by Flyvbjerg (1996) and Yiftachel (1998), which is remarkably underexplored by planning researchers and theorists.

Forecasting, too, has its dark side. It is here we find Wachs's (1989) lying planners. They are busy, not with getting forecasts right and following the AICP Code of Ethics, but with getting projects funded and built. And accurate forecasts are often not an effective means for achieving this objective. Indeed, accurate forecasts may be counterproductive, whereas biased forecasts may be effective in competing for funds and securing the go-ahead for construction. 'The most effective planner', says Wachs (1989: 477), 'is sometimes the one who can cloak advocacy in the guise of scientific or technical rationality.' Such advocacy would stand in direct opposition to AICP's ruling that 'the planner's primary obligation [is] to the public interest' (American Planning Association, 1991: B.2).

Nevertheless, seemingly rational forecasts that underestimate costs and overestimate benefits have long been an established formula for project approval (Flyvbjerg, Bruzelius and Rothengatter, 2003; Flyvbjerg and COWI, 2004). Forecasting is here just another kind of rent-seeking behaviour. Risk is not a result of error but of misinformation. The consequence is a Machiavellian make-believe world of misrepresentation, which makes it extremely difficult to decide which projects deserve undertaking and which do not. The result is, as even one of the industry's own organs, the Oxford-based Major Projects Association (1994: 172), has acknowledged, that too many projects proceed that should not. One might add to this observation that many projects don't proceed that probably should, had they not lost out to projects with 'better' misrepresentation (Flyvbjerg, Holm and Buhl, 2002).

In this situation, the question is not so much what planners can do to reduce inaccuracy and risk in forecasting, but what others can do to impose on planners the checks and balances that would give them the incentive to stop producing biased forecasts and begin to work according to their Code of Ethics. The challenge is to change the rules of the power play that governs forecasting and project development. Here better forecasting techniques and appeals to ethics won't do; institutional change with a focus on accountability and good governance is necessary.

7.8   GOOD GOVERNANCE IN PROJECT DEVELOPMENT

As argued in Flyvbjerg, Bruzelius and Rothengatter (2003), two main types of accountability define liberal democracies: (1) public-sector accountability through transparency and public control, and (2) private-sector accountability via competition and market control. Both types of accountability may be effective tools to curb planners' misrepresentation in forecasting and to promote a culture that acknowledges and deals effectively with risk.

In order to achieve accountability through *transparency and public control*, the following would be required as practices embedded in the relevant institutions (the full argument for the measures may be found in Flyvbjerg, Bruzelius and Rothengatter, 2003: chs 9–11):

1.   National-level government should not offer discretionary grants to local infrastructure agencies for the sole purpose of building a specific type of infrastructure. Such grants create perverse incentives. Instead, national government should simply offer 'block grants', 'infrastructure grants', or 'transportation grants' to local governments, and let local political officials spend the funds however they choose to, but make sure that every dollar they spend on one type of infrastructure reduces their ability to fund another. This prevents the situation where 'free money' seems to be available, seen from the promoter's perspective, a situation likely to result in waste. Instead a situation is created where the promoter's own money is at stake, which should always be the case.
2.   Forecasts should be made subject to independent peer review. Where large amounts of taxpayers' money are at stake, peer review may be carried out by national or state accounting and auditing offices, such as the General Accounting Office in the USA or the National Audit Office in the UK, who have the independence and expertise to produce such reviews. Other types of independent review bodies may be established, for instance within national departments of finance or with relevant professional bodies.

3. Forecasts should be benchmarked against comparable forecasts, for instance using reference class forecasting as described in the previous section.
4. Forecasts, peer reviews and benchmarkings should be made available to the public as they are produced, including all relevant documentation.
5. Public hearings, citizen juries and the like should be organised to allow stakeholders and civil society to voice criticism and support of forecasts. Knowledge generated in this way should be integrated in planning and decision-making.
6. Scientific and professional conferences should be organised where forecasters can present and defend their forecasts in the face of colleagues' scrutiny and criticism.
7. Projects with inflated cost–benefit ratios should be reconsidered and stopped if recalculated costs and benefits do not warrant implementation. Projects with realistic estimates of costs and benefits should be rewarded. Politicians should keep projects at arm's length to be free to stop and reward projects in this manner.
8. Professional and occasionally even criminal penalties should be enforced for planners and forecasters who consistently and foreseeably produce deceptive forecasts. An example of a professional penalty would be the exclusion from one's professional organisation if one violates its code of ethics. An example of a criminal penalty would be punishment as the result of prosecution before a court or similar legal set-up, for instance where deceptive forecasts have led to substantial mismanagement of public funds (Garett and Wachs, 1996). Malpractice in planning should be taken as seriously as it is in other professions. Failing to do this amounts to not taking the profession of planning seriously.

In order to achieve accountability in forecasting via *competition and market control*, the following would be required, again as practices that are both embedded in and enforced by the relevant institutions:

1. The decision to go ahead with a project should, where at all possible, be made contingent on the willingness of private financiers to participate without a sovereign guarantee for at least one-third of the total capital needs.[4] This should be required whether projects pass the market test or not, that is, whether projects are subsidised or not or provided for social justice reasons or not. Private lenders, shareholders and stock market analysts would produce their own forecasts or would critically monitor existing ones. If they were wrong about the forecasts,

they and their organisations would be hurt. The result would be more realistic forecasts and reduced risk.

2. Full public financing or full financing with a sovereign guarantee should be avoided.
3. Forecasters and their organisations must share financial responsibility for covering cost overruns and benefit shortfalls resulting from misrepresentation and bias in forecasting.
4. The participation of risk capital should not mean that government gives up or has reduced control of the project. On the contrary, it means that government can more effectively play the role it should be playing, namely as the ordinary citizen's guarantor for ensuring concerns about safety, environment, risk and a proper use of public funds.

Whether projects are public, private, or public–private partnerships (PPPs), they should be vested in one and only one project organisation with a strong governance framework. The project organisation may be a company or not, public or private, or a mixture. What is important is that this organisation enforces accountability *vis-à-vis* contractors, operators, etc., and that, in turn, the directors of the organisation are held accountable for any cost overruns, benefits shortfall, faulty designs, unmitigated risks, etc. that may occur during project planning, implementation and operations. The governance framework should discourage organisational entrenchment, i.e., the existence of the organisation for longer than it is needed. If the institutions with responsibility for developing and building major infrastructure projects effectively implemented, embedded and enforced such measures of accountability, then the misrepresentation in cost, benefit and risk estimates, which is widespread today, would be mitigated. If this is not done, misrepresentation is likely to continue, and the allocation of funds for infrastructure projects is likely to continue to be wasteful and undemocratic.

7.9 CONCLUSIONS

This chapter presents evidence that a key risk in the development and management of large transportation infrastructure projects is misleading forecasts of demand and cost. Typically such risks are understated or even ignored in infrastructure planning, to the detriment of social and economic welfare.

Risks, therefore, have a doubly negative effect in infrastructure development and management, since it is one thing to take on a risk that one has calculated and is prepared to take, much as insurance companies and professional investors do. It is quite another matter – that moves risk-taking to a different and more problematic level – to ignore or misrepresent risks. This is especially the case when risks are of the magnitude documented here, with many forecasts being off by more than 50 per cent on investments that measure in hundreds of millions of dollars.

Such behaviour is bound to produce losers among those financing infrastructure, be they taxpayers or private investors. If the losers, or, for future projects, potential losers, want to protect themselves, then the study presented above shows that the risk of faulty forecasts, and related risk assessment and management, must be placed at the core of project development and management. The objective of this chapter has been to take a first step in this direction by developing the necessary data and approach.

The policy implications of the findings are clear. First, the results show that a major planning and policy problem – namely misinformation – exists for this highly expensive field of public policy. Second, the size and perseverance over time of the problem of misinformation indicate that it will not go away by merely pointing out its existence and appealing to the good will of project promoters and planners to make more accurate forecasts.

The problem of misinformation is an issue of power and profit, and must be dealt with as such, using the mechanisms of transparency and accountability we commonly use in liberal democracies to mitigate rent-seeking behaviour and the misuse of power. To the extent that infrastructure planners partake in rent-seeking behaviour and misuse of power, this may be seen as a violation of their code of ethics, that is, malpractice. Such malpractice should be taken seriously by the responsible institutions. Failing to do so amounts to not taking the profession of planning seriously.

NOTES

1. Time may be measured by year of decision to build a project or by year of completion. The year of completing a project, with inauguration and start of operations, is historically substantially more manifest than the year of decision to build. Consequently, it has been a great deal easier to obtain data on year of completion than on year of decision to build. Data were available on year of decision to build for only 111 of the 258 projects in the cost sample, whereas data on year of completion were available for 246 projects. Development in cost overrun over time was tested for both sets of data, although when evaluating the dependence of cost overrun on year, it is better to use year of decision to build rather than year of completion; the latter includes length of implementation phase, which has influence on cost overrun, causing statistical confounding.

2. Other methods aimed at reducing inaccuracy and bias are the 'cost estimate validation process' (CEVP) developed by Washington Department of Transportation (Reilly et al., 2004), the 'successive principle' developed by Lichtenberg (2000), and Monte Carlo simulations. These three methods typically use subjective data (normally an expert panel's assessment of uncertainty for each of a number of components making up a planned project). In contrast, reference class forecasting uses empirical data on uncertainty, based on actual, documented performance in previous comparable projects. Kahneman's

142   *Planning and decision-making*

research shows that we should expect significantly more accurate outcomes of forecasts that use empirical data compared with forecasts that use subjective data.
3. The closest we have come to an outside view on travel demand forecasts is Gordon and Wilson's (1984) use of regression analysis on an international cross-section of light-rail projects to forecast patronage in a number of light-rail schemes in North America.
4. The lower limit of a one-third share of private risk capital for such capital to effectively influence accountability is based on practical experience. See further Flyvbjerg, Bruzelius and Rothengatter (2003: 120–23).

REFERENCES

American Planning Association (1991), 'AICP Code of Ethics and Professional Conduct', adopted October 1978, as amended October 1991, www.planning.org/ethics/conduct.html.
Brooks, J.A. and P.J. Trevelyan (1979), 'Before and after studies for inter-urban road schemes', in *Highway Planning and Design: Proceedings of Seminar held at the PTRC Summer Annual Meeting, University of Warwick, England from 9–12 July 1979*, Planning and Transport Research and Computation Co. Ltd, London: PTRC Education and Research Services Ltd: 251–66.
Bruzelius, Nils, Bent Flyvbjerg and Werner Rothengatter (2002), 'Big decisions, big risks: Improving accountability in mega projects', *Transport Policy*, 9 (2): 143–54.
Flyvbjerg, Bent (1996), 'The dark side of planning: rationality and *realrationalität*', in Seymour Mandelbaum, Luigi Mazza and Robert Burchell (eds), *Explorations in Planning Theory*, New Brunswick, NJ: Center for Urban Policy Research Press: 383–94.
Flyvbjerg, Bent (1998), *Rationality and Power: Democracy in Practice*, Chicago, IL: University of Chicago Press.
Flyvbjerg, Bent (2005), 'Measuring inaccuracy in travel demand forecasting: methodological considerations regarding ramp up and sampling', *Transportation Research A*, 39 (6): 522–30.
Flyvbjerg, Bent (2006), 'From Nobel prize to project management: getting risks right', Invited plenary paper, Project Management Institute Research Conference, Montreal, July: 16–19.
Flyvbjerg, Bent and COWI (2004), *Procedures for Dealing with Optimism Bias in Transport Planning: Guidance Document*, London: UK Department for Transport.
Flyvbjerg, Bent, Nils Bruzelius and Werner Rothengatter (2003), *Megaprojects and Risk: An Anatomy of Ambition*, Cambridge, MA: Cambridge University Press.
Flyvbjerg, Bent, Mette K. Skamris Holm and Søren L. Buhl (2002), 'Cost underestimation in public works projects: error or lie?', *Journal of the American Planning Association*, 68 (3): 279–95.
Flyvbjerg, Bent, Mette K. Skamris Holm and Søren L. Buhl (2003), 'How common and how large are cost overruns in transport infrastructure projects?', *Transport Reviews*, 23 (1): 71–88.
Flyvbjerg, Bent, Mette K. Skamris Holm and Søren L. Buhl (2006), 'Inaccuracy in traffic forecasts', *Transport Reviews*, 26 (1): 1–24.
Fouracre, P.R., R.J. Allport and J.M. Thomson (1990), *The Performance and Impact of Rail Mass Transit in Developing Countries*, TRRL Research Report 278, Crowthorne, Berkshire, UK: Transportation and Road Research Laboratory.

Fullerton, B. and S. Openshaw (1985), 'An evaluation of the Tyneside Metro', in K.J. Button and D.E. Pitfield (eds), *International Railway Economics: Studies in Management and Efficiency*, Aldershot, UK: Gower: 177–208.

Garett, Mark and Martin Wachs (1996), *Transportation Planning on Trial: The Clean Air Act and Travel Forecasting*, Thousand Oaks, CA: Sage.

Gilovich, Thomas, Dale Griffin and Daniel Kahneman (eds) (2002), *Heuristics and Biases: The Psychology of Intuitive Judgment*, Cambridge, MA: Cambridge University Press.

Gordon, Peter and Richard Wilson (1984), 'The determinants of light-rail transit demand: an international cross-sectional comparison', *Transportation Research Part A: Policy and Practice*, **18A** (2): 135–40.

Hall, Peter (1980), *Great Planning Disasters*, Harmondsworth, UK: Penguin Books.

Kahneman, D. (1994), 'New challenges to the rationality assumption', *Journal of Institutional and Theoretical Economics*, **150**: 18–36.

Kahneman, D. and A. Tversky (1979), 'Prospect theory: an analysis of decisions under risk', *Econometrica*, **47**: 313–27.

Kain, John F. (1990), 'Deception in Dallas: strategic misrepresentation in rail transit promotion and evaluation', *Journal of the American Planning Association*, **56** (2): 184–96.

Lichtenberg, Steen (2000), *Proactive Management of Uncertainty Using the Successive Principle*, Copenhagen: Polyteknisk Press.

Lovallo, Dan and Daniel Kahneman (2003), 'Delusions of success: how optimism undermines executives' decisions', *Harvard Business Review*, July: 56–63.

Mackinder, I.H. and S.E. Evans (1981), *The Predictive Accuracy of British Transportation Studies in Urban Areas*, Supplementary Report 699, Crowthorne, Berkshire, UK: Transportation and Road Research Laboratory.

Major Projects Association (1994), *Beyond 2000: A Source Book for Major Projects*, Oxford: Major Projects Association.

National Audit Office (1988), *Department of Transportation, Scottish Development Department and Welsh Office: Road Planning*, London: Her Majesty's Stationery Office.

National Audit Office (1992), *Department of Transportation: Contracting for Roads*, London: National Audit Office.

Nijkamp, Peter and Barry Ubbels (1999), How reliable are estimates of infrastructure costs? A comparative analysis', *International Journal of Transport Economics*, **26** (1): 23–53.

Pickrell, Don H. (1990), *Urban Rail Transit Projects: Forecast Versus Actual Ridership and Cost*, Washington, DC: US Department of Transportation.

Priemus, Hugo (2007), 'Development and design of large infrastructure projects: disregarded alternatives and issues of spatial planning', *Environment and Planning B*, **34** (4): 626–44.

Reilly, J., M. McBride, D. Sangrey, D. MacDonald and J. Brown (2004), 'The development of CEVP®: WSDOT's Cost-Risk Estimating Process', *Proceedings*, Boston Society of Civil Engineers, Fall/Winter.

Richmond, Jonathan E.D. (1998), *New Rail Transit Investments: A Review*, Cambridge, MA: Harvard University, John F. Kennedy School of Government.

Richmond, Jonathan E.D. (2001), 'A whole-system approach to evaluating urban transit investments', *Transportation Reviews*, **21** (2): 141–79.

Royal Town Planning Institute (2001), 'Code of professional conduct', amended by the Council on 17 January, available at www.rtpi.org.uk.

Skamris, Mette K. and Bent Flyvbjerg (1997), 'Inaccuracy of traffic forecasts and cost estimates on large transportation projects', *Transportation Policy*, 4 (3): 141–6.

Szyliowicz, Joseph S. and Andrew R. Goetz (1995), 'Getting realistic about megaproject planning: the case of the new Denver international airport', *Policy Sciences*, 28 (4): 347–67.

Van Wee, Bert (2007), 'Large infrastructure projects: a review of the quality of demand forecasts and cost estimations. A review of literature', *Environment and Planning B*, 34 (4): 611–25.

Wachs, Martin (1986), 'Technique vs. advocacy in forecasting: a study of rail rapid transit', *Urban Resources*, 4 (1): 23–30.

Wachs, Martin (1989), 'When planners lie with numbers', *Journal of the American Planning Association*, 55 (4): 476–9.

Wachs, Martin (1990), 'Ethics and advocacy in forecasting for public policy', *Business and Professional Ethics Journal*, 9 (1–2): 141–57.

Walmsley, D.A. and M.W. Pickett (1992), *The Cost and Patronage of Rapid Transit Systems Compared with Forecasts*, Research Report 352, Crowthorne, Berkshire, UK: Transportation and Road Research Laboratory.

Watson, Vanessa (2003), 'Conflicting rationalities: implications for planning theory and ethics', *Planning Theory and Practice*, 4: 395–408.

Webber, Melvin M. (1976), *The BART Experience: What have we Learned?*, Monograph no. 26, Berkeley, CA: University of California, Institute of Transportation Studies.

World Bank (1994), *World Development Report 1994: Infrastructure for Development*, Oxford: Oxford University Press.

Yiftachel, Oren (1998), 'Planning and social control: exploring the dark side', *Journal of Planning Literature*, 12 (4): 395–406.

8. Evolving strategy: risk management and the shaping of mega-projects[1]

Roger Miller and Donald R. Lessard

8.1 INTRODUCTION AND OVERVIEW

Project management is often equated with methods that decompose a project into discrete elements, determine their sequencing, and track their completion. Our review of large-scale engineering projects reveals a different reality. In the early stages in particular, project management consists of a series of shaping episodes, first to explore if there is a project, then to recruit participants and explore potential bases of collaboration among them, then to flesh out a holistic proposal – a script for the project if you will – then to advocate and negotiate more precisely the shape of the project and the roles of the various parties, and finally to reach closure and a final agreement. It is at this point that traditional 'decomposing' project management begins. Along the way, projects are often abandoned, or the process returns to an earlier stage because of obstacles encountered or new insight or interests that develop.

Rather than a 'Microsoft Project', the more apt metaphor is a sequence of real options, each of which is shaped and then either exercised or abandoned. In fact, as is often the case with cutting-edge practice, managers have been successful at creating value through the development and exercise of sequential options without explicitly framing the process in options terms, and without explicitly valuing these options since the emphasis is on whether there is a positive value option that justified going forward rather than determining an exact price.

The real-options framework is based on the same logic as that of financial options as developed by Black and Scholes (1974). It recognises that the decisions that determine project cash flows are made sequentially over many episodes. The key insight of this approach is that uncertainty or volatility may actually increase the value of a project, as long as flexibility is preserved and resources are not irreversibly committed. As a result, the economic value of a project when it is still relatively unformed is often greater than the discounted present value of the expected future cash flows.

Value is increased through the creation of options for subsequent sequential choices and exercising these options in a timely fashion. Thus sponsors seek projects that have the potential for large payoffs under particular institutional and technical circumstances. Our study illustrates the rich varieties of mechanisms through which these options are shaped and exercised over the life of the project – the real management that is integral to real options.

Large engineering projects (LEPs) are high-stakes games characterised by substantial irreversible commitments, skewed reward structures when they are successful, and high probabilities of failure. Their dynamics also change over time. The journey from initial conception to ramp-up and revenue generation takes ten years on average. While the 'front end' of a project – project definition, concept selection, and planning – typically involves less than one-third of the total elapsed time and expense, it has a disproportionate impact on outcomes, as most shaping actions occur during this phase. During the ramp-up period, the reality of market estimates and the true worth of the project are revealed. Sponsors may find that actual conditions are very different from expectations, but only a few adaptations are possible. Once built, most projects have little flexibility in use beyond the original intended purpose. Managing risks is thus a real issue.

The purpose of this chapter is to sketch out the various components of risk and outline ranges of strategies for coping with risks and turbulence based on an assessment of 60 projects as part of the IMEC (International Program in the Management of Engineering and Construction) study. Furthermore, we propose the elements of a governance system to master their evolutionary dynamics. The main finding is that successful projects are not selected but shaped. Rather than choosing a specific project concept from a number of alternatives at the outset based on projections of the full sets of benefits, costs and risks over the project's lifetime, successful sponsors start with project ideas that have the potential to become viable. These sponsors then embark on shaping efforts to influence risk drivers ranging from project-related issues to broader governance. The seeds of success or failure of individual projects are thus planted early and nurtured over the course of the shaping period as choices are made. Successful sponsors, however, do not escalate commitments, and they abandon quickly when they recognise that projects have little possibility of becoming viable.

Two other key concepts related to risk that emerge from the study are governability – the creation of relationships that allow a project to be reconstituted and proceed even after major changes in project drivers and the resulting payoffs to the various parties involved – and turbulence – the tendency for risks to compound dramatically once things begin going off track. In our view, projects are dynamic, iterative and often chaotic systems: project-management architectures must reflect this. While they tend to resemble a spiral more than the classic waterfall, even this metaphor may be too orderly. Projects are better viewed as evolutionary and path-dependent systems composed of episodes displaying different dynamics.

These findings apply equally, albeit in somewhat different ways, to the three distinct classes of risk (in terms of their causes) encountered in most projects: those emanating from the dynamics of the project itself (technical and operational risks); those associated with the markets with which the project interacts (market risks); and those related to the political, social and economic setting of the project (institutional/social risks).

In this chapter, we first discuss the IMEC project and the sample of projects that underlie it. Our focus is mostly on front-end choices. We then describe the nature of risks encountered in projects and assess the various strategies that successful projects employ to cope with these risks. Using these descriptions, we highlight the extent to which project management in the face of risk is a sequence of shaping episodes, and then we draw conclusions.

8.2 THE IMEC STUDY AND LARGE ENGINEERING PROJECTS

The IMEC study grew out of the noted difficulties in project delivery that became public (Miller and Lessard, 2001). As long as governments and businesses were content to rely on traditional financing, governance and methods, there was no need for innovative approaches. However, as public financing became tight and many projects become more financially, politically and socially complex, methods that had served their purpose in the past were no longer sufficient.

IMEC was thus set up to understand the changes that were occurring. To our knowledge, there had been no recent attempts to study, evaluate and present a systematic analysis of the new approaches to large projects except the initiatives of the UK Treasury Board (HM Treasury, 2006), Bent Flyvbjerg and his colleagues on mega-projects and risks (Flyvbjerg et al., 2003) and the book by Thomas Hughes, *Rescuing Prometheus* (Hughes, 1998). To counter the objection that each project is unique and that generalisations are therefore impossible, we decided to undertake grounded research to understand what leads to success or failure, using a sample of 60 LEPs. The goal was to identify the practices that, in the experience of executives involved in projects, really made a difference. The IMEC study was distinctive in several ways. First, it was an international field study. The study sums up the collective experience from Europe, North and South America, and Asia. In general, seven to eight participants – sponsors, bankers, contractors, regulators, lawyers, analysts and others – were interviewed for each of the 60 projects. Second, it involved systemic and strategic perspectives. Particular emphasis was placed on front-end development decisions, but execution and initial ramp-up to operation were also studied. Calling upon a range of disciplines, the IMEC study focused on themes such as coping with uncertainty through risk analysis, institution shaping and strategies. Finally, projects were selected from a range of domains. The 60 projects included 15 hydroelectric dams, 17 thermal and nuclear power plants, 6 urban transport facilities, 10 civil infrastructure investments, 4 oil platforms, and 8 technology initiatives.

Projects differ substantially in terms of the intensity of the social/institutional, technical and market-related risks that they pose to sponsors (see Figure 8.1 for the IMEC sample). For instance, oil platforms are technically difficult, but they typically face few institutional risks because they are built far from public attention and bring high direct benefits to their sponsors and affected parties. Hydroelectric power projects tend to be moderately difficult in so far as engineering is concerned, but very difficult in terms of social acceptability. Nuclear power projects pose high technical risks but still higher social and institutional risks. Road and tunnel systems present very high levels of risk, as rock formations usually hide big surprises and markets are difficult to predict when user fees are applied. Market risks faced by roads, bridges and tunnels are especially high when private sponsors build them under concessionary schemes. Urban transport projects that meet real needs pose average market and social/institutional risks. However, they pose technical risks, as they often involve underground geological work that affects costs. R&D projects present scientific challenges but face fewer social acceptability and market difficulties, as they can be broken into smaller testable investments.

8.3   THE NATURE OF RISKS IN PROJECTS

Risk is the possibility that events, their resulting impacts and their dynamic interactions will turn out differently than anticipated. Risk is typically viewed as something that can be described in statistical terms, while uncertainty is viewed as something that applies to situations in which potential outcomes and causal forces are not fully understood. In this chapter, both risks and uncertainties will be referred to as risks. Risks are multidimensional and thus need to be unbundled for a clear understanding of causes, outcomes and drivers.

In the IMEC study, managers were asked to identify and rank the risks they faced in the early front-end period of each project (Miller and Lessard,

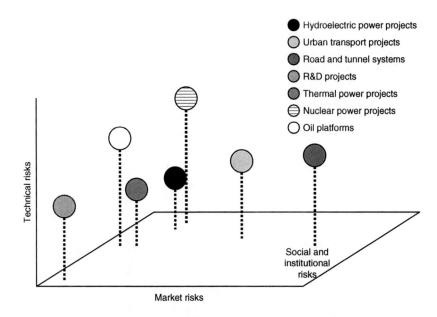

Figure 8.1   A taxonomy of LEPs in the IMEC sample

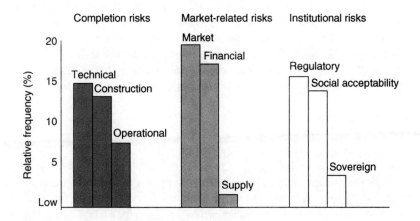

Figure 8.2   Major risks in LEPs, IMEC study

2001). Market-related risks dominated in terms of mentions (41.7 per cent), followed by technical risks (37.8 per cent), and institutional and sovereign risks (20.5 per cent). Figure 8.2 illustrates the frequency of mentions of the risks that managers identified as important in their projects.

Market-related Risks

The ability to forecast demand varies widely, thus creating high levels of risk. The output of oil projects is a fungible commodity sold in highly integrated world markets: probabilistic forecasts are possible. In contrast, many road projects face a specific set of customers; however, users of highways, tunnels, bridges, airports and ports often have alternatives, and forecasting behaviour is extremely difficult. Failures to reach traffic volume seriously threaten business models.

The market for financial inputs depends on prior risk management.[2] Unless all risks have been addressed by sponsors, financial markets are hard to convince. Many projects that offer an adequate prospective return are unable to go forward because of the parties' inability to work out acceptable risk-sharing arrangements. Supply risks are similar to market risks: both involve price and access uncertainties. Supply may be secured through contracts, open purchases, or ownership.

Completion Risks

Projects face technical risks that reflect their engineering difficulties and degrees of innovation: some of these risks are inherent in the designs employed. Construction risks refer to the difficulties that sponsors, prime contractors and contractors may face in the actual building of the project. Execution risks refer to issues that arise from errors or conflicts in the task breakdown, schedule and so on.[3] Operational risks refer to the possibility that the project will not function as expected – for example, that the availability, capacity, or operating efficiency will turn out to be lower than anticipated.

Institutional Risks

The ability of projects to access key resources or to appropriate the returns from operations in order to repay debts and recoup and profit from investments depends on the laws, regulations and norms that govern the appropriability of returns, property rights and contracts. Some countries are governed under constitutional frameworks and the rule of law, while others are led by powerful political parties or clans. Institutional risks refer to unexpected changes in these rules and norms that somehow alter the project payoffs. They are typically seen as greatest in emerging economies – countries whose laws and regulations are incomplete and in a state of flux – although the risks associated with community opposition to projects (the NIMBY phenomenon) or changes in environmental regulations may be as great or greater in highly developed countries.

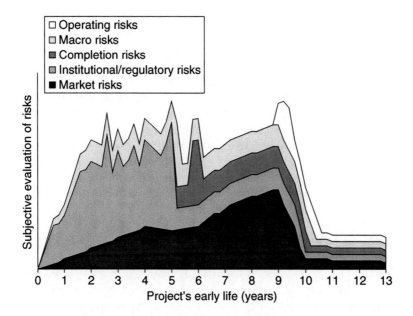

Figure 8.3   The evolution of risks over a project's life

Regulations concerning pricing, entry, unbundling and other elements are presently undergoing major changes in many countries, thus opening opportunities. Social-acceptability risks refer to the likelihood that sponsors will meet opposition from local groups, economic-development agencies and influential pressure groups. Sovereign risks, in turn, involve the likelihood that a government will decide to renegotiate contracts, concessions, or property rights.

Many of these risks emerge only over time. Emerging opportunities or risks may call for changes in project configurations. Benefits may outweigh costs but the reverse can also be true. Projects that appeared sound at one point in time all of a sudden become ungovernable. Events burst out and interact to create turbulence. Figure 8.3 illustrates the evolution of risks that emerge and challenge sponsors. Many risks are linked to the life cycle of the project: regulatory risks, for instance, diminish very soon after permits are obtained, while technical risks drop as engineering experiments are performed.

Turbulence

While strictly speaking not an additional category of risk, one aspect of risk that we observed in many projects was turbulence. Turbulence refers to the way that consequences of events are compounded in unforeseen ways, even if the initial event lies within a range of possibilities that was known in advance, but often more seriously in the case of events that are truly 'surprises'. In the face of such difficulties, some parties have a tendency to leave projects or minimise their losses, perhaps at the expense of other participants. Moves and countermoves lead to a vortex that causes project demise. Without a set of institutional and governance devices to contain degradation, otherwise viable projects sink into deadlocks. In the case of a major civil transportation project, the discovery of geological conditions that were different from those planned for but well within the range of possibilities and did not represent that large a change in overall project economics, for example, allowed opponents to raise multiple issues that ultimately caused the collapse of the entire project.

Opportunity Failures and Oversights

Opportunity failures refer to the risk of missing a good opportunity to improve value or to reduce costs due to error, inadvertence, or even design. While an opportunity failure may be seen as a risk event resulting from a completion or social/institutional cause, the accumulation of such oversights in a project may itself become a cause of a governance crisis. Failures to capture opportunities do not threaten a project's continuity when the public or private sponsors remain unaware of what could have been achieved. When, however, there is a consensus that too many opportunities have been lost, the sponsor or other key players may lose legitimacy in the eyes of others, and the fabric of agreements required to sustain the project breaks down.

Oversight risks are particularly salient when projects are constructed using the traditional mode of contracting, in which the sponsors define expectations in detail and call for bids for execution: since these arrangements typically have no mechanisms for responding to opportunities and changes in circumstances, they generate oversights. In contrast, new modes of governance that rely on partnerships or relational contracts may allow the incorporation of changes and trigger innovative solutions that reduce the likelihood of such oversights.

8.4   APPROACHES TO MANAGING RISK IN LARGE ENGINEERING PROJECTS

Theoretical perspectives on structuring and coping with risks range from narrow, technical analysis to systemic political and institutional approaches.

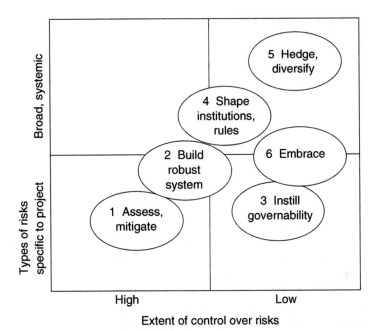

Figure 8.4 Strategies to cope with risk

In the course of the IMEC study, we have observed many innovative approaches to risk management. Sponsors, we have found, strategise to influence outcomes by using six main risk-management techniques: 'decisioneering' to assess and mitigate risks; building robust strategic systems; instilling governability; shaping institutions; hedging and diversifying risks through portfolios; and embracing risks.

Figure 8.4 illustrates the applicability of these strategies to types of risks classified along two axes: the extent to which the risks are controllable and the degree to which they are specific to the project or inherent to the economic system and thus affecting large numbers of actors. When risks are specific to the project and controllable – that is, endogenous – the usual prescription is to mitigate with risk-management approaches. However, if one party has comparative advantage in such mitigation, due to possessing more information regarding the risk or control over the outcomes, the prescription is to shift these risks to that party through contract. When risks are poorly defined but at least partially under the control of affected parties, governments, or regulators, transforming them through institutional influence is the way for sponsors to gain some control. When risks apply broadly but are not under the control of any of the parties, the preferred approach is to transfer them through hedging transactions when markets exist or through insurance when it is priced efficiently. Sponsors must be prepared to embrace the remaining risk, and typically enhance their ability to do so by diversifying exposure through forming portfolios of projects, or equivalently, syndicating out parts of some projects to balance their overall exposure.

Classic Decisioneering Approaches to Assessing and Controlling Risks

Decisioneering approaches view projects as initiatives that can be planned under conditions of calculable risks. Careful analyses of trade-offs between costs and risks, it is argued, can yield good approximations for the appropriate timing of investment in projects. Accelerating a project will increase development costs to the point that there is a danger of sinking it. Proceeding with prudence increases the danger of missing the opportunity that the project aims to capture.

This perspective, typical of much of the project-management literature (Cleland and Ireland, 2006) assumes an environment in which the range of issues facing a project is more or less constant and current quantitative trends can be easily extrapolated into the future. Decisioneering approaches can be grouped into two basic streams. The first are quantitative sensitivity analyses that investigate the impact that possible deviations in some variables, such as anticipated costs, may have on financial performance. The second are probabilistic approaches – using scenario analysis, decision trees, or influence diagrams – that provide more sophisticated alternatives to sensitivity analysis and, in some cases, link the assessment of risk to choices and actions. Sensitivity analysis and similar approaches are helpful for making go/no-go decisions by eliminating the projects with high anticipated performance variability. However, because they focus on aggregate variables, they are less useful for the concrete and detailed shaping of a strategic system through specific choices and actions.

Building Robust Strategic Systems

Sponsors of projects deal with anticipated risks, constraints and issues by creating strategic systems with scope. Large-scale projects potentially face several classes of risks: sponsorship/development, market, social acceptability, regulatory and political, financial, execution and operation. A large portion of the risks are addressed through project-specific strategies to reduce the odds of negative events or the maximal negative impact that such events may have on the project. We identified five classes of strategies

Table 8.1   Devices used in building strategic systems

Information search	Research and studies
	Expert judgements
	Debates, scenarios, risk seminars
	Multidisciplinary strategy teams
Network building and co-optation	Early involvement of financiers, operators and others
	Public–private partnerships
	Alliance of owners sharing equity
	Partnerships with suppliers/contractors
	Coalitions with affected parties
Structures of incentives, and contracts	Risks/decision rights allocation
	Type and number of contracts
	Incentives/penalties
	Frame agreements
	Methods of contractor selection
Project/design configuration	Select geographical location/site
	Complementary investments and linkages
	Contract flexibility, ability to restructure
	Flexible/modular technical solutions
	Flexible contracts/contractual options
Influence and bold actions	Educate regulator, rating agencies, and others
	Side payments: compensation, add-ons
	Pre-emptive action, signals
	Climate of optimism
	Windows of opportunity
	Signal probity (e.g. bidding)
	Seek and improve on legal requirements
	Change laws and regulations

(summarised in Table 8.1): information/selection, co-optation, allocation, design and action.

'Information/selection strategies' refer to the approaches that managers use to gather information about the project and its environment, as well as to shape and approve the project concept, and to identify and decide on the best strategies. We identified three classes of information/selection strategies: studies, private search and relational probing. 'Studies' refers to 'impersonal' and 'objective' information-gathering approaches such as comparative costs estimates, forecasts, tests and simulations. In this class, selection emphasises theoretical models and bureaucratic procedures. The 'private search' class involves the use of a network of personal contacts to obtain 'privileged' information; it often requires a history of previous joint work and trust. Selection takes the form of early commitment to and relentless but flexible pursuit of a single opportunity. 'Relational probing' refers to lengthy face-to-face interactions with potential participants, such as banks, regulators, clients, suppliers, engineering and construction firms, operators and affected parties, during which the information emerges and the concept is directly tested. Like personal searches, relational probing strategies proactively uncover flaws or risks and focus on meeting potential opponents and critics of the project, rather than supporters. Selection relies on iterative discussion and negotiation to expose unworkable alternatives and stimulate the emergence of a better project concept. The information/selection approach used will influence the extent to which risks are identified and the quality of the solutions and strategies that will be produced.

'Co-optation strategies' secure a basic set of 'core competencies', such as technical and construction skills, which will increase the odds for success in critical areas of project execution and ensure access to 'resources' such as markets, financing and even public support. The first step in co-optation is deciding which resources can be provided by the owner's business units or subsidiaries. Some projects, however, require bringing independent participants on board through 'partnership' links – as co-owners, joint-venture partners, or equity investors. Alternatively, resources can be co-opted through contracts and formal agreements such as project financing and tax treaties. Then again, access to some resources may be achieved through informal 'engagement' links with communities and other stakeholders in order to obtain their support.

'Allocation strategies' refer to the detailed ways in which rights, responsibilities, rewards and risks are apportioned between participants through pricing, transfer, penalty, incentive and other contractual clauses. Parties to a contract delimit their respective responsibility areas – what each of them has to provide to the other party, when, and under what conditions. For instance, a joint venture between an electric utility and an independent firm contains agreements that stipulate that the utility provides a site for the gasification plant and guarantees the supply and quality of coal, demineralised water and auxiliary power. The utility has the obligation to accept all the synthetic gas that meets the quality requirements and owns all the by-products that result from the gasification process. Failure to supply the required quantities reliably triggers the payment of penalties.

Price-determination formulas are another frequently used allocation strategy. Cost-reimbursement contracts allocate risks to the owner; fixed-price contracts transfer the cost-overrun risk to the contractor. In cost-incentive and performance-based price-determination schemes, the owners and contractors share the risks and rewards. In many power plant projects the price of the turnkey contract increases if the contractors deliver the plant early or if performance tests reveal that real plant capacity is larger than specified capacity. Other risk-allocation strategies limit the negative consequences for one of the parties to a contract. For instance, utilities often include clauses that allow them to cancel contracts with independent developers if regulators do not allow them to fully recover the contract costs from their customers. Economic-dispatch formulas can be designed to pass on the additional costs resulting from operating a power plant at suboptimal capacity to the electric utility that purchases the power and dispatches the plant.

'Design strategies' involve the use of technical, organisational, scheduling and financial choices to reduce the likelihood and impact of risks. One spectacular example of a technical solution used mainly for political risks is the building of power plants on barges that can be towed away from the host country in case of difficulties. Other examples are technical solutions that reduce the supply risk by providing fuel flexibility and economic development initiatives to gain the support of local communities.

'Action strategies' include confronting opponents using legal or informational means; persuading other participants and stakeholders such as banks, rating agencies, regulators, politicians, publics and opponents; making gestures that legitimate the project in the eyes of the regulators or the communities; developing alternatives to be used if the preferred course of action is blocked by an adverse event; and taking pre-emptive steps to signal commitments. For instance, faced with the prospect of social opposition, the owners of the ITA power plant project in Brazil established a public relations centre in the community and organised town-hall meetings at which the project was explained. Opposition weakened and the population became an ally of the project. Traditionally, engineering firms design projects under a cost-reimbursement contract, and construction is contracted using fixed-price or unit-price contracts. More recently, engineering–procurement–construction and turnkey contracts group these activities together to better align incentives between engineering and construction. BOT (build–operate–transfer)-like schemes, which make a single firm or consortium responsible not only for developing, designing and building the project but also for operating it for a long period of time, propose an even more radical way of aligning incentives. Finally, participant selection procedures may range from invited negotiations to open and public calls for bids.

Instilling Governability

Diligent sponsors do not sit idle, waiting for the probabilities to yield a 'win' or a 'loss', but work hard to influence outcomes and turn the selected initial option into a success. They shepherd their choices in light of changing conditions and often succeed against the odds. Governability is enabled by instilling a series of properties in projects: cohesion, reserves, flexibility and generativity (Miller and Floricel, 2005). These four properties are often contradictory, so a balance must be sought. For instance, strong inter-organisational bonds increase cohesion but limit flexibility. Hierarchical links create inefficiencies, while long-term contracts bring rigidities. Short-term contracts do not provide sufficient stabilisation of the future to induce adequate investment. Increasing flexibility through design and incentives may reduce the efficiency of the project.

'Cohesion' is the property that results in participants' staying with the project and solving the problems caused by turbulence, instead of exiting as crises erupt. The main sources of cohesion are the bonds between project participants resulting from co-optation strategies and informal links created during project execution or early operation. Still other bonds are the result of collateral ties between the organisations participating in a project.

Inadequate cohesion leads to disintegration. Cohesion emerged quite unexpectedly as the basic governability property: one cannot govern a project that is disintegrating; flexibility is clearly not enough. To support cohesion reserves can be built into the institutional arrangements surrounding it. In fact, ownership is the dominant factor in building reserves. Co-optation and sharing, used to deal with anticipated risks, also build in the ability to respond to turbulence. Reserves are frequently incorporated into execution budgets and schedules; contingency allowances in budgeted costs are a common practice for dealing with cost and schedule variability. Finally, reserves can be designed into projects through redundancies and slack resources.

'Flexibility' is the property that enables a project to be restructured as choices, actions and commitments, which initially stabilised the future, change when unexpected events occur. Flexibility can be achieved by using strategies that do not produce long-term constraints, offer other avenues for action, or reduce the costs of restructuring and pursuing alternatives. These costs can be reduced through co-optation and design strategies that emphasise modularity, in which no element of the project is critical by itself. Contractual structures associated with co-optation and allocation strategies are among the main sources of lack of flexibility. The same long-term contracts that reduce market and fuel-supply risks in independent projects may block efforts to respond to new market realities. Contracts often create rigidity at the interface between owner and contractor: as contractors stick to specifications, changes required by the owner will be very expensive.

'Generativity' is the ability to develop creative responses to situations that appear difficult. Response generation presupposes correct sensing and interpretation, as well as the time and attention needed to produce constructive rather than destructive debates. Co-optation strategies, especially those that bring in participants with different competencies, may help. Having many points of view and access to different networks also means that adverse developments will probably be detected earlier and different perspectives will be brought into the discussion. For instance, unlike projects financed on the balance sheet, project financing brings banks, investment advisers, rating agencies and consulting engineers to the heart of project debates. Creative individuals bring in new perspectives from outside the circle of managers who normally participate in the project. With their different experiences, they can sense danger and propose innovative solutions. On the other hand, numerous participants and contractual interfaces hamper creativity, especially when parties focus on contracts instead of problem-solving.

Shaping Institutional Arrangements

Sponsors attempting to anchor projects often find that laws and regulations are incomplete. Many projects serve to unlock new models of project delivery (for example, the first BOTs were developed in the 1980s). One-third of the projects analysed by IMEC required at least one change in laws and rules. Concession rights, property rights, economic regulations, or foreign-investment rules needed to be modified. More than one-quarter required or accompanied changes in property rights: land rights, water rights, monopoly on or improvements to BOT and concession frameworks. Changes to laws and regulations in capital markets were also frequent. A few projects called for new environmental frameworks.

The main function of institutional arrangements is to help anchor projects in their economic and political contexts, and ensure that investments will be repaid and social utility provided. Unless they are solidly anchored, projects will be at the mercy of shifting interests, caprices and opportunistic moves. Sponsors will seek institutional arrangements to buttress LEPs.

Stabilisation of the long-term future to enable investments
Legal and regulatory frameworks, such as sector regulations and concession frameworks, help to reduce risks by minimising opportunities for

clients, communities, or governments to attempt to capture revenues after the investment is sunk. The goal is to create the prospect of secure streams of funds in the long term to cope with the various uncertainties that can affect the project. To secure streams of revenues, the approach throughout most of the twentieth century has been to assign sponsorship and ownership to network operators. Recently, power-purchase agreements, in which the regulator or the state forces network operators to sign long-term supply contracts with independent producers, have been used as a tool for providing revenue flows. Concessions by the state to sponsors also provide a framework for future revenues but are less secure.

Flexibility to face turbulence
During the front-end development of projects, when agreements are negotiated and commitments made, managers develop specific strategies to cope with foreseeable risks; they cannot, however, develop specific ways to cope with 'surprise' events. Turbulence is likely to arise given the long time span required for development. Flexibility is provided by elements of institutional arrangements that enable projects to undergo rescheduling, restructuring, or bankruptcy. The flexibility provided by institutional arrangements helps many projects survive unforeseen events.

Enhancing the legitimacy of projects, participating organisations and agreements
Many projects face opposition from interest groups. Laws, regulations and practices that create well-structured assessment frameworks enable sponsors and interest groups to air their views through public hearings, and even to oppose decisions through appeal procedures. Public-bidding frameworks structure the orderly selection of 'fit' sponsors and provide legitimacy. Practices such as inviting representatives of the public into planning and design meetings and proactively consulting conservationist groups and environmental regulators help to find credible solutions and reduce the likelihood of protest.

Frameworks for structuring voice, decision-making and public trade-offs make it possible to choose public transportation systems, erect power plants and, in some countries, build nuclear facilities. To manage social-acceptability risks in siting of power plants in Japan, for instance, the Three Power Source Laws System was put in place by the Japanese Ministry of International Trade and Industry. This framework structures public consultations and hearings across the country; the population is consulted on choice of eventual sites for projects and their technical features.

Portfolios, Insurance and Hedging

The principle of diversification is applied in projects in many different ways. In many projects, three applications were observed. First, sponsors of risky projects likely to face turbulence from disturbances caused by economic crises or government behaviours build a diversified portfolio across sectors and jurisdictions to balance risks and cash flows. Positive variations in a few compensate for negative outcomes in others. While sponsors may be able to influence some behaviour, these risks – particularly those of overall macro-economic conditions or general policy changes – are by and large beyond the control of project participants. Diversification generally is the sole option. Second, sponsors may hedge against possible losses due to currency fluctuations or commodity exposures by employing financial derivatives or other structures to shift these exposures to 'the market at large', which by definition possesses the maximum diversification potential and hence should demand the lowest premium for bearing such risks. Third, sponsors may protect themselves against political risks by investing in many countries, finding partners in each country, or buying insurance against expropriation. They may also engage in shaping or influencing behaviours by incorporating legitimate stakeholders and/or by being sure that they deliver value to those in control.[4]

Embracing Residual Risks

Of course, not all risks can be mitigated, shaped to sponsors' advantage, or transferred to others through contracts or market transactions. Successful project sponsors and other strategic players understand which risks must be taken in order to seek 'the prize' associated with the project. Through experience, they have developed a clear sense of their comparative advantage in bearing various risks, reflecting their financial strength (their capital base, diversification, access to capital markets, and financial sophistication), their understanding of particular risk domains, and their influence over the relevant events or consequences of those events. In areas where uncertainty is high, sponsors seek partners with comparative advantages in bearing risks.

Efficient risk management requires matching risks and responses, all within a dynamic iterative system. This is typically done through an iterative 'layering process', as depicted in Figure 8.5. For any given risk that is identified, there is a pecking order of responses – for example, mitigating or shaping for risks that are controllable to some extent; applying the principle of comparative advantage to determine who best should bear them given the ability to control coupled with the financial capacity to bear the

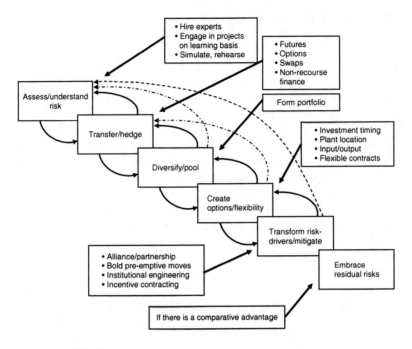

Figure 8.5   The layering process

risk; hedging in the case of risk that can easily be transacted in financial markets; and pooling or diversification for risks that cannot be shaped or traded.

8.5   GOVERNING PROJECTS AS EVOLUTIONARY SYSTEMS

In this section, we will outline a governance framework to manage projects while recognising that they are essentially evolutionary and messy. The actual decision-making processes observed in the projects studied in IMEC were indeed messy, and often chaotic. Projects are often launched by promoters who need to charm potential participants and feel compelled to build convincing but less-than-reality-grounded stories. Expenditures are allocated to soft issues such as opinion research, public affairs and announcements that lay bare issues of politics and power. Decisions are never final but are remade, recast and reshaped. Confrontations often bring deadlocks.

This messiness, as opposed to clear-cut decision-making, has led many observers to argue that LEPs are basically unmanageable, and that success is a matter of luck and improvisation. In reality, projects are better viewed as evolutionary systems where messy decision processes can be structured by a governance framework that combines discipline with creative responses.

Performance of Projects

Traditional perspectives on project management measure performance in terms of meeting projected costs, deadlines and functionality. However, project sponsors buy benefits not artefacts: they evaluate projects by the value and satisfaction they create. Should one adopt an evolutionary perspective, performance becomes the output of processes over which control varies from strong to minimal. Achieved results may be different from initial expectations for a number of reasons:

- The internal governance framework of the sponsoring organisation may have led to initial estimates that were off the mark, wrong, or deceptive, as managers were unwilling to allocate the resources necessary to build solid estimates or tell the truth.
- Capabilities of sponsors or consultants to shape projects or respond to crises may have been inadequate or have faltered. Exogenous or endogenous events may have required competencies that parties did not have.
- Exogenous unexpected events beyond the control of sponsors or partners may have generated turbulence that was difficult to master.
- Sponsors may have changed priorities mid-course, set new goals, or cut budgets, thus triggering endogenous turbulence.
- Bold moves to profit from emerging technical or market opportunities may have led to overruns but with increased benefits. Overall satisfaction may be high, together with a perception of bad management.

Should one adopt an evolutionary perspective, the performance of projects becomes not a comparison with goals stated many years ago but the output of processes of shaping, countermoves and facing emerging risk. The project that has been built differs from the original concept because of unexpected events, imposed redesigns or voluntary changes in the concept.

Progressive Issue Resolution Through Shaping Episodes

Rather than evaluating projects at the outset based on projections of the full sets of benefits and costs over their lifetime, competent sponsors view and shape them in evolutionary perspectives. They start with initial concepts that have the possibility of becoming viable. They then embark on shaping efforts to refine, reconfigure and eventually agree on acceptable concepts. Sponsors cut their losses quickly when a concept has little possibility of becoming viable.

Shaping episodes start with broad hypotheses about what nested problems and risks need to be addressed and what resources are necessary to achieve progress. The shaping process combines deliberate actions with responses to emergent situations. Various intertwined issues have to be resolved one by one by sponsors alone or in cooperation with partners or co-specialised firms. Progress typically involves 'buying in' some stakeholders and 'buying off' others. In some cases, the expectations of stakeholders can be specified in advance. In many cases, though, it is not clear how to accommodate various interests; the leading sponsor uses the front-end period to identify mutual-gains trajectories.

Episodes start with momentum-building, continue with the countering of opposing forces, and iterate until closure can be achieved. As shaping progresses, new options are opened and old ones are closed. At closure, clients and partners agree to commit, thus losing degrees of freedom.

Momentum building

Momentum is built by imagining concepts, promoting legitimacy and selling a project configuration such that partners, affected parties and governments accept what is proposed. Risk seminars and decision conferences are used to shape the value proposition and identify risks. To ensure that investments are protected against opportunistic behaviours, risk-sharing agreements will be developed. To gain legitimacy, consent from affected parties and approval by governments will be sought.

Meeting countering forces

The countering forces that come into play over time can easily sidetrack weak sponsors into wrong choices or lead inexperienced ones to kill good ideas. In each shaping episode, the forces of criticisms and counteractions will be at work. Opponents will call for realism. Experts will challenge cost estimates and risk potentials. Sponsors will respond and take actions that may plant the seeds of later failure or success. In situations of antagonism or when desire to collaborate is mixed with the intention to oppose, parties learn opponents' values, communicate promises and make veiled or overt threats to arrive eventually at meetings of minds.

Sponsors sometimes believe their own overly optimistic assumptions. Weak analyses, incomplete research and the need to show progress lead to the rejection of valid criticisms. Excessive realism, in contrast, leads to scepticism and to the eventual rejection of good opportunities. What is basically a good concept is painted negatively and rejected. Unfavourable judgements drive away parties whose contribution is critical. Doubts, negative stories and emergent problems set in motion self-fulfilling prophecies.

Sponsors often yield to the temptations of unreasonable commitments because they are unaware of particular risks. Blindness generally comes from the inability to form coalitions that confront distinct but relevant viewpoints. Regulatory agencies may refuse to grant permits or change rules during project shaping. Only projects whose leaders and sponsors have the resources, willingness and competencies to counteract destructive forces survive.

Closure
Eventually, imperfectly coordinated but stabilised understandings move toward temporary agreements that are enforceable. Each shaping episode ends with a process of closure that suggests either abandoning the whole project or accepting a temporary agreement on a concept configuration.

Closure takes many forms: memorandum of understanding, business case, negotiated agreement, formal public commitment, sets of formal contracts, and so on. The dangers associated with closure are that choices can be made too early or too late, too rigidly or too flexibly. Missing the boat – rejecting a good opportunity – is just as real a possibility as selecting a bad option or pursuing the wrong project. Premature closure locks a project on a rigid configuration, narrow sets of agreements, or irreversible choices that limit degrees of freedom for the future.

When exogenous or endogenous forces are strong, the agreed-upon closure may be reopened at the start of another shaping episode. For example, emerging technical opportunities may call for reopening IT projects or infrastructure projects. When this occurs, assessing costs against benefits is necessary. Similarly, changes in the business models may call for reconfiguration of the agreement. Figure 8.6 pictures the shaping effort as going up a hill through coalition-building, problem-solving and risk management in the face of counter-dynamics such as cynicism, false expectations and feedback effects.

Projects as Paths of Interdependent Shaping Episodes

Projects are rarely shaped in one over-arching episode. Instead, multiple and interdependent episodes are necessary to resolve issues and arrive at a closure that, though reopenable, can be agreed upon. Episodes are not stages that logically flow from one to the other, but distinct shaping dynamics that are autonomous yet path-dependent. Figure 8.7 illustrates the path

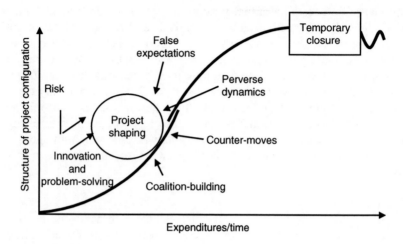

Figure 8.6   Stages in project shaping

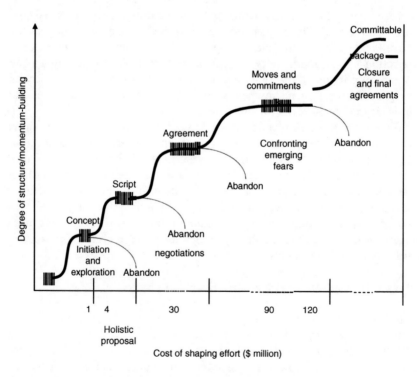

Figure 8.7   A project as a series of shaping episodes

of early front-end shaping episodes for a bridge project that was examined in great detail. Five episodes characterised the progression from initial hypothesis to formal contracts and construction fund release. We will present these episodes in a generic manner:

Initiation and exploration
The initiation episode is usually short (six months to a year) and closes when a credible party conveys to others that the project concept has relevance and should be sponsored. The credible party states openly that it is ready to allocate funds and lead debates on the ways and means of shaping and financing the idea. In the IMEC sample, project ideas were initiated by network operators (32 per cent), entrepreneurial firms (20 per cent), political leaders (20 per cent), technical entrepreneurs (12 per cent) and owners of rights (8 per cent).

Resources of a few million dollars are used to shape the project concept during this episode. Exploratory searches are conducted internally or in collaboration with external parties. In the IMEC sample, the dominant modes of exploration were a team in symbiosis with external consultants (16 per cent); open idea competition (20 per cent), strategic-planning groups (30 per cent), and entrepreneur design (28 per cent). Conceptual closure is achieved when independent studies confirm the viability of the concept. The output is a series of documents sketching out ideas but with an emphasis on technical issues. The most common form is a position paper presented to legitimate authorities, such as ministers or boards of directors.

Development of holistic proposals
The leading sponsors start with 'horseback' assumptions and proceed to develop holistic proposals covering financial and technical parameters, social acceptability, environmental challenges, and regulatory decisions and permits. The central concern is to maintain a perspective that avoids blindness to risks. Sponsors build fully developed scripts addressing pertinent risks and providing concrete solutions. Holistic proposals are presented as business cases to investors or public authorities. Preparing such proposals is expensive: from a few to many tens of millions of dollars. Entrepreneurial sponsors are often unable to fund such efforts.

Extended negotiations
Assuming that a version of the holistic proposal has been selected, the leader works with selected bidders to clear out assumptions concerning risks, revenues, costs, guarantees, engineering design and other factors. Assumptions often need to be reworked. Many sketched relationships have to be made operational. Numerous issues skipped earlier are discovered

and require solutions. Such issues may include definition of property rights to protect sponsors; development of guarantees to protect clients from completion risks faced by sponsors; negotiation of terms of guarantees and covenants to protect banks and investors; determination of the public contribution in the case of projects in which toll revenues are insufficient; determination of pricing structures and conditions of the concession; and identification of rules, regulations and laws that will have to be modified to provide security to the project.

When a government is the sponsor, negotiations of agreements have to meet additional criteria of transparency, probity and accountability. Negotiations often extend over many years because different departments have distinct requirements and expectations. Many winners of competitions, having sketched beautiful holistic proposals, are dismayed when they have to restart negotiations after winning a bid and spend $15–20 million just to work out issues that they thought were resolved.

Confronting emerging fears
As information is made public, pressure groups are triggered. Facing social and environmental fears is a very expensive affair. Sponsors have to bind themselves through actions to gain consent. Promises to engage in future actions are insufficient. Concrete moves to meet expectations and solve social and environmental issues have to be made.

If parties are unable to forge agreements, they must wait for court or government decisions. The presence of public social- and environmental-assessment frameworks is extremely important here in helping to solve dilemmas. Delays are the inevitable consequence of such formal assessments, but the public framework builds legitimacy and forces parties either to make trade-offs or to kill the project.

Closure on a Committable Package
Commitment on a final package can take place when all major issues have been resolved. In many projects, sponsors have spent a few hundred million dollars to shape a holistic proposal, gain consent, solve social and environmental issues, and build agreements. Once the slow front-end shaping process closes on a committable package, the sprint to engineering, procurement and construction may then begin.

The costs of shaping projects and planning to meet risks can be high. For simple projects, around 2–3 per cent of the overall costs will be spent in planning activities. However, for socially complex projects up to 35 per cent of the total costs will be spent in shaping the concept, ensuring good-quality coordination between players and investing to master risks. Leadership tends to be different in each episode. During the initiation period, entrepreneurs or political officials tend to be leaders until a credible client accepts the project as a viable idea. In developing proposals and negotiations, two leaders, the owner and the sponsor/developer, interact. During construction, leadership is shared between the owner and contractors.

Sometimes, the reopening of closure is so powerful that shaping has to return to early conceptualisation. For example, during the construction of the Tucurui dam in Brazil, the extent of rain was such that prior estimates about the flow of water had to be revised and all designs redone during construction. Similarly, progress in clinical research may lead doctors to openly question assumptions embedded in the design of a university hospital.

Governance Frameworks for Shaping Projects as Evolutionary Systems

Various governance arrangements for developing projects have been tried. The rational model for project planning emerged in the twentieth century to replace the entrepreneurial approach. Belief in formal analysis was, and still is, the central pillar of the rational approach. Successful projects are portrayed as the product of advanced planning by experts who carefully weigh forecasts, alternatives and contracts. Project failures are seen largely as resulting from planning errors. Although many studies showed that large projects did not always conform to the rational-system model, the ideal lives on.

The approach proposed here combines rational planning with evolutionary shaping as progress is made on facing issues, risks and opportunities. Governance frameworks can be built at the project level but also at the institutional level to provide the scaffolding around which the various issues of projects can be shaped.

Governance means setting up a structure – a set of decision-making processes and methods for accumulating of knowledge to ensure that creativity and discipline are brought to bear. In conjunction with analytical planning, debates and discussions about risks, value creation and opportunities to reopen projects are kept alive. They make sure that risks are not defined as cost contingencies but that risk-management systems are put in place to trigger the negative feedback loops necessary to counteract the positive loops. The reopening of closed agreements will be subjected to cost–benefit tests.

Participants
Building a structure to shape projects through their multiple episodes requires deciding what parties will be involved. The structure must identify the multiple perspectives from which the project may be viewed, and the multiple tests that it should be subjected to. If the project team is staffed

only with internal technical experts, projects will be configured in technical terms. In contrast, if the project office includes external parties, experienced contractors, lawyers representing opponents, and professional managers with a systemic perspective, risks and opportunities will be addressed. Sponsors who become blind to particular risks do so because they have not brought distributed and differentiated expertise and viewpoints. They fail to form coalitions that can identify the major issues, put in place mechanisms to address them, and not allow commitments to get out of step with the resolution of key risks.

Using a mountain-climbing metaphor, competent public or private sponsors do not rush to climb the mountains that they are best equipped to climb. Rather, they seek to select, equip and train a climbing party. In fact, the game consists in identifying projects that stretch capabilities but that, because of their complexity and risk, offer substantial value and benefits to clients in spite of the costs involved.

Processes

Governance processes set up decision-making frameworks to make sure all the right questions are being asked, to initiate research activities to develop answers, and to outline the hurdles that the project must clear. Large multinational firms have often put in place complex frameworks composed of five or six decision gates in which most issues are addressed. Governmental frameworks are usually less complex, with a few decision moments.

For example, the system instituted by the Royal Ministry of Finance of Norway (see Chapter 9 in this book) includes three gates at which the project concept is tested. Project concepts are developed technically by the relevant ministries but must answer the following questions: what is the value for clients and opponents? Is value created properly shared? What are markets estimates? How will the project be financed? Could it be built using alternatives? What are the major risks and how will they be dealt with? Where are the forgotten costs, especially in risk mitigation? How do estimates compare with other projects in the world? Have competing options such as public–private partnerships been analysed? The initial concept is assessed internally. However, holistic proposals are evaluated in cooperation with external expert evaluators (Samset et al., 2006).

Methods for accumulating knowledge

Without comparative knowledge about costs, contracts, risks and so on, it is very difficult to shape projects. Sponsors who get involved sporadically in large projects find themselves starting anew and building on high levels of ignorance. The accumulation of knowledge has to be organised on a systematic and continuous basis. Sponsors should internally and in cooperation with others build knowledge bases on construction cost estimates, risk-bearing costs, contractual forms, practices for introducing innovation, financial methods for business modelling, and learned best practices.

Powerful sponsors such as governments and large firms may even shape the environments in which projects will be developed. They may decide that ultimate users, engineering contractors or project management firms must build up their capabilities to create value and share knowledge. Improved capabilities will make it possible to answer questions better and work cooperatively to develop superior solutions by engaging in generative thinking and search for innovative solutions.

8.6   CONCLUSION: CREATION AND EXERCISE OF OPTIONS

As we have shown, the succession of shaping episodes that form the front-end process to cope with risks can be reinterpreted as a sequence of creating, shaping, and the exercising or abandoning of real options. Decisions that determine project cash flows are made sequentially over many episodes, and value is often created or preserved in the face of a great deal of uncertainty by ensuring flexibility and limiting irreversible commitments until a final closure is reached, and then 'sprinting' to the finish as quickly as possible. In fact, this process of exploration, shaping, closure and sprinting takes place many times in the complex projects we have reviewed. Value is increased through the creation of options for subsequent sequential choices, and exercising these options in a timely fashion. Thus sponsors seek projects that have the potential for large payoffs under particular institutional and technical circumstances. The study in this chapter illustrates the rich varieties of mechanisms through which these options are shaped and exercised over the life of the project – the real management that is integral to real options.

NOTES

1. This chapter is based primarily on Miller and Lessard (2001) and the underlying IMEC study. However, it also reflects the insights that the two authors have gained from their separate journeys over the last six years. Miller has gone on to define and lead the MINE study, a large-scale project focusing on innovation games based at Ecole Polytechnique de Montréal. Lessard has continued his work on large-scale projects in the oil-and-gas sector as faculty director of the BP Projects Academy and the Major Projects Research Program at MIT.
2. The term 'financial risk' is often used overly broadly to refer to risks with financial consequences – essentially everything. For us, the term applies only to events that have some underlying financial cause.

3. Schedule risk also is often used to identify a risk that has an impact on the schedule. Here, we refer to schedule risks only when they are a cause and not just a consequence. Of course, in episodes of turbulence a schedule impact may become a cause of further unravelling, and hence the distinction becomes less clear.
4. For an excellent recent study of how sponsors deal with political risk in major projects, see Wells and Ahmed (2007).

REFERENCES

Black, Fischer and Myron Scholes (1974), 'From theory to a new financial product', *Journal of Finance*, **29** (2): 399–412.

Cleland, D. and L. Ireland (2006), *Project Management: Strategic Design and Implementation*, 5th edn, New York: McGraw-Hill.

Flyvbjerg B., N. Bruzelius and W. Rothengatter (2003), *Megaprojects and Risk: An Anatomy of Ambition*, Cambridge, MA: Cambridge University Press.

HM Treasury (2006), *PFI Strengthening Long-term Partnerships*, London: HMSO, March.

Hughes, Thomas (1998), *Rescuing Prometheus*, New York: Pantheon.

Miller, R. and S. Floricel (2005), 'Project risks', in André Manseau and Rod Shields (eds), *Building Tomorrow: Innovation in Construction and Engineering*, Aldershot, UK: Ashgate.

Miller, R. and D. Lessard (2001), *The Strategic Management of Large Engineering Projects: Shaping Risks, Institutions and Governance*, Cambridge, MA: MIT Press.

Samset K., P. Berg and O.J. Klakegg (2006), *Front-end Governance of Major Public Projects*, Concept Research Program, Technical University of Norway, May.

Wells, Louis T. and R. Ahmed (2007), *Making Foreign Investment Safe: Property Rights and National Sovereignty*, New York: Oxford University Press.

9. How to overcome major weaknesses in mega-projects: the Norwegian approach

Knut Samset

9.1 INTRODUCTION

A truly successful project is one that has been implemented in accordance with its budget and time schedule, and which significantly contributes to the fulfilment of its agreed objectives. Also, it should have only minor negative effects, its objectives should be consistent with needs and priorities in society, and it should be viable in the sense that the intended long-term benefits resulting from the project are produced. These requirements were first formulated for US-funded international development projects by the USAID in the 1960s. They were subsequently endorsed by the UN, OECD and the European Commission. They are summarised in terms of five requirements or success factors that have to be fulfilled: more specifically the project's efficiency, effectiveness, relevance, impact and sustainability. These are tough requirements that go far beyond the performance measures that are usually highlighted in the media and attract public attention when news about shortcomings in mega-projects hit the headlines. In most such cases the debate is about the projects' efficiency measures, such as their budgetary compliance and progress, and in some cases also their cost-efficiency as compared with similar projects.

However, these efficiency measures are only the first signs and immediate indicators of a project's success. Clearly, they are main features of the contractual arrangements governing the implementation of the project, and therefore essential concerns both for the commissioning party and for the contractors who are made accountable for delays and overrun. It is also a major concern in industry, as well as in government, when large amounts of public funds are involved. This may explain why inadequate efficiency is considered news in the media and therefore gets public attention. But these efficiency measures are insignificant indicators that can only provide a very restricted testimony of a project's success. Clearly, there are many examples

173

of projects that score high on efficiency, but subsequently prove to be disastrous in terms of their effect and utility. And there are also numerous projects that failed to pass the efficiency test but still prove to be tremendously successful both in the short and the long run.

9.2 TACTICAL AND STRATEGIC PERFORMANCE

A crucial distinction is between projects' *tactical* and *strategic* performance. Journalists and the public seem to be more concerned about how projects are being implemented in tactical terms than in their strategic performance in terms of immediate and long-term effects and utility. Strategic performance requires that the anticipated immediate positive effects of the project are produced (*effectiveness*), that these effects are consistent with needs and priorities in society and the market (*relevance*), that there are no major negative effects of the project (*impact*), and that the anticipated benefits resulting from the project prevails as expected (*sustainability*).

Projects that score highly on all the five success criteria mentioned above are those that perform successfully both tactically and strategically. Such projects may be rare. Taking Norway as an example, one type of project

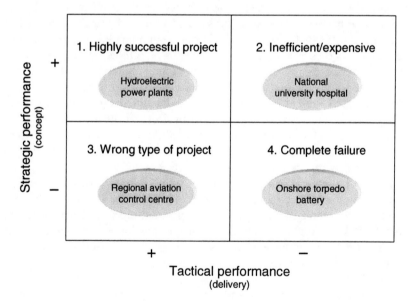

Figure 9.1   *Performance profiles to categorise different projects from*
highly successful (1) to complete failure (4)

that has proved successful and has satisfied all these requirements again and again are hydroelectric power projects. These involve the construction of dams to form large water reservoirs in the high mountain areas, power plants with turbines and electric generators in the valleys below, and huge pipes to carry the water at high speed from the reservoir. In terms of tactical performance the track record of such projects is impressive. One explanation is the existence of a national industry with highly specialised expertise and decades of accumulated experience in delivering such projects on time and within budgets (*efficiency*). In strategic terms, these plants produce cheap and clean energy (*relevance*), enough to cover a sizeable share of the country's electricity needs (*effectiveness*). There is no pollution and no significant adverse environmental effects (*impact*). In economic terms the power plants are extremely viable, and also long-lived (*sustainability*). Most of these projects therefore fit into category (1) in the performance matrix in Figure 9.1: they are highly successful projects.

Projects that might qualify for either of the remaining three categories in Figure 9.1 may be more common. Each of these categories will be illustrated by recent examples from Norway.

Category (2) projects are viable in strategic terms but inefficient tactically. One example would be the national university hospital in Oslo, which was completed in 2000, one year behind schedule and with considerable cost overrun. Newspapers had comprehensive coverage of developments during the construction phase and there were a number of public debates in the media. A public inquiry was subsequently commissioned to establish the causes of the problems. Clearly, the cost overrun was considerable in absolute terms; however, in relative terms it was equivalent to only a number of months of operational costs for the entire hospital, and therefore less significant if seen in a lifetime perspective. Also, the inquiry established that a large share of the cost increase was due to necessary amendments and scope expansions, which have increased the efficiency and utility of the hospital's operations. The designers failed to foresee these needs when the project was planned. In strategic terms, the need for and significance of the project have proved conclusive, and in retrospect it is generally considered a great success.

Category (3) projects are the wrong type of project in strategic terms, but efficient tactically. One example would be the air traffic control centre for the country's central region. It included the construction of a very tall, oversized concrete control tower at Trondheim Airport, which was completed in 2003 in compliance with the project's time schedule and budget. The media attention has been surprisingly limited, despite the fact that the facility was never equipped or taken into operation: because of a restructuring of the national air traffic control system, this particular centre was left redundant. The problem in this case was that the need for this type of project had been overtaken by technological advances in the field of air traffic control. Decision-makers failed completely since the decision to build was already outdated long before it was made.

One example of a conspicuous type of category (4) projects – the total failures – would be a sophisticated onshore torpedo battery built inside the rocks on the northern coast in 2004 with considerable cost overrun and delay. The battery, built to accommodate 150 military personnel for as long as three months at a time, was officially opened with the successful launch of a test torpedo against a ship dummy off shore. However, it was closed down by Parliament only one week later. It was apparent that no potential enemy would expose its ships to such an obvious risk. The onshore torpedo battery concept harks back to the Second World War and was long over-taken by political, technological and military development when the decision to build was taken in 1997, long after the Cold War ended. The project is the unfortunate and wasted result of a strategic blunder.

In summary, taking the projects' performance profiles into account, the politicians, media and the public seems to be more preoccupied with category (2) and (4) projects, which are underperformers in tactical terms, and disregard their strategic potential or performance. What are highlighted are problems deriving essentially from weaknesses in project management decisions. This is a very restricted perspective. The focus should rather be on category (3) and (4) projects – the strategic underperformers. It is a paradox that even projects that prove to be complete failures tend to escape attention as long as they perform acceptably in tactical terms.

9.3   PROJECT LIFE CYCLE AND STAKEHOLDERS

Public mega-projects are typically conceived as the result of politically expressed needs in dialogue between various stakeholders. This is followed by some lengthy process to develop the project and make the necessary decisions. This typically involves government at various administrative levels, as well as political institutions, the public, media, and consultants and contractors in the private sector. Such processes are often complex, shielded and unpredictable, as described and analysed in the in-depth IMEC study of 60 major projects where the focus was on the reconciliation of uncertainty and feasibility in the front-end phase (Miller and Lessard, 2000). The processes can also be deceptive and irresponsible, affected by hidden agendas rather than openness and social responsibility, and dominated by strong stakeholders or coalitions, as discussed for instance by Altshuler and Luberoff (2003), Flyvbjerg et al. (2003) and Miller and Hobbs (2005).

In projects that fail strategically, it is likely that the problem is associated with the choice of project rather than how it is implemented. The choice is decided during what might be a highly politicised process up front. In some cases the problem can be traced back to decisions in the earliest phase where the initial idea was conceived. What happens during the front-end phase is therefore essential for the project's success. A study by the World Bank in 1997, based on a review of as many as 1125 projects, concluded that 80 per cent of the projects with a satisfactory 'quality at entry'[1] were successful while only 35 per cent of those with unsatisfactory quality were successful. Tactical performance tends to be less dependent on the initial choice of concept and more on decisions made during planning and implementation. Keeping the distinction between tactical and strategic decisions is therefore useful in trying to prevent the strategic focus from becoming blurred by project-management concerns during the front-end phase.

Numerous decisions are made during the entire life cycle of a project, resulting from a decision-making process that runs in parallel with an analytic process, which provides input to decision-makers as illustrated in Figure 9.2. The distinction is made between the front-end, the implementation and the operational phases.

The front-end phase is initiated when the initial idea is conceived. It proceeds as a complex and often unpredictable process, aimed to generate information, consolidate stakeholders' views and positions, and arrive at the final decision whether or not to finance the project. During this period, the initial idea is transformed into the choice of concept. This may take years, even decades in some mega-projects. The key stakeholder during the front-end phase is the commissioning party, who is supposedly attempting to arrive at what is considered the best choice of concept in dialogue, and sometimes in opposition, with other stakeholders. Decisions during the front-end phase will clearly have implications for planning and implementation of the project, but more so for its effect and utility. The management

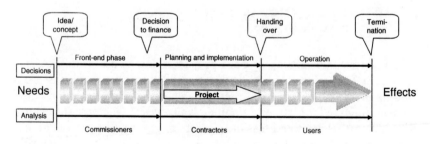

Figure 9.2   Decision and analysis throughout a project's life cycle

perspective is or at least should be secondary up front, and the focus should be on the justification and potential benefits from the anticipated project as seen in the operational perspective. Once this is agreed, subsequent decisions during the front-end phase will tend to have a more restricted effect on the choice of concept as such, but increasingly more on issues that have to do with budgeting, planning and implementation. This is bordering on and merging with what are termed project-management issues.

The implementation phase begins once the decision to finance is made, and includes detailed planning, mobilisation of resources and implementation, resulting in the delivery of the project's outputs. The main stakeholders are the contractors, while the commissioning party's involvement depends largely on the contractual arrangement. The contractors have a restricted view of the project: their motivation is to deliver the agreed outputs according to specifications and at the same time make a profit. For the contractor, the initial choice is of little significance; his responsibility is to implement whatever he is commissioned to.

The operational phase begins once the outputs have been delivered, set in operation or been used. The main stakeholders are therefore termed the users. Decision-makers at this stage are responsible for the operation and will have to make do with what has been produced, with limited possibilities to make strategic changes. The users are just the passengers on the ride, and detached from the foregoing decision processes without any possibility of influence.

In this theoretical model the three groups of decision-makers therefore have different interests and perspectives on the project. They operate in separate sequences without much interaction. Of course, there is a need for some sort of alignment of interests, and in many projects contractors and users may have possibilities to influence decisions during the front-end phase to a limited extent. In reality, there are all sorts of variations of projects and processes that complicate the theoretical case described above.

9.4 CHALLENGES, DECISIONS AND PERFORMANCE

One fundamental challenge in mega-projects is how to deal with problems such as tactical budgeting whereby responsible agencies at various levels tend to underestimate costs in order to increase the chance to obtain government funding for a project. Another challenge is to increase the chance that the most relevant and feasible project concept is chosen. Yet another challenge is to ensure a transparent and democratic process, and avoid adverse effects of stakeholders' involvement and political bargaining. To make the process predictable is also a major challenge since the front-end phase in public mega-projects commonly extends over at least one parliamentary election period. Challenges are abundant and complex. Many of the strategic performance problems facing public mega-projects can be interpreted in terms of deficiencies in the analytic or the political processes preceding the final decision to go ahead, and the interaction between analysts and decision-makers in this process. Below, the distinction is made between decisions to improve the project's tactical versus its strategic performance, and the five success factors or decision criteria mentioned above are applied.

Decisions Determining Tactical Performance

Here decision-makers are charged with the responsibility to secure efficient delivery of project outputs in terms of scope, quality, timing, budgetary compliance, etc. The point of departure is the commissioner's specifications and requirements, as well as the contractual obligations. The main challenge is to translate the specifications into a project design and implementation plan, which is realistically achievable in view of uncertainties that might affect the undertaking. These are project management issues and the tasks are thoroughly described, for instance, by the Project Management Institute in its 'Body of Knowledge' (PMI, 2005). It involves management of project integration, human resources, communications, procurement, design, planning, cost estimation, risk, etc. Although deficiencies in project management may have serious economic implications, the problems may still be marginal seen in a wider strategic perspective, as illustrated above. Examples are the cases of the national university hospital, and the onshore torpedo battery. We will not go further into such project management issues in this chapter.

Decisions Determining Strategic Performance

In order to succeed strategically, four of the five success criteria need to be satisfied, as mentioned above. The project's intended effect should be useful (*relevance*), the effect should be achieved in time (*effectiveness*), there should be no major negative effects (*impact*), and the positive effects should be sustained (*sustainability*). The main challenges for decision-makers are as set out below.

Ensuring that the project is *relevant* is essentially a question of aligning its objectives with needs and priorities that justify the undertaking on the one hand and what can realistically be expected as its effects on the other. This is often impossible. Take the regional aviation control centre as an example of a project that is not relevant. There was no need for the project, since technological development now allows for more accurate monitoring by satellites and computer processing of data. The system can now be more centralised. In fact, Norway, with its population of only four million, has as many as five air traffic control centres. The USA, in comparison, has only four. The regional centre was obviously redundant and should not have been built. This illustrates the point that relevance may change over time. The hydroelectric power projects, on the other hand, are relevant as long as there is a need and a market for electricity and it is used productively. This is clearly the case, and strongly so because alternative sources of energy are both more polluting and expensive.

The next challenge is to ensure that the project's objectives are realistically achievable, in other words, that the intended effect will be realised as planned (*effectiveness*). The issue here is to what extent objectives will be fulfilled given the resources available and the uncertainties facing the project. In purely rationalistic terms, a number of formal requirements have to be satisfied in the strategic design of a project. Objectives should be consistent in the sense of being linked logically in sequence and in parallel. They should be realistic in probabilistic terms; essential risks should be identified and considered. This type of logic- and probability-based analysis is often deficient. This was demonstrated in a study of 30 major Norwegian-funded international development projects that were all designed according to the same strategic format in order to ensure quality at entry. It was found that despite the considerable resources spent on strategic design, all projects had several major design flaws so that the designs were entirely inadequate as a basis for budgeting and planning. The weakest part of the design was the identification of contextual uncertainties that might affect the projects during implementation and operation (Samset et al., 2006).

Securing *sustainability* and avoiding adverse *impacts* is essentially a question of understanding the complexity of the contextual situation in which the project is implemented and operated. This includes its institutional setting, market demands and restrictions, stakeholders' needs and priorities, technological and environmental opportunities, and challenges. The task up front is one of making comprehensive analyses, identifying stakeholders, facilitating communication and involvement. Such activities may delay decision-making, but experience strongly suggests that this often is worthwhile in order to avoid some of the strategic problems encountered.

One huge paradox in front-end management of mega-projects is that these, even many of the public mega-projects, originate as a single idea without systematic scrutiny or consultation. Also, in too many cases, the initial idea will remain largely unchallenged and therefore survive and end up as the preferred concept – even in cases when it subsequently proves to be a strategic underperformer or failure. Improved front-end management is therefore likely to pay off if seen in a wider life-cycle perspective, as evidenced by the IMEC study (Miller and Lessard, 2000). There is much to be achieved by improving quality at entry at the earliest stage of the process. This requires that the initial ideas be challenged, for instance by analysis, extracting and making use of previous experience from similar undertakings, and involving stakeholders. The challenge is to ensure that projects are designed to respond to needs and priorities in society that might be valid throughout their lifetime, that their objectives are realistically achievable, that they are not likely to cause major negative impacts, and that their benefits can be sustained. Clearly, this is not simply a question of making a rational choice up front. The choice may not survive the unpredictable decision process that lies ahead. However, based on experience with such projects, one could assume that since the less rational choice seems to be able to survive, the rational concept might at least have the same ability.

9.5   PRINCIPLES FOR FRONT-END GOVERNANCE OF PROJECTS

Current reforms in public management aim to build effective and accountable institutions in the public sector and facilitate investment and initiatives in the private sector under what is termed good governance. Trends towards increased autonomy of public and private institutions have been followed by a corresponding trend to increase control measures and regulation. The regulatory features of such regimes may represent new restrictions and administrative challenges, in the stricter sense, with more agencies established in order to enforce regulations. In a less rigid sense, regimes are based on degrees of self-regulation with reference to publicly endorsed rules and standards.

The policy instruments available to the public in order to bring about such changes are not restricted to the use of regulations, but would also comprise economic means and information, as discussed by Bemelmans-Videc et al. (1998). The instruments can be either affirmative or negative. Regulations can be either prescriptive and provide rules to be followed, or proscriptive, specifying what is not allowed. Economic means can be either incentives, for instance in terms of benefits or refunding arrangements, or negative sanctions in terms of taxation or fees. Information can be either in terms of advice and encouragement giving guidance of what can be achieved and in which way, or in terms of warnings or description of pitfalls and possible adverse effects. One example is the World Bank's model to enhance state capability (World Bank, 2000), where the regulatory part is described in terms of rules and restraints, the economic part in terms of competitive pressure, and the information part in terms of public 'voice' and partnership.

Governance regimes for mega-projects comprise the processes and systems that need to be in place on the part of the financing party to ensure successful investments. This would typically include a regulatory framework to ensure adequate quality at entry, compliance with agreed objectives, management and resolution of issues that may arise during the project, and standards for quality review of key governance documents.

Miller and Hobbs (2005) have discussed the need for design criteria that should be brought to bear when developing a governance regime for a mega-project, in light of the complexity of such projects. Their assumption is that these would contrast with the traditional conception of governance as a static, binary, hierarchical process. Governance regimes for mega-projects are time-dependent and self-organising. Because the process is spread out over a long period of time, there is an opportunity to transform the governance structure as the project unfolds. Rather than thinking of the design of mega-project governance structures as a search for the one best structure, the design of such regimes can be thought of as a flexible strategic process that will draw on a variety of governance regimes to deal with different issues in different phases of the project life cycle.

Flyvbjerg et al. (2003) discuss ambitions, risk and effects in mega-projects based on a large sample of projects. The authors conclude that the problem with such projects is mainly one of risk-negligence and lack of accountability on the part of project promoters whose main ambition is to build projects for private gain, economical or political, not to operate projects for public benefit. Their suggested cure for what is termed the mega-project paradox is (1) that risk and accountability should be much more centrally placed in mega-project decision-making than is currently the case, (2) that regulations should be in place to ensure that risk analysis and risk management are carried out, (3) that the role of government should be shifted from involvement in project promotion to keeping it at arm's length and restricting its involvement in the formulation and auditing of public interest objectives to be met by the mega-project, and (4) that four basic instruments be employed to ensure accountability in decision-making: by (a) ensuring transparency, (b) specifying performance requirements, (c) making explicit rules regulating the construction and operations of the project, and finally (d) involving risk capital from private investors, the assumption being that their willingness to invest would be a sound test on the viability of the project up front.

9.6   A NORWEGIAN SCHEME TO IMPROVE FRONT-END GOVERNANCE OF MEGA-PROJECTS

One current initiative, or rather an experiment, to improve governance of mega-projects is the quality-at-entry regime that was introduced in 2000 by the Norwegian Ministry of Finance. The focus in the early stage of the regime was to improve budgetary compliance in public investment projects and avoid major cost overrun. From 2005 onwards, the regime was expanded to include quality assurance of the early choice of concept. The intention is to make sure that the right projects get started, and to dismiss unviable projects. In parallel, the ministry initiated a research programme designed to study the effects of the regime and focus on front-end management of public mega-projects, and to help improve the regime continuously.[2]

The Norwegian governance system was designed to improve analysis and decision-making in the front-end phase, and particularly the interaction between the two. One observation was that the necessary procedures for decision-making already existed; however, there were no binding rules that could ensure quality and consistency of analysis and decisions in combination. In a technocratic model for decision-making this would not be necessary. Here decision and analysis follow in a chronological sequence that would eventually lead to the selection and go-ahead of the preferred project without unforeseen interventions or conflicts, as illustrated in Figure 9.3. In reality, the process may to a larger degree resemble an anarchic process affected by various stakeholders, which is complex, less structured and unpredictable. Analysis may be biased or inadequate. Decisions may be affected more by political priorities than by rational analysis. Political priorities may change over time. Alliances and pressures from individuals or groups of stakeholders may change over time. The amount

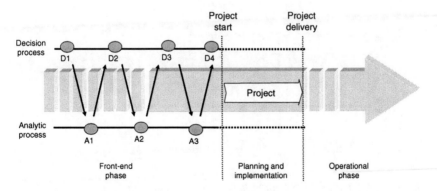

Figure 9.3   Model of technocratic decision-making up front in projects

of information is abundant and may be interpreted and used differently by different parties. The possibility for disinformation is considerable (see Chapter 5 in this book).

The response to these challenges would seem not to be a strict and comprehensive regulatory regime, but rather (1) to establish a distinct set of milestones and decision gates that would apply to mega-projects in all sectors regardless of existing practices and procedures in the different ministries or agencies involved; (2) to ensure political control with fundamental go/no-go decisions; (3) to ensure an adequate basis for decisions, and (4) to focus decisions on essential matters, not on the details. The answer seemed to be (1) to anchor the most essential decisions in the Cabinet; (2) to introduce a system for quality assurance of the basis for decisions that was independent of government and sufficiently competent; and finally, (3) to make sure that the governance regime was compatible with procedures and practices of the affected ministries and agencies.

Under what is termed the quality-at-entry regime, pre-qualified external consultants are assigned to perform quality assurance of the decision basis in all public mega-projects with a total budget exceeding some €60 million. During the first four years, this applied to some 50 projects where cost estimates and decision documents were scrutinised prior to Parliamentary appropriation of funds. Based on the experience gained, the regime was expanded in 2005 to include two separate quality assurance exercises in sequence, that is to secure the decision basis for (1) the choice of concept (QA1), and (2) the budget, management structure, and contract strategy for the chosen project alternative (QA2), as illustrated in Figure 9.4.

QA1 should help ensure that the choice of concept is subject to a political process of fair and rational choice. Since the choice of concept is a

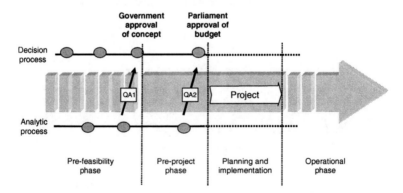

Figure 9.4   The Norwegian quality-at-entry regime for major public investment projects

political one, the consultants' role is restricted to reviewing the professional quality of underlying documents constituting the basis for decision. The decision is anchored in the Prime Minister's Office and will initiate a pre-project to analyse the feasibility of the chosen project. Responsible ministries are now required to explore at least two alternative concepts in addition to the zero alternative (doing nothing). They are supposed to prepare the following documents:

1. *Needs analysis*, which maps all stakeholders and affected parties and assesses the relevance of the anticipated investment in relation to their needs and priorities.
2. *Overall strategy*, which should specify on this basis consistent, realistic and verifiable immediate and long-term objectives.
3. *Overall requirements* to be fulfilled, for instance functional, aesthetic, physical, operational and economic requirements.
4. *Alternatives analysis*, which defines the zero option and at least two alternative concepts, specifying their operational objectives, essential uncertainties and cost estimates. The alternatives should be subjected to a full socioeconomic analysis (see Chapter 6 in this book).

QA2 is performed at the end of the pre-project phase, aimed to provide the responsible ministry with an independent review of decision documents before parliamentary appropriation of funds. This is partly a final control to make sure that the budget is realistic and reasonable, and partly a forward-looking exercise to identify managerial challenges ahead. The analysis should help substantiate the final decision regarding the funding of the project, and be useful during implementation as a reference for control. The focus is on the strategic management document, and the consultants will review its consistency with previous decisions when the concept was decided (QA1) as well as the implications for the project of changes that might have occurred afterwards, and the cost frame, including a necessary contingency to make sure that the budget is realistic.

9.7 DISCUSSION

The quality-at-entry regime is essentially a top-down regulatory scheme that was introduced to enforce a qualitative change in government practice and improve quality at entry of mega-investments. During its first four years it did not interfere with current procedures, but merely aimed to improve on existing documents that are an essential basis in the political decision process. The experience is that although the regime has been controversial, it has also been met with essentially constructive responses from the ministries and agencies involved, which have adopted their practices to meet the new quality requirements, and in some cases also adopted the scheme as a self-regulatory procedure.

This is possibly due to three factors: (1) the regime does not interfere with existing procedures for analysis or political decision-making, but merely aims to lift the professional standard of underlying documents; (2) it does not require altered procedures in the involved institutions; (3) the introduction of the scheme has been supported by establishing an arena for exchange of experience. This is in the sense of meetings at regular intervals headed by the Ministry of Finance, with representatives of involved ministries, agencies, consultants and researchers. This has facilitated openness and cooperation among the parties to discuss standards and practices and develop the scheme further.

Resistance to the scheme seems to be first and foremost rooted in the fact that it challenges the conclusions and professional judgement of the involved agencies, but also that it has given rise to increased attention and media debate about cost estimates and budgetary compliance in public mega-projects.

To date, six years after the scheme was introduced, only a few projects have been completed and it is therefore too early to evaluate its effects. The findings so far are that it has resulted in stochastic cost estimation being applied in all involved ministries and agencies. Over the first years it has been observed that differences in cost estimates between the ministries and the quality assurers have been reduced significantly. What effect this has on costs and cost efficiency cannot be determined at this early stage. Is it perhaps the effect of reduced cost estimates by the ministries or increased cost estimates by the consultants? The same goes for the effect on budgetary compliance. If the situation improves, is it the result of better cost estimates and cost control, or simply because budgets have increased? If the latter, the scheme will not have proved its value. What seems to be the case so far, however, is that there is an increased awareness in ministries and agencies about cost estimation, which might have a positive disciplining effect in the time to come.

The extended quality-at-entry regime, which was introduced in 2005, adds another dimension to the regulatory feature of the scheme, in that it anchors the decision regarding the choice of concept in the Prime Minister's Office. The reason for this is that the choice of concept is considered the single most important decision that will determine viability and utility of a project, and hence the extent to which public funds are being used effectively. Lifting the decision from the administrative to the political level provides a distance from narrow perspectives and professional biases. It also introduces authority, which is expected to have a trickle-down effect on professional conduct at ministry and agency levels. For these reasons, it is expected to be controversial. The response, somewhat surprisingly, seems to be rather coloured by an understanding that this is a sensible and logical step in the right direction, and that the hands-off approach is being appreciated.

One fundamental aspect of the governance regime is that at least three alternative concepts should be considered, and this should be done at an early stage when options are still open. The alternatives should have the same degree of specification, to help to make a fair assessment of alternatives. This has triggered a debate regarding what should be considered a concept. Should it be restricted to a distinction between different technical solutions to the same problem, for instance bridge versus tunnel in an infrastructure project for crossing a fjord, or should it be related to the differences in the combined effects of different projects in the broadest sense? Whatever the answer, since the regime has put this on the public agenda it could have an effect on analysts, politicians and the public in the time to come. This, and the emphasis on socioeconomic analysis, might prove significant in the aim to identify relevant alternative concepts and select viable project alternatives.

In terms of tactical cost underestimation up front, the government agency is now required to come up with a realistic preliminary cost estimate at an early stage, when alternative concepts are being considered. The fact that this estimate will be subjected to a second external review once the pre-study is completed could have a disciplining effect on analysts and help reduce large cost overrun, as we have seen in the past. But again, it is far too early to draw any lessons from this experiment.

Project governance has only recently become an issue in the project-management community. In order to move forwards in this field, numerous questions need to be answered: which are the current procedures applied in different countries and agencies – and what are their effects? What would it take to develop more effective governance regimes at international, government or corporate level to ensure maximum utility and return on investment for society and investors? What would be the optimal mix of regulations, economic means and information in improved governance regimes for mega-projects? What seems to be an issue for the project-management community is to lift their perspective beyond the delivery of the project itself and onto the broader issues of the project's utility and effects. An increased understanding and sensitivity in this area could be of mutual benefit to both the financing and the implementing parties.

NOTES

1. Quality at entry was used as an indicator to characterise the identification, preparation and appraisal process that the projects had been subjected to up front.
2. For further information, see www.concept.ntnu.no.

REFERENCES

Altshuler, Alan and David Luberoff (2003), *Mega-projects. The Changing Politics of Urban Public Investment*, Washington, DC: Brookings Institution Press/Lincoln Institute of Land Policy.
Bemelmans-Videc, M., R. Rist and E. Vedung (eds) (1998), *Carrots, Sticks, and Sermons: Policy Instruments and Their Evaluation*, New Brunswick, NJ: Transaction Publishers.
Flyvbjerg, Bent, Nils Bruzelius and Werner Rothengatter (2003), *Megaprojects and Risk: An Anatomy of Ambition*, Cambridge, MA: Cambridge University Press.
Miller, Roger and Brian Hobbs (2005), 'Governance regimes for large complex projects', University of Montreal, paper for the EURAM 2005 conference.
Miller, Roger and Donald R. Lessard (2000), *The Strategic Management of Large Engineering Projects: Shaping Institutions, Risk and Governance*, Cambridge, MA: MIT Press.
PMI (Project Management Institute) (2005), *A Guide to the Project Management Body of Knowledge* PMBOK® Guide, PMI.
Samset, Knut, Peder Berg and Ele J. Klakegg (2006), 'Front end governance of major public projects', paper presented at the annual European Academy of Management conference, Oslo.
World Bank (2000), *Reforming Public Institutions and Strengthening Governance: A World Bank Strategy*, Washington, DC: World Bank.

10. Public–private partnership and mega-projects

Joop Koppenjan

10.1 INTRODUCTION

Public–private partnership (PPP) in mega-projects has attracted increasing attention worldwide and is seen as a promise for the future (Pollit, 2002). It is often considered to be a third option for preparing and managing public infrastructure projects, in addition to traditional public project development and privatisation.

Traditional preparation and management of public projects consists in general of governments preparing the projects, contracting out the construction and taking care of the maintenance and operation themselves or contracting these out separately. Despite the popularity of PPP, this is still the dominant method of working in, for example, projects in the transport and water sector worldwide.

Although there are examples showing that public service provision is successful, for instance in the field of water management, it is often associated with government failure (Johnstone and Wood, 2001). Public decision-making stands for 'pork-barrel policies' in which public funds are channelled into lobbies of alliances of private company, public organisations and politicians, a selection of uneconomic projects and major budget overspending and time overruns (Bruzelius et al., 2002). The cost overspend of 84 per cent (£3.5 billion instead of the planned £1.9 billion) on the new Jubilee Line extension of the London Underground which was delivered in 2000, six years after the initially intended date, is a well-known example (Joosten, 2005). Public service provision is considered to involve poor quality and efficiency, inadequate innovation and, particularly in developing and transitional economies, low levels of cost coverage, neglect of poor sections of the population and clientism.

Privatisation of infrastructures has been realised worldwide in the telecommunication and energy sectors based on the idea that the market will provide more funds, greater efficiency, better service and more innovation. At the same time there is an increasing awareness that as a result of market failure certain goods and services will not be delivered, the area surrounding infrastructures will be burdened with negative side-effects such as noise and pollution, and other forms of nuisance, and opportunistic behaviour leads to higher prices, inadequate service provision and investments failing to materialise. Extensive regulation is needed in order to control these negative effects (Johnstone and Wood, 2001; Koppenjan and Enserink, 2005).

In areas where privatisation has remained limited up to now, such as in the transport and water sector, PPP is seen as a third option, by means of which it will be possible to avoid both public and market failures. The advantages of involving the private sector in public projects can be combined with the promotion and safeguarding of public values. For political reasons, however, in debates PPP may be positioned in somewhat different ways. In the UK, for instance, PPP is put forward by the Labour government as an alternative to privatisation, whereas in Australia PPP is viewed as a fullyfledged form of privatisation.

The Private Finance Initiative (PFI) model that was developed by the Conservative government in the UK in the early 1990s and taken up by Blair under the name public–private partnership appears to be developing into an important standard worldwide (Osborne, 2000; Pollit, 2002; Spackman, 2002). The UK continues to play a pioneering role in this. HM Treasury (2005) reports a commitment of £42.7 billion by the UK government for 667 PFI projects in 2004. Among other countries, Australia, the Netherlands and South Africa have set up programmes to follow this example.

The spread of PPP worldwide shows that the expectations are high: PPP is supposed to offer the opportunity to avoid government and market failures, and to combine the strong points of public and private involvement, making it a 'marriage made in heaven' (Hodge and Greve, 2005). However, PPP also has a host of critics who think that the construction and management of essential public infrastructures and the public service provision linked with it cannot be trusted to private parties. In the view of these critics, PPP stands for 'problem, problem, problem' (Bowman, 2000).

Given the increasing relevance of PPP for public infrastructural projects, we present an overview of the experiences with regard to this phenomenon in this chapter. We will investigate to what extent PPP lives up to expectations: is it a 'marriage made in heaven' or does PPP in practice stand for 'problem, problem, problem'?

Given the scope of this contribution, we are not able to provide a comprehensive overview of all PPP applications in major public infrastructural projects worldwide. We concentrate in particular on PFI-like arrangements in the transport and water sectors. First of all we will discuss what PPP is about, why PPP is introduced and which PPP models are most commonly used (Section 10.2). We then outline the state of the art of the application of PPP in practice: are the ambitions that underlie the choice of PPP realised (Section 10.3)? After that we discuss a number of typical problems that occur in PPP processes which will have to be dealt with in order to make PPP schemes work (Section 10.4). Finally, Section 10.5 summarises lessons regarding the conditions for successful PPP in mega-projects.

10.2 WHAT PPP IS ABOUT: DEFINITIONS, MOTIVES AND FORMS

The term PPP is used in a catch-all way to denote a large number of relationships between the public sector and the private sector (Whettenhall, 2003). Nevertheless there is a certain consensus about what the term does and does not include.

What's in a Name? Defining PPP

Broadly speaking, a PPP project is understood to be a project in which private parties on the basis of long-term contracts or arrangements are involved in the design, building, maintenance and/or operation of a public infrastructure, and co-finance it (Li and Akintoye, 2003; Spackman, 2002). Forms of innovative contracting such as design and construct, and design, construct and maintenance are not usually seen as PPP; in PPP private parties are expected to take on responsibility with regard to the financing of the project (Van Ham and Koppenjan, 2002).

Motives for PPP: Realising Value for Money

Governments strive for PPP because they think the building and operation of infrastructural projects according to this formula is cheaper, faster and better. The following benefits of PPP are expected (HM Treasury, 1993; Ministerie van Financiën, 1998; Spackman, 2002):

1. *Attracting private investment* Investment in infrastructure is an expensive business and governments' wish lists are long. These desires concern both new infrastructure and the upgrading of existing infrastructure. Public funds are too limited to realise all these desires. By means of PPP, efforts are made to attract private money in order to enable these investments. Under EU financial policy European countries see PPP as an opportunity to realise infrastructural projects

without growing budget deficits, enabling them to meet the requirements of the EU budget policy (Pollit, 2002; Johnstone and Wood,
2001).

2. *More value for money (VfM)*   Private companies are supposed to work
   more cost-consciously and efficiently than the public sector. Moreover,
   with PPP contracts various project components such as design, building, maintenance and realisation are contracted out jointly. Since
   private parties are able to coordinate these phases, design optimisations
   are possible which lead to better quality and efficiency returns.
   Ultimately, the same project can thus be delivered for less money, or
   higher quality can be achieved for the same money. The chances of
   overspend in terms of time and budget decrease, too, because private
   parties are better at project management and contracts discourage
   modifications during the project (Pollit, 2002; Spackman, 2002).

3. *Promoting innovation*   By involving private parties and particularly
   major, international players, in public projects, expertise is tapped
   which governments themselves do not have at their disposal so that
   innovative solutions become possible. Innovations can lead to design
   optimisations with efficiency returns, but also to redefinitions of the
   scope and content of projects, thus increasing its societal value
   (Koppenjan, 2005).

4. *Better decision-making and project management*   Private involvement is
   considered to improve the decision-making on infrastructure because it
   forces the government to clearly delimit and define the project beforehand. PPP also limits the informal lobby activities of private parties
   because they are expected to participate in the risk-bearing. The
   chances of over-optimistic estimates of returns and costs and the selection of uneconomic projects – characteristics of public decision-making
   – decrease, since private financial institutions will monitor the quality
   of investments and project management (Bruzelius et al., 2002).

Forms of PPP: an Overview of Contractual Arrangements

Forms of PPP can be classified according to the extent to which tasks, risks
and responsibilities of former public service provision are transferred to the
private partner (Bennet and Grohmann, 2000; Akintoye and Beck, 2003;
Walker and Smith, 1995). In the literature a wide variety of classifications is
used. Figure 10.1 gives an overview of three frequently used categories of
PPPs. These three models of public sector involvement are elaborated below.

1. *Operation, maintenance and service contracts*   The private sector must
   perform the service for the agreed costs and must meet performance

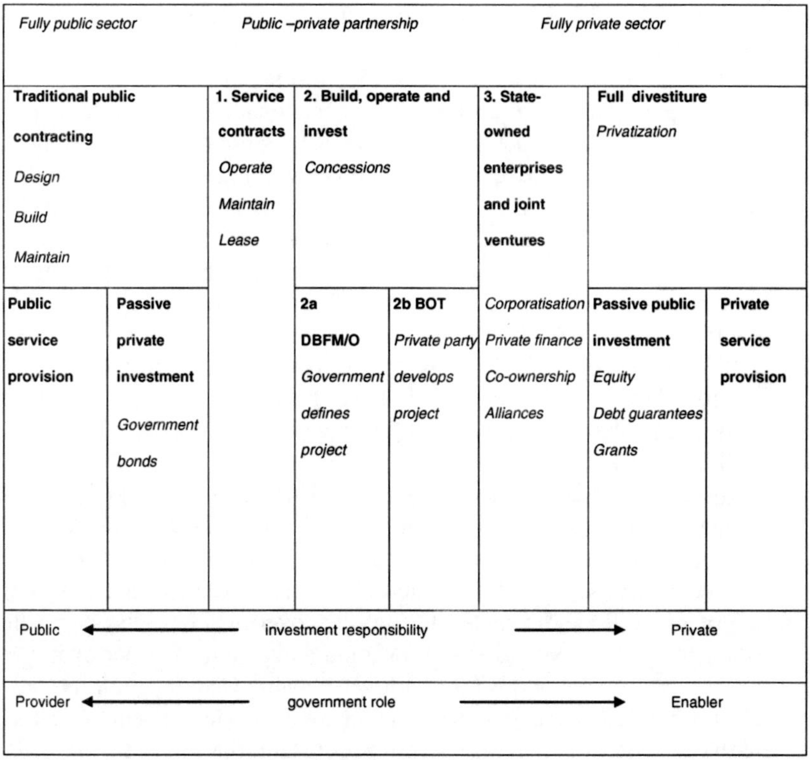

Fully public sector		Public –private partnership			Fully private sector	
Traditional public contracting *Design* *Build* *Maintain*		**1. Service contracts** *Operate* *Maintain* *Lease*	**2. Build, operate and invest** *Concessions*		**3. State-owned enterprises and joint ventures**	**Full divestiture** *Privatization*
Public service provision	**Passive private investment** *Government bonds*		**2a** **DBFM/O** *Government defines project*	**2b BOT** *Private party develops project*	*Corporatisation* *Private finance* *Co-ownership* *Alliances*	**Passive public investment** *Equity* *Debt guarantees* *Grants*	**Private service provision**

Public ⟵————— investment responsibility —————⟶ Private

Provider ⟵————— government role —————⟶ Enabler

Source: Adapted from Bennet and Grohmann (2000).

Figure 10.1   A spectrum of PPP models

standards set by government. Government is responsible for funding any capital investments. These contracts do not solve the problem of limited public budgets, although private parties will have to pay for their concessions, depending upon the possibilities for cost recovery and profit. Transfer–operate–transfer (TOT) arrangements, for example, mean that government-constructed facilities are leased to a private operator who pays a lump sum that makes it possible for government to invest in a new facility (Chang et al., 2003). Operation, maintenance and service contracts lead to greater efficiency. Improvements are limited, however, by the government's ability to provide capital investments and to monitor performance. Chang et al. (2003) suggest that operation and maintenance contracts (such as those applied for sewage treatment plants in Long Tian and Sha Tian townships of Shenzhen City) may be best for cities where facilities have already been constructed. The aim is not to attract private investments but to increase efficiency. This may lead to savings that will lower subsidies and tariffs.

2. *Build, operate and transfer* (BOT) These forms bring private investments into the construction of new infrastructure or the upgrading of existing infrastructure. Combining construction and operation makes design optimisations possible. Because private parties accept financial responsibilities, they become receptive to financial incentives provided by government. Private parties may receive government payments or user payment, depending on the kind of contract involved. Concession contracts (e.g. design, build, finance, maintain and/or operate – DBFM/O) are publicly developed projects, for which consortia of contractors, financers and operators have to be found to realise them. This is the model that is known as PFI (Private Finance Initiative) in the UK (Pollit, 2002).

In these contracts up-front financing from private parties is needed to pay for the construction of the project. They can then recover the costs on this investment through a 'user-pay' system in which users have to pay for the use of the infrastructure or the service provided or, if that is not possible or desirable, through a 'government-pay' system: the government then pays a one-off or annual availability or performance fee. An example of this is the shadow toll, which can be put into operation when toll charging is not possible owing to the existence of alternative connections or legislation preventing the charging of tolls. Depending on whether the contractor has borne the cost of realising the infrastructure and is able to recover the costs on this investment at a profit, this party pays for the concession. If excess profits are anticipated, benefit-sharing arrangements between government and private parties can be entered into. Furthermore, contracts can contain bonus and penalty provisions in order to ensure that there are incentives for the private party to continue to perform during the building, maintenance and/or operation phases.

DBFM/O contracts require that governments have the expertise and regulatory capacity to develop viable projects and manage complex contracts. If this expertise and capacity are not available, as is the situation in many developing countries and countries with economies in transition, the build, (own,) operate and transfer (BO(O)T) model may be an alternative. If this model is used, private parties are responsible for the development of the project. The ownership of the project remains with the government. After an agreed period for operation, in which private parties have to recover their investment costs, the project is then transferred to government. Sometimes also the ownership is in the hands of the private parties during the concession period (BOOT contracts). Fully fledged concessions such as those used for water supply in Manila may result in increased service delivery, which is of great value to poorer households (Johnstone and Wood, 2001).

3. *State-owned enterprises and joint ventures*   Governments may decide to incorporate the realisation and/or operating of an infrastructure project in a special-purpose vehicle (SPV), a private-law body whose shares are entirely in the hands of the government. The advantage of this is that it places the project development and operational management at arm's length from the political sphere so that it can occur in a business-like way. A state-owned enterprise (SOE) of this type can be financed with public funds, which can subsequently be recovered via toll charges. This is the mode of operation used in the realisation of the multi-billion euro projects at Great Belt (a toll bridge in Denmark) and the Oeresund (the combined rail and road link comprising a tunnel and bridge between Denmark and Sweden) and the – less costly – Westerscheldt Tunnel in the Netherlands. Bruzelius et al. (2002) advocate that SOEs of this type should be forced to attract private financing because private control mechanisms would thus be activated which better ensure the cost-effectiveness and control of the project.

Joint ventures are SPVs in which both government and private parties invest. This model makes it possible for both parties to cooperate intensively during some or all phases of infrastructure development and operation. This model, sometimes referred to as 'alliance model' or 'institutional PPP', to more clearly distinguish it from the 'concession model' or 'contractual PPP', is particularly suited to complex, innovative and uncertain projects that cannot be precisely defined beforehand (Van Ham and Koppenjan, 2002; EU, 2004). By sharing risks, costs and benefits, it becomes possible to develop and operate these projects jointly and to realise innovative infrastructures and services. Some authors consider this arrangement to provide the conditions for real partnerships, enhancing the intensive forms of collaboration needed to develop the high-quality infrastructures which the current complex network society demands. Concession contracts in their opinion do not add much to genuine outsourcing arrangements (Klijn et al., 2007).

These three forms of PPP differ in the extent to which (commercial) risks are transferred from the public to the private sector (Bennet and Grohmann, 2000). In addition, they place increasing demands on the skills and capacities of the public procuring agency responsible for designing and managing the contract. The choice of the PPP model therefore is contingent upon both the nature of the project and the regulatory capacity of government.

10.3 EXPERIENCES WITH PPP: DOES IT LIVE UP TO EXPECTATIONS?

To what extent did PPP in mega-projects live up to expectations regarding the realisation of private investments, value for money, innovation and better decision-making?

Are Private Investments Realised?

Experiences in several countries, and especially the UK and the Netherlands, show that it is hard to get PPP projects off the ground. In the UK the first initiatives date from the 1980s, but only from the middle of the 1990s onwards did the number of PFIs increase, due to efforts of the Treasury and the establishment of specific units within government promoting PFI. Pollit (2002) cites the example of the Channel Tunnel Rail Link (the link between the Channel Tunnel and London) and the Skye Bridge (a PFI toll bridge in Scotland) (NAO, 1997). In 2004 there were 667 signed PFI schemes in the UK with a total capital value of £42.7 billion. Half of the projects by value were transport projects (HM Treasury, 2005). In the Netherlands from 1998 onwards a large number of PPP initiatives were taken, but the number of PPP contracts that are actually signed remain rather limited, although the Ministries of Finance and Transport are committed to PPP. More common are partnerships in the form of formal or informal alliances, for instance in city revitalisation projects (Klijn et al., 2007). In Denmark PPP is not developing due to the adverse attitude of the Ministry of Finance. The public funding of projects is considered to be cheaper and more appropriate. Overall one can conclude that PPP needs active promotion and specific government units and regulations in order to be accepted as an alternative to the traditional public preparation and management of infrastructural projects.

Nevertheless, in the area of transportation and water management worldwide, some governments do succeed in attracting private capital and thus in realising projects that, without private money, would be considerably delayed or would not be realised at all. Boxes 10.1 and 10.2 give an overview of the PPPs in these two areas.

BOX 10.1   THE USE OF PPPs IN TRANSPORT PROJECTS

In Europe, Spain and France are known for their extensive network of toll roads, built and operated by private companies. However, the ownership of many of these companies has passed over to government, since the private companies that originally built the roads performed poorly as operators (Flyvbjerg et al., 2003). Only recently in France has reprivatisation been considered. Currently, the UK, Spain, Portugal, Finland and the Netherlands have advanced PFI arrangements. In Portugal, BOT arrangements have been used since the early 1990s. Economic growth resulted in an increased demand for basic infrastructure such as motorways, bridges, railways and pipelines. PPP was pursued in order to get private investment. In Finland, the first DBFO project, the Lathi Motorway, was started in 1997 (Akintoye and Beck, 2003). In Germany, about 12 road projects and one railway project were financed by DBFO schemes, involving DM 4.6 billion (Flyvbjerg et al., 2003). As mentioned in the introduction, Australia and South Africa are also committed to PFI programmes. Australia is expected to realise A$20 billion on PPP projects during the period 2002–7 (Gray, 2002).

In the USA and Canada, PPP has mainly developed at the county and municipal level, especially in the fields of public schools, welfare programmes, inner-city redevelopment and wastewater treatment operation. In California, four toll roads have been realised by BOT schemes, without state or federal funds (total value $2.5 billion). Since the mid-1990s Canada has selectively applied PPP (in Canada: P3) to large infrastructure projects in Nova Scotia (Akintoye and Beck, 2003).

In the developing world there is a strong regional concentration of PPP in Latin America and South East Asia. In Mexico, development franchises were tendered for the construction of 5400 km of motorway in the period between 1984 and 1994.

In Asia, BOT-like schemes have been used in China, Thailand, the Philippines, Malaysia, Vietnam, Korea and Japan (Akintoye and Beck, 2003). The BOT contracts in Hong Kong have been significant sources of inspiration. The first major BOT project was the Cross Harbour Tunnel (CHT) under Victoria Harbour which links Hong Kong Island with Kowloon. The building of the project started in 1969 and cost US$56 million. The CHT has been successfully operated since then, and four further tunnels have been realised in this way. All these projects had a concession period of 30 years in which the investors will need to recoup their costs by means of toll charges (Kumaraswamy and Zhang, 2001).

BOX 10.2   THE USE OF PPPs IN THE AREA OF
           DRINKING-WATER SUPPLY AND
           WASTEWATER MANAGEMENT

Haarmeyer and Coy (2002) provide an overview of projects in the field of drinking-water supply and wastewater management over the whole world, and show that although public service provision remains dominant in this sector, in numerous countries projects are being realised under PPP. Whereas in the UK water and sewerage are privatised, France and Spain are using long-term concessions. In the Netherlands sale-and-leaseback constructions were popular during the 1990s since tax rules made them financially attractive. Recently a large wastewater treatment facility in Delfland has been realised, using a DBFM concession of 30 years (Expertise Centrum PPS, 2004). In the Eastern European capitals of Sofia and Bucharest, 25-year concessions have been issued by means of a public tendering process for the operation and improvement of extensive drinking-water and wastewater systems. In China, Vietnam, Korea, the Philippines and Thailand, too, important BOT and BOOT contracts have recently been entered into with regard to drinking-water supply and wastewater treatment. In South America, many BO(O)T projects in this area have been delivered, with Argentina in the forefront: 70 per cent of the drinking-water supply is controlled by private providers. In the USA, 85 per cent of the drinking-water supply and 95 per cent of the wastewater treatment is in public hands. In the coming years, however, huge investments are needed to meet the increasingly stringent requirements that are being imposed on drinking water and wastewater (Haarmeyer and Coy, 2002; see also Johnson and Moore, 2002).

Although there are many infrastructural projects for which private financing has been found, there is also a great deal of evidence that governments find it difficult to introduce PPP as a new institutional practice. In addition, it is important to note that PPP does not guarantee private investments. In their evaluation of 76 North American PPP projects, Boardman et al. (2005) state that substantial private investment was realised in less than half of these projects. Five projects in the field of transport, drinking-water supply and waste processing were fiascos, with private parties wanting to be fully compensated for commercial risks and threatening bankruptcy to prevent losses, while the public authorities did their utmost to ensure that the projects were continued.

Some authors point out that many PPP contracts such as DBFM and DBFO chiefly concern pre-financing. PPP involves either the purchase of infrastructure through users' credit cards, or the introduction of a mechanism whereby a one-off public capital expenditure is replaced by a series of small, annual expenditures (Hodge and Greve, 2005). Especially with regard to PFI schemes, the emphasis on generating new private investments recently seems to have lost importance in favour of the other PPP advantages (Klijn et al., 2007). In developing countries, generating private investments obviously remains an important motive.

Is Value for Money Realised?

Do PPP schemes deliver better value for money than publicly developed and managed infrastructural projects?

Hall (1998) examined a number of early PFI projects in the UK and ascertained that in road projects and prison projects considerable savings had been achieved. Although calculations were surrounded by uncertainty, he found that there were nevertheless 'some grounds for optimism'. Moreover, an analysis of 29 PFI projects commissioned by the Treasury Task Force identified efficiency advantages of 17 per cent with respect to the public sector comparator (Arthur Andersen and Enterprise LSE, 2000). In 1999, the National Audit Office (NAO) examined ten PFI projects and found that in every project the best offer had been selected, and in eight out of ten cases good value for money was achieved. The NAO reported a 10 to 20 per cent efficiency return on seven projects (NAO, 1999). An influential report from the Institute for Public Policy Research (IPPR, 2001) concluded that PFI had been successfully applied in road construction and prisons; but was less successful in delivering hospitals and schools. Mott Macdonald (2002) and the NAO (2003) found that PPP delivers on time far more often than infrastructure projects realised with public funding. Pollit (2005) finds this too: projects under PFI 'are [now] delivered on time and to budget a significantly higher percentage of the time'.

Hodge (2005) examined 48 Australian projects, three of them in depth, and found that these projects were well managed from a commercial point of view. By means of a 34-year BOT concession, the A\$2.1 billion City Link project in Melbourne was contracted out, whereby risks were successfully transfered and value for money was achieved. With regard to PPP in human service contracting in the USA, Martin (2005) found a significant improvement in contractor performance thanks to the use of performance-based incentives. In the Netherlands, the conversion of a regional road into

Planning and decision-making

a motorway (the A59) by means of a PPP arrangement underlined the potential of performance-based incentives.

However, the assessment of PPP as successful in realising value for money and improved project management is not unchallenged. Although some PPP projects were successful and delivered value for money, others did not. The Skye Bridge in Scotland, which opened in 1993, turned out to be more expensive than if it had been realised with public funding. In the Netherlands the PPP road tunnels which were built in the early 1990s proved to be more expensive than public construction too. In the UK, PPP did not deliver value for money in the case of hospitals and schools (IPPR, 2001; NAO, 2003).

What is more, the methods used for calculating value for money – the Public Private Comparator (PPC) and the Public Sector Comparator (PSC) – are heavily criticised. Hall (1998) states with respect to his positive findings that the furnishing of proof is weak because an accurate and non-controversial public-sector comparator is lacking. The complex contracts are surrounded by uncertainties and, in addition, the outcomes of long-term contracts are always uncertain. Moreover, data may have been adjusted because it was politically advantageous to imply efficiency returns. Shaoul (2005) mentions manipulation of the PSC process. In the Dutch High Speed Rail Link project and the N31 road project the assumptions used in conducting these studies were chosen in such a way as to justify the choice of PPP (TCI, 2004; Buck, 2004). Bloomfield et al. (1998) mention a lease contract at a correctional facility in Massachusetts of a 7.4 per cent more expensive deal than using conventional financing, disguised by 'inflated sales pitches'. Fitzgerald (2004) shows with regard to eight PPP projects in Victoria, Australia, that the finding of value for money is highly sensitive to the choice of the discount rate. If this were set at 5.7 instead of at 8.65 per cent, the outcomes would be reversed. With regard to four early PFI road projects in the UK, the NAO (1998) determined that an inappropriate discount rate was used. Ultimately it appeared that public construction would have been cheaper. Even more uncertainties are involved in the use of the PPC and the PSC; for example, the question of to what extent costs, benefits and risks have been included in the calculations. Boardman et al. (2005) examined 76 major 'P3' projects in North America and ascertained that it is difficult to take account of the transaction costs of PPP projects – which can be high – when making a comparison with traditional public implementation.

These latter observations show that it is difficult to conclude beyond any doubt that PPP schemes deliver better value for money. As far as they do, it is clear that this depends on the specific circumstances of projects and policy areas. Following the reasoning of Pollit (2002), we can conclude that in some policy areas and some countries, parties involved seem to have gone through a learning circle by which they have gradually succeeded in mastering the PPP process, while others still have not.

Do PPP Schemes Result in Innovation?

Do PPP projects result in more innovation than public projects? Pollit (2002) ascertains that substantial innovation is realised both with respect of the physical assets of projects as well as in governance methods, contract forms and financial constructions.

However, some authors state that the potentials of PPP with regard to innovations are not fully realised, due to the preference for PFI-type contracts in which the government defines the project in advance and draws up clear specifications for design. Within the constraints which then apply, the design scope for private parties is limited to design optimisations. For more innovative contributions, a collaborative development process is necessary for which joint ventures are more appropriate (Klijn et al., 2007; Van Ham and Koppenjan, 2002).

Within PFI contracts the design scope is often further limited because the specifications for design are not formulated at the level of functional requirements and parties endeavour to exclude all risks by means of detailed contracts. This trend is reinforced by the fact that both public and private parties do not yet have the skills needed for PPP. For example, the project organisation that led the procurement process for the Dutch High Speed Rail Link project until far into the contract negotiations was geared towards the conventional tendering of projects. Content-driven expertise dominated and detailed referential designs were used.

Moreover, it appears that the participation in the tendering process of foreign companies, from whom innovation is anticipated, is often disappointing. For instance, in the Dutch High Speed Line project foreign companies participated only in two of the ten contracts involved. Companies find it difficult to meet the legislation and regulations of countries that are unfamiliar to them. Also, national governments and industries do not warmly welcome foreign companies to their national markets (TCI, 2004).

To sum up, in some PPP projects innovations are realised. In other projects they are prohibited by inflexible procurement procedures and the use of detailed rather than functional requirements. PFI-like contracts restrict innovation to design optimisations. These contracts leave little room for improvements with regard to the content and scope of projects, since the PFI approach implies that projects are defined up front by government without private involvement.

Does PPP Improve the Quality of Decision-making and Project Management?

Do PPP schemes contribute to better decision-making on infrastructural projects and fewer budget and time overruns?

PFI indeed seems to encourage governments to clearly define performance requirements and to introduce financial penalties for failure to perform. Since private parties carry financial risks, it is more likely that projects will start on time and meet requirements because the contractor does not get paid until he delivers. Furthermore, PPP brings in private management skills, innovative design and risk management expertise, conditions for better decision-making and better project management (Klijn et al., 2007).

On the other hand, there are examples of governments and private companies engaging in PPP schemes without clear up-front project definitions or realistic assumptions and calculations. In the Netherlands, privatisation did not appear to have a disciplining influence on the planning processes pertaining to the three major rail projects in which PPP was applied, i.e. the High Speed Rail Link, the Betuwe Link and the Zuiderzee Link. On the contrary, the argument that private parties would want to co-finance was used to convince Parliament that the projects were socially profitable. Furthermore, private parties do not always base their decision to participate on rational arguments either. For example, in promoting the construction of the Zuiderzee Link in the Netherlands, Siemens aimed at bringing its maglev technique into practice even though the project was commercially uneconomic (TCI, 2004).

The quality of decision-making seems to be threatened by problems with regard to transparency, accountability and democratic legitimacy. Walker and Walker (2000) criticise the 'off-balance sheet PPP infrastructure deals' as misleading accounting trickery. In addition, they criticise the high returns on investments of private parties in the Sydney Airlink BOOT project, in which the private consortium anticipates a profit of 21 to 25 per cent while the government is fobbed off with 2 per cent. In the case of Sydney's M2 Motorway, private investors achieved a pre-tax return on investment of 24.4 per cent. They are of the opinion that under PPP, accountability towards Parliament and the public is rendered difficult. Johnston and Romzek (2005) find the same thing with regard to short-term service contracts in North American water projects. Hodge (2005), too, ascertains in the Australian projects studied that arrangements are non-transparent, the government for political reasons presses ahead with the hurried construction of projects, and seems keener to protect the interests of the private investors than public interests or the interests of the citizens. In the Melbourne City Link BOT contract, which was successful in terms of value for money, Parliament was hardly involved; the project is problematic from the point of view of transparency and legitimacy. Other authors also mention high deal complexity and low PPP transparency, resulting in accountability problems (Fitzgerald, 2004; Hodge and Greve, 2005).

To sum up, PPP may contribute to better decision-making and project management, but this is not guaranteed. PPP even introduces new challenges with respect to transparancy, accountability and democratic legitimacy.

Lessons from Mixed PPP Experiences

It is difficult to pass an overall judgement on the success or failure of PPP as a method of working. Successes appear to lie chiefly in the sphere of effectiveness (private investments; value for money, improved project management and innovation). The problems arise especially in the sphere of transparency, legitimacy and accountability. But owing to the complexity of projects and contracts, the uncertainties with which they are surrounded and the limitations of the assessment methods used, the successes are not unquestioned. As far as they hold, they are closely bound up with the skills that governments have managed to develop in specific policy areas with regard to the procurement process and contract management.

10.4   ISSUES IN THE FORMATION AND OPERATION OF PPP PROJECTS

It does not seem wise to go further into the endless debate on the success or failure of PPP, and the highly normative and therefore unsolvable question of whether governments should engage in PPP or not. Since PPP is a practice that is adopted in a growing number of countries, it seems wiser to address the question of what typical problems parties face when engaging in PPP processes. In doing so, we may identify some of the critical conditions that influence the success or failure of PPP and that must be addressed in order to reduce the chance of failures or disadvantages, and to improve the quality of the development and management of PPP projects in practice.

Issues in the Formation of PPP Projects

Since currently a reasonable number of PPP contracts have been concluded, the international literature on PPP provides us with a fairly good account of the typical issues that parties involved face in the formation phase of PPPs.

Chaotic and lengthy procurement processes

The procurement processes by which PPPs are brought about are characterised by lengthy, erratic contract negotiations among a small number of
bidders, and considerable cost inflation during the bidding process, resulting
in questionable risk properties. In the UK this pattern has been found in, for
instance, road projects and the London Underground, and in the High Speed
Rail Link and the A59 and N31 road projects in the Netherlands (NAO,
1998; 1999; 2003; Joosten, 2005; Koppenjan and Leijten, 2005).

In the design and construct and DFBM contracts for the High Speed Rail
Link, for instance, the private bids were between 43 and 80 per cent higher
than anticipated. What followed were improvised, chaotic negotiations
aimed at driving the bids down via cutbacks and the taking back of risks
(TCI, 2004). Governments' determination to develop PPP contracts puts
them in a weak negotiating position compared to private parties, running the
risk of entering into complex contracts which they don't fully comprehend
and ending up taking back risks that they originally wanted to transfer.

High transaction costs

The transaction costs of PPP deals appear to be high for both government
and private parties. Governments are often forced to hire external expertise
at high rates (Pollit, 2002). In the Dutch High Speed Rail Link project,
foreign consultants received over €45 million. Due to the project-based
application of PPP, learning effects with regard to PPP are often not institutionalised within standing organisations and may easily get lost after the
project is finished. Knowledge management aimed at institutionalising
learning effects is an important strategy in trying to reduce transaction
costs.

Companies complain about the costs they have to incur for bids while not
knowing if they will be remunerated. These experiences lead to pleas for a
reduction in the number of parties who are allowed to make bids, private
parties being reimbursed for their design expenses and the standardisation
of procedures and contracts (TCI, 2004; Buck, 2004). Each of these solutions has institutional implications and drawbacks. So at this point is is far
from clear how they should or could be brought into practice.

Lack of competition

PPP presupposes competitive tendering to stimulate private parties to
produce their best bids. Open tenders, or at least competitive dialogues,
should prevent 'shotgun marriages' and 'sweetheart arrangements'. This
requirement also implies that competition between (consortia of) banks,
constructing firms and service providers exists. The practice of PPP
shows in many cases a remarkable lack of competition, governments often

creating legal monopolies in favour of their private partners (EU, 2004; Koppenjan and Enserink, 2005).

For instance, the tender procedure for the Dutch High Speed Rail Link was started at a time when there were already many major infrastructural project under construction. Constructing firms had little capacity available and the prices of building materials were high. The competition was further limited by the scale of the project: only a small number of large firms were capable of doing the job. Collusion on the side of the firms, leading to illegal agreements on the height of the bids and the division of the market, reduced competition even further (TCI, 2004).

Late involvement of private parties

The earlier private parties are involved, the greater the chance that innovative contributions will be delivered. In practice, however, it appears to be difficult to achieve this early involvement. The preference for PFI-type contracts in which governments define projects up front restricts the possibilities for private parties to participate in early project stages. The market consultations governments use to involve private parties in early project stages are highly voluntary by nature and there are disincentives for private parties to invest in these activities. The tendering policies of governments, and especially those of the EU, even deter early involvement because it might lead to exclusion from the competitive tendering process.

Strategic use of PCC and PSC

In theory, the choice of PPP is made dependent on the added value which this method of working has compared to traditional, public project preparation. In the UK a converse burden of proof is used: the public scenario is only raised after it has become apparent that PPP does not deliver more value for money. The PCC and the PSC are used to determine this (Pollit, 2002). As argued in Section 10.3, evaluation research has shown that the outcomes of these instruments are not rock-solid but vary according to the assumptions used. The PCC and PSC are often used to legitimise the choice of PPP. This does not mean that these instruments could not play a useful role in the development of PPP, however. De Bruijn and Leijten (2004) suggest that although the outcomes of these instruments are not reliable enough to be used to underpin decisions regarding the use of PPP, they do offer governments information that can be used as a starting point in the negotiation process with private parties.

Dealing with representative bodies and stakeholders

PPP schemes for major infrastructural projects result in high complexity and low transparency. This leads to accountability problems: representative bodies such as parliaments or municipal and provincial councils are scarcely involved and have difficulty in understanding and exerting control over PPP schemes. Careful coordination between the project and representative bodies – before, during and after the conclusion of contract negotiations – is highly important. Of course Parliament will claim the right to take the final decision on the project. Uncertainty for contract partners cannot be eliminated. At most, parties can make agreements about how they will deal with any changes to their contractually agreed relations (De Bruijn and Leijten, 2004). In addition, the lack of transparancy and legitimacy also raises the question of how stakeholders can be involved in PPP projects. There are examples of PPP projects that were quite succesful in this respect (Van Ham and Koppenjan, 2002).

Issues in the Contract Implementation Phase of PPP

The track record with regard to the implementation of PPP contracts, which often have a duration of 25 or even 30 years, is limited. Most of the recent proclaimed PPP victories refer to contract closure or at best to the finalisation of the construction phase. It remains to be seen which issues will arise during the contract implementation phase and whether parties are equipped and capable of handling these. This depends on the content and quality of the contract. The contract should for instance include conditions that further a proper transfer of the project at the end of the contract period

But since contracts almost by definition will be incomplete, this is not enough. Governments need to organise the regulation and management of the PPP contract. Furthermore, due to the long contract periods, it is clear that PPP schemes will be vulnerable to changing conditions in the environment of the project (e.g. technologies, physical environment, economy, policies) which may jeopardise the public interest involved as well as private parties' return on investments. International accounts of the implementation of PPP contracts suggest that the parties may expect the following problems (Koppenjan and Enserink, 2005).

Ex-post **contract dependence: strategic behaviour**
Long-term contracts and arrangements between government and private parties frequently create private monopolies. These evoke typical forms of strategic or opportunistic behaviour by private concessionaires: raising charges, reducing the quality of the service provision, cutting down on maintenance, and avoiding investments in uneconomic project components ('cherry-picking'). In the Netherlands, for example in urban development projects, it turns out to be difficult to get private parties to invest in public

project components such as parks, public transport and road infrastructure (Koppenjan and Enserink, 2005). One way out of this problem is to prevent parties from raking in their profits too soon. For example, the contract with the private infrastructure provider for the London Underground requires that during the first years of the contract, period investments only are made; cost recovery can only occur later (Joosten, 2005; NAO, 2004).

Renegotiating contracts: adapting to circumstances or hold-up?

In water concessions in South America the renegotiations by means of which private providers try to get out of their contractual obligations to connect poorer districts to their physical networks are notorious (Johnstone and Wood, 2001). This is an example of the 'hold-up' phenomenon. If one of the two parties has made asset-specific investments, asymmetrical dependence relations develop, allowing the other party to change contract conditions to his advantage. In addition, private parties can threaten bankruptcy or actively aim for it. Since the government ultimately has an interest in a completed project which will be operated properly, it will feel compelled to intervene in order to save the project. The course of events regarding the bankruptcy of the Channel Tunnel Rail Link in the UK is an example of this (Pollit, 2002).

To prevent hold-up, arrangements should ensure that all involved parties make asset-specific investments so that they all have a common interest in making the project a success. Also, since during the operation of long-term contracts circumstances are likely to change, contracts and contract partners should be prepared for dealing with interim contract modifications. The extent to which these general remedies in practice can be realised, and how this can be done, is a challenge for practitioners and an interesting subject for future research.

Manifest political risks

An important cause for the failure of PPP projects is the tendency of governments to modify contract conditions during development or operation. The consequences of this are budget and time overruns, private bankruptcies, or lengthy legal procedures entailing compensation claims. The Bangkok Elevated Transport System project in Thailand, for example, collapsed in the early stages of building because the government decided to opt for a tunnel (Tam, 1999). One of the reasons for the budget overspend on the Channel Tunnel was that the French and UK governments were able to impose a whole range of safety requirements during development, while the costs lay with the private parties. This was compensated by an extension of the concession period, but currently the concessionaire is still teetering on the edge of bankruptcy (Flyvbjerg et al., 2003).

These experiences demonstrate that PPP projects need to be protected against the tendency of governments to keep interfering in an uncoordinated way with the development and operation of a project. This imposes requirements on the contract but also on a government as a professional procurer of products and services, and its capacity to coordinate the policies and strategies of the various public bodies that are inevitably involved in major projects.

10.5   CONCLUSION: CONDITIONS FOR PPP IN MEGA-PROJECTS

From the overview of the problems public and private parties encounter in formation and implementation of PPPs, the following picture emerges: in PPPs a large number of parties are involved; contract negotiations and renegotiations are erratic and lengthy; transactions costs are high; uncertainties about technologies, developments and forecasts are huge; transparency is lacking; and both public and private actors behave strategically, trying to create beneficial advantages by the way costs, benefits and risks are allocated. Parties often have unrealistic expectations of each other and are not very professional in playing the PPP game both in the phase of formation and in the implementation of PPP schemes. Apparently parties are not very well prepared and equipped to deal with the reality of PPP in infrastructure projects, as a result of which the high expectations of PPP in many instances are not realised. Parties lack the proper skills and expertise, the operation procedures of their organisations do not fit PPP requirements and, above all, as far as governments are concerned, they do not want to lose their control over mega-projects.

So the day-to-day reality of the marriage between public and private parties can hardly be described as heavenly. PPP imposes stringent requirements on both partners. In order to make this relationship work, it is not enough to develop proper contract forms and schemes; investments have to be made in the institutional condition for governing these working methods: the development of skills and expertise; improvement of the role performance by governments as professional procurers and process managers, and private parties as contractors; and the redesign of organisations to support these new roles.

Experiences from real-life cases teach us that the introduction and development of PPP in mega-projects follows a learning curve: it is only by actually engaging in a series of PPP projects that parties learn to master the PPP process. In some sectors and some countries the learning process has advanced further than in others.

The fact that PFI-type contracts seem to be developing into a new standard may be considered beneficial for this learning process. Standardisation reduces complexity, thus increasing the understanding and quality of the PPP process. Giving the erratic tender procedures and contract negotiations, and the high transactions costs, both public and private parties call for standardisation, which according to them helps to reduce the uncertainties and the costs of involvement in PPP processes.

This standardisation has a price, however. Mega-projects are far from standard. They have unique characteristics, which make them worlds apart. Just as some projects will be less suited for involving private partners than others (for instance when the project is highly controversial, when competition is lacking or when there is no good business case), when PPP is considered, it is far from obvious that one PPP model fits all. As shown earlier, there are different PPP models, developed for different purposes and different projects. Some aim at a more efficient operation, others at realising private investments, still others at developing innovative, high-quality projects.

As far as PFI is concerned, there is a remarkable tension with some essentials of large infrastructure projects. PFI assumes the up-front specification of project requirements by governments and risk transfer to private parties. These schemes seem to be especially appropriate for known, standard projects, like some road schemes or water treatment facilities. Large, complex infrastructure projects, however, are new, unique and surrounded by a high degree of uncertainty. Governments find it hard to specify their requirements in advance. Private parties are supposed to bring in their expertise and creativity at an early stage. Uncertainties mean that instead of riks-transfer, risk-sharing is sensible. In such cases the alliance model is perhaps more attractive than PFI-like schemes.

All in all, there are reasons to argue that the current emphasis on PFI-like models in the world of mega-projects should be complemented by experiments with other models: the variety of mega-projects calls for the development of a variety of PPP options, which makes the task for parties to learn to handle these options even more challenging.

REFERENCES

Akintoye, A. and M. Beck (eds) (2003), *Public Private Partnerships: Managing Risks and Opportunities*, London: Blackwell Publishers.

Arthur Andersen and Enterprise LSE (2000), 'Value for money drivers in the private finance initiative', report commissioned by the Treasury Taskforce, www.treasuryprojects.gov.uk/series_1/andersen.

Bennet, E. and P. Grohmann (2000), *Joint Venture Public Partnerships for Urban Environmental Services. Report on UNDP/PPPUE's Project Development Facility 1995–1999*, New York: UNDP and Yale University.

Bloomfield, P., D. Westerling and R. Carey (1998), 'Innovation and risks in a public–private partnership: financing and construction of a capital project in Massachusetts, *Public Productivity and Review*, **21** (4): 460–71.

Boardman, A.E., F. Poschmann and A.R. Vining (2005), 'North American infrastructure P3s: examples and lessons learned', in G. Hodge and C. Greve (eds), *The Challenge of Public–Private Partnerships. Learning from International Experience*, Cheltenham, UK and Northampton, MA, USA: Edward Elgar: 169–89.

Bowman, L. (2000), 'P3; problem, problem, problem', *Project Finance*, **206**; 25.

Bruijn, J.A. de and M. Leijten (2004), 'Publiek–private samenwerking bij infrastructuurprojecten', in TCI, no. 10: 232–48 (in Dutch).

Bruzelius, N., B. Flyvbjerg and W. Rothengatter (2002), 'Big decisions, big risks: improving accountability in mega projects', *Transport Policy*, **9** (2): 143–54.

Buck Consultants International (2004), *Evaluatie DBFM Rijksweg 31*, The Hague (in Dutch).

Chang, M., M.A. Menon and H. Imura (2003), 'International experience of public–private partnership for urban environmental infrastructure, and its application to China', *International Review for Environmental Strategies*, **4** (2): 223–48.

EU (2004), *Green Paper on Public–Private Partnerships and Community Law on Public Contracts and Concessions*, COM(2004)327.

Expertise Centrum PPS (2004), *Voortgangsrapportage 2004*, The Hague: Ministerie van Financiën (in Dutch), www.minfin.nl.

Fitzgerald, P. (2004), *Review Partnerships Victoria Provided Infrastructure, Final Report to the Treasurer*, Melbourne: Growth Solutions Group.

Flyvbjerg, B., N. Bruzelius and W. Rothengatter (2003), *Megaprojects and Risk. An Anatomy of Ambition*, Cambridge, MA: Cambridge University Press.

Gray, J. (2002), 'Going private: a twenty bn shake up', *Australian Financial Review*, **1**: 52–3.

Haarmeyer, D. and D. Coy (2002), 'An overview of private sector participation in the global and US water and wastewater sector', in P. Seidenstat, D. Haarmeyer and S. Hakim (eds), *Reinventing Water and Wastewater Systems*, New York: John Wiley and Sons: 3–28.

Hall, J. (1998), 'Private opportunity, public benefit?', *Fiscal Studies*, **19** (2): 121–40.

Ham, J.C. van and J.F.M. Koppenjan (2002), *Publiek–private Samenwerking bij Infrastructuur: Wenkend of Wijkend Perspectief*, Utrecht: Lemma (in Dutch).

HM Treasury (1993), *Breaking New Ground: The Private Finance Initiative*, London: HMSO.

HM Treasury (2005), *PFI Signed Project Lists*, London: HMSO.

Hodge, G. (2005), 'Public–private partnerships: The Australasian Experience with Physical Infrastructure', in G. Hodge and C. Greve (eds), *The Challenge of Public–Private Partnerships. Learning from International Experience*, Cheltenham, UK and Northampton, MA, USA: Edward Elgar: 305–31.

Hodge, G. and C. Greve (eds) (2005), *The Challenge of Public–Private Partnerships. Learning from International Experience*, Cheltenham, UK and Northampton, MA, USA: Edward Elgar.

IPPR (2001), *Significant Reforms of PPPs Necessary for Labour to Deliver on Public Services: Current Topics*, www.ippr.org.uk, 25 June.

Johnson, R.A. and A.T. Moore (2002), 'Improving urban water infrastructure through public–private partnerships', in L.W. Maus (ed.), *Urban Water Supply Handbook*, New York: McGraw-Hill: 3.1–3.21.

Johnston, J.M. and B.S. Romzek (2005), 'Traditional contracts as partnerships: effective accountability in social service contracts in the American states', in G. Hodge and C. Greve (eds), *The Challenge of Public–Private Partnerships. Learning from International Experience*, Cheltenham, UK and Northampton, MA, USA: Edward Elgar: 117–43.

Johnstone, N. and L. Wood (2001), *Private Firms and Public Water. Realising Social and Environmental Objectives in Development Countries*, Cheltenham, UK and Northampton, MA, USA: Edward Elgar.

Joosten, W. (2005), 'London Underground Limited. Een casusstudie van de grootste PPS van het Verenigd Koninkrijk', Delft Thesis, Faculty of Technology, Policy and Management, Delft University of Technology (in Dutch).

Klijn, E.-H., J. Edelenbos and M. Hughes (2007), 'Public–private partnerships: a two headed reform; a comparison of PPP in England and the Netherlands', in C. Pollitt, S. van Thiel and V. Homburg (eds), *New Public Management in Europe: Adaptation and Alternatives*, Basingstoke, UK: Palgrave Macmillan.

Koppenjan, J.F.M. (2005), 'The formation of public–private partnerships: lessons from nine transport infrastructure projects in the Netherlands', *Public Administration*, **83** (1): 135–57.

Koppenjan, J.F.M. and B. Enserink (2005), *International Best Practices in Private Sector Participation in Sustainable Urban Infrastructure. Thematic report and policy recommendations*, Delft/Stockholm/Beijing: CCICED Taskforce on Sustainable Urbanisation Strategies.

Koppenjan, J.F.M. and M. Leijten (2005), 'Privatising railroads: the problematic involvement of the private sector in two Dutch railway projects', *The Asia Pacific Journal of Public Administration*, **27** (2): 181–201.

Kumaraswamy, M.M. and X.Q. Zhang (2001), 'Governmental role in BOT-led infrastructure development', *International Journal of Project Mangement*, **19** (3): 195–205.

Li, B. and A. Akintoye (2003), 'An overview of public–private partnership', in A. Akintoye and M. Beck (eds), *Public–Private Partnerships: Managing Risks and Opportunities*, London: Blackwell Publishers: 330.

Martin, L.J. (2005), 'United States: human services', in G. Hodge and C. Greve (eds), *The Challenge of Public–Private Partnerships: Learning from International Experience*, Cheltenham UK and Northampton, MA, USA: Edward Elgar: 144–162.

Ministerie van Financiën (1998), *Meer Waarde door SamenWerken* (eindrapport) The Hague (Ministerie van Financiën) (in Dutch).

Mott MacDonald (2002), *Review of Large Public Procurement in the UK*, London: Mott MacDonald.

National Audit Office (1997), *The Skye Bridge*, HC5 Parliamentary Session 1997–8, London: HMSO.

National Audit Office (1998), *The Private Finance Initiative: The First Four Design, Build, Finance and Operate Roads Contracts*, HC 476, 1997/1998, London: HMSO.

National Audit Office (1999), *Examining the Value for Money Deals under the Private Finance Initiative*, HC 739, Parliamentary Sessions, 1998–9, London: HMSO.

National Audit Office (2003), *PFI Construction Performance*, HC 371, Parliamentary session 2002–3, London: The Stationery Office, www.nao.org.uk. publications/nao_reports/01-02/0102375/pdf.

National Audit Office (2004), *London Underground: Are the Public–Private Partnerships likely to work successfully?*, Report by the comptroller and the auditor general, HC 644 Session 2003–4: 17 June 2004, London: The Stationery Office.

Osborne, S. (ed.) (2000), *Public–Private Partnerships: Theory and Practice in International Perspective*, London: Routledge.

Pollit, M.G. (2002), 'The declining role of the state in infrastructure investments in the UK', in S.V. Berg, M.G. Pollit and M. Tsuji (eds), *Private Initiatives in Infrastructure: Priorities, Incentives and Performance*, Cheltenham, UK and Northampton, MA, USA: Edward Elgar.

Pollit, M.G. (2005), 'Learning from UK Private Finance Initiative experience', in G. Hodge and C. Greve (eds), *The Challenge of Public–Private Partnerships. Learning from International Experience*, Cheltenham, UK and Northampton, MA, USA: Edward Elgar: 207–30.

Shaoul, J. (2005), 'The Private Finance Initiative or the public funding of private profit', in G. Hodge and C. Greve (eds), *The Challenge of Public–Private Partnerships. Learning from International Experience*, Cheltenham, UK and Northampton, MA, USA: Edward Elgar: 190–206.

Spackman, M. (2002), 'Public–private partnerships: lessons from the British approach', *Economic Systems*, **26**: 283–301.

Tam, C.M. (1999), 'Build–Operate–Transfer model for infrastructure developments in Asia: reasons for success and failures', *International Journal of Project Development*, **17**: 377–82.

TCI (Tijdelijke Commissie Infrastructuurprojecten) (2004), *Grote projecten uitver-groot. Een infrastructuur voor besluitvorming* [Large projects under the magnifying glass. An infrastructure for decision-making], Tweede Kamer, 2004–2005, nos 1–10, The Hague: Sdu Uitgevers (in Dutch).

Walker, B. and B.C. Walker (2000), *Privatization: Sell Off or Sell Out*, Sydney: ABC Books.

Walker, C. and A.J. Smith (1995), *Privatised Infrastructure: The Build Operate Transfer Approach*, London: Thomas Telford.

Whettenhall, R. (2003), 'The rhetoric and reality of public–private partnerships', *Public Organization Review: A Global Journal*, **3**: 77–107.

PART III

Innovation, Competition and Institutions

11. Innovations in the planning of mega-projects

Werner Rothengatter

11.1 SOME LESSONS LEARNED FROM GOOD AND BAD EXPERIENCES

The first big railway projects (Stockton–Darlington in the UK, 1825 and Nürnberg–Fürth, 1835, in Germany) were purely business-oriented undertakings. In the second half of the nineteenth century the state came in, not only to solve the problems with bankruptcy of some major players in the railway business, but in the first instance to coordinate the manifold railway initiatives associated with heterogeneous infrastructure and rolling stock as well as the different types of organisation. Friedrich List (1841) was the protagonist of spatial development policy through railway infrastructures, and his vision was to improve accessibility of the German regions so radically through an efficient railway network that Germany would catch up with the UK economy, which at that time was far ahead because of the Commonwealth.

It is obvious that the various spatial impacts stemming from a mega-project in the sense of Friedrich List cannot be captured by the project company. This justifies the state coming in and forming a public–private partnership. Other reasons for the state's participation are high risk, reduction of external effects or social balance (e.g. for regional development). As soon as the state comes in, however, the race is opened for all kinds of rent-seeking activities. Naturally, the private investors are interested in using state bodies and politicians as promoters for the project, and they will try to hedge their risk and gain supernormal profits through the construction work and the financial business. The political players are interested in passing popular stories to the voters, such as increase of competitiveness, improvement of regional economic structure, better employment or enhanced quality of life.

Three examples of mega-projects in the transport sector are exhibited in Table 11.1, summarising the most important experiences so far. The major lessons learned are as follows:

Table 11.1   Characteristics of some mega-projects (see Flyvbjerg et al., 2003)

Project	Function	Critical problems	Major benefits	Procurement
Channel Tunnel	Link UK to the mainland; passenger, freight trains and rolling motorway	Promotion by construction industry; cost overrun 80%; financing cost 140% higher than forecasted	Private finance, low public contribution; strengthening corridors London–Paris/Brussels	Unprofessional procurement in the first phase; financial consolidation after establishment of Eurotunnel in 1994
Great Belt Bridge and Tunnel	Link East Denmark to mainland; rail and road transport	Cost overrun 54%; complementary with Oeresund but competitive with Fehmarn Belt projects	Together with Oeresund linking Sweden and East Denmark to mainland	Weak cost control; dominance of public-type procurement
Oeresund Bridge and Tunnel	Link South-West Sweden to East Denmark; provide development axis for the Copenhagen agglomeration; establish transnational joint ventures (ports)	Cost overrun 26%; overestimation of demand; reduction of user charges necessary to achieve planned patronage; lower revenues than expected	Good example of public–private partnership; positive impacts on regional development; increase of public transit	Efficient procurement; project company business oriented; publicly set car/truck tariffs too high at start; change to two-part tariff

1. In the case of public procurement there is a tendency to underestimate costs and overestimate benefits.
2. In the case of public procurement there is little interest and little chance to perform *ex-post* evaluations.
3. If private institutions have to take risk, then the expectations for the project outcome tend to be more pessimistic. Short- and medium-term returns dominate the benefit calculation.

4.   Private institutions tend to underestimate the network and other externalities.
5.   The public and private actors in general apply different cost and benefit calculation schemes, often based on different forecasting approaches, as soon as the private actors have to bear part of the risk.

Beyond the three mega-projects in Table 11.1, Flyvbjerg et al. (2003) list a number of projects procured worldwide that have shown dramatic cost overruns and shortfall of traffic demand. In particular, for rail the actual costs of projects are on average 45 per cent higher than estimated (with a standard deviation of 38).

Looking at the reasons for planning failures for mega-projects, one can identify five major problem areas:

1.   Public procurement schemes are characterised by rewarding project appraisal optimism. To steer a project successfully through the barriers of a public decision process it would be fatal to estimate costs and benefits realistically. Project appraisal serves to promote the project. Therefore there is no interest in *ex-post* comparisons for actual and estimated figures.
2.   Public procurement schemes don't include risk estimations. The same holds for private schemes if the state gives sufficient guarantees. In such conditions the financial calculation follows the 'EGAP' principle (everything goes according to plan).
3.   The planning calculations of public and private actors look completely different. The public applies cost–benefit analysis, which is based on a comparative-static analysis of project impacts for a long time horizon. The private investors will prepare rate-of-return and cash-flow figures with high emphasis on the short and medium term if they have to bear part of the financial risk.
4.   The transport consultancies, which are in charge of cost–benefit or financial calculation, will generate results according to the preferences of their clients. In most cases their honorarium is independent of the accuracy of their forecast. This leads to a biased data environment for a mega-project.
5.   The contract scheme is in many cases too rigid and does not react to unplanned changes in the environment. For a mega-project contracts have to be signed some eight to ten years before the operation is opened.

The main source of procurement problems is institutional.[1] This means that a proper choice of procurement scheme can help to avoid major mistakes.

A second source is methodological and can be treated by better assessment techniques once the institutional settings are right. Of course the stakeholders will only be interested in applying new assessment methods if the procurement scheme will reward more economically rational behaviour. In this sense introducing truth-telling incentives is a major challenge to innovation in the planning of large-scale projects.

The chapter is organised as follows: Sections 11.2, 11.3, 11.4 and 11.5 discuss the basic requirements for a revised institutional setting which seems necessary for improvements to the procurement scheme. This includes the involvement of private risk capital, a professional project company, proper risk allocation and the exposure of major players to risk, including the consultants. Once these necessary conditions for institutional improvements are in place, some innovations in decision support systems can help to find commonly accepted project layouts, as presented in Sections 11.6 and 11.7. Section 11.8 shows how the system dynamic model approach can be enriched to encourage truth-telling. Section 11.9 will conclude the findings.

11.2   INSTITUTIONAL INNOVATIONS: THE PROJECT COMPANY AND INVOLVEMENT OF PRIVATE RISK CAPITAL

Project Company

Flyvbjerg et al. (2003) have pointed out that in the case of mega-projects, politicians often act as promoters rather than as neutral welfare-maximisers so that the normative planning scheme in which the state takes all-important decisions from an objective and neutral position ('benevolent dictatorship') will not work. The question is whether political decision-makers are expected to change their attitude to please voters in the short run while neglecting the long-run economic consequences. The answer is: certainly not. Promotion of prestige projects and political appearances for opening ceremonies with a high level of public attention are part of political business. Only if the procurement regime can be changed from the beginning is there a chance to bring in a more economically rational calculation into the scheme. Two basic requirements are:

1.   Establish a project company under private law.
2.   Let private investors bear a substantial part of the economic risk.

A project company under private law, which is obliged to work under defined public objectives and constraints on the one hand and has some entrepreneurial freedom to achieve good business results, on the other hand, would take responsibility for the management of the process. It is most important to hire professional managers, not (former) politicians or administrators, for this job and link their salaries to the achievement of contracted performance criteria. As the project should be defined in functional terms by the political side, enough entrepreneurial freedom should arise to design a project according to economic principles. The DBFO (design–build–finance–operate) scheme of public–private partnership seems to be the most promising form to integrate private creativity in developing the project.

If a private management company takes responsibility, along with some individual risk, then transparency can be provided from the beginning with respect to two basic aspects: the scoping of the project and the roles of the private and the public stakeholders. The importance of a proper scoping of PPP-financed projects has been demonstrated by a number of cases, which are readily taken by opponents of private project finance as examples of its inappropriateness. The M1 project in Hungary, which closed a gap on the motorway between Budapest and the Austrian/Hungarian border, is a good example. While the project management performed well with time and cost discipline for the construction, the project failed because the revenues were much too low after the project opened. The main reason was a massive diversion of traffic to the secondary network because of the high user fees. The scoping failure was to limit the concession to the 40 km stretch, which had to be newly built, and not to the link between the border and Budapest. In the latter case the charges per km would have been much lower and the traffic diversion could have been minimised.

European and national legacy don't allow for widening the scope of privately co-financed projects to avoid fragmentation and improve on financial viability. Therefore it is difficult to procure a project so that user finance is sufficient for private profitability.

If the concession does not allow for sufficient revenues, then a negotiation on public contributions is necessary. Public support can consist of various measures:

- grants for financing the investment costs;
- guarantees for loans and their interest rates;
- fixed payments for particular user classes (shadow tolls);
- free provision of access links;
- guarantee of no competing projects in the future;
- extension of the concession to value-added services (e.g. land development at intersections, stations or airports).

Involvement of Private Risk Capital

Such a scheme is more easily established if there is eventually a substantial involvement of private risk capital with a lower bound of about one-third of the total capital invested. Private investors will be a better guarantee of economic viability of a project rather than cost–benefit analysis, with its various possibilities of manipulation and appraisal biases. In such a regime the probability increases that the entrepreneurial freedom that is offered through a DBFO scheme is used to develop an economic project design. The participation of private capital may serve as an economic truth-telling constraint in a public environment that is less accustomed to economic thinking.

While calling for private capital involvement seems very natural in order to avoid public 'X-inefficiency', it will not be easy to find a good compromise with other public objectives. One example is fostering free competition for the transport infrastructure. Often the charges from infrastructure use are not the main source of business profits; rather the profit arises from the use of the capacity itself for producing services for the customer. This holds for railway tracks as well as for airport facilities. If participation of private capital is open, then the transport service companies in particular might be interested in buying a fixed and guaranteed part of the capacity for their own use. An example is the new airport terminal Munich II, co-financed by Lufthansa. It is interesting for the regulator to explore to what extent such a regime creates a new possibility for grandfathering. Limiting the participation of service companies to 30–50 per cent and guaranteeing free access of third parties to the slots if they pay the same fees as the incumbent companies might solve this problem. In any case a strong regulation authority will be needed in such a situation.

11.3 INSTITUTIONAL INNOVATIONS: INTEGRATION OF SHAREHOLDER GROUPS IN THE PROCUREMENT PROCESS

The challenge for institutional solutions is not only economic. Critical groups will almost certainly oppose any kind of mega-projects. These groups can be classified into four categories:

1. Potentially affected residents who try to stop the project because it might prove detrimental to their living conditions.
2. Land owners who resist as long as possible, in order to maximise the compensation that has to be paid for the loss of property.

3. Green organisations, which fight for a minimisation of environmental disturbance.
4. Radical groups that fight against any big project.

The strategy to be followed is to integrate groups (1) and (3) as soon as possible into the planning process while trying to keep the power of opponents in groups (2) and (4) low. In the traditional planning scheme the analysis of environmental impacts would follow after the economic performance has been confirmed. Practice shows, however, that a project can rarely be stopped if the economic criteria have proven very positive, such that project promoters are encouraged to manipulate environmental data to make the project pass the public evaluation checks. Against this background it is important to analyse the environmental impacts at the beginning of the planning process. For instance, in the recently revised German standard evaluation scheme for transport infrastructure investments, an environmental risk analysis is obligatory at the beginning of the process. Therefore necessary mitigation measures can be defined at an early stage of the planning process and enter the economic evaluation. In the process of project procurement the environmental and social issues can be treated from the beginning in parallel with the technical and economic issues, such that incompatibilities and barriers are identified as early as possible.

11.4 INSTITUTIONAL INNOVATIONS: RISK-TAKING OF CONSULTANTS

Consultants play a big role in the procurement process as forecasts of demand development and economic/ecological/social impacts strongly influence the decision-making. In many cases the consultants are hired by the promoters of a project or are at least heavily influenced by them. Then, the major objective of a consultant is not to prepare the best forecast, but to maximise the probability of getting the next contract. A good example of this type of behaviour is the procurement of two maglev projects in Nordrhein–Westfalen ('Metrorapid') and in Munich (Transrapid Airport Shuttle), after the big maglev project Hamburg–Berlin had failed for financial reasons. The federal government then dedicated the financial subsidy, originally planned for Hamburg–Berlin, to the two successor maglev projects in Nordrhein–Westfalen and Bavaria, which then competed for these funds. For legal reasons a cost–benefit analysis had to be prepared for both projects, to be integrated into the federal transport investment programme. It was in the interest of the former red/green federal government that the Metrorapid would be evaluated not worse than the Munich Transrapid to justify the major part of federal funding going to Nordrhein–Westfalen, which at that time was also governed by the same political colours. Against this background it was not surprising that the consultant came out with a cost–benefit ratio of 1.5 for both projects. To achieve this result some changes of the standard CBA procedure and a number of strange evaluation approaches were necessary. Taking the comments of neutral experts, none of these projects should have passed the threshold of 1 for benefit over costs, while the Munich Transrapid was regarded the better of two non-viable projects.

There are two possible ways to set consultants' incentives properly. First, contracts can be given in parallel to several consultancies so that a competitive situation arises. Then different country experiences can be used, as happened for instance in the case of the Montreal–Ottawa high-speed rail corridor in Canada. This procedure is appropriate for the pre-feasibility phase. When preparing a feasibility study, confidential information usually has to be included, so that the number of consultants can be kept low. In this phase the consultant in charge will be inclined to forecast the most likely development if a bonus is paid for forecasting accuracy or a penalty in case of large deviations of the actual from the forecasted demand/cost development. Of course the long life of transport investment projects will make it difficult to apply this principle for the whole project life. But it could be exercised for instance for the first five years after the start of a project. If private financial institutions are involved in the procurement as risk-takers, such contracts will automatically become standard tools to foster truth-telling in consultancies.

11.5   INSTITUTIONAL INNOVATIONS: APPROPRIATE RISK ALLOCATION STRATEGIES

Public–private partnership for mega-projects requires a proper risk allocation to private and public bodies. Risks can be classified into:

- construction risk
- operation risk
- demand risk
- financial risk
- political risk
- *force majeure* risk.

In any case the private investor should bear the part of the risk that can be privately managed. Asset liability management provides some interesting principles for the management of different types of risk. While it is clear that construction and operation risk should be allocated to private parties, it is not so obvious with demand and financial risk. Long-term demand development can not be forecasted with high accuracy, so the contract between the state and the project company should include some flexibility. In the case of some recent Spanish motorway projects, this problem was dealt with in that the contract was based on a defined range for the demand development. As soon as the actual development comes out higher, the company has to pay higher concession fees to the state. If it comes out lower, re-contracting is possible (see Bel and Fageda, 2005). In the case of financial risk, a hedging strategy for treating long-term risk on interest rates might be very expensive and boost the costs of the project. In this case the state can guarantee interest rates because it is the only institution that can diversify this risk over a very long period. Political risk naturally has to be allocated to the public. The Channel Tunnel is an example of wrongly assigning parts of political risk to private actors, which at that time was accepted in a phase of euphoria about the European dream project. *Force majeure* risk must be allocated to a partner that can diversify this risk, usually the state. Only in the case of network companies (e.g. the Austrian ASFINAG which is responsible for the whole Austrian motorway and expressway network) can *force majeure* risk be allocated to the company.

11.6 INNOVATIVE DECISION SUPPORT: COPING WITH THE PREFERENCES OF DIFFERENT STAKEHOLDER GROUPS

There seem to be two major requirements of the planning process that have not been fulfilled by an appropriate methodology. The first is derived from the existence of a number of stakeholders who can influence the progress of a project in one way or the other. The second is a more holistic and dynamic approach to the evaluation of projects, contrasting the partial approach of traditional CBA which usually ends up with incomplete comparative-static comparisons. The first issue will be dealt with in this section; the second issue is the topic of Section 11.7.

The involvement of various parties with different goals leads to a complex interaction mechanism. Stakeholders have to be integrated in a timely fashion into the process and it has to be taken into account that they might have different preferences. The European Investment Bank, together with the EU Commission, has published a study on the evaluation of railway projects with participation of several stakeholder groups (RAILPAG,

2005). The basic concept is a traditional CBA, which is carried out according to the particular objectives of the different groups.

The classified stakeholders are the users, the transport service operators, the insurance companies, the contractors and suppliers, the infrastructure managers, the non-users and the government. A further sub-classification leads to 20 stakeholder groups. The effects are classified by user service, operation, assets and external effect; considering the sub-classifications results in 30 effect types. These effects of a railway project are screened in the form of an SE (=stakeholder×effects) matrix, which includes 20 × 30 cells. Although many cells are empty, going through the overall analysis can be very tedious, although the evaluation procedure for each cell seems simple.

The SE matrix can be regarded as a possible approach to treat the multidimensionality of the planning process. But it might be questioned whether it is wise in an early stage of the process to force the parties to reveal their preferences in an explicit manner, in order to prepare a complete CBA for all stakeholder groups. As long as there is a negotiation situation, the parties might be inclined to avoid a rigid fixing of their positions. Furthermore, it is not clear to what extent the SE matrix might help in the case of diverging results.

An alternative approach starts from the assumption that there are a few powerful stakeholder groups in the game that base their positions on a few characteristics of the project. For example, the environmentalists will fight against additional environmental burdens caused by a project; industry will stress better accessibility of industrial locations; and the regional government will be interested in employment effects. There are only two groups that will be interested in applying a complete calculation. First, the federal government will require an estimation of all costs and benefits arising from the project. Second, the investors/operators will need an estimation of long-run demand/revenues/costs to check financial viability. For both sides the results from traditional CBA are not sufficient to support their decisions in the case of a mega-project, which is a singularity for the decision-makers and not one of thousands of marginal investments to be ranked by a standard CBA procedure. Therefore we suggest a staged approach to the decision problem, adjusted to the stage of maturity of the project.

In a first stage, i.e. in a phase of pre-feasibility analysis for the project when the final design is not decided, it will be sufficient to prepare rough calculations for basic indicators of the social and business appraisals. The preferences of the other stakeholder groups can be summarised by a comparison of the minimum positions of the groups with the expected performance indicators of the project. The result can be represented in the form of a simple spider diagram, which can be used as a basis for the mediation process and the further design of the project.

A more sophisticated method is CLP (constraint logic programming), which is an embedding of constraints in a host programming language. The constraint programming approach is to search for a state of the world in which a large number of constraints are satisfied at the same time. The CLP methodology has been developed within the framework of artificial intelligence, while its logical roots are closely related to operations research (Heinitz, 2000; Liedtke, 2006). Constraints are formulated, variables and their domains defined and the search for solutions carried out by optimisation calculation or heuristics. The heart of the method is the constraint solver, which computes variable domains that satisfy the set of constraints.

For practical application the preferences of the parties are formulated as functional constraints. This means that the parties are asked to define a minimum threshold for every important decision criterion. A mediation process is used to explore which of these constraints are soft and which are hard. CLP then finds out the minimum change of soft constraints to achieve a feasible solution.

Figure 11.1 shows how CLP can be used to facilitate the negotiation process. The stakeholder parties are asked to formulate the conditions under which they would accept the project. CLP constructs the feasible

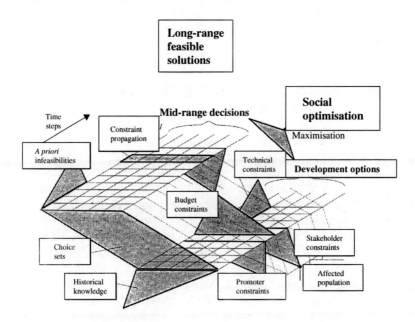

Figure 11.1   Principal structure of constraint logic programming (see Heinitz, 2000)

domain, which, as expected, is empty at the beginning. Exploring soft constraints and possibilities for trade-offs, the process can be guided to generate first feasible solutions, which the parties might accept – usually under specific conditions. If a set of feasible solutions is identified, then a design of project alternatives can follow, which concludes the pre-feasibility phase.

It is not the CLP method itself, but rather the placing of the method in the context of a mediation process that brings an innovative element into the procurement. The economic rationale is to apply the Kaldor–Hicks criterion in an explicit manner. This rule says that a project is beneficial to society if the advantaged parties can compensate the disadvantaged parties and enjoy a surplus at the end. In traditional CBA this rule is applied only in a virtual way, i.e. the benefits of the advantaged are compared with the costs of the disadvantaged: if the difference is positive, the net benefit of a project is proven. However, compensation is not actually given to the disadvantaged, which explains the strong resistance of negatively affected groups even if the CBA results are positive. In the case of mega-projects it seems to be wise to apply the Kaldor–Hicks criterion in its original form to increase acceptability. Furthermore, this will separate the constructive groups from the destructive groups, which may generate more political options for the process. Finally it leads the planners to rethink the technical alternatives and the possibility of removing hard constraints (see Box 11.1).

BOX 11.1   MEGA-INVESTMENT AT FRANKFURT AIRPORT

Fraport AG is planning a €3.4 billion investment, consisting of a new terminal, a new maintenance/repair hall for the Airbus A 380 and an additional starting/landing track. While other alternatives were confronted with manifold complaints of stakeholders, the north-west track suffered from a hard constraint: the starting/landing route would cross the location of a chemical plant, which is infeasible for safety reasons. After a tedious mediation process it was decided to relocate the chemical firm and compensate for the costs, which is estimated at almost €700 million.

This example underlines the point that constraints often have to be reconsidered during the mediation process, so creativity should concentrate in the pre-feasibility phase on the treatment of soft and eventually also hard constraints.

11.7 INNOVATIVE DECISION SUPPORT: SYSTEMS APPROACH TO DYNAMIC ASSESSMENT OF MEGA-PROJECTS

In most cases mega-projects are evaluated by traditional CBA, sometimes extended by a regional economic impact analysis. While CBA is a useful tool for preparing a ranking for a set of small and medium-sized projects, a warning should be given about the application of this instrument in the case of mega-projects. The reasons are:

1. CBA is based on partial analysis, deriving the economic impacts from traffic changes on the link considered. In the case of mega-projects the indirect impacts distributed through the networks and the economic sectors might dominate the picture.
2. CBA uses average values for important impacts, such as time savings. While these values might work for the whole set of transport investments on average, they can be wrong for the special case.
3. CBA applies a comparative-static analysis, only looking at the start and end situations with and without the project. As the time horizon for the life of a mega-project is in general very long, many changes can occur in the time in between; in particular the benefit stream for the mega-project will not be independent of other network changes.
4. CBA assumes that the financial side does not matter. This is not true for mega-projects. The benefit streams can be strongly dependent on the method of finance.
5. CBA starts from the hypothesis that there is one year for opening the operation of the whole project. In many cases, however, a mega-project is composed of a number of sub-projects, which are started sequentially. The benefit stream can be dependent on a number of other decisions within the time horizon of project life such that the whole time profile of benefit development is needed instead of a point-to-point forecast.

There have been several attempts to extend CBA in the context of the European Framework Programme. The IASON project (IASON, 2004) investigated spatial computed general equilibrium (SCGE) models and system dynamic models, while the TIPMAC project (TIPMAC, 2004) focused on combinations of econometric/transport modelling approaches (E3ME) in comparison with system dynamic models (SDM). Every new approach mentioned brings in a wider systems view and is therefore more appropriate than traditional CBA for estimating indirect economic impacts. Taking the present versions of the model developments, one can conclude that the SDM approach is best suited to cope with the special problems of mega-projects. This is because of the following features:

1. SDM is intrinsically system-based and dynamic, i.e. constructed to model feedback mechanisms between sub-systems.
2. As SDM works sequentially, there is no difficulty in modelling staged project realisations.
3. SDM can be based on micro behaviour, which may be aggregated by micro–macro bridges.
4. SDM can integrate macro, regional and sectoral indicators such that it can be adjusted to the project scale.
5. SDM provides a closed framework in which all major reactions are modelled in a consistent way.
6. SDM can be calibrated for every module and every level (meso, macro, regional, sectoral), based on available data.
7. SDM can be easily combined with a transportation model to estimate the transport reactions most accurately in the feedback processes between transport and economic sectors.
8. SDM can allow for breaks in trends in so far as the dominant feedback mechanism may change over time. Example: decoupling processes from GDP for energy consumption or for road transport.

Box 11.2 gives a brief summary of the basic features of SDM approaches, and the weaknesses that might limit the scope of applications.

BOX 11.2 STRUCTURE, STRENGTHS AND WEAKNESSES OF SDM APPROACHES

SDM was developed by J. Forrester in the late 1960s and consists of four basic components: feedback theory (cybernetics), numerical simulation, decision theory and mental creativity techniques. Mathematically, it consists of a system of (eventually non-linear) difference equations, which are solved sequentially by applying numerical integration techniques. This makes it possible to treat large dynamic systems including complex interactions, which implies a number of advantages. Efficient solutions techniques are available in commercial software packages, such as VENSIM or POWERSIM, to solve large models, but also software with nice graphical tools (e.g. ITHINK) can be applied to support management or political decision-making.

As modelling is less rigid compared with equilibrium models in economics, there are advantages of flexibility on the one hand, but high risks of wrong applications or interpretations on the other hand. Some problems are listed below:

1. Setting *time intervals* and choosing *numerical integrators* Depending on the type of difference equations, the setting of parameters for numerical simulation can influence the results of computation substantially.
2. Defining the *endogenous* and the *exogenous parts of the system* This determines the possible feedback mechanisms and can have high impacts on long-term processes.
3. Constructing *bridges between different modules* of the system While the equations inside a module in most cases can be estimated econometrically, this is in general not possible for the bridge equations. Example: modelling the transmission of time savings from the transport module to the regional and macroeconomic modules, which is done in ASTRA through the productivity variables of the production functions.
4. Filling gaps through *mental creativity* Overcoming the disadvantages of partial modelling implies that relationships have to be included for which the empirical information is not sufficient for a statistical estimation. This implies high risk of introducing subjective value judgements into the quantitative framework and exposes the SDM to fundamental critique. See the justified critics of the first world model of Dennis Meadows developed for the Club of Rome and the book *Limits to Growth*, published in 1972.
5. Applying different methods of *calibration* As an SDM may include different sub-models (e.g. a decision model for haulage companies with aggregation through a calibrated distribution function, and a macroeconomic model for the main economic indicators, calibrated on the base of time series), the calibration of the single modules and of the complete system can be a tedious process. While Rogelio (2003) demonstrates the difficulties with calibration, Schade (2005) has shown that it is possible to calibrate a very large-scale system like ASTRA in the form of a staged adjustment process. At the end of the calibration ASTRA simulates 15 years of the past (1990–2004) at a defined level of accuracy, before it starts on the future.

Figure 11.2 shows the SDM model ASTRA, which consists of eight modules. ASTRA contains 29 countries (EU 27, Norway, Switzerland) with the following features. The population module (POP) treats the development of population by age groups. The macroeconomics module (MAC) is composed of the macroeconomic indicators and their relationships within the national accounts. It includes among others an input–output table with 25 sectors, the employment situation and productivity development. The foreign trade module (FOT) describes the trade flows between the countries.

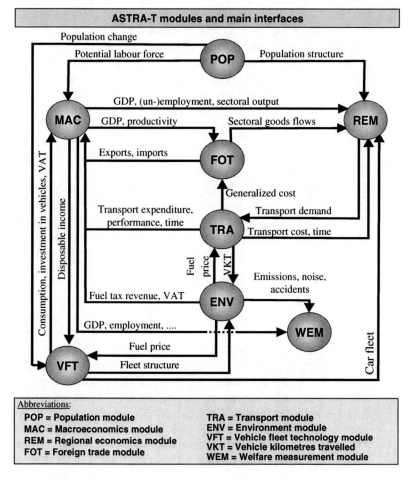

Source: TIPMAC (2004).

Figure 11.2   Structure of the SDM ASTRA

The regional economics module (REM) is for modelling the regional economy and prepares the interfaces with the transport model. The transport module (TRA) is a functional representation of the transport system of a country, which can be linked to a national or international transport model. The vehicle fleet technology module (VFT) treats the development of vehicle technology over time. The welfare measurement module (WEM) calculates characteristic welfare indicators to prepare a final assessment.

After several years of development, ASTRA has made available a large-scale model with some 200 000 dynamic variables and 1 million static relationships. Nevertheless this model has to be prepared and tuned for every application. In the context of the TIPMAC research ASTRA has been adjusted to the problem of assessment of TEN investments, including the financial side. This means that in contrast to the traditional CBA, the financial source of investments had to be defined and integrated in the model context. Financing can be done by taxes, user charges or credits, and every method of finance will influence the benefit stream of a mega-project. In TIPMAC, taxes or user charges have been investigated, because credit finance can be performed by a number of different financial instruments, which were not the focus of analysis.

Figure 11.3 shows the investment activity that was assumed following the TEN definition of the van Miert group and of the Commission. It was assumed that the priority projects would be realised as soon as possible so that a characteristic expenditure stream followed for each EU country (at the

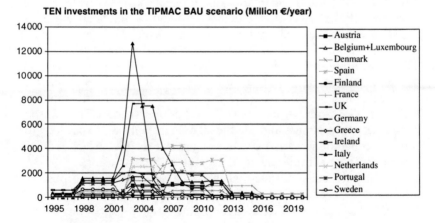

Source: TIPMAC (2004).

Figure 11.3   Expenditures for high-priority projects of TEN in EU 15, 1995–2020

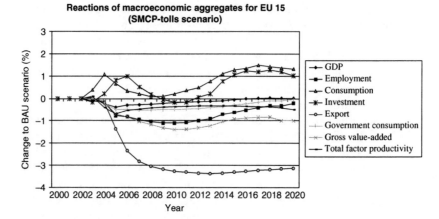

Source: TIPMAC (2004).

*Figure 11.4   Impacts of TENs and their finance on aggregate economic
indicators, 2000–2020*

time of analysis for the EU 15). Italy has a number of large-scale projects,
for instance the Messina Bridge, Lyon–Turin, the Brenner Base Tunnel and
other high-speed links. The UK shows an early peak in investment activity
for the West Coast railway line, while in Spain there is a more continuous
high level of investments for the Pyrenees crossing and a number of railway
projects (changing to the standard gauge for interoperability reasons).

In the TIPMAC scenarios different assumptions for financing of the
TENs have been analysed. Without going into details of these scenarios, it
can be seen from Figure 11.4 and Table 11.2 that the overall impact of the
TENs on European GDP is marginal. Table 11.2 underlines that there will
be winners and losers. For instance, Portugal is most likely to win because
it will enjoy high benefits from the projects without contributing much to
the funding instruments, such as fuel taxes or user charges. The transport
companies of the Netherlands on the other hand will have to pay high fuel
taxes or congestion charges on the congested networks, which will slow
down international trade activity using land transport means.

The general results indicate that there is a high risk of overinvestment
in mega-projects on the TEN priority list. If the procurement process for
the TENs were governed by economic considerations, then the next step
after presenting the van Miert list would have been to investigate the
mega-projects more carefully, checking for parallel investment and substi-
tutive effects among projects. Instead, the Commission has put political
promoters in charge of every project to remove any remaining national bar-

Table 11.2   Impacts of TENs on GDP and employment in the EU 15 for different finance scenarios

Values for 2020 (%) change to BAU	GDP			Employment		
	TEN+ Fuel	TEN+ SMCP	SMCP- Tolls	TEN+ Fuel	TEN+ SMCP	SMCP- Tolls
Austria	0.23	3.74	3.61	0.02	−0.00	0.04
Belgium+ Luxembourg	0.27	0.75	1.09	0.08	0.41	0.54
Denmark	0.01	−0.90	−0.92	0.01	−3.44	−3.37
Spain	1.44	−3.67	−4.81	0.57	−1.68	−2.06
Finland	−0.20	2.73	3.20	−0.08	−0.34	0.06
France	0.04	−0.42	−0.10	−0.00	−0.69	−1.06
UK	0.22	0.95	0.78	0.22	0.38	0.25
Germany	0.06	0.88	0.94	0.08	−0.37	−0.09
Greece	−1.45	−3.22	−3.15	−0.39	−2.47	−2.54
Ireland	0.01	−0.04	−0.01	−0.01	−0.02	−0.01
Italy	0.04	−0.38	−0.14	0.01	−1.20	−0.91
Netherlands	0.01	−5.44	−5.42	0.00	−1.70	−1.48
Portugal	0.65	7.03	7.09	0.28	1.35	1.24
Sweden	−0.09	2.98	3.66	−0.07	0.92	1.29
EU 15	**0.18**	**−0.09**	**−0.06**	**0.12**	**−0.62**	**−0.61**

Notes:
BAU = business as usual.
Fuel = fuel tax.
SMCP = social marginal cost pricing.
.SMCP-Tolls = combination of social marginal cost pricing and vignette payments.

Source: TIPMAC (2004).

riers and to overcome financial problems. This is just the opposite of the recommendations given in Flyvbjerg et al. (2003). The reduction of the TEN budget 2006–2013 from more than €20 billion to about €8 billion Euro might provide a chance to bring more economic realism into the political scenery.

11.8   ENRICHMENT OF THE SDM APPROACH TO ENCOURAGE TRUTH-TELLING

Every appraisal method is subject to manipulation. The SDM (system dynamic model) approach can be made more robust against this risk by integrating the basic aspects of the financial appraisal for possible private investors. The process of data generation for the social and private-type project assessment, as it is designed in the context of an SDM, provides a wide interface for the two types of evaluation. Of course, the objectives are different. While the public sector is interested in social rentability, including internal and external effects wherever they occur, the private investors will focus only on the rentability of financial capital invested, on risk and cash-flow indicators related to the particular project.

Let us examine this interface more closely. Important inputs for both types of evaluation are:

1. Transport demand pattern, demand for other types of project use ('value-adding services').
2. Investment costs and related current costs for the project.
3. Investment costs and related current costs for complementary projects (e.g. access links).
4. Willingness-to-pay figures for time savings and reductions of operating costs (tariff elasticity of demand).
5. Spatial economic impacts and indirect benefits (induced transport demand for the project).

Point (1) is a central issue for transport modelling. It underlines that there is a close interdependence between transport and economic modelling. To satisfy this requirement of a close integration of these fields, the ASTRA software provides an interface for exchanging data with a transport model. IWW[2] is running ASTRA in combination with the transport model VACLAV, which is based on NUTS 3 regions for the EU 27 + 2 and all interregional links for all traffic modes. On this basis transport demand for the project that stems from interregional flows can be forecasted within a consistent framework of socioeconomic developments.

Point (2) relates to the problem that the public decision-maker might be more interested in an EGAP (everything goes according to plan) forecast of cost, while the private investor would prefer an MLD forecast (most likely development) eventually modified by risk considerations.

In several mega-project procurements the necessary additional investments for access links have simply been neglected in the CBA. This failure should be avoided by implementing point (3). As such costs can be substantial, they must be included and their allocation must be made explicit. Steps (1), (2) and (3) relate to the problem of allocating risks.

Point (4) relates to the fact that often the average values for time savings and reductions of operating costs are not adjusted to the region, its industrial sectors and its population structure. ASTRA offers the possibility to simulate impact chains following from savings of general costs endoge-nously so that the valuation factors in the assessment step can be made con-sistent with the simulated economic impacts.

Spatial impacts and repercussions through a sequence of feedback processes are hard to predict: point (5). Nevertheless there are a number of findings of the World Bank (1994), Vickerman (1987), SACTRA (1999), Lakshmanan and Anderson (2002) as well as the statistical tests of Biehl (1975; 1991) or Rothengatter and Schaffer (2005) that underline that a boost of the regional economy surrounding a mega-project cannot automatically be expected. A number of conditions must hold to identify a realistic chance of stimulation of economic growth, and for regions lagging behind it will be necessary to add substantial further social capital to catch up the develop-ment gap. ASTRA offers an interface in the regional economic module for integrating such considerations in the system dynamics context. If a high probability of fostering the regional economy is identified, then induced transport activities will follow, which are relevant for the transport forecast and the related benefit/cash-flow estimations. This would create a positive feedback process, increasing the indirect benefits of the project.

11.9 CONCLUSIONS

Mega-projects have been a playing field of rent-seeking industrials and incompetent public managers in the past. As long as there is enough public money available, the financial disasters associated with some mega-projects will not make the players nervous. For publicly financed projects in general there is no sufficient financial control after the final approval by parlia-ments. The auditor general can control the legality, but not the economic efficiency, of spending public money. Often it is impossible to get data from the authorities on the performance of the projects after realisation. This holds in particular if several public bodies (federal and state governments, public enterprises) are involved. If private capital is involved, the financial success becomes more transparent. In this case it is dependent on the mag-nitude of private risk-taking whether private involvement will lead to a higher discipline of money spending.

This chapter has focused on aspects of new institutional arrangements and innovative assessment tools to improve on the performance of the planning process for mega-projects. With respect to the institutional side, the main messages are:

1. Establish a project company, hire a professional project manager and allocate a substantial part of the risk to private investors.

2. Provide a proper scheme of risk allocation.
3. Public guarantees should be handled with care. In general they should be dedicated to reduce financial risk (interest guarantee).
4. Contracts could be set up in a more flexible way to treat demand risk (data corridor, flexible concession fees, recontracting).
5. Consultants could be offered a bonus or be subject to a penalty in their contracts, depending on the accuracy of their forecasts.
6. Constraints and barriers, eventually set by particular stakeholder parties, can be integrated from the beginning of the procurement process (e.g. environmental constraints).

The use of extended assessment methods can help to discover inconsistencies and avoid appraisal biases. First, it is recommended to control the constraints and barriers of the stakeholder groups permanently by constraint logic programming. This guarantees that feasible steps are discovered and the main blocking arguments are treated early in the process. This will reduce friction in the procurement process. Second, it is suggested to use a large-scale system dynamics tool as a base platform for the generation of all data relevant for decision-making. The main advantages are:

1. Using a system dynamic approach (SDM), all affected sectors can be integrated in a holistic way (contrasting partial analysis with CBA) and consistent feedback schemes can be constructed to analyse the potential impacts of the mega-project.
2. SDM can be extended by coupling it to transport simulation and regional economic impact models to generate the basic input data for evaluation.
3. If the same SDM platform is used for public evaluations (social rentability) and private evaluations (rate of return), then a truth-telling mechanism is built in in the sense that the countervailing interests are balanced.

In this chapter we have not dealt with aspects of risk and of proper contracting in much detail. The basic message is that increased success of mega-projects is not so much a matter of better methods or more accurate calculations. The major progress can be achieved by changing the institutional environment so that the incentives of the stakeholders work in the direction of generating real economic benefits within the budget to be spent. Once the incentives are set right, the players will almost automatically be interested in using the best technologies and methods, as suggested.

NOTES

1. We are not focusing here on the intrinsic problems associated with mega-projects, such as long life, high risk or unexpected changes, but rather on general concepts of procurement to cope with these problems appropriately.
2. Institute of Economic Policy Research of the University of Karlsruhe.

REFERENCES

Bel, G. and X. Fageda (2005), 'Is a mixed funding model for the highway network sustainable over time? The Spanish case', in G. Ragazzi and W. Rothengatter (eds), *Procurement and Financing of Motorways in Europe*, Amsterdam: Elsevier: 187–204.

Biehl, D. (1975), *Bestimmungsgruende des regionalen Entwicklungspotentials: Infrastruktur, Agglomeration und sektorale Wirtschaftsstruktur* (Influencing Factors for Regional Development: Infrastructure, Agglomeration and Sectoral Structure), Kiel: Kieler Studien, Bd. 133.

Biehl, D. (1991), 'The role of infrastructure for regional development', in S. von Hartard and C. Stahmer (eds), *Sozio-ökonomische Berichtssysteme für eine nachhaltige Gesellschaft*, Marburg: Metropolis: 42–65.

Flyvbjerg, B., N. Bruzelius and W. Rothengatter (2003), *Megaprojects and Risk. An Anatomy of Ambition*, Cambridge, MA: Cambridge University Press.

Heinitz, F. (2000), *A Constraint Logic Programming Approach to Travel Demand Modelling*, Karlsruhe Papers on Economic Policy Research, 10.

IASON (2004), 'Methodology for the assessment of spatial economic impacts of transport projects and policies', Deliverable 2 of the IASON project funded by the 5th Research Framework of the European Commission.

Lakshmanan, T.R. and W.P. Anderson (2002), *Transportation Infrastructure, Freight Services Sector and Economic Growth*, White Paper for the US DOT and FHWA, Boston, MA.

Liedtke, G. (2006), *An Actor-based Approach to Commodity Transport Modelling*, diss. thesis, Universität Karlsruhe (TH).

List, F. (1841), *Das nationale System der politischen Ökonomie* (The National System of Polical Economy), Stuttgart: Verlag der J.G. Cottáschen Buchhandlung.

RAILPAG (2005), *Railway Appraisal Guidelines*, Brussels and Luxembourg: European Commission and European Investment Bank.

Rogelio, O. (2003), 'Model calibration as a testing strategy for system dynamics models', *European Journal of Operational Research*, **151**: 552–68.

Rothengatter, W. and A. Schaffer (2005), 'The impact of transport infrastructure and other immobile production factors on regional competitiveness', paper prepared for DG Regio, Karlsruhe.

SACTRA (Standing Advisory Committee for Trunk Road Assessment) (1999), *Transport and the Economy*, Report to the Department of Transport, London.

Schade, W. (2005), *Strategic Sustainability Analysis: Concept and Application for the Assessment of European Transport Policy*, Baden-Baden: NOMOS.

TIPMAC (2004), *ASTRA-T: Results of the TIPMAC Policy Scenarios*, Report to the European Commission for the Research Project TIPMAC, Karlsruhe.

Vickerman, R.W. (1987), 'The Channel Tunnel and regional development: A critique of an infrastructure-led growth project', *Project Appraisal*, **2** (1), March: 31–40, Guildford: Beech Tree Publishing.

World Bank (1994), *An Overview of Monitoring and Evaluation in the World Bank*, Report 13247, Operations Evaluation Department, Washington, DC.

12. The cost of the technological sublime: daring ingenuity and the new San Francisco–Oakland Bay Bridge

Karen Trapenberg Frick

12.1 INTRODUCTION

Mega-projects are often captivating to political leaders and the public because of their colossal size and the technical hurdles they overcome. This feature of major infrastructure in the landscape has been termed the 'technological sublime' (Marx, 1964; 2000; Nye, 1994). This chapter uses the concept of the sublime to contribute a new dimension to understanding the evolution of mega-project design and optimism bias. The case of the new San Francisco–Oakland Bay Bridge in Northern California is used to demonstrate how the technological sublime dramatically influenced bridge design, project outcomes, public debate, and the lack of accountability for its excessive cost overruns.

According to David Nye (1994: xvi), the technological sublime 'is about repeated experiences of awe and wonder, often tinged with an element of terror, which people have had when confronted with particular natural sites, architectural forms and technological achievements'. In the Bay Bridge case, the goal of developing a sublime, new structure became the focal point of the public debate and drove the design and funding process. The project's initial purpose was to replace the bridge's east span, which collapsed during the 1989 Loma Prieta earthquake. Debate focused on designing a 'signature' bridge – a bridge that signifies the technological and aesthetic triumph of the region over the San Francisco Bay, a geologically complicated body of water, and thereby leave a unique signature on the landscape. This daring ingenuity spoke to the interest of many in the Bay Area, but not all, to create a sublime new bridge. The concept of the 'technological sublime' provides a theoretical context for interpreting underlying motivations, optimism and rhetoric of political leaders and participants advocating for not only a mega-project, but a 'mega-landmark'. The basis for the analysis is the results of in-depth interviews with approximately 45 key participants and extensive review of project-related documents and media accounts.

First, the background on mega-project characteristics and the technological sublime is reviewed. Then an overview of the existing Bay Bridge and the design process for the new bridge is provided. The chapter concludes with observations about the impact of the technological sublime on the planning process, project design and implementation, as well as implications for analyses of other mega-projects.

12.2   SETTING THE STAGE: MEGA-PROJECT CHARACTERISTICS

Typical characteristics of major transportation infrastructure projects come to light in the mega-projects literature (see Frick, 2005 and Chapter 2 in this book). These characteristics are termed the 'Six Cs' for the purposes of this chapter, and reveal that mega-projects are often:

- *Colossal* in size and scope, whereby there is major facility expansion or reconstruction, which may be a new tunnel, bridge, airport or rail system. These projects are highly visible after construction starts and the public witnesses these monumental endeavours.
- *Captivating* because of the project's size, engineering achievements and possibly its aesthetic design. This trait is related to the characteristic of 'colossal'. However, the project's design and technical accomplishments may generate a sense of awe and wonder in the project beyond its size and scope. It may also capture the imagination and attract the attention of participants and observers who typically may not follow a transportation project, such as architects, developers and the broader general public. Little attention has been devoted to this characteristic in the mega-projects literature; however, the 'technological sublime' literature often focuses on large-scale infrastructure projects.
- *Costly*, in that costs are often underestimated and increase over the life of the project. Mega-projects typically cost at least $250 million to $1 billion (Altshuler and Luberoff, 2003: 2). As discussed in this book, 'optimism bias' may be at play in cost estimating and the resultant cost increases.
- *Controversial*, as project participants negotiate funding and mitigation packages, engineering and aesthetic design plans, and pursue construction. Controversy may brew in part because of a project's

potential displacement or impacts to nearby businesses, residences and the physical/built environment.

- *Complex*, which breeds risk and uncertainty in terms of design, funding (as project costs are high and often covered by numerous funding sources) and construction.
- Laden with *control* issues related to who the key decision-makers are, what agency/agencies manage/operate the project, and who the main project funders are and what restrictions they put on it.

These characteristics are interrelated and evolve during mega-project development. In particular, mega-projects tend to be colossal and in turn become costly endeavours even under the best of circumstances. Since they are of a colossal nature and highly visible, they captivate a broader set of stakeholders and citizens who typically do not follow more standard transportation projects. In turn, these multifaceted projects become controversial because of the additional interests and the complexity associated with unpredictable issues due to risk and uncertainty with project funding, design and implementation. They also become controversial in terms of potential impacts to existing businesses, residences and their adjacent surroundings. Control issues then arise from this generally described situation because numerous stakeholders with differing vested interests assert their perspectives and attempt to steer the project's course.

These characteristics are illustrative of a mega-project's many facets, and provide a framework for evaluating specific cases and mega-projects in general. This case study focuses on how the 'captivating' and 'colossal' characteristics of the technological sublime affected the new Bay Bridge's regional design process.

12.3 THE TECHNOLOGICAL SUBLIME: A FIELD GUIDE

A key aspect of the bridge process revolved around the new bridge rhetoric related to creating a captivating 'signature' bridge – a bridge that signifies the technological and aesthetic triumph of the region in earthquake country. The debate became infused with notions of designing a bridge that is different. Not a bridge 'that could be anywhere', according to Oakland Mayor Jerry Brown, but a bridge that should be 'a spectacular structure that expresses the daring of human ingenuity and symbolizes the splendor of Oakland and the East Bay' (Brown, 1998).

This ingenuity captured the imagination of some, but not all, to create a sublime geographical landmark. The concept of the technological sublime provides a tool for understanding some of the motivations and rhetoric of political leaders and participants to advocate for such a landmark. It also proves useful to other researchers and policy-makers examining major infrastructure projects who seek to interpret underlying motivations in the design and implementation of major infrastructure projects/mega-projects as this concept has not been addressed in depth in the mega-projects literature.

The notion of technological sublime can be found in the work of historians Leo Marx and David Nye (see also Upton, 1998: 165–8). Marx labels America's fascination with technological advances of the nineteenth century as the 'rhetoric of the technological sublime' in which language was used, particularly in literature and public speeches, to convey a sense of the USA's unlimited potential in the area of progress. According to Marx, democracy fuelled American pursuits of new technology and inventions because it 'invites every man to enhance his own comfort and status. To the citizen of democracy inventions are vehicles for the pursuit of happiness' (Marx, 1964: 205). With respect to transportation technology, Marx comments, 'To look at a steamboat . . . is to *see* the sublime progress of the race. Variations on the theme are endless; only the slightest suggestion is needed to elevate a machine into a "type" of progress' (Marx, 2000: 203).

Following the work of Marx, historian David Nye traces the technological sublime in the USA by examining the impact that railways, skyscrapers, bridges and electricity had on the American psyche in the nineteenth and early twentieth centuries. These projects used technological means never seen before to achieve an end, be it faster travel or traversing difficult geographical territory. According to Nye, America's fascination with technology and major public works is connected to the 'sublime', an eighteenth-century aesthetic notion that was developed in literary and artistic works about nature, particularly Western natural landscapes such as the Grand Canyon, Yellowstone and Yosemite. From the nineteenth century to the present, advances in technology have been able to conquer nature and cause both fascination and terror in its viewers. He equates new technologies with national destiny, 'just as the natural sublime once undergirded the rhetoric of manifest destiny' (Nye, 1994: xvi, 282). Related to this perception of destiny, one of the first American experiences of technological sublime was through the Western expansion of the railways, which 'dramatized the unfolding of a national destiny' (ibid.: 76).

Nye (ibid.: 282) acknowledges: 'Despite its power, the technological sublime always implies its own rapid obsolescence, making room for the wonders of the next generation.' As a result, obsolescence fuels the development of new technologies to accomplish an even greater technological achievement. The idea of progress creates a political dimension that can capture the imagination of political leaders and the public. This aspect of the technological sublime is critical to note for major infrastructure projects because it is not just a psychological response to a major technological achievement, but a political tool that can be used to bolster position statements, increase public awareness and/or fulfil personal interests. In turn, these motivations may shape the design and outcome of a project. This political dimension of the technological sublime is not specifically addressed in the mega-projects literature and yet it plays a critical role in generating a realm of project optimism and momentum.

The technological sublime contributes to our understanding of major infrastructure projects because of its political, aesthetic and functional implications. It adds a personal dimension to mega-project design and implementation. The concept of technological sublime is used in this chapter to examine the debates that centred on bridge aesthetic and function, and how the design process and outcome were shaped as a result.

12.4 THE BAY BRIDGE IN BRIEF

The State of California owns and operates the Bay Bridge through its State Department of Transportation, also known as Caltrans. The San Francisco Bay Area's regional planning agency, the Metropolitan Transportation Commission (MTC), has also had increasing management authority over the Bay Area's seven toll bridges, including the Bay Bridge. The MTC manages the Bay Area's state-owned toll bridges through a separate entity, the Bay Area Toll Authority (BATA), whose board is identical to the MTC board. For the purposes of this chapter, BATA's approval actions on the new Bay Bridge are referred to as MTC actions as BATA was established during the new Bay Bridge design process. A different regional entity, the Golden Gate Bridge, Highway and Transportation District, own and operates the internationally known Golden Gate Bridge, which is in close proximity and can be seen from the Bay Bridge.

The Bay Bridge was completed in 1936 at a cost of $77 million, and the technological sublime aspect of the bridge loomed large (see Figure 12.1). According to Caltrans, the bridge was

> the greatest bridge in the world for its cost, length, quantities of steel and concrete, weight, depth, and number of piers, the size of the bore of the tunnel on YBI (Yerba Buena Island), and the versatility of its engineering. Seven of its piers were deeper than any others in the world. New technologies were created to construct the foundations. The submarine work was the greatest underwater engineering task ever undertaken. The steel for the superstructure was said to constitute the largest steel order ever placed. (East Span FEIS, 3-104 to 3-105)

Figure 12.1   Original Bay Bridge under construction

The bridge consists of a west span built in a suspension bridge design
between San Francisco and Yerba Buena Island, a tunnel through Yerba
Buena Island, and an east span in a cantilever/truss design between the
island and the Oakland shore (see Figure 12.2). The bridge is a double-deck
structure and currently contains ten travel lanes – five lanes for westbound
traffic on the upper deck and five lanes for eastbound traffic on the lower
deck. Travellers on the upper deck have enchanting views of the Bay and
San Francisco, while travellers on the darker lower deck proceed with
restricted views to the East Bay. The total bridge length including
approaches is 8.25 miles (13.28 km). The current bridge toll for round-trip
crossing is $4.00.

In general terms, the east span is approximately two miles (3.22 km) in
length and has three main sections: (1) a cantilever section located adjacent
to Yerba Buena Island (with a centre span of 427 metres or 1400 feet each);
(2) an overhead truss system east of the cantilever portion (five spans of 154
metres or 504 feet each); and (3) a deck truss system similar to a viaduct (14
spans of 89 metres or 288 feet each). For the cantilever section, three of the
four piers hit bedrock or have sunken caisson foundations. Remarkably, one
of the piers (Pier E3) is suspended above bedrock at about 70 feet (21 metres)
from the bottom of the caisson. For the overhead and deck truss system's
foundations, Douglas Fir timbers are used to provide support and were
installed by cofferdams that were left in place, filled in with concrete, and

Note: The existing Bay Bridge's western suspension bridge is in the foreground and the eastern cantilever/truss bridge is in the background. A tunnel on Yerba Buena Island connects the bridges.

Source: © Barrie Rokeach 2007.

Figure 12.2 Existing San Francisco–Oakland Bay Bridge

'much larger than required to actually support the bridge' (Caltrans, Replacement vs. Retrofit, 3-3 to 3-6). Importantly, the span's structure is a function of the bay's geology. The cantilever span allows the bridge to cross a deep-water shipping channel, and the trusses allow for the bridge to traverse an area of the bay with soft soils and mud. Bedrock along the bridge's length is not found until at least 300 feet (91 metres) below the waterline near Yerba Buena Island to almost 440 feet (134 metres) near the Oakland shore.

A portion of the east span's upper deck collapsed during the 1989 Loma Prieta earthquake, whose magnitude was 7.1 on the Richter scale with an epicentre 60 miles (97 km) away from the bridge (see Figure 12.3). With two major faults located significantly closer, energy from a maximum credible earthquake (MCE) with a magnitude of 8 on the Richter scale for the San Andreas fault could be 30 times that of the Loma Prieta earthquake. Energy generated from an MCE on the Hayward fault of magnitude 7.25 could be of a level similar to the Loma Prieta earthquake. With the US Geological Service estimating a 70 per cent chance of a 6.7 or greater magnitude earthquake by 2030, 'the risk (to the bridge) is real!' exclaimed Denis Mulligan of Caltrans (California Transportation Commission, Transcript of 11 May 2000 meeting: 1).

Source: Courtesy of the California Department of Transportation.

*Figure 12.3   Collapse of Bay Bridge's east span, Loma Prieta
             Earthquake, 1989*

Finally, the Bay Bridge is one of the most travelled facilities in the region
and operates at capacity during the morning and evening weekday peak
travel periods. Extensive public transport is also provided with buses, rail
and ferries. Approximately 288 000 vehicle trips and 590 200 person trips
are made on an average weekday in the corridor (MTC, 2002: 10–11).

As a result of the geological and seismic concerns as well as the bridge's
prominence as a vital transportation artery, the pursuit of upgrading the
facility evolved into a complex high-profile endeavour, particularly as aesthetic considerations came into play.

12.5   PUBLIC DESIGN PROCESS AND REDUX

Under normal circumstances, the State of California would lead the public
design process for its own structure. However, as discussed below, the new
bridge's design underwent two main cycles of intense public debate:

● the 'regional mega-landmark phase' during the years of 1997 and
  1998, in which the east span's design was selected by a different agency
  – the region's transportation planning agency, the Metropolitan
  Transportation Commission (MTC). As discussed below, this signified

a fundamental change in California and regional decision-making on one of the State's largest and most expensive transportation infrastructure projects;

- the 'State tinker toy phase', during the years of 2004 and 2005, in which the State advocated bridge redesign a few years after construction had started. This position was largely in response to a likely major cost increase resulting from the sole bid submitted for a contract to build the bridge's landmark tower segment. Critics of the State's position dubbed this the 'tinker toy' approach after the children's toy because the State considered exchanging a highly complex design midstream with another that it believed would be less difficult and costly.

The several intervening years were also filled with controversy due to staggering cost increases or contentious issues primarily related to the bridge's alignment. (For an in-depth discussion, see Frick, 2005.)

Regional Mega-Landmark Phase

The new Bay Bridge's regional design process began in 1997 when the State of California decided to replace the existing east span rather than seismically retrofit it in part due to a set of studies that showed similar replacement and retrofit cost estimates at approximately $900 to 1.5 billion (Jordan, 1997). The existing span would be demolished after the new bridge's completion.

The State's preferred replacement alternative was an unadorned viaduct (also known as a 'skyway') between the Oakland shore and Yerba Buena Island, with two steel-reinforced concrete structures containing ten lanes of traffic (five lanes in each direction) estimated at $1.5 billion (see Figure 12.4). It also provided a preliminary design of a double tower cable-stay structure for which the Bay Area could pay an additional $221 million if it so chose (McCormick, 1997). The final bridge design and alignment would be resolved during the environmental process. 'There is no question that the replacement option will give the people of California the best bridge at the best price,' said James W. van Loben Sels, then Director of Caltrans, as quoted in Caltrans's press release. 'Normally, if the cost of the retrofitting exceeds more than half the cost of the replacement, then it often makes economic sense to spend a little more for a new structure that incorporates the latest technology and offers the prospect of a much longer life span' (California Department of Transportation, 1997: 3).

With this announcement unveiled, public attention focused on the bridge's appearance and whether the State's proposed alternatives were

Note: The simulation illustrates Caltrans's proposed viaduct.

Source: Courtesy of the California Department of Transportation.

Figure 12.4 Early 1997 east span alternative by Caltrans

worthy of the site, particularly given the prominence and proximity of the world-renowned Golden Gate Bridge and the Bay Bridge's west span, which both have suspension designs. '[The] Bay Area may need to make a fateful choice themselves. Accept a stripped-down model of a span – or commission a lasting Bay crossing that may be equal of the Golden Gate Bridge,' stated the *San Francisco Chronicle* (1997). Across the Bay, the *Oakland Tribune* added:

> We think the design of the bridge is even more important than cost. We see this as a rare opportunity for the East Bay to insist on a graceful, even majestic design that the entire region can be proud of, not some utilitarian roadway. Let's make this a splendid front door to the East Bay ... the bridges spanning San Francisco Bay are a world-class attraction that have made our Bay Area a living postcard. Let's keep them picture perfect. (*Oakland Tribune*, 1997)

Due to increasing opposition over the initially proposed designs, state officials asked MTC to facilitate a public involvement process to develop regional consensus on a seismically safe and aesthetically pleasing new east span. Importantly, the Bay Area would design only half of the overall bridge – the east span. The west span's suspension span would undergo seismic retrofit. MTC established the Bay Bridge Design Task Force using a subset of its board to oversee the process. Of the viaduct design, Caltrans's preferred option, Supervisor Mary King, the Task Force's chair, commented: 'While we appreciate [that] the governor [Governor Wilson] has offered vanilla ice cream, we want chocolate sauce on top' (Oakes, 1997). In other words, MTC and many in the region were interested in developing a signature bridge design and rejected the viaduct bridge offered by Governor Wilson.

The Task Force's recommendations were based on another committee created for the design process, called the Engineering and Design Advisory Panel (EDAP). It consisted of approximately 35 members who were technical experts in bridge engineering, architecture and geology. EDAP was charged with the mission of 'reconciling design and engineering considerations so that the residents of the Bay Area can be assured that they will have a world class bridge' (Hein, 1997). EDAP chair Joseph Nicoletti commented: 'It is a very exciting thing we are about to do. What we come up with will result in a landmark that will last for 100 years' (Nolte, 1997). MTC's EDAP and Task Force committee meetings became the key political and technical arena in which the Bay Bridge's design was debated.

With these committees established, MTC and Caltrans focused on the following issues:

- How should the new bridge be designed? How do different bridges compare in terms of seismic performance? How does the new design incorporate signature features so that it will become a new Bay Area landmark/icon? Does it compete with or complement the Bay Bridge's west span and the Golden Gate Bridge?
- What should be the alignment of the new bridge? How do alignment options affect the bridge's termini at Yerba Buena Island and the Oakland shore?
- Should there be a rail line, cycle path, and carpool lane on the new bridge?

Decisions on these issues would come at a financial and political cost as each item competed for limited funds that would later become available through a complex funding arrangement between the State and the region (see Frick, 2005). In addition, many of these issues would challenge Caltrans's primary project objective, which was to provide a seismically safe new bridge as quickly as possible. According to Denis Mulligan, then with Caltrans:

> I always like to point out why we're doing this project. The San Francisco Oakland Bay Bridge East Span Seismic Safety Project is not a project designed to remove an ugly bridge from the Bay or a project designed to interfere with

someone's economic development. It is a public safety project. The Bay Bridge was damaged in the Loma Prieta Earthquake in 1989. (California Transportation Commission, 2000: 1).

Public outreach generally involved public meetings and formal hearings, informal polls, press coverage, and letters, emails and telephone calls received from the public. MTC and Caltrans held over 30 spirited meetings to discuss the east span's design from March 1997 to June 1998 (Heminger, 1997).

12.6   BRIDGE DESIGN: FORM AND FUNCTION

At the beginning of their deliberations, EDAP and the Task Force developed design review criteria. In addition to seismic safety, the bar was set high for creating a landmark bridge. The Bay Bridge Coalition, an ad hoc advocacy group with representatives from EDAP and other design/engineering organizations, recommended:

> The design should reflect the Bay Area's optimism, international status, and positive attitude toward technology. Statements about fashion, style, details, modernism, post-modernism, and whether or not form indeed follows function should be de-emphasized in the design criteria. Instead, the emphasis should be on the quality of the design and construction. Please realize that this bridge will define the style of the beginning of [the] next millennium, not react to it. (Bay Bridge Consortium, 1997)

Many participants were concerned about how the Bay Bridge's east span would relate architecturally to the often-noted 'elegant' or 'graceful' suspension bridge of the Bay Bridge's west span and the Golden Gate Bridge. A key issue was whether the new span should compete with these bridges or complement them. Some felt that the east span should complement those bridges. Others thought that was unnecessary. EDAP member Chris Arnold (1997) commented:

> I do not think the east [span] solution should be compromised by the need to 'harmonize' with an existing span developed under quite different site conditions and separated by an island. Rather, I think the East and West spans should be considered a 'progressive' series of experiences for the motorist (as it already is) and if the driver has an experience beneath the large vertical trusses of the west span there is no reason why he or she should not have an equally interesting, and even contrasting, experience beyond the island.

With this backdrop, the Task Force and EDAP reviewed design proposals, first those submitted by bridge experts and members of the public, and then later in a limited competition between two teams within one firm.

Design options generally fell into three categories: (1) suspension; (2) cable-stay; and (3) viaduct. Most tower designs had one to two towers located near Yerba Buena Island and were connected to a viaduct for the majority of the bridge's length. In addition, members of the public and others proposed creative and sometimes unorthodox designs that were rejected during the early stages. For example, a proposal called the 'Unity Towers of the East Bay' recommended that office buildings serve as bridge towers and that a third deck have parking and pedestrian/cycle access. 'Each office tower would be a city unto itself,' stated the proposal's author, Michael Longo (1997).

The cable-stay bridge design appeared to be the favourite among many EDAP and Caltrans participants because it was the bridge type of choice throughout the world. However, as a surprise, a self-anchored single tower suspension design won EDAP approval in May 1998 (see Figure 12.5). Elements of the EDAP-recommended bridge included:

- the new east span should have a single tower self-anchored suspension span because it is similar to the Bay Area's other suspension spans (the Golden Gate Bridge, the Bay Bridge's western spans, and the forthcoming new Carquinez Bridge);
- the suspension design should be asymmetrical, with the main span east of the tower about twice the length of the back span west of the tower;

Source: Courtesy of the California Department of Transportation.

Figure 12.5 MTC/EDAP-recommended self-anchored suspension span

- the bridge's viaduct portion should have a variable depth (haunched) profile built in concrete or a constant depth profile built in steel. The minimum span length would be 525 feet (160 metres), except near the viaduct's endpoints at Yerba Buena Island and the Oakland shore;
- a cycle/pedestrian pathway should be included and located on the eastbound deck's south side.

Several EDAP members commented that since the reported cost and seismic strength of the cable-stay and suspension bridges were similar, their decisions were made subjectively based on aesthetics and other factors, such as constructability and the east span's relationship to the west span and the Golden Gate Bridge. Many EDAP members appeared impressed with the uniqueness of the suspension bridge type because it had achieved a far greater asymmetry than the cable-stay bridge at EDAP's final decision meeting on the bridge type (with a 385-metre main span and 180-metre back span for the suspension span, and a 275-metre main span and 215-metre back span for the cable-stay bridge). Similarly, several key interviewees noted that the SAS bridge's increased asymmetry was the main reason in their opinion for EDAP's support of this bridge type over the cable-stay bridge. Support for the SAS bridge was further elevated as its asymmetry was viewed as better structurally because 'not only visually appealing . . . it shifts the tower west to a better foundation further up the rock shelf near Yerba Buena Island and results in a shipping channel with more than a 1,000 feet of horizontal clearance', according to EDAP's recommendations.

On the selection of the suspension bridge type, several interviewees also commented that their opinion was swayed because the bridge designers noted that the SAS bridge design echoed the suspension designs of the Bay Bridge's west span and the Golden Gate Bridge, but with a 'modern flair'.

However, not all EDAP participants were pleased with these recommendations. EDAP member T.Y. Lin commented that a 'suspension bridge represents an ignorance in engineering' (recorded at the meeting of 18 May 1998) and that 'it will be a testament to our ignorance. We'll be the laughing stock of the whole world' (Diaz, 1998). An EDAP member who was interviewed interpreted Mr Lin's statements as reflecting his substantial concerns about how the SAS bridge type was more difficult to construct than a cable-stay bridge and that there were less expensive and easier options, such as a cable-stay bridge, which Mr Lin proposed to the *San Francisco Chronicle* in 1997.

Opposition from elected officials on both sides of the Bay escalated against the recommended SAS bridge. East Bay elected officials opposed the design for aesthetic reasons and over concern for how rail was being incorporated into the design. An opposition letter to MTC from several elected officials was issued and a press conference was held. These officials stated:

> We, the undersigned East Bay community leaders, are expressing our mutual concerns that the Bay Bridge Eastern Span design process has not produced a *world class design* that establishes a sense of gateway and place for the East Bay. The East Bay communities expect and deserve a *world class design* that is oriented towards people and provides quality public access and amenities. (Emphasis added; letter of 18 June 1998)

According to the Berkeley Mayor of the time, Shirley Dean, a signatory of the letter; 'We're saying time out, we don't need to rush. We need to do the job right. People are going to remember this decision for decades, and our children and grandchildren will have to live with what we decide now for a long time' (Hamburg, 1998). Oakland Mayor Jerry Brown also joined the opposition. He recommended an international design competition to develop a new design in part because

> The recommended design – half of a suspension bridge attached to a bland viaduct – speaks of mediocrity, not greatness. It does not respect the site or reflect the incomparable beauty of the place. It mocks the principle of the suspension bridge by eradicating its most beautiful part: the freely suspended towers. It copies the past rather than pulling us to the future. It fails to rise to the challenge which the setting and the new millennium demand. It could be anywhere. (Brown, 1998)

The *San Francisco Chronicle* and the *San Francisco Examiner* similarly followed suit and suggested a delay in the region's decision to allow for design reconsideration (editorials 21 and 22 June 1998).

In response, MTC and Caltrans stated that the bridge decision could not be delayed because the project needed to continue and be completed quickly for seismic safety reasons. Further, with respect to aesthetic design, the agencies responded that the Bay's geology dictated the bridge type in that a deep-water shipping channel near the island was the only logical place to locate a tower, and that a tower or series of towers in the soft shallow soil closer to the East Bay shore would be costly and unnecessary. EDAP vice-chairman John Kriken commented, '[Mayor] Jerry Brown, I'm sorry you can't wave your magic wand and put rock over there. There's no way to build a tower closer to Oakland. If you're anchored only in mud, you want to keep the bridge profile as low as possible' (Adams, 1998). In the end, MTC approved the EDAP-recommended design of a steel single-tower self-anchored suspension span connected to a viaduct. According to those involved in the bridge design, Rafael Manzanarez, Brian Maroney and Man-Chung Tang, 'When built, this will be the largest self-anchored suspension span in the world.' The estimated cost was $1.5 billion to $1.65 billion.

State 'Tinker Toy' Phase

Over the next several years, Caltrans completed a protracted and contentious environmental review process mainly due to disputes over the perceived impacts of the bridge's proposed alignment (see Frick, 2005). It also entered into numerous construction contracts, and the bridge's cost started rising. By mid-2004, Caltrans planned to contract out the bridge's last major component, the self-anchored suspension tower. Only one bid was received, submitted by a consortium led by the American Bridge Corporation. The bid, which ranged from $1.4 billion to $1.8 billion, was twice as high as Caltrans's contract estimate of approximately $750 million. The State then officially announced that the new span's overall cost had doubled to approximately $5 billion. Caltrans cited several factors that contributed to the increase: insurance and bonding costs had continued to increase due to concerns about terrorism; steel prices had increased by 50 per cent in the last few years; technical experts and staffing needs were greater than anticipated; project construction took longer and was more difficult than expected, particularly due to marine construction activities; and construction costs generally had increased industrywide. In addition, there was limited capacity on the part of the construction industry to bid on the east span's suspension tower contract. Importantly, it was asserted that approximately half of the east span's cost increase was related to the self-anchored suspension tower. However, others strongly disputed the extent to which the signature tower span was to blame for the cost increase.

As a result, Governor Arnold Schwarzenegger and his administration proposed that the bridge's 'signature' suspension tower should not be built and that a viaduct should be constructed in place of the tower. The Administration's stated goal was to reduce financial/construction-related risk and project costs by $300 to $500 million (roughly 5 per cent of the total east span cost) by pursuing a more standard design. According to Will Kempton, Caltrans Director, 'There are some challenges [with the skyway design]. But there are few unknowns with the skyway. This is a much simpler kind of design, and we are very familiar with this type of work' (Cabanatuan, 2004). The Administration's news came as a shock to many because the bridge's viaduct segment was approximately 70 per cent complete and a portion of the suspension tower's foundation was under construction. Critics of the Administration's recommendations argued that cost savings would not be realised and that the bridge process would get lost in endless environmental, design and permit delays if the viaduct option were selected. Many were sceptical of Caltrans's ability to make such recommendations given its track record to date. California State Senator Don Perata commented: 'The same agency that botched the last estimate is the same agency recommending we build the skyway, saying it won't take any longer and promising it will save money. I'm not sure there's a lot of confidence in Caltrans there' (Cabanatuan, 2004). With respect to the overall project, California State Senator Tom McClintock of Ventura County later stated: 'It's the biggest fiasco in California transportation history. This was a simple retrofit of that bridge that has been botched beyond anyone's wildest imagination' (CNN, 2005).

Numerous duelling studies were completed comparing suspension, cable-stay and viaduct alternatives, and each side interpreted the studies' results in line with their initial positions (see Frick, 2005). State legislation was finally signed in 2005 to cover the cost increase and allow the Bay Bridge project to move forward as designed. Through a toll increase, refinancing and other measures, the Bay Area would fund a large part of the additional costs, but it also agreed to assume major oversight responsibilities for the Bay Area's state-owned toll bridge programme. 'We're ready to move forward with a bridge that will be beautiful, that will keep the people of our state safe and that will keep commerce flowing across a very, very important state bridge,' stated California State Assemblyperson Loni Hancock, bill author of the legislation. The new tower's contract was awarded to a joint venture between American Bridge Company and Flour Enterprises in April 2006, nearly two years after the original single-tower bid had been submitted. The total bridge cost is currently estimated at $5.4 billion (plus an additional $900 million contingency), a far cry from the initial 1998 estimate of approximately $1.5 billion. It is expected to open to traffic in 2013.

12.7 OBSERVATIONS, IMPLICATIONS AND RECOMMENDATIONS FOR MEGA-PROJECT DEVELOPMENT

The case of the new San Francisco–Oakland Bay Bridge exemplifies the allure and potential of the technological sublime to consume a public planning and decision-making process. It fuelled an optimism that engineering and design can conquer nature while at the same time blinding many stakeholders to the complex realities of building a colossal project 'on time and on budget' – a mantra that should be at the forefront of every milestone during project planning and delivery. Instead, the underlying theme driving the process was that this is history in the making because the bridge would become a 'once-in-a-lifetime' landmark. As a result, the stage was set for a wide variety of participants to voice differing perspectives about bridge design and even harness this theme to promote additional elements, such as a cycle/pedestrian facility and reinstitution of rail service on the bridge. Arguments for these modes often focused on increasing capacity for alternative transport; however, the advocacy was often bolstered with the sentiment that the bridge could not be 'world class' unless it provided rail or new cycle/pedestrian access. A feeding frenzy then occurred in which the bridge project became a magnet to resolve other issues plaguing the region such as: traffic congestion; air quality; tourism, economic development and city revitalisation; and lack of pedestrian/cycle access. The one unexpected benefit of the sublime's impact was that it created a small knowledgeable, yet sceptical, group of Bay Area officials later willing to support maintaining the bridge's signature tower in the face of the Schwarzenegger Administration's recommendation to replace it with a viaduct or cable-stay tower. Except for this particular benefit, the overall results are threefold: unrealistic implementation schedules, underestimated costs and lack of accountability. Together these results fuelled heightened public scepticism and distrust as nearly a quarter of a century will have passed between the 1989 earthquake and the bridge's projected completion in 2013.

Why did notions of the sublime influence the Bay Bridge process and outcomes? The answer boils down to two words: project definition. Conflicts over this two-mile bridge erupted over major unresolved differences of opinion between the various players over the project's basic premise. Was the new bridge simply a seismic improvement endeavour, or was it supposed to become a sublime 'mega-landmark' that demonstrates the Bay Area's aesthetic and engineering sensibilities? Should the new bridge provide additional travel capacity for cycles, pedestrians, bus and rail transit, and/or possibly even cars? According to an MTC commissioner interviewed:

> [T]his bridge became for people somehow a place on which to hang all of their anger, hopes, frustrations, dreams, whatever around the transportation problems of the Bay Area when really it was a safety measure and the part that got so frustrating for me because if you could look at it clearly and understand why we were doing it, if you could remember the reason we were doing it, you remember the day that the bridge collapsed and that government has some obligation to public safety.

With the technological sublime as the turbulent undercurrent to unresolved problem definitions, efforts to achieve the sublime evolved in two interrelated ways: one that affected the bridge's aesthetic features and one that affected the bridge's functional aspects of design and structural integrity. These aspects are labelled the 'aesthetic sublime' and the 'functional sublime' for the purposes of the chapter. The aesthetic sublime addresses how officials and other participants often tailored their passionate public testimony to maximise the visual and experiential aspects of the design. Their stated motivations were to maximise the potential for a new awe-inducing Bay Area landmark and, in some cases, to garner inclusion of different bridge elements they felt were needed for a 'world-class' structure.

The functional sublime is related to achieving a bridge design that would address the site's immense physical requirements in terms of seismic and geologic constraints while also becoming a symbol of technological progress in bridge engineering. Based on interviews with MTC's technical committee members and others, the technical design participants had seismic safety at the forefront of concern. However, an overwhelming sense prevailed that the bridge should benefit from the latest technology and serve to advance new design and construction techniques when appropriate. Nowhere is this clearer than in the selection of the self-anchored suspension span, a design never before built at this scale in a seismic zone. From a functional perspective, a towerless viaduct bridge could have been the bridge of choice; however, the aesthetic backlash against the design removed this as a legitimate contender. In effect, the design itself symbolises a hybrid effort to accomplish both the aesthetic and functional technological sublime – a signature tower connected to a viaduct. The tower provides the potential for landmark recognition and the viaduct represents the physical realities of the site affecting the design.

A major 'leap of optimism' in accomplishing the sublime occurred at the project's onset and had an everlasting effect on the design process and outcome. The State did not sufficiently anticipate and plan for the Bay Area's strong opposition to the viaduct as the preferred alternative and the belief that the region should pay for bridge enhancements. MTC's Executive Director at the time, Lawrence Dahms, commented in February 1997: 'Until today, I don't think anybody thought about what the next step would be after Caltrans made the announcement. So everybody's scurrying around trying to figure out what's next' (McCormick, 1997). Some interviewees and others point to this approach as the debate's fire-starter for the region, never fully considering the State's towerless viaduct as a viable option. Alan Hess of the *San Jose Mercury News* observed:

[W]ith a ham-fisted introduction by Governor Wilson, the skyway solution came across instantly as the bargain basement version. This is what the state will pay for, he said in his take-it-or-leave-it taxcutter's monotone. If the Bay Area wants upgrades with cables or towers, it will have to pay for it, he said. By presenting

it as the Motel 6 of bridges, Wilson guaranteed that it would be D.O.A. ['Dead
on arrival', meaning that the skyway viaduct design would be rejected outright].
(Hess, 1998)

Further, the State optimistically thought that a public design process for
such a complicated structure could be completed in six months even though
it had taken seven years to recommend bridge replacement over retrofit.
The region tentatively agreed, but then later argued that the process should
be extended. Then, several agencies within the bridge's vicinity advocated
for an even longer decision-making process as the regional decision was
looming in mid-1997, and continued to argue against it during the environmental process lasting several years thereafter. As a result, the project's
delivery was regularly delayed and often viewed as 'behind schedule'.

What could be done differently that would be instructive in the development of future mega-projects? A cost-estimating tool called 'optimism
bias uplift' could be expanded to address the potential problem definition
conflicts and schedule delays that develop in design processes resulting
from the technological sublime. For an optimism bias uplift, 'reference
class forecasting' is used whereby a contingency dollar amount is added to
a project's estimated cost based on other similar projects. This technique
is based on the work of Daniel Kahneman and others, who analysed the
psychological reasons for the development of overly optimistic estimates
of a project or situation's duration (see Chapter 7 in this volume; Flyvbjerg
and COWI, 2004). A similar optimism in schedule estimation occurs in
mega-projects, as demonstrated in the Bay Bridge case. Thus optimism
bias analyses for mega-projects would benefit from explicit identification
of a 'contingency schedule uplift' to budget sufficient time to address the
political impacts of the technological sublime on schedule delay and estimated costs. A more realistic timeframe could be developed based on other
high-profile mega-projects to allow for adequate public involvement up
front and throughout implementation as construction complexities
surface. The schedule uplift would also allow for the time needed to complete required environmental processes and negotiate the 'Christmas tree'
effect of projects in which elements are added to address public concerns
or for mitigation purposes. Thus project appraisals would account for a
'cost uplift' *and* an explicit 'schedule uplift'. Both uplifts could be com-
municated directly to the public and decision-makers to provide improved
cost estimates and project completion schedules, thereby directly confronting the need for projects to be 'on budget and on schedule'. The
schedule would allow time for 'the unpredictable' even if the specifics of
predicting the unpredictable could not be fully scoped at the beginning of
project development. Of course, care should be taken to ensure that dollar

costs attributed to a schedule uplift are not assumed as immediately available for the project.

Similar to Flyvbjerg's recommendation that the implementing agency should fund any cost uplift used, it also should be held accountable for the schedule uplift. A simple yet clear way to demonstrate schedule adherence is currently employed in a regular feature of the *San Francisco Chronicle* about failing public infrastructure of all sizes called '*Chronicle*Watch'. Each instalment features the following: project(s) in need of repair or upgrade, such as street repaving and intersection improvement; the responsible public agency; a photograph of the lead staff person; and the number of days since the project was identified. When the situation is resolved, the agency and project are likewise identified. A similar form of regular public notice could be published through the media and on appropriate websites for local mega-projects. The project's schedule as well as costs – budgeted, the uplift amount and actual to date – could be identified, thereby providing a transparent means for assessing whether the project is on budget, on schedule and who is held accountable, and, it is hoped, later applauded when projects are successfully implemented.

12.8   WRAPPING UP THE SUBLIME AND FUTURE RESEARCH CONSIDERATIONS

The new Bay Bridge case raises several important additional dimensions that should be considered in policy analyses of mega-projects: the sublime, aesthetics and funding. First, the technological sublime clearly played an instrumental role in the decision-making process. As future mega-projects are pursued, it would be instructive for project sponsors to recognise that the technological sublime may consume some public processes and in turn affect project design, budgets and schedule. On the one hand, the sublime has the potential to fuel creative design, engineering and public involvement. On the other hand, it may negatively affect cost and project schedules as optimism persists about the ability of design and engineering to overcome the technical complexities and risks associated with implementing large-scale projects. Additional case study analyses should be undertaken to examine the extent to which pursuit of the aesthetic and functional sublime affects other mega-projects, and whether similar or divergent themes emerge in project development and implementation.

Second, the Bay Bridge case reveals several issues related to the legitimacy and level of appropriateness of using public funds on the aesthetic dimensions of a project. The Bay Area elected to make a public statement with a signature bridge and chose to pay for the initial higher cost difference to build a bridge that was not simply a utilitarian 'bare-bones' viaduct. The region's path generates a set of interesting policy questions for mega-projects as well as other publicly funded projects in general. Should the government be expected to invest in aesthetics beyond the basic design of such a project? Is it reasonable to argue that there is an aesthetic value in simplicity and cost minimisation itself? Should the level of government paying the basic costs have the full responsibility for the extra cost, or is it legitimate to argue that those additional costs should be the responsibility of the units of government who will gain from the imagery? Further, if cost increases occur, how do the various levels of government cover the additional cost among themselves? These various dimensions of a larger policy debate ought to be further considered as policy-makers and researchers gain a deeper understanding of mega-projects.

Overall, achieving the technological sublime in mega-projects should be recognised as a potentially critical element in project development, whether or not the designs result in endearing landmarks or engineering marvels. As in the Bay Bridge case, the sublime may provide participants with the personal motivation and interest to heighten their involvement and/or with a political tool that at a minimum provides pithy soundbites that capture the attention of the media and larger public. Implementing agencies would best be served to acknowledge the unpredictable, chaotic nature that the sublime may contribute to a process and budget sufficient time to address it, rather than assume all will go according to plan. Such recognition would improve project performance and public debate by reducing the prevailing optimism in delivery schedules for projects that require substantial funding and time, and in the end, will change the way we travel and perceive the landscape.

ACKNOWLEDGEMENTS

The author gratefully acknowledges the support and guidance of Martin Wachs and Elizabeth Deakin. They provided unlimited assistance, guidance and wisdom during the research and writing phases. Martin Wachs also reviewed several drafts in detail and provided insightful contributions throughout the chapter. In addition, the research was generously supported by assistance from the US Department of Transportation through the Dwight D. Eisenhower Program, the University of California Transportation Center, the Women's Transportation Seminar and the University of California, Berkeley.

REFERENCES

Adams, Gerald D. (1998), '2nd tower? No way, say bridge designers', *San Francisco Examiner*, 5 July.

Altshuler, A. and D. Luberoff (2003), *Megaprojects. The Changing Politics of Urban Investment*, Washington, DC: Brookings Institution Press.

Arnold, Chris (1997), 'Building systems development, Palo Alto', Memorandum to Joe LaClair regarding 'Bay bridge criteria', 21 April.

Bay Bridge Consortium (1997), Technical Advisory Committee signed by Perry A. Haviland. Letter to Metropolitan Transportation Commission, 22 April.

Brown, Jerry (1998), Mayor-Elect, City of Oakland, '"There" needs to be a more fitting bridge', *San Francisco Chronicle*, 22 June.

Cabanatuan, Michael (2004), 'The new Bay Bridge proposal: simpler? Definitely. Cheaper? Maybe', *San Francisco Chronicle*, 11 December.

California Department of Transportation (1997), 'Wilson Administration recommends replacing Bay Bridge', press release, 13 February.

California Transportation Commission (2000), *Transcript of Item 4.11B, Update on Eastern Span of Bay Bridge Replacement, Including Comments from U.S. Navy, Meeting of the California Transportation Commission* (Sacramento, California), 11 May.

CNN International.com (2005), 'Bay Bridge project California's "biggest fiasco"', 16 March.

Diaz, Sam (1998), 'Opinion on bridge changes: single tower: revised model also allows bikes, walkers', *San Jose Mercury News*, 30 May.

Flyvbjerg, Bent and COWI (2004), *Procedures for Dealing with Optimism Bias in Transport Planning*, Guidance Document, London: UK Department of Transport, June.

Frick, Karen Trapenberg (2005), 'The making and un-making of the San Francisco–Oakland Bay Bridge: a case in megaproject planning and decision-making', unpublished doctoral dissertation, University of California, Berkeley, CA.

Hamburg, Laura (1998), 'S.F. Joins 11th-hour stick over bridge design: Treasure Island Plan could suffer', *San Francisco Chronicle*, 19 June.

Hein, William F. (1997), Metropolitan Transportation Commission. Memorandum to EDAP regarding 'Future role and process of EDAP', 9 June (Agenda Item #4 for 16 June 1997, EDAP meeting).

Heminger, Steve (1997), Metropolitan Transportation Commission. Memorandum to Bay Bridge Design Task Force regarding 'Summary of public comment', 17 June (Agenda Item #4 of 24 June 1997, Bay Bridge Design Task Force meeting).

Hess, Alan (1998), 'A bridge to take us from whimsy to expensive looniness', *San Jose Mercury News*, 5 April.

Jordan, Edward G. (1997), California Transportation Commission. Letter to State of California Senator Deidre Albert, 10 March.

Longo, Michael (1997), Santa Cruz, 'Unity Towers East Bay Bridge', New East Span Proposal Submitted to MTC Bay Bridge Design Task Force, 6 May.

Mauzanarez, Rafael, Brian Maroney and Man-Chung Tan, *San Francisco–Oakland Bay Bridge*, T.Y. Lin International and Moffat & Nichol.

Marx, Leo (1964; 2000), *The Machine in the Garden*, Oxford: Oxford University Press.

McCormick, Erin (1997), 'Cost vs. aesthetics: bridging the gap', *San Francisco Examiner*, 14 February.

Metropolitan Transportation Commission (MTC) (2002), *San Francisco Bay Crossings Study*, Oakland, CA: Metropolitan Transportation Commission, July.
Nolte, Carl (1997), 'Case made against "prima donna" span', *San Francisco Chronicle*, 10 April.
Nye, David E. (1994), *American Technological Sublime*, Cambridge, MA: The MIT Press.
Oakes, Robert (1997), 'Bay Area residents have until July to pick Bay Bridge design', *Contra Costa Times*, 19 February.
Oakland Tribune (1997), 'A new front door to the East Bay', editorial, 19 February.
San Francisco Chronicle (1997), 'A new Bay Bridge, but what design?', editorial, 14 February.
Upton, Del (1998), *Architecture in the United States*, Oxford: Oxford University Press.

13. Provision and management of dedicated railway systems: how to arrange competition

Didier van de Velde and Ernst F. ten Heuvelhof

13.1 INTRODUCTION

Since the 1980s, an intensive debate has been going on about the optimal institutional design of the rail transport sector (train and metro). For decades, activities in this sector were organised in vertically integrated enterprises. 'Vertically integrated' means that the various links in the production chain, particularly infrastructure and transport services, were united in one hand. This gave rise to vertically integrated monopolists. Particularly in continental Europe, governments owned these vertically integrated monopolists.

In the 1980s, doubts were cast on this arrangement. The absence of competition and the dominance of governments were no longer seen as a guarantee for reliable and cheap service delivery. Many argued that more competition and the introduction of private ownership would generate incentives to improve the performance of this industry. This argument was raised in many network-based industries. The idea is that productive efficiency will rise after the introduction of competition and privatisation (see, e.g., Winston, 1993; Megginson and Netter, 2001; Letza et al., 2004; Donahue, 1989: 57–78).

One condition that was considered vital for changes of this kind was the unbundling of the various links in the production chain. Infrastructure and services should no longer be united in one hand as a matter of course. Unbundling would allow the introduction of competition in links that do not require monopolistic ordering. This unbundling would also allow the private sector more room, since links in which competition was introduced would be able to switch to private ownership.

The perceived need for competition was so big that forms of competition *on* or *for* the market were developed even for links that were regarded as natural monopolies. Public–private arrangements became the fashion and plenty of experiments were conducted with new forms of contracting (competition *for* the market).

However, the high degree of interdependence between the technical design of the infrastructure (including tracks, energy provision and signalling system) and that of the trains as vehicles using the infrastructure generates critical interface problems that require specific attention when the use of competition is contemplated for parts of a railway system.

A large variety of competition-based arrangements for the provision and management of railway systems can be observed. This chapter suggests in its second section a framework for the classification and analysis of competition-based arrangements in the railway sector. This framework takes into account the design, build, operate, maintain and finance stages commonly found in recent (competition-based) contractual arrangements and combines them with the complexity of the railway sector through the conceptual layers that characterise transport infrastructures, such as the civil engineering work and its equipment (tracks, signalling, energy supply) and vehicles.

An essential purpose of this chapter is to present to a non-specialised public the variety of ways in which contractual and competition-based arrangements can be incorporated in the provision of rail infrastructures and train operations.[1] Our focus is on the realisation of new railway systems (infrastructure *and* transport services on these infrastructures) with one main transport service provider. This means that we do not address issues related to track capacity allocation in competitive train operations.

Before drawing a few conclusions in the last section of the chapter, we present in Section 13.3 the framework as applied to a few European cases. This is done to illustrate in a synthetic way the variety of arrangements that can be found in recent European cases where competition was used to provide and manage new railway infrastructures.

13.2   A GRID FOR THE ANALYSIS OF CONTRACTUAL ARRANGEMENTS IN THE RAILWAY SECTOR

Two main perspectives are used to establish a grid for the presentation and analysis of (competition-based) contractual arrangements in the railway sector. The first is the life-cycle stage. This is the traditional division between design, build, operate, maintain and finance. The second is a division into the main components that characterise railway systems, with infrastructures (track and stations) and vehicles forming the main inputs in the production of transport services.

Design, Build, Finance, Operate and Maintain

Numerous activities are required before transport services can be provided to customers. Various assets (infrastructures and vehicles) need to be produced; these assets need to be managed and maintained in order to deliver usable infrastructure capacity and usable vehicle time. These intermediate outputs constitute inputs in the production of transport capacity. Various marketing activities have to be deployed first to conceive and then to sell this transport capacity into individual transport services to passengers.

These activities differ sharply, as do the competencies required to complete them successfully. However, in the rail industry they were until recently performed by the same enterprise – the state railway company or the municipal metro company – which had specialised units to carry them out.

Recently, debate has arisen as to whether, and to what extent, other organisation forms can bring better results. Each of the activities mentioned above could, in principle, be contracted out to different companies specialising in the relevant activities. For example, asset *design* may be outsourced to firms of consulting engineers, *build* to building contractors and *operate and maintain* to specialised operators. The problem with such decompositions is that optimal choices for each of the individual activities do not necessarily combine into an optimal set for the global package; poor performance in one activity could indeed have serious subsequent (but delayed) impacts on other activities.

More innovative forms of contracting out are also conceivable that try to address this issue (see, e.g., Hann and Mack, 2005; De Ridder, 1998; Vollaard and Witteveen, 1999), such as: BO contracts (build and operate in one hand), DB contracts (design and build in one hand) and DBFOM contract (design, build, finance, operate and maintain in one hand). The essence is that several phases are then entrusted to one contractor, who can, from his own expertise and in response to the set of incentives resulting from the combination of several phases into one contract, make economic trade-offs between the various phases of the project so as to improve overall project efficiency. A typical example is the trade-off that may exist between additional building costs and possible lower maintenance costs in the future.

For the clarity of the presentation, we group the traditional stages design, build, operate and maintain (DBOM) into two main types of activities: 'conception' and 'utilisation' (see Figure 13.1). In the design stage principals can confine themselves to indicating functionalities of the activities contracted out, leaving their detailed design and arrangement to the contractors. Note, however, that the extent to which the contractor is in

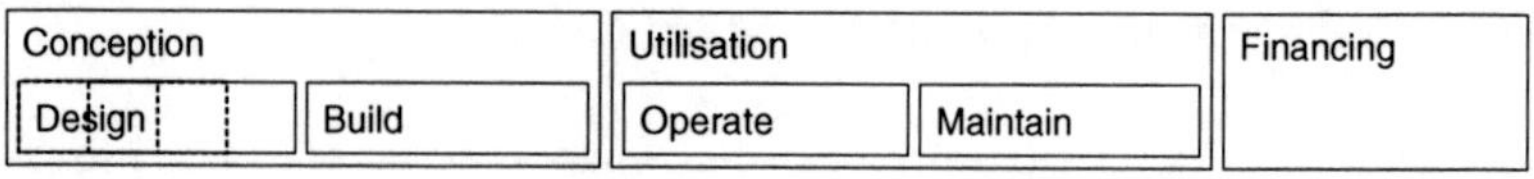

Conception			Utilisation			Financing
Design		Build	Operate	Maintain		

Figure 13.1   DBOM and finance

charge of the full design varies from case to case. This is represented by the dotted lines in Figure 13.1.

An essential feature of public–private partnerships and competition-based arrangements is the mobilisation of private sector capital to realise infrastructure projects. Linking private participation in the DBOM stages to private financing and risk-taking is meant to enhance the incentives to which contractors are subjected to realise the project aims. Numerous possibilities exist in this respect, but covering these options falls outside the scope of this chapter (see, e.g., Hann and Mack, 2005 for various project financing structures and options, such as equity, debt and bonds).

Components of the Railway System

The elements presented in Figure 13.1 form the first dimension of the grid of analysis suggested in this chapter. However, this is not sufficient to present the complexity of (competition-based) contractual arrangements in the railway sector, as railway systems are composed of several components (see Figure 13.2) for which different contractual and competition-based arrangements can exist. This forms the second dimension of the grid of analysis suggested here.

We distinguish *essential components* from *additional components*. The *essential components* are those features that are indispensable for providing transport services to customers. These include fixed installations (infrastructures) and moving components (trains) that are the main inputs to service provision. *Additional components* are those that are not essential to realise transport services, even when closely linked to the rail transport system. These are, e.g., commercial spaces located at the stations and surrounding real estate. We need to include these components in our analysis, as they are potential sources of substantial funding for the provision and management of rail infrastructures and their operations.

Fixed installations are the track infrastructure and the station infrastructure. The track itself is composed of the civil engineering infrastructure (rail bed, tunnels and bridges) the rails themselves, the electrical power supply for traction (in the case of electric railways) and the infrastructure part of the signalling and safety system (beacons, sensors, signals located alongside the track, etc.) The complementary part of the safety system is

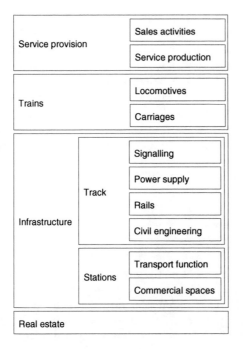

Figure 13.2   Components of railway systems

located inside the train (receivers, computers, human interface, etc.) The station infrastructure comprises the space needed for realising transport services: loading and unloading spaces (such as platforms for passenger transport), transfer spaces and waiting spaces for passengers or storage spaces for freight.

The *moving components* (i.e. the trains) can further be divided into traction units (locomotives) and passenger or freight transport units (carriages or wagons). Unlike freight trains, most modern passenger trains are made up of train sets (electrical multiple units or EMUs) in which traction and transport are integrated into a single device by locating the motor units underneath the vehicles.

Service provision refers to the conception or design of transport services, i.e. identifying (potential) demand and supplying transport services that suit demand. This includes on the one hand the conception and production of transport services (including the design of all related quality aspects and bearing related production-cost risks) and the commercial part, such as fare design and sales activities (including bearing commercial risks), on the other hand.

The various components and sub-components are linked by input–output relationships that constitute basic steps in chains of production that ultimately lead to the sales of rail transport services. Human resources are used at each of these steps. The various asset components (stations, tracks, trains) need to be designed, built, operated and maintained. This leads to the production of infrastructure services (rail 'paths', station 'slots') and vehicle services (the availability in time of rolling stock, well maintained and fit for purpose). These are combined by a service provider who puts the available rolling stock to productive use on specific infrastructures. This delivers transport capacity that can be sold as transport services to customers (see also Schaafsma, 2001; and Van Twist et al., 2003 for similar approaches).

A General Framework of Analysis

Combining both dimensions introduced above leads to a table (Figure 13.3) as a general framework of analysis enabling a comparison of the variety of arrangements that can be encountered in railway systems. The table also includes an additional column referring to the actor taking the *initiative* for the respective component of the whole system. In most cases, at least in Europe (transport) authorities or companies belonging to them take the initiative to create new rail systems.

This framework is meant to illustrate and help explain some of the complexities of such arrangements in the railway sector. From this table, it is clear that one cannot simply talk about 'design, build, operate and maintain' for the railway sector. The various parts of the production process (station, track building, track equipment, train or service provision) could be entrusted to one or to several actors and, furthermore, different DBOM arrangements could be chosen for each of these. The choice of the best set of arrangements (integration of all sub-components or not, contractual relation or not, competition-based or not) for a specific railway project will have to take at least the vertical and horizontal dimensions in the table into account.

The *vertical dimension* refers to the choice of whether or not to allocate the various steps in the production of the train transport services to several organisations, and whether or not to subject them to different arrangements (contractual or not, competition-based or not). The choices made in this dimension will influence system-wide optimisation, since one of the characteristics of the railway system is the high degree of interdependence between the technical design of the infrastructure (including the civil engineering work, the tracks, the energy provision and the signalling system) and that of the trains using the infrastructure.

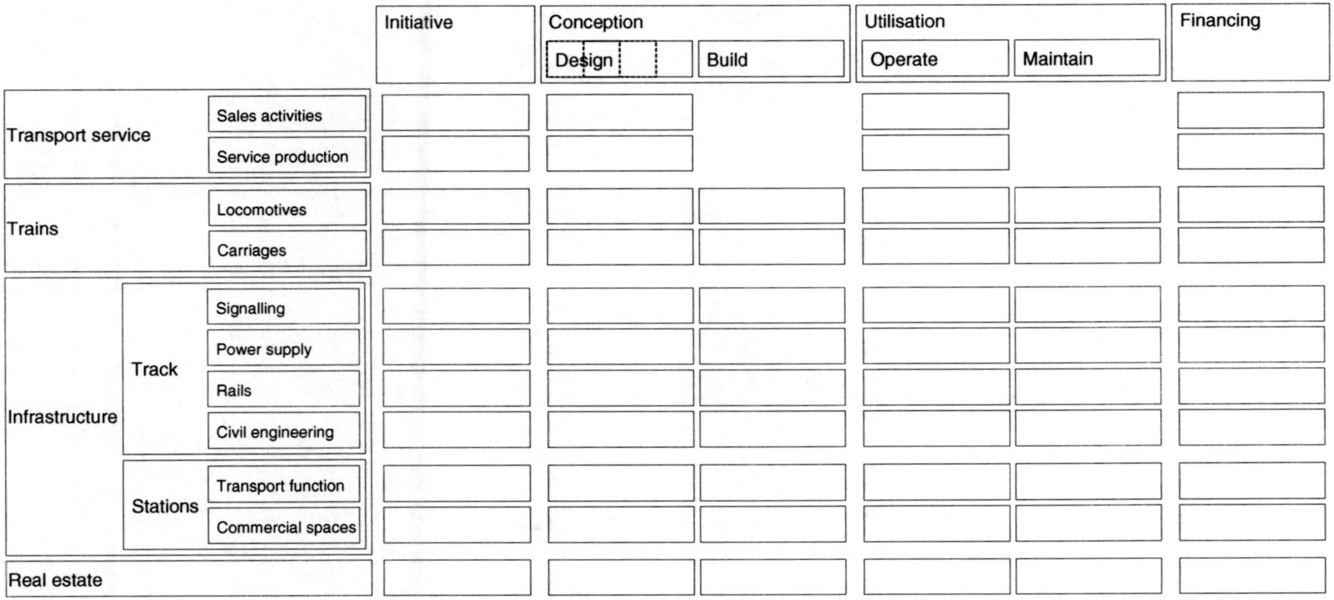

Figure 13.3 General framework of analysis

The *horizontal choice* whether or not to separate the design, build, operate and maintain stages will affect the extent to which and the way in which trade-offs between building costs and maintenance costs can be realised (including life-cycle cost optimisation). This issue is present for every single step of the production process represented in the vertical dimension.

These horizontal and vertical splits refer to the existence or absence of specific contractual relations between separate contracting parties, as opposed to the more traditional integration of all (or most) steps within one organisation, such as a state railway company. Various award procedures can be designed to establish such contractual relations, such as open tenders, restricted tenders, negotiated awards and auctions. The call for tenders can be designed more or less 'functionally', leaving more or less design freedom to the bidders at the time of bidding, as represented by the dotted lines in the 'design' box of the table. Various sets of incentives can be designed for the bidding period and for the contract period. In the case of contracts for the provision of transport services (upper part of the vertical dimension), the operator can also be granted more or less redesign freedom during the contract period (see, e.g., Van de Velde, 1999, for a classification of various options). Finally, the resulting contracts can get various legal classifications (concession, contract, etc.), giving them various rights or obligations.

13.3   CASES OF COMPETITION IN THE PROVISION OF RAIL INFRASTRUCTURES AND THE OPERATION OF TRAIN SERVICES

Looking at the realisation of new railway systems over the last decade, we can observe a growth in the usage of competition-based arrangements and of multiple contractual relations within the vertical and horizontal dimensions presented in the previous section. The purpose of this chapter is not to provide a full review of all possible arrangements. Rather, the three examples presented here have been selected such as to illustrate the extreme diversity in such arrangements in recent European practices:

- the TFM Madrid Metro extension case illustrates a fully integrated outsourcing;
- the HSL South high-speed line case in the Netherlands illustrates perhaps in its most extreme form the splitting up of the production chain into individual contracts; while

- the Copenhagen Metro (Ørestad) case is positioned somewhere in between, by having separate contracts in the conception phase, with more integration in the utilisation phase and in the finance/risk part.

Further cases can be encountered, such as the metro concession in Rouen (France), the Arlanda rail link in Stockholm (Sweden) or the Heathrow Express in London (the UK). This could indeed illustrate further variations upon the typical arrangements presented in this chapter, but the main variations are covered in the cases selected here.

Further in-depth studies of these and other cases would be required before we could identify the relative performance of these different arrangements, but that is not the purpose of this chapter. For some of the projects, it might still be too early to be able to draw conclusions, as they are only nearing completion (e.g. the HSL South case).

Metro Madrid: TFM Metro Extension (Line 9)

The concession which led to the 20 km extension (three stations) of Line 9 of the Madrid Metro, using an existing railway alignment, was awarded to the winning Consortium 'Transportes Ferroviarios de Madrid' following a competitive procedure. This concession lasts for 30 years (until 2029) and requires the winner to design, build, operate, maintain and finance the project. The consortium is formed by the public operator of Madrid (Metro de Madrid SA: 42.5 per cent), a bank (Caja Madrid: 25 per cent) and building companies (FCC 12.2 per cent, Acciona (Necso) 12.2. per cent and ACS 8.1 per cent). The project is financed for 20 per cent by shareholding through the consortium partners and 80 per cent by a loan led by Caja Madrid in collaboration with the European Investment Bank. The income of the project is made up of passenger receipts and a subsidy based on a (yearly declining) subsidy per passenger that is supposed to cover the difference between the fare charged to the passengers and the total costs of the project per passenger (including operational costs, amortisation, payment of the principal and the interests, and profit) (ICEX, 2006: 20). This subsidy payment is based on the number of passengers realised, up to a maximum number of journeys determined by the concession holder in the tendering process for each year of the contract. Project planning started in 1996; the line was opened in 1999 (CRTM, 2005: 10).

What characterises this concession is the integrated way it was granted. All layers distinguished in our framework form part of a single concession contract (see Figure 13.4). The exception is real estate, which remains outside the concession's scope. Each consortium member is in charge of its speciality within the realisation of the project.

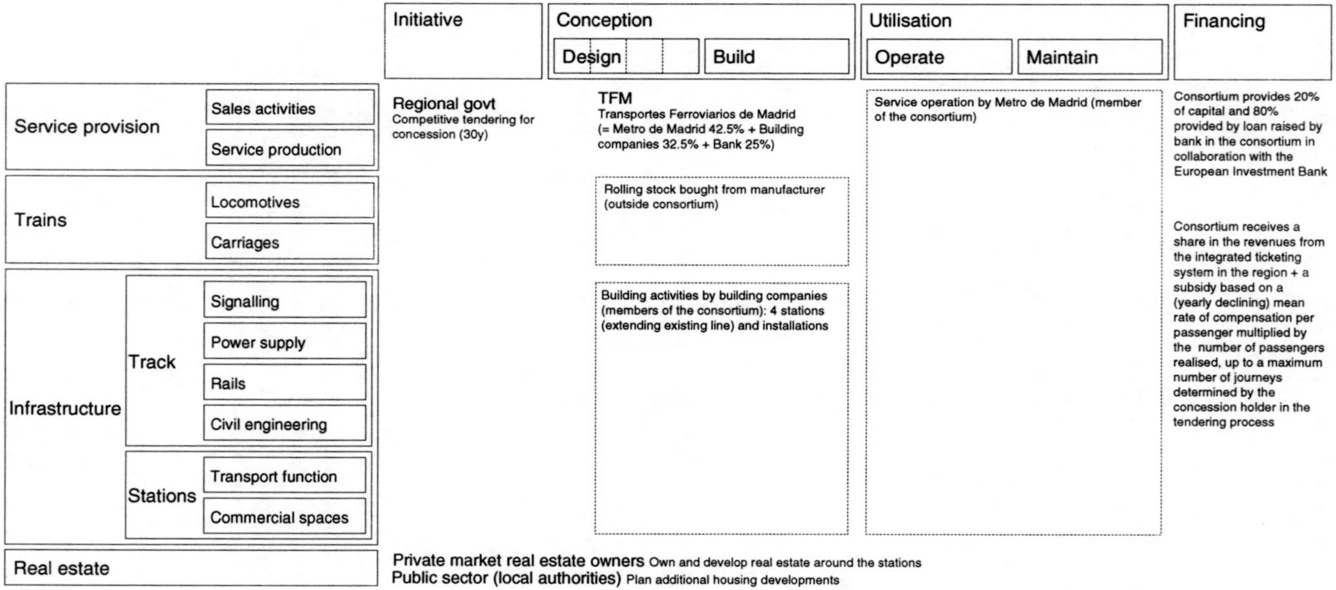

Figure 13.4   TFM (Metro Madrid – Extension Line 9)

Ørestad Metro Line

The Ørestad Development Corporation (established in 1993) is owned 55
per cent by the Municipality of Copenhagen and 45 per cent by the Danish
Ministry of Transport and Energy. It was set up to plan, develop and sell the
land in the Ørestad area. This mainly undeveloped area that was granted to
the Corporation is located between the city centre and Copenhagen
International Airport. The Corporation also has to build a new metro
system linking this area to Copenhagen (in three phases, of which the
example presented here is only the first phase), and to invite tenders and
enter into contract for the operation of the metro. The building of the metro
and the infrastructure of the Ørestad were financed by loans guaranteed by
the Danish state and the participating local and regional authorities. The
basic principle of the Ørestad development is that the new transport infrastructure (metro) would be paid for by the value increases generated in the
surroundings by this infrastructure. The Corporation's debt is to be repaid
through its share of the profits from the metro, through revenues from the
sale of land in the Ørestad area and – until the Corporation is free from debt
– through the reversing of land tax and service charges from the land sold
(Ørestadsselskabet, 2006a: 10–12). The sale of land started in 1997. The first
section of the metro was opened in 2002. It is expected that the debt will be
paid back by 2038 (Ørestadsselskabet, 2006b).

   The Ørestad Metro line (Copenhagen) is a typical example of synergetic
development of real estate with a new transport infrastructure. This rail
project differs substantially from the Madrid example. Two contracts are at
the core of the project here. The first is a civil work contract, won by the
COMET consortium of construction companies, to realise the civil engineering part of the metro (stations and tunnels). The second is an integrated transport system contract, won by Ansaldo Trasporti (see Figure
13.5). This contract covers the realisation of the whole transport system
(tracks, signalling, rolling stock) in a vertically integrated fashion, and the
first five years (2002–7) of operation and maintenance of that system,
including the stations and tunnels. Ansaldo was recently granted a contractually foreseen three-year contract extension until October 2010
(Ørestadsselskabet, 2006a: 30). Ansaldo subcontracted this operation and
maintenance contract to Metro Services (Serco) during the first five years.
This will now be transferred to a consortium composed of Ansaldo and
ATM (the public operator of the Milan metro) in October 2007 for the
second phase of the contract.

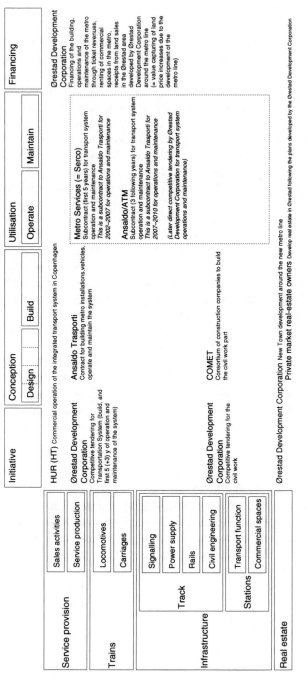

Figure 13.5   Copenhagen Metro

High-speed Line Amsterdam–Belgium (Netherlands)

The decision to build a high-speed railway line from Amsterdam via Rotterdam to Brussels (to connect it to the existing high-speed line to Paris) was taken in 1996 after many years of discussion. The building of the line started in 2000 and trains are expected to run in 2008, following some delays.

The contracting for the realisation of the new high-speed train service is divided into three main blocks (see Figure 13.6). The first is the more traditional outsourcing of the civil engineering work to build the civil work of the line. The second block is a concession for providing a functioning track infrastructure. In this block, which is the largest public–private partnership ever signed in the Netherlands, the concessionaire has to design, build, operate, maintain and finance all track equipment (rails, safety and signalling system, energy system, etc.) for a period of 25 years. It is paid by the state for the realised availability of the track. The track concessionaire has no commercial responsibility for the usage of the track capacity. This concession was awarded to the Infraspeed consortium, established in 1999 and composed of construction companies and institutional investors (Fluor Infrastructure, Siemens Nederland, Koninklijke BAM Groep, Innisfree and HSBC Infrastructure) (Projectorganisatie HSL-Zuid, 2007). The third block is the transport contract. This is a 15-year concession awarded in competition by the state to the HSA (High-Speed Alliance) consortium, composed of NS (Dutch Railways) and KLM. HSA has to provide its own trains and operate at least the minimum required number of train services, and do this on a commercial basis (i.e. without subsidy). This consortium also has to pay the state for the right to use the track. This sum, which is in fact a charge for infrastructure usage, was maximised in a competitive tendering process.

This case represents perhaps one of the most extreme forms of separation of both horizontal and vertical steps in the framework presented. Another particularity of this case is the presence of several other actors. The Dutch rail infrastructure manager (ProRail) and the station operator of the national railway company (NS Stations) are both present and perform parts of the infrastructure tasks.

13.4 CONCLUSIONS

The main issue, identified as the vertical dimension in our framework of analysis, is whether production stages that are conceptually separable (such as infrastructure management and train operations) should be separated,

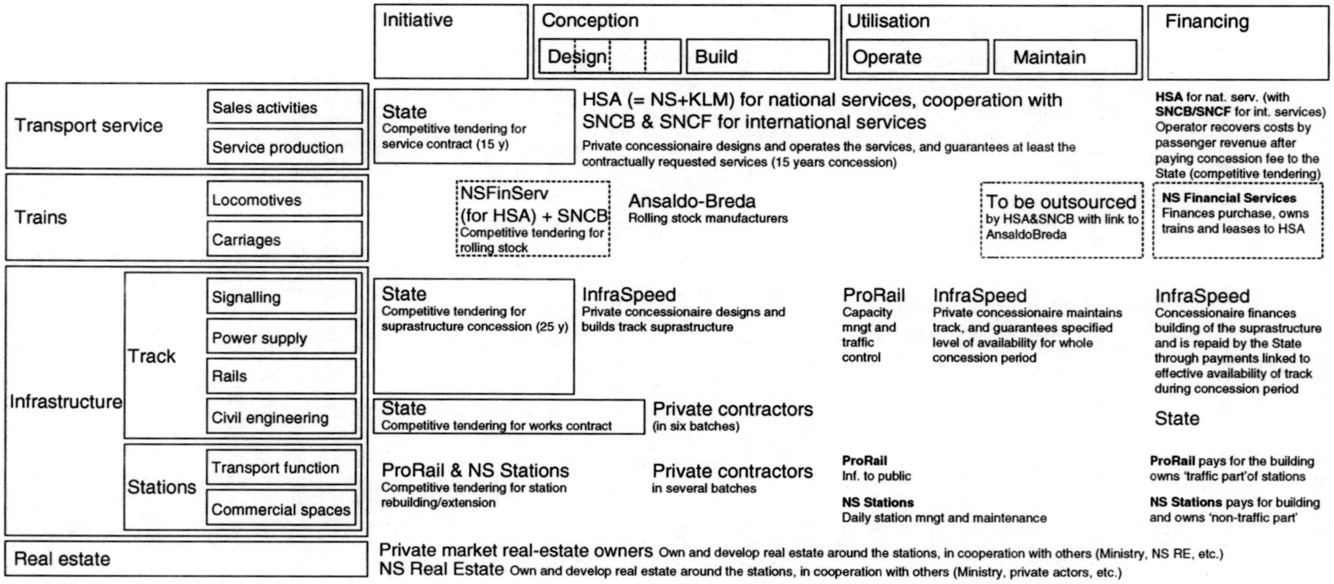

	Initiative	Conception — Design / Build	Utilisation — Operate / Maintain	Financing
Transport service (Sales activities, Service production)	**State** Competitive tendering for service contract (15 y)	**HSA (= NS+KLM) for national services, cooperation with SNCB & SNCF for international services** Private concessionaire designs and operates the services, and guarantees at least the contractually requested services (15 years concession)		**HSA** for nat. serv. (with **SNCB/SNCF** for int. services) Operator recovers costs by passenger revenue after paying concession fee to the State (competitive tendering)
Trains (Locomotives, Carriages)	**NSFinServ (for HSA) + SNCB** Competitive tendering for rolling stock	**Ansaldo-Breda** Rolling stock manufacturers	**To be outsourced** by HSA&SNCB with link to AnsaldoBreda	**NS Financial Services** Finances purchase, owns trains and leases to HSA
Track (Signalling, Power supply, Rails)	**State** Competitive tendering for suprastructure concession (25 y)	**InfraSpeed** Private concessionaire designs and builds track suprastructure	**ProRail** Capacity mngt and traffic control — **InfraSpeed** Private concessionaire maintains track, and guarantees specified level of availability for whole concession period	**InfraSpeed** Concessionaire finances building of the suprastructure and is repaid by the State through payments linked to effective availability of track during concession period
Infrastructure (Civil engineering)	**State** Competitive tendering for works contract	**Private contractors** (in six batches)		**State**
Stations (Transport function, Commercial spaces)	**ProRail & NS Stations** Competitive tendering for station rebuilding/extension	**Private contractors** in several batches	**ProRail** Inf. to public — **NS Stations** Daily station mngt and maintenance	**ProRail** pays for the building owns 'traffic part' of stations **NS Stations** pays for building and owns 'non-traffic part'
Real estate	**Private market real-estate owners** Own and develop real estate around the stations, in cooperation with others (Ministry, NS RE, etc.) **NS Real Estate** Own and develop real estate around the stations, in cooperation with others (Ministry, private actors, etc.)			

Figure 13.6 High-Speed Line South (Netherlands)

or whether interdependencies between these or other stages require integration to guarantee optimisation. These critical interface problems require specific attention. This is also a fundamental issue of transaction-cost economics and essentially a classic question, examined by Coase (1937) in his famous article where he raised the question whether coordination should come about through the market mechanism or through the hierarchy in a firm.

A main aim of using contracting under competition in the case of infrastructures was the introduction of additional incentives for budget control in infrastructure realisation and for better inclusion of trade-offs between various project stages, such as building and maintenance costs in infrastructure design and operation. But many of the newly introduced contracting and competitive practices go beyond simple outsourcing, as they also introduce several non-hierarchically related initiative-takers along the various components of railway systems, adding to the complexity and requiring further coordination between these new actors. A characteristic of some of the current reform practices in the European railway sector in general ('the separation between infrastructure management and train operations') is that they are, to a large extent, more dictated by political or economic dogma rather than by optimal outsourcing decisions.

Intensive debate is going on as to whether vertical integration in rail transport has, or does not have, positive effects (see, e.g., Mulder et al., 2005). The costs of vertical separation are relatively high (Bureau of Transport and Regional Economics, 2003) and it seems that the benefits only outweigh the costs if separation brings sufficient competition. A conclusion in a recent overview of institutional changes in the railway industry is that introducing competition through vertical unbundling has proven more problematic than introducing competition with vertical integration (Gómez Ibáñez, 2006: 3). However, this conclusion is not shared by all the other authors of the book in which the overview is presented. Apparently, there are exceptions to this general rule. We think that introducing the horizontal dimension of the framework suggested in this chapter may clarify why some examples of vertical unbundling are effective in introducing competition and others are not.

Further questions present themselves in our framework of analysis in a horizontal sense: to what extent should the various activities (designing, building, operating, maintaining) and their financing be kept in one hand and how much room should private parties be given in their role as contractors? Here, the following considerations play a role:

- Optimising phase by phase might hamper an optimal arrangement across all phases. A classic example is that cheap building might cause expensive maintenance (Zoeteman, 2004). Slightly more expensive building may bring such savings on maintenance costs that, from an integral perspective, this would be a better policy.

- Private contractors who receive a fully specified call for tender have hardly any room to perform this task in the best possible way. They have only one interest, which is to perform the specified activities as cheaply as possible, exactly matching the agreed quality level. Consequently, these contractors' extensive expertise is utilised only partially.

- Although the integration advantages are important, it is doubtful whether they apply to all activities. For example, there would seem to be a close link between building and maintenance, so close that their integration in one hand must yield unmistakable advantages. The advantages of integrating building and operations are, on the contrary, less manifest. It is highly questionable whether and to what extent the advantages of integration outweigh its disadvantages in this case.

- A government can invite tenders for both the process and the product, giving the contractor room to carry out those tasks optimally. Yet, by giving this room, the government loses possibilities for steering and adjusting. This may be a disadvantage from the perspective of the tender-inviting government, but an advantage from the perspective of society as a whole. Infrastructures and services tend to involve politically and societally sensitive processes about which there is almost constant debate. Handing over control of everything makes it either impossible or very expensive for the government to follow the direction in which this debate is moving.

- One of the problems in traditional contracting is that principals have an information disadvantage compared with contractors. The latter know more, which makes it difficult for principals to steer and check contractors. Allowing contractors more room and, in addition, making them responsible for several activities, increases the principals' information disadvantage even further and makes it even more difficult to steer and check contractors.

What did these innovative forms of contracting bring us? The picture is somewhat vague. In Chapter 10, Koppenjan concludes that it is difficult to judge the success or failure of these new forms of contracting. Successes appear to be scored mainly in effectiveness, better project control and innovation. Most problems occur in the areas of transaction costs, transparency, legitimacy and accountability. Many of the disadvantages might perhaps have been prevented if the process had been better organised.

NOTE

1. The railway system presents a number of particularities when compared with other network infrastructures. While utilities such as electricity, gas or water distribution networks can usefully be compared with passenger and freight transportation networks, the necessity of the use of vehicles (trains, cars and lorries) in passenger and freight transportation makes the economics, the operation and the regulation of these networks substantially more complex. While water, gas or electricity networks provide a continuous flow of uniform goods to a set of tapping points, passenger and freight transport networks, on the contrary, only allow the movement of non-substitutable individuals, groups of passengers or items of freight on largely non-substitutable origin–destination pairs. Furthermore, these movements require the use of vehicles and components such as containers to protect individual shipments. Moreover, these vehicles and components need to be continuously repositioned in the network to serve demand where it is located.

REFERENCES

Bureau of Transport and Regional Economics (2003), *Rail Infrastructure Pricing: Principles and Practice*, Report 109, Canberra: Australian Government, Department of Transport and Regional Services.

Coase, R. (1937), 'The nature of the firm', *Economica*, New Series IV: 386–405.

CRTM (2005), *Madrid 2005 – A World Reference*, Madrid: Consorcio Regional de Transportes de Madrid.

De Ridder, H.A.J. (1998), 'Modern Bouwproces vraagt Integrale Contractvorm' (Modern Building Process demands Integral Contract Form [in Dutch]), *Land + Water*, 3: 39–41.

Donahue, J. (1989), *The Privatisation Decision*, New York: Basic Books.

Gómez Ibáñez, J.A. (2006), 'An overview of the options', in J.A. Gómez Ibáñez and G. de Rus (eds), *Competition in the Railway Industry: An International Comparative Analysis*, Cheltenham, UK and Northampton, MA, USA: Edward Elgar: 1–22.

Hann, N. and T. Mack (2005), 'A banking perspective on transport', in K.J. Button and D.A. Hensher (eds), *Handbook of Transport, Strategy, Policy and Institutions*, Amsterdam: Elsevier: 299–324.

ICEX (2006), *Transporte ferroviario urbano en España Madrid*, Instituto Español de Comercio Exterior.

Letza, S.R., C. Smallman and X. Sun (2004), 'Reframing privatisation. Deconstructing the myth of efficiency', *Policy Sciences*, 37: 159–83.

Megginson, W. and J. Netter (2001), 'From state to market: a survey of empirical studies on privatization', *Journal of Economic Literature*, 39: 321–89.

Mulder, M., M. Lijesen, G. Driessen and D.M. Van de Velde (2005), 'Vertical separation and competition in the Dutch rail industry – A cost–benefit analysis', in G. Alexandersson and S. Hulten (eds), *Third Conference on Railroad Industry Structure, Competition and Investments*, Stockholm, 20–22 October.

Ørestadsselskabet (2006a), *Annual Report 2005*, Copenhagen: Ørestadsselskabet.

Ørestadsselskabet (2006b), www.orestadsselskabet.dk/okonomi, 28 February.

Projectorganisatie HSL-Zuid (2007), www.hslzuid.nl, 28 February.

Schaafsma, A.A.M. (2001), *Dynamisch railverkeersmanagement: besturingsconcept voor railverkeer op basis van het Lagenmodel Verkeer en Vervoer* (Dynamic rail traffic management: management concept for rail traffic on the basis of the Layer Model Transport and Traffic [in Dutch]), TRAIL thesis series, T2001/7, Delft: DUP Science.

Van de Velde, D.M. (1999), 'Organisational forms and entrepreneurship in public transport (Part 1: classifying organisational forms)', *Transport Policy*, 6: 147–57.

Van Twist, M.J.W., A.W. Diederen, B.P.A. van Mil, M.A.R. van Roost and M.M. Timmermann (2003), 'Tussen droom en daad . . . Marktordening en publieke belangen rond vitale transport-infrastructuren', voorstudie van Berenschot voor de Raad voor Verkeer en Waterstaat, The Hague: Raad voor Verkeer en Waterstaat (in Dutch).

Vollaard, B.A. and W. Witteveen (1999), *Innovatief aanbesteden: naar een hoger maatschappelijk rendement van overheidsinvesteringen* (Innovative contracting: towards a higher social return of public investments), The Hague: Ministerie van Economische Zaken (in Dutch).

Winston, C. (1993), 'Economic deregulation: days of reckoning for microeconomists', *Journal of Economic Literature*, 31: 1263–89.

Zoeteman, A. (2004), *Railway Design and Maintenance from a Life-Cycle Cost Perspective: A Decision-Support Approach*, Delft: TRAIL Thesis Series, TRAIL Research School.

14. Rail infrastructure at major European hub airports: the role of institutional settings

Moshe Givoni and Piet Rietveld

14.1 INTRODUCTION

The development of rail links to airports can be compared with the development of rail links to ports. 'Prior to the advent of road and air transport, the main form of transport for overseas journeys was a combination of rail and sea . . . [therefore] railways were built directly into the seaports' (Stubbs and Jegede, 1998: 56). However, when airports substituted seaports for overseas journeys the share of rail in surface transport was in decline and the share of the private car on the rise, resulting in good connections of airports to the road network and not the rail network. A notable development is that more recently this is changing, and as the air transport industry continues to grow the number of rail connections to airports increases.

The main rationale for railway connections to airports is the need to bring passengers to (or from) the airport when they begin (or end) their air journey. This need increases with growing congestion on roads, which is often especially severe around airports, and the growing awareness to the need to reduce car dependent travel. The development of the high-speed train (HST), which can increase airports' catchment area and on some routes can substitute the aircraft, provides another important incentive to connect airports with the (HST) rail network. From a transport policy perspective, the importance of integration between transport modes and transport networks provides the main justification to invest in rail services to airports.

The above is reflected in the increased number of railway connections to airports. In 1998, 62 rail connections to airports existed in the world and 116 were planned (in Europe, 40 existing connections and 49 planned and in North America, 14 existing and 32 planned connections – IARO, 1998). In addition to an increase in the number of rail connections to airports, there is an increase in the quality of these connections. At many airports, local, regional, national and international rail services are provided, by both conventional and high-speed rail, and airlines can use the rail network as an integral part of their route network.

The notion of integration seems to be a prerequisite for an effective and beneficial role of the railways in air transport, and vice versa. By examining three cases, London Heathrow Airport, Amsterdam Schiphol Airport and Paris Charles de Gaulle (CDG) Airport, this chapter aims to investigate air–rail policies as part of transport policy and examine how these translate into infrastructure investments in terms of railway services at airports. The benefits of air–rail integration and the role the railways can play in the future of air transport have been described by Givoni and Banister (2006; 2007) and are therefore briefly described here. The aim of this contribution is more to explain why, despite these recognised potential benefits from railway services at airports, the degree of air–rail intermodality still varies between Europe's largest airports.

Before the three cases are described, Heathrow Airport in Section 14.3, Schiphol Airport in Section 14.4 and CDG Airport in Section 14.5, a short overview of rail connections to airports is given in Section 14.2. In Section 14.6, possible reasons for the differences in the levels of intermodality and rail infrastructure at different European hub airports are discussed. In Section 14.7 conclusions are drawn.

14.2   RAILWAY CONNECTIONS TO AIRPORTS[1]

Airports can be connected to the railway network in several ways. Based on the geographical coverage of the rail service from the airport, the following categorisation is suggested (Table 14.1). At the lower level are services that connect the airport with the city centre only, usually by special trains (with special facilities for luggage) that provide fast and frequent connections to the city centre, but often at premium fares. Examples include the Arlanda Express in Stockholm, the Heathrow Express in London, and the Narita Express in Tokyo. At a higher level, the airport is connected to the city metro system, providing a wider geographical coverage but usually a lower standard of service in terms of travel time to the city centre and capability to cater for airport passengers (mainly in terms of luggage space). This is the most common type of rail link to an airport (IARO, 1998). Examples include the London Underground connection to Heathrow (the Piccadilly line) and the RER (Réseau Express Régional) connection of CDG to Paris.

At the regional level, the airport is connected to the regional rail network. These connections can vary in terms of the number of destinations directly served by the airport, and as a consequence the geographical

Table 14.1   *Categorisation of rail links to airports based on geographical coverage*

Geographical coverage	Category according to Stubbs and Jegede (1998)	Category according to IARO (1998)	Examples
City centre	Special line	High-speed dedicated links	Heathrow Express service from Heathrow to London
City	Metro line	Metro links	Piccadilly line service from Heathrow
The airport region	Spur line, branch line	Accidental links	Manchester airport rail station; Prestwick airport rail station
National/ international	Main line	Regional links, high-speed networks	HST services: Frankfurt Airport to Stuttgart and CDG to Brussels

Source: Reproduced from Givoni and Banister (2007).

area covered by these services. Often, airports happen to be built close to rail lines and thus a connection is 'accidental', and serving the need of the airport passengers is not the station's main purpose (IARO, 1998). In addition, the demand for rail services is not high enough to make the airport station an important stop on routes passing through or near the airport. In this case, a change of train is required to access the main railway network, and the rail connection to the airport will usually be a spur or a branch line from the main line (Stubbs and Jegede, 1998).

Large airports located along a main-line rail route will usually generate enough demand for rail services to become an important stop on the routes passing through the airport (i.e. a through station), as all trains will stop at this station and many destinations could be reached by a direct rail service. Such services will usually provide access to the airport from the boundaries of the airport catchment area. Gatwick Airport rail station is an example of such a railway connection. As the area covered by rail services from the airport increases beyond the airport region and the typical airport catchment area, rail services become more than just an access mode to the airport. Rail services to airports present the potential for the airport to compete with other (regional) airports and can be a potential replacement for short-haul flights. Such rail connections will be categorised in the upper level of the geographical coverage. CDG, Frankfurt and Schiphol airports benefit from this type of railway connection. Major hub airports will often have more than one type of rail service. CDG, for example, will have railway services covering all the geographical areas mentioned in Table 14.1 after the new railway service to the city centre, similar to the Heathrow Express service, is completed in 2012 (Mott MacDonald, 2003).

In addition to the type of rail connection to the airport, the location and configuration of the airport station in relation to the air terminal(s) is important in determining the attraction of railway services to passengers and other airport users. In general, two broad configurations can be identified: one is to build the interchange under the existing air terminal complex, and the other is to build it adjacent to the air terminal and at the same level (Buchanan and Partners, 1995). Schiphol, London Stansted, Zürich and Tokyo Narita airports follow the first configuration, while Frankfurt, CDG, London Gatwick and Manchester airports are examples of the second configuration. 'Many would consider the best location for a rail/air interchange is under the air terminal complex . . . The location of the rail station under the terminal has the additional benefit of making the airport and rail station appear well integrated, which is an important perception for air passengers when making a mode choice' (Buchanan and Partners, 1995: 6–20). More important is, however, the level of inconvenience associated with the transfer between the aircraft and the train, which is determined by the distance and change of level between the (aircraft) gate and the (train) platform, and the means provided to the passenger to overcome those, e.g. travelators, elevators, people movers, etc.

The relationship between the rail and air transport networks was traditionally based on the railway as a provider of access services to the airport, thus on a limited cooperation between the modes and in practice cooperation between the railways and the airports. Yet close cooperation could increase the role of the railways in air transport to the benefit of both industries, while competition between the industries might be counterproductive for passengers as the benefits of cooperation would be avoided. When railway services to/from airports become important to the airlines, cooperation between the air and rail industries can reach the level at which air and rail services are fully integrated. In this case, the railway is an integral part of air transport and the differences between the airlines and the railways become smaller, as they both provide a complete transport service.

Whether cooperation or competition between the air and rail modes is more desired depends on the relationship between the respective networks. When two networks are parallel to each other, competition is usually considered more beneficial, as it leads to more choice and lower fares for passengers. In serial networks (when the networks are used one after the other, such as when the train is used to access the airport), cooperation is considered more beneficial (Borger and Proost, 2007). However, when considering the capacity constraints at major hub airports and the high environmental impact from aircraft operation, in the case of the parallel HST and aircraft networks, cooperation might be more beneficial than competition, as Givoni and Banister (2006) suggest.

Demand for rail services at airports usually comes mainly from passengers and thus from the terminal area. However, at large airports significant demand is generated by employment at the airport area, which is often spread around a much larger geographical area than the terminals, and this could lead to conflicts in deciding where to locate the rail station or, alternatively, may require more than one rail station.

The high demand generated for railway services at large airports, by passengers but also by people who work, shop, recreate or meet there, makes these airports similar to city centres. Moreover, people do not live in these cities, but have to travel to/from them each time they need to carry out an activity in the city. This view of the airport as a city, from a railway planning perspective, underlines the discussion of intermodality policies in the three case studies described below.

14.3 LONDON HEATHROW – THE BYPASSED CITY

London Heathrow Airport is the main UK airport and the largest in the world outside the USA in passenger volume (see Table 14.2). UK air transport policy is very much focused on development at this airport, and the airport plays a major role in securing air transport's socioeconomic benefits. Heathrow's importance to the UK stems from the level of services it provides (direct services to about 190 destinations), which is partly possible by its international position as a hub airport. 'Heathrow's extensive route network is only viable because of the large number of international passengers transferring through the airport . . . As a result, UK travellers and businesses benefit from having direct flights to more destinations and [at] higher frequencies. This is a leading factor in attracting inward investment to the whole of the UK. Regional travellers benefit from having an increased range of destinations served one-stop via a hub' (DfT, 2003a: 15).

*Table 14.2   Profile of London Heathrow, Amsterdam Schiphol and Paris
             CDG airports (2003)*

Category	London Heathrow	Amsterdam Schiphol	Paris CDG
Air transport movements (global/ regional ranking)	460 748 (12th/2nd)	392 997 (19th/4th)	515 025 (6th/1st)
Passengers in millions (global/ regional ranking)	64.26 (3rd/1st)	39.96 (8th/4th)	48.12 (7th/3rd)
Cargo in metric tonnes (global/ regional ranking)	1 300 420 (15th/4th)	1 353 760 (14th/3rd)	1 481 200 (11th/2nd)
Number of runways	2	5	4
Terminal size (m²)	291 041	370 000	542 300
Gates	141	89	124
Check-in counters	515	300	543
% of international passengers	88.0	99.6	90.0
% of transfer passengers	34.0	40.9	58 (2000)
% of hub carrier passengers	40.9 (BA)	51.5 (KLM)	57.2 (AF)
Number of destinations	190	245	N/A
Passengers/movement	139	102	93
Movements per day	1 262	1 077	1 411
Daily gate utilisation (passengers)	1 249	1 230	1 063
Employees	4 000	2 231	4 071
Shareholders	(from 2006) 100% Ferrovial Consortium (Spanish)	The state: 75.8%, City of Amsterdam: 21.8%, City of Rotterdam: 2.4%	Aéroports de Paris: 100% (from 2005 a 'société anonyme' (corporation))

Sources: Various.

Heathrow's contribution to the UK depends on the level of service it provides, but also on the level of access to its services, which from the UK can be by air, road and rail. Access by air to Heathrow's international route network is relatively limited. In 1990, 18 UK destinations were served from

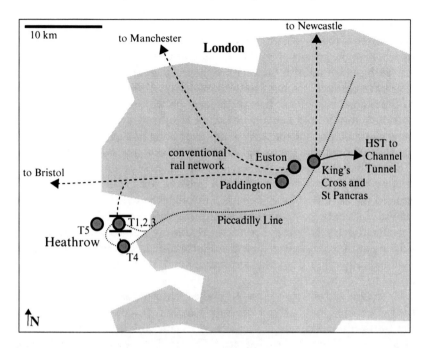

Figure 14.1   Rail service to and around Heathrow

Heathrow by 118 round trips per day, but these figures fell to only 8 destinations and 84 round trips per day in 2004 (CAA, 2005). In 2003, Schiphol
Airport served 16 regional airports in the UK, and Paris and Brussels
served 11 and 8 respectively (House of Commons Transport Committee,
2003). Access to Heathrow by road is increasingly compromised by congestion; the roads around Heathrow often have relatively high levels of congestion compared with the rest of the network, and journeys to Heathrow
from the central business district are delayed throughout the day by over 50
per cent compared to the free-flow speed. This results in travel time of more
than an hour, compared to just over 40 minutes at free-flow condition, for
the 15 km from London's city centre to Heathrow (Eddington, 2006). In
terms of railway services, Heathrow Airport offers good connections with
London (Figure 14.1), which include an express service to London city
centre, the Heathrow Express (this line also serves several intermediate
stops between the airport and the city centre – the Heathrow Connect
service), and a connection to London's metro system (the Piccadilly line).
Despite its size and importance, Heathrow Airport offers very limited
railway services to destinations outside London, and these are through a
bus transit between the airport and nearby railway stations.

Heathrow Airport handles more than 40 million non-transfer passengers per year and, together with the number of employees and visitors making their way to the airport every day, the potential demand for railway services at Heathrow is that of a major European city centre railway station. In a European context, it is hard to think of a city of this size that is bypassed by the rail network, regardless of its location with respect to the main rail corridors and the rail network. Making Heathrow a stop on the UK rail network could provide the way to improve access to Heathrow from within the UK. It could also secure the airport socioeconomic contribution to the UK and limit its impact on the environment. These potential benefits from making Heathrow a stop on the rail network are greater after a plan to expand the airport runway capacity, through the construction of a third runway, had to be postponed for environmental reasons (DfT, 2003b). The benefits from better railway services at Heathrow are also greater when considering airlines' preference to use available runway capacity to serve international rather than domestic destinations and the limitations in improving access to Heathrow by increasing road capacity.

There are currently no plans to make Heathrow an important stop on the rail network, and air–rail intermodality is not an option considered for the future development of the airport. There are several rail plans for Heathrow at different planning stages. Those that are most likely to materialise are aimed at extending the current Heathrow Express and the metro system services to the new Fifth Terminal (T5) which is now under construction. The configuration of these connections means that Heathrow's five terminals will be served through three different railway stations with no direct rail connection between all of them. Other planned rail lines which include Heathrow are the Crossrail and Airtrack projects. The Crossrail line is a new east–west line across London and is considered as the 'transport spine needed to underpin the most rapid economic growth areas of London and is the most critical addition to the transport network' (Mayor of London and Transport for London, 2006: 80). The line is planned to include stations at Stratford, and at Ebbsfleet, where HST services from London to Europe will stop, but plans to make Heathrow a stop on the Crossrail line have changed to include 'an option to serve Heathrow Airport' through a link to the Crossrail main line (Crossrail, 2005). Still, the London Plan states that 'Crossrail will also facilitate journeys from Heathrow to London's business districts, thereby improving the Capital's international gateways' (Mayor of London and Transport for London, 2006: 80), but with Crossrail serving Heathrow through a link, the London areas served by Crossrail will lack direct access to the range of air services Heathrow provides. Thus the benefits from the Crossrail connection to Heathrow could have been greater. The Airtrack project is planned to provide rail connections between the new terminal and the regional rail network south of the airport, and it will offer services to South London (Waterloo, Clapham Junction, Richmond) and towns near Heathrow such as Staines, Reading and Guildford.

The rail plans for Heathrow described above represent the limited role the railways are expected to play in the future of UK air transport. In 2003, the UK published its air transport policy for the next 30 years in *The Future of Air Transport* White Paper (DfT, 2003b). In its contribution to the debate leading to the White Paper, the Strategic Rail Authority (SRA)[2] limited the railways' role in the air transport industry to improving access to airports. It stated that 'the work that the authority has carried out is not intended to suggest which airports are most suitable for growth . . . But the authority would like to set out the main rail surface access issues that need to be considered' (SRA, 2003: 4). Whether rail could play a role in the future of air transport very much depends on the airports chosen for expansion and their location with respect to the rail network. Rail services at Heathrow, current and planned, also represent the UK government vision of the role of rail in air transport. The government view is that, for example, new rail lines can reduce demand for air transport between cities (e.g. London–Manchester) but not between cities and airports (e.g. Manchester–Heathrow) (Dft, 2003a), although connection of airports such as Frankfurt and CDG to the (HST) rail network proved that rail can substitute aircraft in such a market.

The long-term planning of Heathrow on the one hand, and the UK railways on the other hand, does not envisage an upgrade of the railway service at the airport. The White Paper considered a horizon of 30 years but, as noted, it did not venture to change significantly the level of service other than improving the access services from the airport's immediate surroundings. In its contribution to the White Paper, the SRA makes notes on a possible future south–north HST line and proposes that Heathrow will be connected to this line through a branch line (SRA, 2003), and not a station on the line. This means that for passengers to enjoy the services on the new HST line, they would have to use a service to a station on the HST line and transfer there. Before its demise in 2004, the SRA planned to launch a consultation on a future south–north HST and in connection with this a *High Speed Line Study* was published (Atkins, 2004). Also, a suggestion was made there to connect Heathrow through a link to the high-speed line.

Since the publication of the White Paper, the nature of air–rail planning in the UK has not changed. At the end of 2006, a special report on transport policy, termed the Eddington Report (Eddington, 2006)[3] was submitted to the government. The report identifies that in economic and social terms investments in improving access to the main UK international gateways will have the highest welfare return on investments, mainly since access to these gateways is currently congested. In the recommendation part, the report proposed to increase road capacity around the main gateways and specifically around Heathrow Airport. Improving rail access to Heathrow is not mentioned as a recommendation.

The importance and benefits of rail services at airports such as Heathrow do not seem to be recognised in the UK. The debate on the future of air transport, as reflected mainly in the consultation leading to the White Paper, gives the impression that the rail and air transport industries seek to minimise the interaction between them. This is against a background where other European hub airports have already invested in high-quality railway stations (see Sections 14.4 and 14.5). In the UK air transport policy debate, much focus is placed on runway and terminal developments at Heathrow's main hub rivals (DfT, 2003a; 2003b; Vandermeer, 2001), but their rail developments are overlooked.

Stubbs and Jegede (1998) reviewed air–rail transport in mainland Britain and concluded that the approach to intermodality, at the time, lacked the necessary national coordination to capitalise on the benefits of air–rail intermodality. In 1998, following the change of government in the UK (from Conservative to Labour), a new transport policy was published (DETR, 1998). The new policy was based on two main objectives: integrated and sustainable transport. Integrated transport was still an objective of transport policy when the air transport White Paper was published, but this is not apparent in it.

Heathrow Airport is only about 2 km from one of the UK main rail corridors, the Great Western Main Line – the line from London to the West – and about 15 km from another main line – The West Coast Main Line connecting London with the north-west including Manchester and Glasgow (Figure 14.1). These features of the rail network, Heathrow's potential demand for rail services and the benefits such services could provide the airport all suggest that in the UK some barriers to air–rail intermodality exist. Attempts to identify these barriers will be made after considering the other case studies.

14.4   AMSTERDAM SCHIPHOL – A CITY ON THE (RAIL) NETWORK

Amsterdam Schiphol Airport is among the world's largest airports and is Europe's fourth largest (Table 14.2). Due to the Netherlands' geography and demography, its international position, especially in the competition with the other major European airports, is much more important in securing air transport's socioeconomic benefits to the country. Unlike at Heathrow, where the reliance on international traffic drives domestic passengers away from the airport, in the case of the Netherlands it is the airport's international hub position that provides the Dutch with access to an air transport network of 245 destinations, compared with 190 at Heathrow.

Schiphol Airport started operation in 1916. At that time the rail network already had in place the main rail lines from Amsterdam to the south (Figure 14.2): a line to Utrecht and another line to Rotterdam, passing about 10 km from where Schiphol would later be established and through the cities of Haarlem, Leiden and The Hague (Rietveld and Bruinsma, 1998). Rail services from Schiphol to Amsterdam began in 1978; and in 1996 as part of expanding the terminal buildings an underground rail station, located just under the main terminal building, was opened (van Wijk, 2007). Rail services passing through Schiphol are on the third rail line going south from Amsterdam, joining the first Amsterdam–Rotterdam line at Leiden (Figure 14.2).

Currently, Schiphol rail station provides national and international railway services (the quality of the international rail services will improve

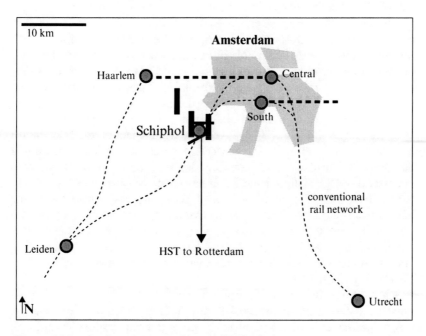

Figure 14.2   Rail service to and around Schiphol

significantly with the completion of the HST line to Belgium), and it is a central node on the Dutch rail network. From the airport station, 54 stations on the Dutch rail network (out of about 350 stations) can be reached directly and another 169 stations can be reached via one transfer. With up to two transfers, more than 95 per cent of the stations on the Dutch network can be reached. Debrezion (2006) measured the rail service quality index for all the stations of the Dutch network[4] and found Schiphol airport station, as a departure station, to be fifth in the Netherlands in service quality. The most recent development in rail services to Schiphol is the new connection, opened in 2006, between Schiphol and the rail line Amsterdam–Utrecht, which allows direct access to Schiphol from, for example, Utrecht Central, the station with the highest service quality index in the Dutch network (Figure 14.2; this recent connection is not accounted for in Debrezion, 2006).

Railway services at Schiphol are also utilised directly by the airlines, to expand their network of destinations and to substitute the aircraft with train services on some routes, for example to Brussels. Following the new rail connection to Utrecht, KLM stopped flight services from Eindhoven to Schiphol (they are now used to connect Eindhoven with CDG, the other hub in the Air France–KLM network; see KLM et al., 2006). In the case of Schiphol, rail access is recognised to have a strategic importance in competition with other airports, especially Frankfurt and Brussels. It therefore also has strategic importance for KLM, the hub carrier at Schiphol. With no rail connections to Schiphol, Frankfurt Airport could have been an option for people between Frankfurt and Amsterdam, especially considering the excellent railway service at Frankfurt Airport and the complete air–rail integration (Givoni, 2005). Furthermore, with good rail connections Schiphol can also extend its catchment area in the direction of Brussels (airport). IATA (2003) investigated the effect of the HST-South line, which will allow HST services between Amsterdam, including Schiphol, and Brussels (and therefore also Paris and CDG), on the connectivity of CDG, Schiphol and Zaventem (Brussels) airports using IATA's connectivity model. It found that for all these airports completion of the line will substantially increase connectivity, including hubbing connectivity. The increase in connectivity was greater when the airport was directly connected to the HST line (CDG and Schiphol as opposed to Zaventem), and the analysis showed that Schiphol will benefit the most from the completion of the HST line.

Schiphol has no unique location attributes that make it the fifth most important station on the network; rather it is its function as an international gateway and its size (in terms of potential rail travellers) that make the airport, in terms of railway services, one of the largest cities in the

Netherlands. In many respects, from a planning perspective Schiphol is seen within the Randstad region as a city (van Wijk, 2007). The success of Schiphol as an airport city or cityport (terms often used in the Dutch planning debate) is evident in the fact that it has the highest office rents among the Randstad cities, higher than downtown Amsterdam; it is the eighth most productive cityport in the Randstad (measured in million euros per square km), out of 23 places compared (which probably also means eighth in the Netherlands); and it has the highest node value of the Randstad's cityports (van Wijk, 2007).

In conclusion, rail services at Schiphol are a direct result of policy and planning, and the recognition that airports generate significant demand for rail services, enough to make them a stop on a main line. The reference to Schiphol Airport as a city (in terms of rail planning) is justified by the position of Schiphol railway station on the Dutch rail network.

14.5 PARIS CDG – ESTABLISHING A CITY ON THE (RAIL) NETWORK

France's main airport, Charles de Gaulle (CDG, also known as Roissy) was opened in 1974. In 2003, it was the biggest airport in Europe (sixth in the world) in terms of aircraft movements and second biggest in Europe (seventh in the world) in terms of passengers (Table 14.2). For many years CDG followed Heathrow's example in terms of intermodality policy and specifically rail access. This changed in the 1990s 'transforming CDG airport from a buffer between transport modes into a facility serving linked intermodal travel' (Perl, 1998: 189).

Rail access to CDG (Figure 14.3) from Paris is through the commuter rail system, the RER. Line B connects the airport with central Paris, including one of the main rail terminals. In 2012, an express service to Paris city centre, similar to the Heathrow Express, is scheduled to open (Mott MacDonald, 2003). Regional, national and international rail access to the airport is through the HST station. The compatibility of the French HST (the TGV – train à grande vitesse) with the conventional rail network means that rail services from the airport are not limited to destinations on the (French) HST network. The HST services at CDG and the good transfer facilities between air and rail services (probably second only to the facilities at Frankfurt Airport) mean that air–rail integration is very much exploited and there are increasing numbers of airlines pursuing integration of rail services into their route network. Naturally, Air France is the main airline utilising rail services. After signing an agreement with SNCF (Société Nationale des Chemins de Fer – French Railways) in 1999, Air

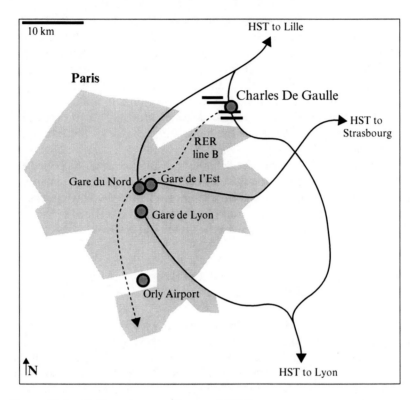

Figure 14.3   Rail service to and around CDG

France launched the 'TGV Air' services, where SNCF serves CDG airport from a half-dozen of relatively close destinations, including international destinations as part of the airline route network (Zembri, 2007). This agreement includes services from CDG to Lyon and Brussels, where the TGV replaces some of the airlines' flights. For foreign airlines, the connection of CDG to the (HST) rail network allows them access to the domestic market, which otherwise would not be possible due to the dominant position of Air France in this market. Emirates, American Airlines and United Airlines have code-share agreements with SNCF which allow them such access to the French domestic market (IATA, 2003).

Understanding the transformation process at CDG is a key to understanding the differences between Heathrow and Schiphol with regard to air–rail intermodality and rail infrastructure. This process is very much related to the institutional settings of the bodies responsible for the development of the airport and (HST) rail network.

What Perl (1998) calls the 'institutional roots of intermodal indifference' in French transport planning stem from the institutionalised boundaries and institutional norms inside the organisations responsible for the airport and rail network development, Aéroports de Paris (ADP) and SNCF respectively. These norms led to a pattern of solving problems based on an internal inertial logic, 'neither ADP or SNCF took responsibility for integrating France's premier gateway into the nation's transport network, because this task fell outside their logic of appropriate action' (Perl, 1998: 190). For ADP, airport accessibility and economic integration with the surrounding region were perceived as costs, rather than benefits. For SNCF, locating CDG's airport rail station at an equidistance from all airport facilities in order to facilitate airport workers' access to and from their trains rather than facilitate passenger's access is the evidence for its intermodal indifference.

The situation changed when ADP and SNCF faced competition and realised that there are new opportunities for them. Following deregulation of European air transport services, CDG started to compete for traffic and for a dominant position as a hub airport. In addition, governments, airlines and national business elites started to view airports as an important variable in their particular fortunes and this influenced airport authorities such as ADP to reassess their organisational practices. For SNCF, the development of the HST in France, but also in Europe, brought the opportunity to play a major role in rail development on a European scale and created a competitive dynamic to planning high-speed projects (mainly competing with Germany for dominance in this market). 'Losing the race to become one of Europe's principal international air gateways would undermine ADP's credibility, just as allowing other high speed rail technologies to overtake the French Train à Grande Vitesse [TGV] would threaten SNCF's reputation' (Perl, 1998: 190). At this point, ADP and SNCF joined forces because both were engaged in new forms of infrastructure development that generated mutually advantageous opportunities for collaboration.

Parallel organisational thinking was a necessary but not sufficient condition for formalising inter-organisational collaboration between ADP and SNCF. To progress beyond informal interaction, a forum in which the organisations could negotiate was needed, one that would allow them to avoid the exposure to government bureaucracy. France's traditional use of high-level working groups to initiate new policy options offered that. In 1985, the Funel commission laid the foundations for a TGV interconnection line that would encircle Paris. The commission recommended that this line would include three stations in the Ile-de-France region placed south, east and north of Paris. The northern station was intended to be located in the vicinity of CDG, with the exact location decided by inter-organisational consultation between ADP and SNCF (Perl, 1998). In 1994, an HST station opened at CDG, directly under Terminal 2 (and to be linked to Terminal 1 by a people-mover). The station became the sole point at which all branches of France's high-speed rail network intersect.

The fact that airlines and railways in the new realties were both targeting international business travellers could have led to rivalry between the industries, but ADP and SNCF forged a collaborative partnership to interconnect France's air and high-speed rail networks at CDG. The mutual advantages of a TGV interconnection facility beneath CDG appeared sufficient to justify the financial and organisational demands of this cooperative venture (Perl, 1998).

14.6 POSSIBLE REASONS FOR THE DIFFERENCES IN RAIL INFRASTRUCTURE AT MAJOR EUROPEAN HUB AIRPORTS

In terms of intermodal policies and more specifically rail services at airports, the cases of Schiphol and Heathrow probably represent two extremes, like CDG before and after intermodality was adopted as a policy. At Schiphol, the picture emerging is one in which every development of the airport on the one hand, and the rail network around it on the other, was done in full coordination considering the mutual benefits to air transport and the Netherlands (especially the Randstad region). At Heathrow, the picture emerging is one of isolation between the airport development and the rail network development, with no appreciation of possible mutual benefits and with efforts to limit cooperation between rail and air transport. All three airports considered above, certainly Heathrow, generate enough demand for rail services to justify high-quality railway services and a train station which is a through station on a main line. Therefore institutional settings, or institutional barriers, seem to be more plausible reasons to explain the different approaches to intermodality which are reflected in different levels of rail infrastructure.

The importance of institutional settings in the (success or failure of) implementation of transport policies and decisions on infrastructure investments was recognised in the EU TIPP project (Transport Institutions in the Policy Process). The TIPP findings suggest that problematic implementation of certain transport policies can in many cases be due to inappropriate and/or ineffective government institutions and organisations, and that these institutions and organisations might even themselves impose barriers or constraints on implementation. The successful or unsuccessful implementation of transport policies depends on institutional structures (and also on institutional processes) in which nine elements seem of most importance. Among them are: the role of national government, the degree of centralisation, institutional consolidation, the role of the private sector, the degree of regulatory intervention and the coordination across modes (Niskanen, 2005). All these elements can be recognised in the description of the three case studies, especially that of CDG.

The institutional settings played an important role in the transition witnessed at CDG and can explain much of the differences between Heathrow and Schiphol. At one extreme, according to Perl (1998), public authority is absent and collaborative possibilities are precluded. When public authority exists but is not absolute, collaborative potential increases. In this range, private organisations can interact informally and negotiate discretely, but retain confidence that their agreements can be enforced publicly if necessary. Yet, in higher doses, public authority becomes a constraint on inter-organisational collaboration, as deliberations become more formalised, open to wider scrutiny, and subject to challenge by third parties. It can be argued that in the case of Heathrow there is an absence of public authority while at CDG in the early days there was too much of it. In contrast, the situation at Schiphol and at CDG (when the environment became more intermodal oriented) can be considered as one where there is a sufficient balance between public authority and organisational independence to allow coordination between organisations without the bureaucracy trap.

By the 1970s, in most of the world, transport had become a largely public sector activity. This changed in the 1980s when transport policy moved progressively in the direction of the market approach and widespread privatisation of transport operations took place. The UK was one of the main pioneers in adopting these changes when it deregulated its express coach services in 1980 and, following that, of other transport services and infrastructure (Nash, 2005). The British Airport Authority was privatised in 1986 with the private company, now called BAA, controlling the three largest London airports (Heathrow, Gatwick and Stansted). In 1987, the UK flag-carrier British Airways was privatised and the national railway, British Rail, was privatised in 1996 (split into an infrastructure company, Railtrack, and 25 Train Operating Companies). In the Netherlands, government and local authorities still have considerable control of the airport and the railway. The government also used to have considerable control of the airline, KLM, but this is much less so at present, especially following KLM merger with Air France.

The situation in the Netherlands makes coordination across industries and modes relatively seamless. The government involvement in the development of the airport and its adoption of the mainport concept (i.e. seeing

Schiphol as more than just an airport) as a policy is seen by the industry as one of Schiphol's advantages (KLM et al., 2006). In contrast, in the UK coordination will be even harder to achieve at times of crises, such as those undergone by the rail industry in the UK (several train accidents, bankruptcy of the infrastructure company and finally the demise of the SRA) and the air transport industry (security, increasing fuel costs, SARS). Naturally, at times of crisis cooperation between industries will be low on the agenda or removed from it. Privatisation probably also means shifting the balance, in managing the industry, from the long term (planning and strategy) to the short term (profitability and return on investment). The separation of the industries also means that, as in the case of CDG, solutions to problems are sought within the organisation and in such an environment the costs of possible cooperation would be perceived to outweigh any potential benefits. In such an environment, the principle that 'where a rail project also benefits non-airport rail users the broad aim will be to divide the costs between the airport and [the] SRA' (SRA, 2003: 11), i.e. between the air and rail industries, does not seem to provide enough incentive for cooperation.[5]

Also, under privatisation, transport industries are still governed by public policy, usually through the ministries of transport and finance. In the case of the UK, the planning forum/coordination body for the air and rail industries is supposed to be the Department for Transport (DfT). Yet in practice, work at such departments is very often uni-modal in nature, the result of a uni-modal approach to transport planning. This means that instead of coordination between the different modes, competition for resources takes place, mainly between the different network administrations (i.e. road, rail, aviation and maritime) (Niskanen, 2005).[6] With privatisation of the transport industries, when each industry lobbies for its own narrow interests and immediate needs, ministries such as the Department for Transport might be even more limited in adopting intermodal philosophy, and this could lead to a situation where the industry influences the ministry of transport more than the other way round. Furthermore, for the fragmented UK rail industry, as noted before, the lack of a body like the SRA makes it difficult for the industry as a whole to see the potential in intermodality.

Surface access to the main UK airports has been recognised by the UK government as a problem and an important planning issue that needs to be addressed. In response, the major airports were instructed to establish surface access forums in which different stakeholders within the airport area take part. In 1996, the Heathrow Area Transport Forum was established to create partnerships of private and public sector bodies (mainly the airport operator, its users and local authorities surrounding the airport) to improve accessibility and tackle car dependence to and around Heathrow (BAA, 2002). Naturally, such a bottom-up approach can only deal with local issues concerning access to Heathrow, and mainly access by employees, but it cannot suggest or progress any strategic decisions on access infrastructure. Furthermore, the forum objectives, as outlined above, focus on access issues only, overlooking issues of integration between the surface and air transport networks, and overlooking the economic integration (through transport infrastructure) of the airport with its surroundings (the approach so dominant at Schiphol).

The (regional) market position of each of the airports described might also provide an explanation, as well as the competition (or lack of it) between the air and rail networks. At CDG and Schiphol the development of the HST network and services led to overlap in the catchment areas of these airports with other airports (particularly Frankfurt – the main hub competitor in addition to Heathrow). Heathrow is still isolated from this competition, and traffic lost at Heathrow is probably gained at Gatwick and Stansted, but these airports are owned together with Heathrow by the same company. The situation would change if HST services between London and CDG were provided (Eurostar has announced intentions to start such a service – Brown, 2004). For passengers originating in Kent (through which the HST line from London to the Channel Tunnel passes), which is at the heart of Heathrow's catchment area, CDG Airport might be easier and quicker to access. In some circumstances, this might also apply to other areas south-east of London (e.g. East Sussex, Surrey and South Essex).

In terms of competition between the modes, the size of the Netherlands means that there is (almost) no competition between the modes on domestic routes, while in France the HST has probably captured most of the market on the routes where it can offer comparable travel times to aircraft – effectively winning the competition and leading airlines to give it up and instead cooperate with the railways on these routes (the Paris–Brussels route is also an example of this). In the UK, in contrast, the two industries are still very much in competition; this is mainly noticeable on the London–Manchester route, probably the most profitable in terms of railway operation in the UK and domestic air travel.

14.7 CONCLUSIONS

The development of rail networks around the world is directly linked to the development of urban centres – the cities. The reason is the high demand generated for railway services, to begin with, especially at the city centres. Large airports generate demand equal to, and often larger than, city centres. Airport cities are high-density cities, with almost all 'residents' walking distance away from the station. They are cities where all 'residents' need to travel, often relatively long distances, making them ideal for railway services. Still, connection of the world's largest airports to the rail network is a relatively recent development, particularly in Europe but much less so in North America.

The principle in developing the railway network, whether an intermediate place (e.g. a city) is connected to a transport line is a function of its revenue-generating ability and the cost of deviating from the least-cost route (Black, 2003), somehow does not seem to be always applied in the case of airports, as the Heathrow case study reveals. Yet it certainly seems to apply in some (European) airports, as the Schiphol and CDG case studies reveal.

The different degrees of rail development at airports which are big enough to justify investments in rail infrastructure depend strongly on the specific context. Nevertheless, the constant and consistent development of railway services at Schiphol, the construction of an HST station at DCG, and in contrast the absence of such developments at Heathrow, point to some underlying reasons which are more generic in nature. The evidence from Heathrow, Schiphol and CDG points to the importance of institutional settings within which the industries operate, and here the level and form of privatisation seem to be crucial while the institutional settings of the government body responsible for transport (i.e. the ministries of transport) seem to be of less importance in determining the extent to which air–rail opportunities are explored.

The effect of the competitive environment in which the air and rail industries operate is not clear. In the case of CDG, introduction of competitive forces was the main incentive to consider air–rail cooperation, but in the case of the UK the competitive environment in which the industries operate might be a deterrent to considering, at this stage, cooperation between the industries. In the Netherlands, the relatively low level of competition faced by the rail industry and the airport (on the domestic front) might facilitate cooperation between the industries. Thus the competitive environment is certainly important, but its effect is not clear. The competitive environment in this case also includes competition between the industries and that between the airports and nearby airports through the land transport network.

Givoni and Banister (2006) provided evidence for the benefits of providing high-quality rail services at Heathrow. These benefits merit further consideration and evaluation, such options should be considered in light of the future development of the airport, but this is not taken up by the actors concerned. The process described by Perl (1998), in which the CDG

Airport was transformed from a buffer between transport modes into a facility serving linked intermodal travel, can be the guide in the case of the UK. Perhaps what is missing in the UK is the type of forum provided to ADP and SNCF to meet and discuss intermodality. A need for such a forum was recognised by Eddington (2006), with regard to transport policy in the UK.

> Government needs to ensure the delivery system is ready to meet future challenges, including through reform of sub-national governance arrangements and reforming the planning process for major transport projects by introducing a new Independent Planning Commission to take decisions on projects of strategic importance. (Eddington, 2006: 7)

The fragmented nature of the UK rail industry and the absence of a single body, like the SRA at the time, to represent it probably makes cooperation between industries even harder to achieve. In addition to that, as Perl (1998) recognised in the case of CDG, parallel organisational thinking is also necessary to promote inter-organisational collaboration between the air and rail industries, and such 'thinking' seems to be absent in the case of the UK air and rail industries.

In conclusion, in countries with large airports and a developed rail network, airports should be a stop on the main rail lines. This approach is in line with securing air transport socioeconomic benefits and limiting its environmental impact. Air and rail transport infrastructure should not be developed in isolation from each other. One way to achieve this is to recognise large airports as cities, where the role and function of these cities in a regional–economic perspective depend on their connection to the surface transport network.

ACKNOWLEDGEMENT

We are grateful for Martijn Smit for producing the maps.

NOTES

1. This section is based on Givoni and Banister (2007).
2. The public sector body responsible, following privatisation of British Rail, for setting the strategy for the development of the UK railways. In 2004, the closure of the SRA was announced as part of plans for restructuring the UK railway industry.
3. Written by Sir Rod Eddington, former CEO of British Airways.
4. The index included attributes such as the number of trips generated from the station, number of trips attracted to the station, and the level of service provided. The level of

service was measured by a generalised travel time indicator which accounts for service frequency and travel time, including penalties for having to transfer, to all other stations on the network.

5. In the case of the HST services to CDG, the financial burden was split as follows: SNCF paid for the track (probably since even without the airport station the line would have been built) and the station was paid for by ADP (45 per cent), SNCF (45 per cent) and the Ile-de-France region (10 per cent) (Perl, 1998).

6. The TIPP project reached these conclusions mainly based on the case study of Finland (case study 7), but it seems to apply to the UK as well.

REFERENCES

Atkins (2004), *High Speed Line Study – Summary Report*, October, www.dft.gov.uk/stellent/groups/dft_railways/documents/page/dft_railways_032564.pdf (24/02/2005).

BAA (2002), *Heathrow Delivering for London and the Regions: A Surface Access Strategy for Heathrow – The Next Five Years*, BAA, Annual Progress Report, May.

Black, W.A. (2003), *Transportation – A Geographical Analysis*, London: The Guilford Press.

Borger, B. de and S. Proost (2007), 'Transport pricing when several governments compete for transport tax revenues', in P. Rietveld and R. Stough (eds), *Institutions and Sustainable Transport: Regulatory Reform in Advanced Economies*, Cheltenham, UK and Northampton, MA, USA: Edward Elgar: 211–30.

Brown, R. (2004), *High Speed Rail in the UK: Achievements and Prospects*, ILT André Bénard Lecture by Eurostar Chief Executive, Cavendish Conference Centre, London, 6 May.

Buchanan and Partners (1995), *Optimising Rail/Air Intermodality in Europe*, European Commission – DG VII, London, November.

CAA, Civil Aviation Authority (2005), *CAP 754 UK Regional Air Services*, CAA Economic Regulation Group, February, www.caa.co.uk/docs/33/CAP754.pdf (28/11/2005).

Crossrail (2005), www.crossrail.co.uk (23/02/2005).

Debrezion, G. (2006), *Railway Impacts on Real Estate Prices*, PhD thesis, Amsterdam: Vrije Universiteit.

DETR (Department of the Environment, Transport and the Regions) (1998), *A New Deal for Transport: Better for Everyone – The Government's White Paper on the Future of Transport*, London: DETR, July.

DfT (Department for Transport) (2003a), *The Future Development of Air Transport in the United Kingdom: South East*, 2nd edn, London: Department for Transport, February.

DfT (Department for Transport) (2003b), *The Future of Air Transport*, White Paper, London: Department for Transport, December.

Eddington, R. (2006), *The Eddington Transport Study – The Case for Action: Sir Rod Eddington's Advice to Government*, London, December.

Givoni, M. (2005), 'Aircraft and high speed train substitution: the case for airline and railway integration', unpublished PhD thesis, London: University College.

Givoni, M. and D. Banister (2006), 'Airline and railway integration', *Transport Policy*, **13**: 386–97.

Givoni, M. and D. Banister (2007), 'The role of the railways in the future of air transport', *Transportation Planning and Technology*, **30** (1): 95–112.

House of Commons Transport Committee (2003), *Aviation*, House of Commons Transport Committee, Sixth Report of Session 2002–03, Volume I, HC 454-I, London: The Stationery Office, July.

IARO (International Air Rail Organization) (1998), *Air Rail Links – Guide to Best Practice*, International Air Rail Organization, Air Transport Action Group, Airports Council International, September.

IATA (International Air Transport Association) (2003), *Air/Rail Intermodality Study*, IATA, February.

KLM, Air Traffic Control and Schiphol Group (2006), 'Connecting cities – a strong mainport to sustain the Netherlands' competitive edge', in W. Salet (ed.), *Synergy in Urban Networks? European Perspectives and Randstad Holland*, The Hague: Sdu Publishers: 111–35.

Mayor of London and Transport for London (2006), *Transport 2025 – Transport Vision for a Growing World City*, London, November, www.tfl.gov.uk/tfl/downloads/pdf/T2025-new.pdf (07/01/2007).

Mott MacDonald (2003), *Key European Hubs – Comparison of Aviation Policy*, Mott MacDonald, Report to the House of Commons – Transport Select Committee, May, www.parliament.uk/parliamentary_committees/transport_committee/transport_committee_reports_and_publications.cfm (18/06/2003).

Nash, C. (2005), 'Privatisation in transport', in K.J. Button and D.A. Hensher (eds), *Handbook of Transport Strategy, Policy and Institutions*, Amsterdam: Elsevier: 97–114.

Niskanen, E. (2005), *Towards Efficient and Effective Implementation of Transport Policy*, TIPP Final Report, November.

Perl, A. (1998), 'Redesigning an airport for international competitiveness: the politics of administrative innovation at CDG', *Journal of Air Transport Management*, **4**: 189–99.

Rietveld, P. and F. Bruinsma (1998), *Is Transport Infrastructure Effective?*, Berlin: Springer.

Stubbs, J. and F. Jegede (1998), 'The integration of rail and air transport in Britain', *Journal of Transport Geography*, **6** (1): 53–67.

SRA (Strategic Rail Authority) (2003), *Statement by SRA – The Future Development of Air Transport in the United Kingdom: South East*, SRA, June.

Vandermeer, R.Q.C. (2001), *The Heathrow Terminal Five and Associated Public Inquiries – Main Report*, Department for Transport, Local Government and the Regions, November, www.planning.dtlr.gov.uk/callins/terminal5/pdf/mainrep01.pdf and www.planning.dtlr.gov.uk/callins/terminal5/pdf/mainrep02.pdf (22/12/2001).

Van Wijk, M. (2007), 'Airports as Cityports in the city region', *Netherlands Geographical Studies*, **353**, Utrecht.

Zembri, P. (2007), 'The spatial consequences of air transport deregulation: an overview of the French case since 1995', in M. van Geenhuizen, A. Reggiani and P. Rietveld (eds), *Policy Analysis of Transport Networks*, Aldershot, UK: Ashgate: 235–56.

15. Drawing institutional lessons across countries on making transport infrastructure policy

W. Martin de Jong

15.1 INTRODUCTION

The growth of the global movement of people, goods and data has, in its wake, increased transnational policy dependence and the exchange of knowledge and information among policy-makers and specialists. Both bilateral learning by representatives of one country from another and multilateral learning within transnational expert networks in Europe and elsewhere have made the phenomenon of 'policy transfer' or 'institutional transplantation' across countries and regions more salient (Dolowitz, 1999; Rose, 1993; 2005; Stone, 2000; 2004; Van Bueren et al., 2002; De Jong et al., 2002; De Jong and Edelenbos, 2007). Policy-makers rate the performance of their own countries in terms of investment levels, congestion levels, modal split and many other indicators against that of their neighbours, and attempt to copy elements from the institutional framework of countries they consider their benchmarks. In the world of transport infrastructure investment the proponents of comprehensive policy analysis may admire the German 'Standardisierte Bewertung' ('standardised appraisal'), which has been in existence there for decades and want to emulate its procedures at home (De Jong and Geerlings, 2005). Those with a strong preference for direct democracy may choose to study the Swiss or Californian practices of consulting individual voters on specific transport issues through the ballot box. Those reluctant to accept high levels of public spending in public transport are more favourably inclined towards a purely economic approach to investment and look at the practice of involving the private sector which occurs in the UK (Nash and Preston, 1991; Pakkala, 2002). Singapore's transit system and its curbs on free motor vehicle ownership, on the other hand, are a source of inspiration for those who believe in alternative forms of globalisation and the responsible use of natural resources (Cervero, 1998).

The cross-national transplantation of policy ideas and arrangements holds both opportunities for the improvement of the performance of one's own policy system and serious institutional challenges when it comes to the viability of the transplant in its new environment. The opportunities derive from the fact that one's own country has in the course of its own historical path developed its own particular solutions to investment challenges, with all their advantages and disadvantages. Since other countries have followed other paths, they are likely to have found other path-dependent solutions to the same or similar policy problems. Policy ideas, models and institutions taken from elsewhere therefore represent a promising, handy and relatively cheap source of inspiration for institutional self-improvement (Rose, 2005). Copying, imitation or even the transformed adoption of ideas, models or institutions from elsewhere is, however, not something that occurs automatically by decree. It is highly improbable, especially if they are solely decreed, that such transplants will fulfil their function properly and be successfully deployed in their new institutional environment (Watson, 1993; Jacoby, 2000). The policy issues that the country of adoption is faced with may not be the same. The availability of funds to make investment programmes a success may be lacking. The legal context in which new regulations have to operate may differ fundamentally from how they worked in the country of origin. Policy-makers and citizens in the adopting country may be decidedly less or more respectful of institutional rules. The customers of transport services may, alternatively, have completely different preferences when it comes to choosing their transport mode or price/quality considerations. If cities in South Africa desire a subway system as in New York or Washington DC, will they be able to gather the required financial means together for such a large-scale construction and refurbishment? Policy-makers in countries in continental Europe hoping to adopt the UK planning policy guidelines for environmental issues to boost the flexibility of their decision-making processes are likely to encounter problems, particularly if they want to give them a similar function at home. Their legal systems are stricter about the distinction between what is official legislation and what is not. Similarly, transport authorities in Northern Europe committed to the introduction of toll roads along the lines of Southern Europe and Latin America to cover the funds necessary for their construction may find that in countries where no such tradition of *péage* or *pedágio* exists, public resistance completely thwarts their initiatives. Policy transplantation, therefore, involves many subtleties which cannot lightly be discarded.

In this chapter, the question of how to learn constructively from other countries on promising institutional arrangements for investment in transport infrastructures is addressed by considering the following sub-questions, each in a separate section:

- *How do existing institutional structures affect the viability of transplanting policy ideas, models and institutions from elsewhere?* What are institutional structures, what do they consist of and how do they affect the behaviour of public and private actors involved in the policy-making process? And, as a consequence, when a new institutional element is introduced into the system, what reactions can be expected? The above issues will be the subject of Section 15.2.
- *What types of institutional structures exist in reality in the world of decision-making on transport infrastructures and what are their characteristics?* We systematically study the essential characteristics of institutional systems and provide a general typology of institutional structures for investing in road and rail infrastructure, as well as studying how they impact on actor behaviour in these systems. This subject is dealt with in Section 15.3.
- *What examples can be given of promising policy transplants from a selection of European countries and what challenges would their adoption probably pose in other countries?* The knowledge acquired in Sections 15.2 and 15.3 will be of great help in answering this particular sub-question, since a prediction of actor behaviour in the adopting country and legal, cultural and other challenges resulting from the types of institutional structure in the country is relevant here, along with idiosyncratic aspects for the specific case at hand. The sub-question is dealt with in Section 15.4.
- *What are general dos and don'ts in policy transplantation regarding the decision-making on transport infrastructure projects that can be gleaned from this chapter?* These concluding lessons will be drawn in Section 15.5.

15.2   INSTITUTIONAL STRUCTURES AND THEIR EFFECT ON POLICY TRANSPLANTATION

Policy actors do not think and act in a void when they draw up plans, allocate funds, negotiate and make choices. Their thoughts and actions are strongly influenced by both formal and informal heuristics or rules of the game telling them what is and what is not allowed, what is and what is not appropriate or adequate in specific circumstances, what is the correct thing to do and what is not (March and Olsen, 1989). Even though at first sight it may seem that such 'institutions' are an impediment to intelligent or flexible action, the fact that they allow actors to make choices in an established, routine manner is a definite advantage. Institutions are often solutions that were found to similar problems in the past, making it unnecessary to reinvent the wheel each time one is presented with the same or very similar problems (Nelson and Winter, 1982; North, 1990; Mantzavinos, 2004). Time and attention, which are always limited, can then be directed to new problems for which clear-cut solutions have not yet been found.

The more conspicuous institutions have a formal character, meaning that they have been given a visible legal or organisational form. Or, put differently, governmental or other authorities have taken them through a process of official enactment as a result of which they have achieved formal applicability. All legislation regarding investment in transport infrastructure and commonly known organisational structures are a reality for policy actors and represent the formal rules of the game in this field. This applies to the property rights, powers and competencies each of the actors has been granted in the policy area, how the service rates for customers of public transport facilities or roads are to be determined, which companies are shareholders for what percentages in public or private transport enterprises, what environmental and noise zonings have to be respected in new and existing runways or port terminals, and so on. It is the formal institutions that are often discussed in political debates and it is to them that policy-makers often turn when they want to change or overturn existing policies or develop completely new policies and policy instruments.

There is also, however, something that could be described as the cultural side to the institutional structure: the informal institutions. Informal institutions have never been officially enacted and can rarely be found in any guidebook on rules and heuristics, but they do have a strong impact on how policy actors behave towards each other, to what extent and in what form they exchange information when formal regulations require them to, if and how they sanction civilians and citizens who do not comply with official norms. They can encourage actors to compensate the loss of sensitive areas by 'planting new forests' even if this is not laid down in any public law or act. Informal institutions can take the shape of conventions, moral codes or social norms: actors feel compelled to follow them or are pushed by others to follow them, but if not backed up by formal institutions, they are not enforceable.

Formal and informal institutions can either reinforce each other, have no impact on each other or can weaken each other's effects. If the first is the case, then official policies and regulations can expect solid support from policy actors and affected groups in the policy area and there is little impetus to change anything. If the second option applies, no complications arise as long as informal institutions are not sabotaged by small defecting minorities (in which case an outcry for formal arrangements is likely to arise) or as long as the enforcement of formal institutions is not hampered by large-scale informal evasion (in which case authorities will either revoke the policy or invest heavily in enforcement measures). If formal institutions and informal institutions work against each other and push in opposite directions, one can speak of 'incongruence'. Policy-makers could then either (1) decide to strictly enforce the formal institutions and thus evoke strong public resistance and make themselves unpopular, or (2) fail to enforce without officially renouncing the policy and leave things as they are, which is the easiest option and happens most frequently, or (3) officially revoke the policy and give in to the dominance of informal institutions, which means acknowledging policy failure.

Congruence between formal and informal institutions, therefore, or the lack of it, has major repercussions on the viability and effectiveness of new policies.

An interesting example to demonstrate this point is that of a particular measure taken in metropolises suffering from smog in hot summers. It has become common to curb motor vehicle use in such periods by allowing car drivers with even number-plates to drive on one half of the day and those with odd numbers on the other half. The typical Scandinavian public policy-maker imposing such a rule will meet with a comparatively benevolent public and a critically respectful attitude towards this emergency measure. Other policy actors will react mildly and citizens will comply, because informal compliance with formal regulation is high, by and large. The city government of a typical South European or Latin American metropolis will be confronted with a very different situation, however. These countries are known for much lower rates of interpersonal and inter-organisational trust, and low faith in the operations of their public authorities. Many car users there will anticipate these new policies differently and ensure that they have two number-plates available in their garage, one with an even number for half the days and one with an odd number for the other half. In Scandinavian culture such behaviour may be judged irresponsible, but most Latins think that it is clever and admire agile ways of evading government regulation. Combating this behaviour is quite a challenge. Strict enforcement is costly, practically demanding, complicated and highly unpopular. As a consequence, the necessary follow-up to make the policy measures really environmentally effective is hard to implement. One can see that the adoption of similar formal institutions in two different informal institutional environments has a hugely different effect in the two places.

Exactly this congruence (or lack of it) between the formal regulatory framework and the informal institutional environment in which it has to function becomes crucial in exercises of policy transplantation. One could consider the adoption of a foreign policy idea, model or institution to be a specific subset of all policy changes, namely those inspired by examples taken from abroad (Rose, 2005). Even if the example were successful in its country of origin, it is far from certain that it would lead to the same achievements in its country of adoption. There, in contradistinction to the circumstances in the model country, financial means to effectively implement an action programme may be lacking, the positive effects of a new legal framework may not arise but the interaction with necessary auxiliary regulations is different and less helpful, the cultural values and norms regarding the desirability and acceptability of using public transport by the more privileged may be different, or practical or geographical issues may prevent similar positive effects from appearing. Normally, institutional systems have particular strengths and weaknesses making the implantation of specific types of transplants possible, but not others. Many Dutch policy-makers in the area of transport infrastructure investment, for instance, have long admired the comprehensive German appraisal method for evaluating infrastructure projects, based on social cost–benefit analysis, and especially its systematic application and actual political impact on the decision-making processes (Bundesministerium für Verkehr, 1993). They saw it as comparing quite positively with their own practice (until recently, when a home-grown economic model obtained wide recognition and became institutionalised) in which some more limited models were only used some of the time for some decisions. Yet, at the same time they praised the flexibility of their own institutional structure and the prevalence of political primacy, while the German system in their eyes was characterised by rigidity and technocracy. But one cannot eat one's cake and have it too. If German policy-makers are willing to accept the outcomes of studies that only experts can completely understand and base their decisions on them, it is because they feel politically committed to these studies and hold on to their outcomes even when this is less convenient. This inherently implies a certain level of consistency and belief in analytical procedures, which is less common in the Netherlands. Conversely, German policy-makers have regularly expressed their delight in the looseness and flexibility of Dutch decision-making practice, but it is probable that, where they are confronted with the regular adjustments and changes in direction common in the Netherlands, they will find them opportunistic, sloppy and 'not serious'.

Congruence can also become an issue when formal institutions are transplanted from countries belonging to another political or legal 'family of nations' (Castles, 1993; Zweigert and Kötz, 1998; Newman and Thornley, 1996; Lijphart, 1999). In such cases, pieces of new legislation or organisational framework do not fit easily with other endogenous institutions and will become alien, often dysfunctional, bodies in their new environment. UK planning policy guidelines regarding transport planning, for instance, which are commonly praised for their flexible use at home (in a common-law country working on the basis of precedent law), become much stricter legislation when incorporated in continental civil-law systems. There, the 'law' is simply to be applied and enforced. Guidelines then cease to be 'guidelines' in the UK sense of the word.

Congruence, both between formal and informal institutions and between old and new formal institutions is an important issue and not something that develops automatically. Lack of congruence between the original policy transplant and the informal institutional environment does not however make transfer impossible, since the form in which the original idea, model or institution is adopted is susceptible to adaptation to make it suitable for its new context. In previous work, the author has distinguished six factors which, if taken into consideration, are conducive to minimising this incongruence and making successful transplantation more likely (De Jong et al., 2002):

1. *One model or several models*   If the idea, model or set of formal institutions is taken from just one country, too much value is attached to one particular problem-solving approach and chances are missed to learn from a wider array of solution repertoires. Developing creative syntheses from various models is preferable.
2. *Literal copying or free interpretation*   If the idea, model or set of institutions is copied literally, no attempt is made to bend and adjust it to preferences and perceptions of relevant players and institutional conditions in the adopting country. Creative interpretation is also preferable since it allows policy actors more space for necessary political and conceptual manoeuvres during negotiations.
3. *Detailed legal framework or general idea*   If detailed procedures are studied for adoption, the odds are that implementation issues will be focused on even before a fundamental debate on the why and how of the transplant has taken place. Using a general approach as a source of inspiration allows policy actors in the adopting country to mould the model in their own way and increase its functionality.
4. *Business as usual or strong sense of urgency*   If there is a strong sense of urgency in the adopting country, meaning that the institutional system and its performance are felt to be in a state of crisis (or if such feelings can be evoked), the position of those wanting change is strengthened and that of the defenders of the status quo weakened.
5. *Adjustment for structural and cultural differences*   If the legal and political systems (formal institutions) and the cultural norms and values (informal institutions) in the country adopting a transplant are comparatively similar to those in the country of origin, adoption is likely to be easier. However, in both cases serious discounting of even small and subtle institutional differences is necessary to avoid policy failure.

6. *Pushed by donor or pulled in by adopter*   If changes in the adopting
    country are pushed too strongly by policy-makers from the donor,
    resistance among potential opponents is more likely to develop and the
    position of proponents compromised by all-too-enthusiastic outsiders
    knowing what's 'best for you'. Adopting actors who pull in and evalu-
    ate options independently and accept only solicited advice fare better.

   Below, we shall bear in mind the clues for successful policy transplantation when looking at the promising foreign ideas, models and institutions
for investing in transport infrastructure.

15.3   TYPES OF INSTITUTIONAL STRUCTURES FOR INVESTING IN TRANSPORT INFRASTRUCTURES

In a study conducted for the Dutch Ministry of Transport by the author
(Ministry of Transport, Public Works and Water Management, 1999; De
Jong, 1999), which has been updated and extended with two extra countries
in De Jong and Geerlings (2005), a relatively complete picture has been
given on the deliberation procedures and practices for the prioritisation of
transport infrastructure investments in eight Western countries. The analysis distinguished the following four institutional dimensions, based on 30
characteristics (see Appendix 15.1), for which the institutional structures in
the countries were tested:

1. *Federalism–unitarism*: the more a country's institutional structure
    encourages administrative layers other than the top layers to organise
    veto powers against proposals initiated by the top layers and the more
    initiatives they can take, the more federalist a country is. Higher levels
    of federalism imply higher level of checks and balances in an institu-
    tional system when it comes to the creation of information.
2. *Democracy–technocracy*: the more the institutional structure encour-
    ages societal groups – pressure groups and citizens – to question expert
    judgement from professional or academic circles, the more democratic
    a country is. High levels of democracy also imply higher levels of
    checks and balances in an institutional system when it comes to the cre-
    ation of information.

High scores on dimensions (1) and (2) reflect high levels of checks and balances in the institutional structure and therefore a much more even distribution of power among actors.

312

Innovation, competition and institutions

3. *Integralism–reductionism*: the more the institutional structure promotes the involvement of as many infrastructure-related aspects as possible in trade-off issues, the more integralist a country is. Higher levels of integralism imply that a greater variety of information delivered to the institutional system is effectively taken into account when choices are made.

4. *Corporatism–pluralism*: the more the institutional structure encourages actors to feel obliged to each other after reaching agreement and therefore to adopt a less opportunistic attitude towards each other, the more corporatist a country is. Higher levels of corporatism imply that a greater variety of information delivered to the institutional system and effectively taken into account when choices are made.

High scores on the dimensions (3) and (4) reflect stronger incentives for cooperation, thereby increasing levels of information exchange and the realisation of co-productions with various parties contributing to projects.

The scores of the eight countries (Sweden, Denmark, Germany, Netherlands, Switzerland, France, the UK and the USA) on each of the four dimensions were obtained at an ordinal scale (high, medium, low) and are shown in Table 15.1.

Although some similar patterns can be observed when these scores are compared with the families-of-nations typology developed by several authors mentioned above, the scores in this table are specific for the field of transport infrastructure investments and can be placed at the policy sector rather than constitutional level.

Table 15.1 becomes more meaningful when it is placed in the context of types of institutional structures, in which interaction between players/

Table 15.1 Institutional characteristics of eight countries regarding infrastructure policy

Country/dimension	Federalism	Democracy	Integralism	Corporatism
Sweden	MEDIUM	MEDIUM	HIGH	HIGH
Denmark	MEDIUM	MEDIUM	MEDIUM	MEDIUM
Germany	MEDIUM	MEDIUM	HIGH	HIGH
Netherlands	LOW	MEDIUM	MEDIUM	MEDIUM
Switzerland	MEDIUM	HIGH	HIGH	HIGH
France	MEDIUM	LOW	MEDIUM	MEDIUM
UK	LOW	LOW	LOW	LOW
USA	HIGH	HIGH	LOW	LOW

organisations occurs along different patterns. Four types of institutional structures can be distinguished, shown in Table 15.2. Here, we can see that dimensions (1) and (2) (on checks and balances) constitute one axis and dimensions (3) and (4) (on cooperation) the other.

The four types of institutional structures distinguished in Table 15.2 can be described as follows.

Type 1. Cooperative Interactors

This type of institutional system has a wide range of interdependent actors, who also maintain durable relationships. It demands a combination of creation of various ideas and extensive sharing of them. Both checks and balances and cooperative structures have been realised, leading to a high degree of information exchange over time between actors. This limits the extent to which actors 'blind one another with science' during the evaluation process, since they can acquire clear insight into each other's calculation methods. The standardisation, acceptance and wide applicability of the models allow them to be used repeatedly without the need for continual redesign or modification to deal with new cases.

Type 2. Benevolent Dictators

This type of institutional system comprises relatively few actors monopolising most of the resources, who maintain lasting relationships with each other. As a market form, one could claim that this structure resembles an oligopoly with strong cartel formation. Information comes from only a small number of sources, but it is widely shared. Actors have cooperative inclinations, but power is not really evenly spread among them.

Table 15.2   Four types of institutional structures

Key aspects as to the use of information	Many checks and balances	Monopoloid power structure
Incentives for cooperation	*Type 1* Cooperative interactors	*Type 2* Benevolent dictators
Incentives for competition	*Type 3* Individualist competitors	*Type 4* Hierarchical determinators

Source: De Jong (2001).

Type 3. Individualist Competitors

This institutional system comprises a very wide range of actors, who maintain only volatile relations between themselves. As a market form, this structure resembles a market with a relatively large number of players on the supply and demand sides, who do not succeed in reaching collusion or agreement because these are mainly focused on direct individual utility. There is a great deal of individual innovation, but this innovation is only standardised after the event or not at all. There are a great many checks and balances, but cooperative structures among the actors are missing.

Type 4. Hierarchical Determinators

This institutional system has a relatively small number of different actors of which one or two dominate the debate. Moreover, these actors maintain few relationships. A dominant market leader sets the agenda and tries to impose it on the other actors without the need or willingness to listen to any of them. He/she is focused on direct utility and the speed of decision-making.

Connecting the data obtained in Tables 15.1 and 15.2 led us to conclude that Sweden, Switzerland and Germany come closest to approaching institutional structure type 1, the USA to type 3 and the UK to type 4.

The Swiss and German institutional structures are rather federal, democratic, integralist and corporatist. In terms of informal behaviour, Swiss and German policy-makers rarely deviate from their formal structure. Before acceptance the formal structure takes a long time to mature, but then fits well with the informal structures. Reasoning in the UK is much more hierarchical and automatically departs from the informal structure. British policy-makers, especially English ones, are prepared to adapt the formal structure if the informal structure so requires. What is striking for the USA is the high democracy score. Perhaps contradictory to the idea that exists about the functioning of representative democracy, direct democracy appears to be alive and kicking. The ethos of individual freedom and property rights is translated into informal practice; that a structure sometimes appears to be missing is hardly a problem. Just as striking is the strong resemblance to the UK regarding the integralism and corporatism indices, and the extreme differences on federalism and democracy. The combination of the distribution of power and competitive orientation leads to fundamentally different politics than a combination of power concentration and competitiveness. Despite cultural similarities between the two Anglo-Saxon states, the differences in state and organisational structure have major consequences.

The positions of Denmark, France and the Netherlands are slightly more complicated because the Netherlands and France cross each other when it comes to federalism and democracy. French citizens and pressure groups are relatively less powerful, but lower tiers of government can bar central government decisions better through a system of osmosis and double functions. The Netherlands has more provisions for citizens to speak out their opinions, but provinces and municipalities have hardly any funds when it comes to transport investments. France and the Netherlands, each other's mirror images, are improbable candidates for a type 1 or type 3 position, but both could swing to be types 2 or 4, depending on the circumstances.

Denmark appears to have medium scores on all dimensions. Both Sweden and Denmark have a stronger tradition of local autonomy than the Netherlands (Rose and Stahlberg, 2002) and in addition to that, Sweden is also more integralist and corporatist. The latter is evident mainly from the concreteness and reliability of agreements, similar to those in Germany. Cervero's case study of the Stockholm metro (1998) offers a splendid example: it is a kind of model state, whose policy models and approaches are either difficult or impossible to imitate. Denmark is explicitly known as somewhat less strictly managed and 'more liberal' than Sweden (Leleur, 1995). Its scores on integralism and corporatism indicate this and bring Denmark closer to flexible and opportunist practice. This is clear from both Cervero's case study of Copenhagen (1998) and from Flyvbjerg's study into decision-making in Aalborg (1998).

As is now clear, cross-national institutional variety essentially refers to having different positions in the table of types of institutional structures. Regularly having similar scores in them, such as Germany and Switzerland, does not mean having exactly the same formal and informal decision-making institutions, but it does mean that styles of decision-making are roughly comparable and that a transplant is likely to be received in more or less the same way in both countries. As mentioned before, the success of cross-national institutional transfers is not guaranteed. The fit with the rest of the institutional framework must be reasonable to good, and the concomitant informal practices must grow around it to make it effective and prevent it from becoming a paper tiger.

15.4 EXAMPLES OF PROMISING POLICY TRANSPLANTS AND HINTS FOR THEIR SUCCESSFUL ADOPTION

In this section, stylised descriptions of four potentially promising institutional transplants are offered, taken from different countries. The advantages in their countries of origin are given, after which some well-reasoned speculations are made regarding adoption of those transplants elsewhere and what it would take to make them operate successfully. These four promising transplants are:

1. Public referenda on infrastructure initiatives or complete investment packages.
2. Public procurement policies for the selection of private funding and contracting.
3. Institutionalised appraisal methods developed in an interactive multi-actor process.
4. Five-year plan-contracts with earmarked budgets between state and regions.

The usefulness of the characterisation of types of institutional structures for fathoming the feasibility and possible congruence of institutional transplants will then become apparent.

1. Public Referenda on Infrastructure Initiatives or Complete Investment Packages

The strongest forms of direct democracy worldwide can be found in Switzerland and some states in the USA, such as California. Their scores on the relevant institutional dimension in Section 15.3 also made this point clearly, and they are strongly embedded in national or regional administrative cultures with decade- or sometimes century-old traditions. The introduction of referenda or propositions submitted to the ballot box elsewhere is therefore no *sine cura*. Switzerland, for instance, has not one but actually three types of non-consultative referenda in the field of transport infrastructure. These are (1) public votes on investment packages exceeding certain amounts of public sums made obligatory by law, (2) votes on running government actions forced through by certain numbers of citizens showing support through their signatures and (3) votes on policy initiatives proposed by citizens who managed to garner a certain number of supporting signatures.

Much can be said in favour of the above form of radical democratisation. Public debate is stimulated, citizens are made more responsible for what their governments do and feel more connected to them. Referenda of this type are also a successful tool to bring deeply felt public emotions or dissatisfaction out into the open in a controlled fashion when the political and bureaucratic classes have remained impervious to them. A radical policy change in the field of infrastructure investment occurred, for instance, when through a *Volksinitiativ* (people's initiative) the Swiss electorate decided to ban freight lorries exceeding 28 tons, often foreign ones from using Swiss motorways through sometimes environmentally sensitive areas. The outcome was both courageous and inconvenient for the Swiss government, who saw its relations with European partners endangered and felt compelled to have all lorries transported on piggyback trains through the Alps, requiring huge investments in an Alpine tunnel system. The investment package resulting from this new government initiative required public approval through a referendum, which was granted for an amount of 16 billion Swiss francs. Unfortunately, when the construction costs proved to exceed the approved budget by far, this pushed public officials to economise but also made them apprehensive about whether they should seek renewed public approval by referendum for this higher sum. Another referendum would not only be costly and make postponement necessary, but what should be done if the new proposal were to be rejected in a referendum? Direct democracy certainly strengthens the link between elector and elected, often pushes authorities to take the voice of the public seriously and impels them to find creative policy solutions when the budget is limited by the vote (high-speed tilting trains on existing tracks instead of constructing new tracks, for instance). On the other hand, it may also lead to political and bureaucratic stalemates, and limited space for manoeuvre by officials.

Introduction of referenda of this sort in countries that have no strong tradition of democracy is no easy matter. The requirement to achieve a 'HIGH' score on the democracy dimension (see Table 15.1) would not only make this legally possible, but also create a favourable climate for it, which would curb many privileges public authorities are accustomed to and bestow greater responsibility on citizens than they are used to. Furthermore, it would require citizens to show serious interest and involvement in public matters to avoid irresponsible outcomes. In short, it would require public authorities, involved private parties as well as a large majority of the electorate to be cooperative interactors, a situation that cannot happen overnight. Lastly, it would require authorities to accept outcomes for votes even if the initial turnout were low (say 20 per cent or less), to accommodate the wishes of passionate minorities and convince all that voting does make a difference and that participation next time could be beneficial for them. It is obvious that exact replicating of the Swiss model or even looking only at that model is far from commendable. Each of the countries interested in moving in that direction should also look at the Californian and Swiss experiences and then make proposals moulded for their own societies.

2. Public Procurement Policies for the Selection of Private Funding and Contracting

A growing number of countries have chosen to give the private sector a much greater role in the design, funding, construction and maintenance of transport infrastructures (Flyvbjerg et al., 2003; Pakkala, 2002; Pakkala et al., 2007). The underlying philosophy is often that private companies can do things cheaper and better, but also that there is a great deal of creative innovative potential left unearthed among designers, engineers and bankers if public regulations determine the how and what of infrastructure development. The UK was among the first to experiment with this new line of public management, soon followed by countries such as Australia, New Zealand and later Sweden, Finland and Norway. The most radical version was adopted in the UK, where new road and railway tracks were contracted to a private consortium who were to design, build, finance and operate (DBFO) them for a period of 30 years and then lease them back to the public sector. Less radical solutions were adopted in New Zealand and Australian states (generally for a period of ten years, including maintenance). Even more moderate was the version adopted in the Nordic countries (for only three or four years with possible extensions, with design and the rest often kept in separate packages to prevent collusion, and excluding construction in the case of Sweden where 'public–private partnerships were never accepted politically). Experiences have obviously varied in each of the countries, but experts generally agree that public expenditure on transport infrastructure for similar projects has decreased substantially and that speed and flexibility of decision-making have increased. As regards innovation, creativity and the improvement of quality performance levels, the evidence is still unclear. The reason why these benefits have occurred is likely to have been the realisation of economies of scale by contracting with large consortia in which banks and insurance companies, designers, construction companies, engineering firms and consultants have joined forces. Another benefit is likely to have been the displacement of many risks to those private firms, who subsequently work according to business principles, take the benefits from the rising value of land and real estate around new infrastructure links, and ensure that possible commercial activities around these links are exploited to the full. Listed as a final gain is the fact that these procurement constructions often allow for the introduction of tolls, through which the user rather than the taxpayer is charged for transport services. The latter depends, however, on the specific institutional arrangement chosen, for the Nordic counties continue to refund the private consortium through the public purse.

This is not to say that there are no public policy risks involved in this move towards increased private sector involvement. Three main arguments are relevant here. Concerns have been raised about the tendency of cartels to develop between the few contractors involved in this business. In Sweden, one case of illegal price agreements was proven (De Jong, 2003), and few would deny that this market can be characterised as strongly oligopolistic. This places special responsibilities on procurement offices and competition regulators. Second, certain policy goals as agreed in plans and public statements (promotion of intermodal policies, optimisation of transport network effects, most environment-friendly option chosen) can in theory all be upheld in negotiations between the procurement agency and contractors, but they can be compromised in the final contracts. Even if they are included, they may be ignored with relative impunity since intervening in the way in which contracts are respected is not easy. Finally, public policy concerns and priorities may and will change in the course of the years: the further the public sector has distanced itself from direct involvement with infrastructure projects, the fewer the chances that any (financially affordable) intervention and infraction in the contract is possible to accommodate these concerns and interests.

Transplantation of public procurement in its various forms as described above has been popular since the late 1990s. Many of the institutional characteristics in the corporatism dimension have been altered in a more competitive, individualistic direction. In fact, the various Anglo-Saxon countries have eyed each other closely, and the Nordic states have studied both the Anglo-Saxon and each other's models. Australia's and New Zealand's arrangements are rather similar, and so are Finland's and Norway's. In all of these cases, the precepts for successful policy transplantation were taken into account. This was often because the initiatives were pushed forward in periods of financial crisis, generic action programmes rather than legal procedures were followed, and because various alternative models were studied. In the case of the Nordic countries, the Nordic Road Federation proved a useful forum for a systematic exchange of experiences. The decision-making logic underlying this sort of institutional transplant shows a tendency towards stronger incentives for competition, meaning that it should work best in individualist competitor or hierarchical determinator types of institutional structures. Although it is true that this form of transplant certainly originated there, it has also caught on in some Nordic countries (not Sweden) and is under consideration in some countries in continental Europe. Adoption there will probably prove less easy, since it will require countries to alter central features in the integralism and corporatism dimensions that they may be quite attached to, such as integrated transport planning and soft and warm relations among various actors. On the other hand, the solutions found in some Nordic countries which have made these relations more business-like and distant,

but not a modern form of cut-throat competition, will presumably be
greeted with more enthusiasm than the UK model.

3. Institutionalised Appraisal Methods Developed in an Interactive Multi-actor Process

In order to make the investment choice from among multiple alternatives,
some form of evaluation and weighing is always necessary. Even though the
actual decision-making is to a very large extent a political and interest-
ridden decision, appraisal methods are nearly always used to generate an
overview of the effects of various options. In relatively politicised institutional systems such as France, analytical studies may be conducted, but in
actual practice (as opposed to the world of paper) their outcomes play a
relatively minor role when political priorities are set in the negotiation
process among various policy actors. In more technocratic systems such as
the German one, on the other hand, political decision-makers show a high
level of commitment to the outcomes of integrated analytical policy
studies. Whereas the former increase the chances of producing negotiated
nonsense enjoying a substantial amount of political support, the latter
severely restrict decision-makers' freedom of manoeuvre to accommodate
information not contained in the study or obliges them to sell alternatives
that may not arouse much excitement among other actors.

In some places, such as in certain Metropolitan Planning Organizations
(MPOs) in the USA, and in certain states in Australia and Finland, an
intriguing middle ground has been sought and found by having a public
agency take the initiative in setting up a process to develop an appraisal
method or evaluation procedure in which the indicators or criteria were
developed and ultimately approved by all the involved actors in the field, both
public and private. In Northern California, for instance, the regional MPOs
for the San Francisco Bay Area hosted brainstorming and interactive decision processes in which local governments, counties, port and airport authorities, the state government, transport companies and social, environmental
and business pressure groups collectively developed an appraisal method
suitable for their region. In the first instance, all were invited to contribute the
evaluation criteria on which they wanted projects submitted for funding to
be judged. Later on, all actors participated in a voting procedure in which
they were to decide collectively which of these criteria were to be incorporated in a generally applicable appraisal model and what weight each of them
would get. This resulted in a report comprising a comprehensive list of criteria for which projects submitted to the MPO could score a certain number of
points. The total number of points scored would decide whether the submitted project would qualify for funding and what priority it should get.

The outcomes of this and similar other interactive appraisal method development processes are remarkable for a number of reasons. The appraisal method generated was, in terms of its contents, quite different from traditional ones based on cost–benefit economics. It consisted sometimes of very practical elements, such as the sizes and heights of bridges, or the presence of money reserved for environmental compensation measures. Second, after some bargaining all involved actors in the region agreed to apply the MPO consistently to all submitted projects. In response to this process, the State of California took the unusual step of devolving all funds for projects of regional size to the MPO and giving it free rein as long as it spent the funds in accordance with the agreed method. In addition, some other actors in the region also entrusted their funds for investment in infrastructure to the MPO, making it a real regional pooling of funds. Finally, during the process solidarity among the various actors had grown enormously, even to the extent that they considered each other partners and the transport networks in the region an intermodal whole. Since then, several other MPOs in the USA have followed suit.

It is not straightforward to come up with powerful caveats against this potentially promising transplant, other than that economists or engineering experts may criticise the contents of the model on scientific grounds or that widespread support can only be produced in quite propitious circumstances. The relevant actors in a region, state or country are not always so predisposed to collaborate, a facilitator is not always capable of producing a useful outcome, and in many cases the authority responsible for funding projects may not be willing to give up its own discretion on allocation decisions. On the other hand, once a critical mass of support has been generated for such an initiative, social pressure on opponents will rise and they may end up getting committed. Interestingly, as an institutional transplant, the requirements for its introduction are in fact a constellation of institutional features taking institutional systems generally in the direction of more federalism, more democracy, more integralism and more corporatism. The choice in favour of these changes will, however, almost always follow after the appraisal method and the regional solidarity have been created, when the climate for making the required formal institutional changes will have become much better. The final result should then be a type 1 institutional structure (cooperative interactors), both highly desirable and hard to obtain.

4.   Five-year Plan-contracts with Earmarked Budgets between State and Regions

Making a national transport plan which includes all the main existing and newly intended infrastructure hubs and links, and connecting this plan as consistently as possible with the actual implementation of projects, is the preferred policy of most continental European countries, at least officially. Two of them, France and Germany, have made major strides in making this connection as systematic as possible, albeit under different names. They have national plans in place for transport infrastructure investments, called *Schéma directeur* and *Bundesverkehrswegeplan*, respectively, which lay out the government's general policy intentions for the coming decades. In these, the reader will also find a list of all the actions that the government, based on suggestions given by various policy actors considering the future, think require serious consideration. This does not yet guarantee construction, for only some of the projects mentioned in this national plan are actually transferred to the *contrat de plan* (plan contract) in France or the *Bedarfsplan* (need plan) in Germany. The five-year agreements signed by both the national or federal government on the one hand, and the regional or state government on the other, do contain those projects whose implementation has been secured. Not only are general sketches given of the spatial and environmental shape the new road, rail or waterway connection will acquire and how it is connected to the entire intermodal network; the financial arrangements for the next five years are also taken care of to make sure annual adjustments of the budget are not necessary. Since these five-year plan contracts have been negotiated and are approved by both relevant partners, discordance is much less likely to arise and certainty about the financial flux is no longer an issue.

Compared to the three previous types of promising policy transplants, this one has very different advantages and disadvantages. Particularly strong points are the comparatively transparent overview of missing links in the national and regional transport networks and the translation of some of them into actual projects to be implemented. Since the signatories enter into a legally binding partnership with clear-cut financial consequences for many years, certainty, security and acceptance are generated in relation to their implementation and construction. Haggling each year over the funding is not necessary; only large-scale reviews after five years are required. The political and administrative requirements of living up to this demanding system are substantial, and obviate flexibility and alterations should actors change their opinions in the course of the process. Also, adoption of any of the previous three transplants is precluded if this system is in place. Since this approach is rather supply-oriented, the voices of transport users and citizens are weak and space for possible privatisation and liberalisation is limited.

Adoption of this type of transplant involves a relatively federal, integralist and corporatist institutional structure. If several of those components mentioned above are already present in a disconnected fashion, strong political leadership aiming for agreement to systematise the decision-making process and massaging the various governmental levels may be sufficient. But should these components be largely absent, as in Anglo-Saxon countries, should the various tiers of government not consider each other more or less as equals, or should a drive for a comprehensive consistent framework not exist, chances of successful introduction will be quite small.

Combining the second type of transplant (public procurement policies for the selection of private funding and contracting), requiring a more competitive spirit, and this one, which necessitates a more cooperative style, will be nearly impossible to achieve.

15.5   CONCLUSIONS

Institutions and institutional systems are hard to change, but, especially when policy actors feel that their performance or legitimacy is at stake, it is not impossible. When congestion on the infrastructure networks has grown out of hand, when annual investment or maintenance costs are considered to be out of control, or when citizens feel they should be more involved in the decision process, drawing lessons from policies in other countries can prove helpful as a source of inspiration for institutional changes at home. This does not imply, however, that following good examples from elsewhere also results in policy successes at home. Political, legal, administrative and cultural practices differ among countries, and so do their economic, geographical and practical potential. In the end, each country can benefit immensely from experiences abroad, but policy actors will always have to take into account that a transplant has to function in a particular institutional context, in its own practical circumstances and in collaboration with other domestic policy actors. If policy models are copied literally and without giving due consideration to necessary amendments, the chances of success are low. The four examples of promising policy transplants described in Section 15.4 – (1) public referenda on infrastructure initiatives or complete investment packages; (2) public procurement policies for the selection of private funding and contracting; (3) institutionalised appraisal methods developed in interactive multi-actor process; and (4) five-year plan contracts with earmarked budgets between state and regions – reflect very different developmental institutional trajectories and were derived from very different national examples. All four may prove invaluable sources of inspiration for policy entrepreneurs apt to provoke changes in their national systems for infrastructure decision-making, albeit in quite different directions. But in none of them can transfer be considered as automatic. It requires political and policy struggles among proponents and opponents, and in all cases intelligent thought and careful manoeuvring in negotiations, which leads the transplants to deviate substantially from their examples. Since histories, needs and preferences also differ, this is a blessing rather than a curse.

APPENDIX 15.1   LIST OF INSTITUTIONAL CHARACTERISTICS

FED (federalism index):

1. Number of financing actors
2. Importance of territorial distribution
3. Importance of consultation rounds
4. Juridical role of sub-national government
5. Organising role of regional authorities

DEM (democracy index):

6. Role of referenda
7. Room for participation procedures
8. Openness of societal discussion
9. Role of societal groups on assessment criteria
10. Representative role of public authorities

INT (integralism index):

11. Interdepartmental nature of plans
12. Formal importance of environmental impact reports
13. Informal importance of environmental impact reports
14. Broadness of assessment framework
15. Importance of spatial translation
16. Belief in the supply approach
17. Public nature of reports
18. Nature of public–economic prioritisation
19. Importance of assessment in territorial context
20. Extensive formulation of assessment criteria

COR (corporatism index):

21. Intermodal nature of plans
22. Intermodal nature of legislation
23. Importance of actor commitment
24. Formal role of assessment procedures
25. Importance of prior standardisation
26. Promoting network effects
27. Equal distribution over modes
28. Reliability of financial promises
29. Avoidance of privatisation tendencies
30. Strength relationship infrastructure – servicing

REFERENCES

Bundesministerium für Verkehr (1993), *Gesamtwirtschaftliche Bewertung von Verkehrswegeinvestitionen; Bewertungsverfahren für den Bundesverkehrswegeplan 1992*, Schriftenreihe, Heft 72, Bonn.

Castles, F.G. (1993), *Families of Nations: Patterns of Public Policy in Western Nations*, Aldershot, UK: Dartmouth.

Cervero, Robert (1998), *The Transit Metropolis: A Global Inquiry*, New York: Island Press.

Dolowitz, D. (1999), *Policy Transfer and British Social Policy: Learning from the USA*, Buckingham, UK: Open University Press.

Flyvbjerg, Bent (1998), *Rationality and Power: Democracy in Practice*, Chicago and London: The University of Chicago Press.

Flyvbjerg, Bent, Nils Bruzelius and Werner Rothengather (2003), *Mega-projects and Risk: An Anatomy of Ambition*, Cambridge, MA: Cambridge University Press.

Jacoby, Wade (2000), *Imitation and Politics: Redesigning Modern Germany*, New York: Cornell University Press.

Jong, Martin de (1999), *Institutional Transplantation: How to Adopt Good Transport Infrastructure Decision-making Ideas from Other Countries*, Delft: Eburon Press.

Jong, Martin de (2001), 'The impact of institutional structures on transport infrastructure performance: a cross-national comparison on various indicators', *European Journal of Transport and Infrastructure Research*, **1** (2): 169–96.

Jong, Martin de (2003), 'Wegenonderhoud in Zweden en Finland', in Ernst ten Heuvelhof, Martin de Jong, Martijn Kuit and Helen Stout (eds), *Infrastratego: Strategisch Gedrag in Infrastructuurgebonden Nutssectoren*, Utrecht: Lemma, pp. 99–114 (in Dutch).

Jong, Martin de and Jurian Edelenbos (2007), 'An insider's look into policy transfer in transnational expert networks', *European Planning Studies*, **15** (5): 687–706.

Jong, Martin de and Harry Geerlings (2005), 'Exchanging experiences between Denmark and the Netherlands on transport infrastructure policies', *International Journal of Technology, Policy and Management*, **5** (2): 181–99.

Jong, Martin de, Konstantinos Lalenis and Virginie Mamadouh (2002), *The Theory and Practice of Institutional Transplantation. Experiences with the Transfer of Policy Institutions*, Dordrecht/London/Boston: Kluwer Academic Publishers.

Leleur, Steen (1995), *Road Infrastructure Planning: a Decision-Oriented Approach*, Lyngby: Polyteknisk Forlag.

Lijphart, A. (1999), *Patterns of Democracy: Governance Forms and Performance in 36 Countries*, New York and London: Yale University Press.

Mantzavinos, C. (2004), *Individuals, Institutions and Markets*, Cambridge, MA: Cambridge University Press.

March, James G. and Johan P. Olsen (1989), *Rediscovering Institutions*, New York: The Free Press.

Ministry of Transport, Public Works and Water Management (Ministerie van Verkeer en Waterstaat) (1999), *International Comparison of Decision-Making on Infrastructure*, Research Series of the Directorate for Strategy and Coordination, The Hague.

Nash, C. and J. Preston (1991), 'Appraisal of rail investment projects, recent British experience', *Transport Reviews*, **11** (4): 295–309.

Nelson, R.R. and S.G. Winter (1982), *An Evolutionary Theory of Economic Change*, Cambridge, MA: The Belknap Press of Harvard University.

Newman, P. and A. Thornley (1996), *Urban Planning in Europe: International Competition, National Systems and Planning Projects*, London: Routledge.

North, Douglas, C. (1990), *Institutions, Institutional Change and Economic Performance*, Cambridge, MA: Cambridge University Press.

Pakkala, Pekka (2002), *Innovative Project Delivery Methods for Infrastructure: An International Perspective*, Helsinki: Finnish Road Enterprise.

Pakkala, Pekka, Martin de Jong and Juha Aijo (2007), *Performance Indicators and Innovative Contracting for Roads – International Results*, Helsinki/Delft: Finnish Road Administration/Foundation Next Generation Infrastructures.

Rose, L.E. and K. Stahlberg (2002), 'De Noordse landen: het "beloofde land" voor het lokaal bestuur', *Bestuurswetenschappen*, **6**: 525–44.

Rose, Richard (1993), *Lesson-Drawing in Public Policy: A Guide to Learning Across Time and Space*, London: Chatham House.

Rose, Richard (2005), *Learning Lessons in Comparative Public Policy: A Guide to Analysis*, London: Routledge.

Stone, Diane (2000), 'Non-governmental policy transfer: the strategies of independent policy institutes', *Governance: An International Journal of Policy and Administration*, **13** (1): 45–70.

Stone, D. (2004), 'Transfer agents and global networks in the "transnationalization" of policy', *Journal of European Public Policy*, **11** (3): 545–66.

Van Bueren, Ellen, Frederic Bougrain and Thomas Knorr-Siedow (2002), 'Sustainable neighbourhood rehabilitation in Europe: from simple toolbox to multilateral learning', in M. de Jong, K. Lalenis and V. Mamadouh (eds), *The Theory and Practice of Institutional Transplantation: Experiences with the Transfer of Policy Institutions*, Dordrecht/London/Boston: Kluwer Academic Publishers, pp. 263–82.

Watson, Alan (1993), *Legal Transplants: An Approach to Comparative Law*, Athens and London: The University of Georgia Press.

Zweigert, K. and H. Kötz (1998), *An Introduction to Comparative Law*, Oxford: Clarendon Press.

Index

340 *Index*